WRITERS, READERS, AND OCCASIONS

Writers, Readers, and Occasions
Selected Essays on Victorian Literature and Life

Richard D. Altick

Ohio State University Press
Columbus

" 'A Grammarian's Funeral': Browning's Praise of Folly?" originally appeared in *Studies in English Literature* 3 (1963); "The Symbolism of Browning's 'Master Hugues of Saxe-Gotha' " in *Victorian Poetry* 3 (1965); "Lovers' Finiteness: Browning's 'Two in the Campagna' " in *Papers on Language and Literature* 3 (1967); " 'Andrea del Sarto': The Kingdom of Hell Is Within" in *Browning's Mind and Art* (Edinburgh: Oliver and Boyd, 1968); "Carlyle's *Past and Present*: Topicality as Technique" in *Carlyle and His Contemporaries: Essays in Honor of Charles Richard Sanders* (Durham, N.C.: Duke University Press, 1976); "Education, Print, and Paper in *Our Mutual Friend*" in *Nineteenth-Century Literary Perspectives: Essays in Honor of Lionel Stevenson* (Durham, N.C.: Duke University Press, 1974); "*Bleak House*: The Reach of Chapter One" in *Dickens Studies Annual* 8 (1980); "The Sociology of Authorship: The Social Origins, Education, and Occupations of 1,100 British Writers, 1800–1935" in *Bulletin of the New York Public Library* 66 (1962); "Varieties of Readers' Response: The Case of *Dombey and Son*" in *Yearbook of English Studies* 10 (1980); "English Publishing and the Mass Audience in 1852" in *Studies in Bibliography* 6 (1953–54); "The Literature of an Imminent Democracy, 1859" in *1859: Entering an Age of Crisis* (Bloomington: Indiana University Press, 1959); "From Aldine to Everyman: Cheap Reprint Series of the English Classics, 1830–1906" in *Studies in Bibliography* 11 (1958); "*Cope's Tobacco Plant*: An Episode in Victorian Journalism" in *Papers of the Bibliographical Society of America* 45 (1951); "The Reading Public in England and America in 1900" in *Literature and Western Civilization: The Modern World II: Realities* (London: Aldus Books, 1972); "Four Victorian Poets and an Exploding Island" in *Victorian Studies* 3 (1960); " 'Our Gallant Colonel' in *Punch* and Parliament" in *Bulletin of the New York Public Library* 69 (1965); "An Uncommon Curiosity: In Search of the Shows of London" in *Quarterly Journal of the Library of Congress* 38 (1981); "Victorians on the Move; or, 'Tis Forty Years Since" in *Dickens Studies Annual* 10 (1982). Grateful acknowledgment is made to the respective editors and publishers for permission to reprint these essays here.

Library of Congress Cataloging-in-Publication Data
Altick, Richard Daniel, 1915–
  Writers, readers, and occasions.

  Bibliography: p.
  Includes index.
  1. English literature—19th century—History and
criticism. 2. Books and reading—Great Britain—
History—19th century. 3. Great Britain—Social
life and customs—19th century. I. Title.
PR 463.A48 1989   820'.9'008   88–5112
ISBN 0–8142–0459–7

Printed in the U.S.A.

9 8 7 6 5 4 3 2 1

Contents

Foreword

Richard Altick recalls that his baptism in Victorian literature (it turned out to be total immersion, not a mere trickle on the head) was in 1941 when, as a beginning instructor, nervous under the weight of a brand-new Ph.D., he was told that he was to teach Victorian poetry that semester, although his qualifications were confined to some desultory reading of the novels of Dickens and his memories of a course in Victorian prose taken in his undergraduate days. It indicates how slightly the period was then valued that the course was so capriciously assigned, but his elders picked better than they knew. The near half century since then has been the period of maturation for Victorian studies, and it has also been the setting for Altick's long writing career. It is no accident that the two have coincided, for as much as any scholar in that time he has been responsible for the serious study of the literature of our grandfathers.

Ever since he taught that first tentative course in Victorian poetry, Altick has been hard to classify as a member of any particular school of criticism because his method is usually as individual as his subjects. He has never been a slave to movements. Although he was still a downy chick when the New Criticism swept over the study of poetry like a tidal wave, he managed to keep his head above water, looking around him without feeling that he had to take part in the splashing and frolicking. And in more recent years, as school after school has succeeded the structuralists and the deconstructionists, he has retained a tolerant, genial interest in ways of thinking with which he has little in common. If he is not a follower of movements, neither does he waste time in deploring, for he knows that no form of criticism is without value so long as it stirs the minds of critics and scholars. As to his own practice, it would not be far off the mark to say that in his attitudes to English literature, he has been less influenced by Continental thought than by English—and often Victorian at that.

One of the essays in this volume is called "Adventures of an Annotator," in which Altick lightheartedly demonstrates the passion for obscure knowledge that has run like an unbroken thread through his writing. So much of his work is devoted to making clear to us what the Victorians understood without explanation that there would be some justice in calling him the annotator to an age, so long as it is understood that, for him, annotation is far from dreary assembly of irrelevant fact, for his purpose is not exhumation but revivification. During the course of his career "intensive biographical and historical scholarship has profoundly affected the way Victorian texts should be read if they are taken to be more than autonomous linguistic events occurring independently of author and milieu." Elsewhere he mentions that although "annotation is, in the first instance, a handmaiden of elucidation, in the end it serves the higher cause of interpretation."

Two of the essays included here were written specially for this volume, and the rest are brought together from scattered earlier publications, the earliest of them from 1951. A few have appeared in volumes of essays with other contributors, the remainder in scholarly journals. Twenty essays of this quality, if equally distributed among four or five young scholars, would ensure the academic promotion of the whole lot; taken together, they demonstrate the remarkable range and continuity of Altick's scholarly curiosity. My only regret is that the method of selection necessarily excludes portions from any of the numerous books that Altick has written about matters Victorian. I should, for example, greatly have enjoyed reading here almost any chapter of his wonderful *The Scholar Adventurers*. (But it is even better to reread the entire book, which has recently appeared in a paperback edition.)

Throughout it is clear that Altick values literature for the same qualities the Victorians did, its moral seriousness, its relevance to the life of man on earth (and perhaps beyond, although that hope diminished as the period wore on), its capacity to amuse as well as to instruct, its illumination of manmade institutions, and its ability to warm the affections. In short, for its humanity.

One of the first things a reader of these essays will notice is the prominence of persons in Altick's examination of the past. Books are not abstractions but documents that are written, published, and read, a process that postulates human beings to take part in each of its stages. From his early essays on, he has been determined to find out who these human beings were, what they thought, what they were like, for on the answers to those questions hangs our understanding of why the books became what they are.

Even in more purely critical essays, Altick is clearly attracted to Browning, Dickens, and Carlyle, the poet, novelist, and essayist of the age who were most conspicuously identified with the examination of human character and idiosyncrasy. The first essay in the book, although really about point of view in "A Grammarian's Funeral," springs from Altick's instinctive awareness that the then-received beliefs about the meaning of the poem were inconsistent with what he knew of the personality and attitudes of Browning.

I am particularly fond of the last section of this book, "Occasions," in which the author turns from writers, publishers, and readers to the literary scholars who study them; in this section he uses his own experience to bring to light the hidden joys of the scholar's life, unsuspected by anyone who has never undertaken research and literary investigation. For the distinguishing quality of Professor Altick's scholarship has always been intellectual pleasure. No doubt every budding scholar begins in enthusiasm for his project, but few retain it for a lifetime, and fewer still know how to convey their own enthusiasm to the reader. Richard Altick's work has obviously given him what Hopkins called "a fine delight," which shines forth from the printed page more luminously with each succeeding year, so that the mature scholar is even more youthful in his joyous enthusiasm than that just-hatched Ph.D. in 1941.

ROBERT BERNARD MARTIN
PROFESSOR EMERITUS
PRINCETON UNIVERSITY

Preface

The tripartite title this volume bears is the most inclusive I could devise to represent the variety of its contents. The divisions have at least a rough logic, although several pieces are equally eligible to be assigned to any of the three. Part One comprises essays on Browning, Carlyle, and Dickens, the trio of Victorian writers in whom I have had a special interest, as well as a statistical analysis of the authorial profession at large in nineteenth-century England. Part Two is concerned with the people they wrote for—the reading public as a sociological entity, the corporate manifestation of (always controversial) popular taste, and, in economic terms, a steadily expanding market for the commodity of the printed word.

The "occasions" memorialized in Part Three are a mixed bag, ranging from the eruption of Mount Krakatoa in 1883 to a retrospect of the first forty years of Victorian studies as a scholarly and critical "field" (1942–82). At first glance, it would appear to be stretching things to enter under the same rubric my profile of the borough of Lincoln's gift to *Punch* and Parliament, Colonel Sibthorp, although to consider him as the odd man out would be peculiarly fitting in view of his sublimely eccentric intransigence. But if the reader will consult page 271, he will find that the Colonel belongs right where he has been placed, because every time he rose to his feet in the House of Commons was an occasion of sorts, whether it elicited anticipatory laughter or a collective groan.

Across the years, my name has come to be associated with writings on the rationale and practice of literary scholarship, and so I have thought it appropriate to include in this collection, for the particular interest of such fresh recruits to the profession as might come upon it, three reminiscent pieces that illustrate some aspects of scholarly inquiry in action. One, on the pleasures of gathering out-of-the-way materials for my book *The Shows of London*, has been published before. The others, on the growth by slow accretion of the essay "Four Victorian Poets and an Exploding Island" and on lessons learned while preparing the Riverside edition of Carlyle's *Past and Present*, are printed here for the first time.

Except for a little touching up, usually to clarify a point, improve an occasional inept turn of phrase, remove a dated reference or update another, the essays are printed without change. I have not attempted to reflect or incorporate into them whatever has subsequently been published on their respective subjects. A few newly added notes are enclosed in brackets.

R. D. A.

WRITERS

1
"A Grammarian's Funeral": Browning's Praise of Folly?

Is "A Grammarian's Funeral" what it has virtually always been said to be: a paean of praise for the dead gerund-grinder? In a fashion, yes; for such an interpretation can be supported by citing parallel doctrine in other familiar Browning poems. For example, the grammarian did what he wanted to do, and we know that Browning heartily approved of a man's following the promptings of his instincts. Again, the grammarian left to God the task of making "the heavenly period / Perfect the earthen," and we inevitably hear echoes of Andrea del Sarto's view of the function of heaven. The poem can be read as one more celebration of success in the midst of apparent failure. It is easy to regard the grammarian as a typical Browning hero, a Rabbi Ben Ezra of the verb-endings.

But our response cannot be merely one of placid assent to the attitude of the student-chorus. Today we are too much aware of Browning's personal ambivalences, which so often find reflection in his presentation of character, to accept unreservedly the traditional reading of the poem.[1] Seldom does Browning wholly condemn a character—even seemingly lost souls have a few redeeming features; but seldom, on the other hand, does he praise a character without qualification. Furthermore, the device of the dramatic mask enables him, as we learn from every fresh intensive study of his best monologues, to indulge his ambivalences by talking out of both sides of his mouth. And slowly we are coming to realize that his gift of satire was both more considerable and more cunning than either his immediate audience or later critics knew. Such considerations necessarily complicate the reading of "A Grammarian's Funeral," a poem that is not as simple or transparent as has usually been thought.

The crucial point is that the ideas of the poem are uttered by personae whose objectivity is gravely suspect. The chorus is composed of students who will become, for better or worse, the grammarians of the next generation. In their admiration for their deceased master, they reveal themselves as pedants off the old block. Their subscription to the grammarian's view of life defines their own limitations. Heaven, and Robert Browning, forbid that we should assent wholeheartedly to the assumptions that underlie their praise:

He knew the signal, and stepped on with pride
   Over men's pity;
Left play for work, and grappled with the world
   Bent on escaping:
"What's in the scroll," quoth he, "thou keepest furled?
   Show me their shaping,
Theirs, who most studied man, the bard and sage,—
   Give!"—So he gowned him,
Straight got by heart that book to its last page:
   Learned, we found him!

                                (43–52)

Oh, such a life as he resolved to live,
   When he had learned it,
When he had gathered all books had to give;
   Sooner, he spurned it!
Image the whole, then execute the parts—
   Fancy the fabric
Quite, ere you build, ere steel strike fire from quartz,
   Ere mortar dab brick!

                                (65–72)

Yea, this in him was the peculiar grace
   (Hearten our chorus)
Still before living he'd learn how to live—
   No end to learning.
Earn the means first—God surely will contrive
   Use for our earning.

                                (75–80)

Was it not great? did not he throw on God,
   (He loves the burthen)—
God's task to make the heavenly period
   Perfect the earthen?
Did not he magnify the mind, shew clear
   Just what it all meant?
He would not discount life, as fools do here,
   Paid by instalment!
He ventured neck or nothing—heaven's success
   Found, or earth's failure:

"Wilt thou trust death or not?" he answered "Yes:
Hence with life's pale lure!"

(101–12)

The grammarian was the type of "high man" who "with a great thing to pursue, / Dies ere he knows it" (115–16); who, "aiming at a million, / Misses an unit" (119–20); who "throws himself on God, and unperplext / Seeking shall find Him" (123–24). "This man," in sum, "decided not to Live but Know" (139).

Beyond question the grammarian is the *students'* hero, but Browning scarcely means him to be ours—certainly not to the same uncritical degree. Far from following Browning's customary advice that man should live life to the utmost, he withdrew from life, preferring to read about it (and in the end not even doing that). To be sure, he aspired, was devoted to a cause. But one may question whether, in Browning's own terms, his special aspiration was praiseworthy, his particular cause worth the sacrifice of a whole lifetime. His goal, though superficially lofty, actually was low. And when he does go up the mountain, it is not under his own power, but as a corpse borne on the shoulders of his disciples.

The note of removal from common life is struck at once. The students bear the dead master away from "the common crofts, the vulgar thorpes" (3), "the unlettered plain" (13)—up a mountain "cistied to the top, / Crowded with culture" (15–16). "Culture" may be interpreted as "artificial, decadent, sophisticated life"—the sort of civilization Browning disparaged through the complacent figure of Cleon. The students thus are symbolically completing the process begun early in the grammarian's lifetime, of separating him from the human sources of strength. They are about to ensconce him in the sort of remote mausoleum from which the guilty Soul, in Tennyson's "The Palace of Art," finally flees to seek renewal in "a cottage in the vale." As Lionel Stevenson has shown,[2] Browning, in his autobiographically significant *Paracelsus* and *Sordello*, had moved steadily away from the romantic exaltation of self-sufficient egocentricity to the familiar Victorian position that art—and learning—must have social usefulness, that the artist and the scholar must maintain a vital contact with common life. Numerous passages of *Paracelsus*, indeed—far too many to list here—serve as illuminating glosses for "A Grammarian's Funeral." The "still voice," for instance, urges Paracelsus to "know, not for knowing's sake, / But to become a star to men forever"; and Festus inquires of Paracelsus,

How can that course be safe which from the first
Produces carelessness to human love?
It seems you have abjured the helps which men
Who overpass their kind, as you would do,
Have humbly sought. . . .

(Act I)

Thus the grammarian's biography, as revealed by the students, is one of progressive detachment from life and increasing neglect of his duty to society at large: a course of which Browning, and not alone the youthful Browning of *Paracelsus*, could hardly have approved. Moreover, his choices involved denial of the ethical values that Browning himself most cherished. Born with the brightest conceivable prospects, the "face and throat [of] / Lyric Apollo" (33–34), he failed utterly to realize his promise. Paracelsus accurately described, by anticipation, not only his own failure but the grammarian's as well:

And men have oft grown old among their books
To die case-hardened in their ignorance,
Whose careless youth had promised what long years
Of unremitted labor ne'er performed.

(Act I)

To have wasted God-given physical attributes, to have scorned the rich potentialities of youth and talent and preferred instead the dusty existence of a hermitic philosopher may be admirable in the eyes of the students, but not, one would suppose, in those of the poet who wrote "Fra Lippo Lippi." The grammarian's youth, in any event, passed; spring turned at once to winter, without the normal intervention of the fruitful summer. Instead of living, he "grappled with the world / [which was] Bent on escaping" (45–46)—not the world of direct personal experience, but life as reflected in books.[3] Nor were the books themselves the reports of first-hand experience; instead, they were the observations of "the bard and sage": not men of action, but men who, like the grammarian, had studied or described life rather than participated in it—the poet, sculptor, and composer of "The Last Ride Together," whom Browning chided for growing "poor, sick, old ere your time" by devoting themselves to art instead of to life. Thus there is an extra irony: the grammarian is not one but two removes from actuality. And as his life wore on, he moved, like a crab, backward, ever farther from the (to Browning) precious realm of here-and-now existence.

•••6•••

From line 50 onward, the essence of the poem is contained in the ironic counterpoint of the words "know," "learn," and "book," on the one hand, and "life" and "live" on the other. The grammarian grew "learned," but his knowledge of life (symbolized as a "book") was second- or third-hand, and it was completely uninspired, mechanical ("got by heart"). Urged to leave off learning and, before it is too late, live (note how in lines 55 and 57 the words "taste" and "actual" intensify the force of "life"), he was scornful: "Grant I have mastered learning's crabbed text, / Still, there's the comment" (59–60). And so, taking up the fine-print commentary, he moved even farther from actual life and devoted himself to books about books. In terms of what, in Browning's view, should have been his central concern—immediate, personal, intense experience of life—he steadily learned more and more about less and less. "Let me know all," he cried (61), but no amount of vicarious knowledge can atone for failure to live. The students praise their master's heroic passion for learning, but to Browning it is a misdirected passion insofar as it contravenes God's intention that life be used for living. The grammarian put the cart before the horse; while acknowledging the desirability of living, he pedantically chose to read all about it first. Nor, although at first glance it seems a praiseworthy ideal, was he right in his decision to "image the whole, then execute the parts" (69). Browning, with his candid awareness of human limitations (as well as his presence in a Victorian culture which preferred systematic, cautious induction to the romantics' visionary aspiration toward the grand synthesis), probably was of two minds about it, as he seems to have been about other alleged virtues of the grammarian. On the one hand, he would have applauded the heroism of the sentiment ("a man's reach . . ."); on the other, he would have deplored the grammarian's lack of realism. Aprile told Paracelsus:

> Knowing ourselves, our world, our task so great,
> Our time so brief, 't is clear if we refuse
> The means so limited, the tools so rude
> To execute our purpose, life will fleet,
> And we shall fade, and leave our task undone.
> We will be wise in time: what though our work
> Be fashioned in despite of their ill-service,
> Be crippled every way? 'T were little praise
> Did full resources wait on our good will
> At every turn.

> (Act II)

Knowledge of "the whole" comes not in a single glorious vaulting of the mind but through a more prosaic fitting together of pieces. Only through viewing the prismatic colors, to recall an image of which Browning was fond, can one hope eventually to gain a vision of the white light into which they blend.

To the others' urging, "Live now or never," the grammarian retorted, "What's Time? leave Now for dogs and apes! / Man has Forever" (83–84).[4] Another fine sentiment, except that Browning elsewhere maintains that the Now must be taken full advantage of if man is to have the further benefit of Forever. Making the most of the possibilities that life offers is normally a prerequisite for more splendid opportunities in the hereafter. *Vivere est orare:* this, if anything, is the contention underlying Browning's recurrent attacks on asceticism—and the grammarian is as much of an ascetic as, say, Friar Lawrence's colleagues. The antiprocrastination parable of the unlit lamp and the ungirt loin is as apropos here as it is in "The Statue and the Bust." The idealism described (97 ff.) in terms that to most interpreters have signified Browning's approval, is a perversion of what Browning seems, on the evidence of other poems, to have believed. It may be "God's task to make the heavenly period / Perfect the earthen," but God cannot be relied on to do so without man's cooperation. To venture "neck or nothing" is a fine histrionic sentiment, but confidence in eternity must be manifested by performance in time. Those who "discount life . . . / Paid by instalment" are fools to the student-bearers, but Browning himself would not use so strong a term. Nor, certainly, would any true Browning hero put so meager a value on life as the grammarian does with his brusque "Hence with life's pale lure!" (112)

The contrast, in lines 113–24, between the "low man" and the "high man," must be read against the narrow frame of reference the students have acquired from their teacher. The grammarian is a high man, and his purpose is "great," only in their special scale of value. To understand the comparative aims of the two men one must remember that the grammarian's—to master the commentary on "learning's crabbed text"—is far less exalted than the students admit. A man's reach should exceed his grasp, to be sure, but what is being reached for makes some difference. And even if we accept the students' standard of value, we return to the unblinkable fact that man's capacity for achievement is limited. The low man's aim is more in accordance with the human being's powers. "Success is naught, endeavor's all," Browning wrote later (*Red Cotton Night-Cap Country,* 4.766), in one more statement of the conviction embodied in Andrea del Sarto's deathless rhetorical question; "but," he hastened to add,

> intellect adjusts the means to ends,
> Tries the low thing, and leaves it done, at least;
> No prejudice to high thing, intellect
> Would do and will do, only give the means.

"That low man seeks a little thing to do, / Sees it and does it": but doing it, however little, is something, as the Carlyle whose ideas Browning so often echoed had eloquently urged. "This high man, with a great thing to pursue, / Dies ere he knows it": has he, in the end, won God's blessing? Full marks, no doubt, for selfless and total dedication, but certainly not for any reasonable view of what he can and cannot hope to accomplish as a mortal man. Ironically, his vocation was fulfilled solely in the achievement of a low man's goal—something "little," such as formulating the doctrine of the enclitic *De*, which *could* be done. And if his works are inadequate, when measured against his initial ambition, so too is his faith. The grammarian "throws himself on God, and unperplext / Seeking shall find him" (123–24): but, we learn in the lines immediately following, even while "the throttling hands of Death" tightened about his throat—once that of lyric Apollo, now attacked by tussis—the "seeking" took the form of still more obsessive grammar-grubbing. It is no more auspicious a deathbed than that of the Bishop of St. Praxed's.

The grammarian's choice was, in effect, a denial of the very premise and spirit of Renaissance humanism, which Browning so much admired: the harmonious blending of living and learning, the study of the classics not as an end in itself but as a guide to a richer life. To the Renaissance humanist, settling *Hoti*'s business and properly basing *Oun* were important pursuits, but only if viewed in broad perspective, as means to a higher end. As the years went by, the grammarian's vocation, originally lofty, degenerated into something perilously close to mere occupation: instead of keeping his eyes fixed on the sunlit mountain that was still to climb, he burrowed ever deeper into the dark mines. His energies were devoted to means, self-sufficient and picayune, which he increasingly mistook for ends. Browning's point is not far removed from Carlyle's and Matthew Arnold's criticism of "machinery."

Nor is it unconnected with the figure of Erasmus, who appeared, in the words of Browning's caption, "shortly after the revival of learning in Europe," and indeed typified the noble strivings of humanism by his devotion to grammatical and related studies *as a means to an end*. The grammarian is a woefully incomplete Erasmus, a man whose scholarship deteriorates into mere pedantry for its own sake instead of serving as the necessary framework for momentous enterprises such as translating the New Testament. That Erasmus hovers somewhere in the background of "A Grammarian's Funeral" was suggested long ago,[5] but the implications of his possible presence have not been fully appreciated. They become clearer if we are aware of the resemblances Browning's poem bears to *The Praise of Folly.*

"A Grammarian's Funeral," like *The Praise of Folly,* belongs to the species *encomium* of the rhetorical genus *oratio.* Both are delivered on an academic occasion (of sorts), and Browning's students, like Folly, may be presumed to be gowned. But *The Praise of Folly* is a *mock* encomium; it is an adaptation and perversion, for satirical purposes, of the genuine article. And so too, I think, is "A Grammarian's Funeral." The true encomium has the serious aim of eulogizing the generally acknowledged public accomplishments of a great and wise man. Erasmus's figure of Folly, on the other hand, praises—folly, the converse of wisdom. Browning's students praise a man whose public accomplishments have been nil, and of whose wisdom, in the world's eyes, there is grave doubt. Both Erasmus's prose work and Browning's poem are, in a way, exercises in self-praise on the part of the speaker: Folly lauds herself, and the students, in lauding their master, of whom they are younger replicas, flatter themselves, their ambitions, their limitations.

In the midst of a great deal of nonsense, of obvious nonwisdom, Erasmus manages to have Folly occasionally deviate into sense. The two passages in *The Praise of Folly* which most specifically link it with "A Grammarian's Funeral" associate compulsive pursuit of learning with folly. In one, which is said to describe Thomas Linacre, Erasmus, speaking through his mouthpiece, Folly, says:

> I used to know a certain polymath versed in Greek, Latin, mathematics, philosophy, and medicine, and a master of them all, then some sixty years old; laying aside all the others, he vexed and tortured himself with grammar for more than twenty years, deeming that he would be happy if he were allowed to live until he had settled with certainty how the eight parts of speech are to be distinguished, a thing which none of the Greeks or Latins succeeded in doing definitively. It becomes a matter to be put to the test of battle, when someone makes a conjunction of a word which belongs in the bailiwick of the adverbs. . . . Do you prefer to call this

madness or folly? It is no great matter to me; only confess that it is done with my assistance . . .[6]

On an earlier page, Folly compares "the lot of the wise man with that of the fool":

> Fancy some pattern of wisdom to put up against him, a man who wore out his whole boyhood and youth in pursuing the learned disciplines. He wasted the pleasantest time of life in unintermitted watchings, cares, and studies; and through the remaining part of it he never tasted so much as a tittle of pleasure; always frugal, impecunious, sad, austere; unfair and strict toward himself, morose and unamiable to others; afflicted by pallor, leanness, invalidism, sore eyes, premature age and white hair; dying before his appointed day. By the way, what difference does it make when a man of that sort dies? He has never lived. There you have a clear picture of the wise man.[7]

The ironic inflection in Folly's voice is unmistakable: the "wise man," the "pattern of wisdom" is in truth a fool. That Folly here speaks for Erasmus is fairly clear. Admittedly, apart from the phrase "morose and unamiable to others," the latter passage is, as the late Hoyt Hudson observed, "an excellent self-portrait." But only as far as it goes; for it omits those very qualities that Erasmus possessed and the grammarian lacked. "The temper of Erasmus," Hudson continued, "did not accord with that of Folly's despised scholar. A favorite word with him was *festivus*—festive, companionable. He refused to allow his scholarship to kill his humanity. And thus Folly's gird has point, even as used by her: the halfwit is understandably human, all too human, while the scholar may verge toward something inhuman or anti-human."[8]

In both *The Praise of Folly* and (if I am right) "A Grammarian's Funeral" the personae express opinions that, for the most part, are not those of the respective authors. But the Erasmian strategy of occasionally allowing Folly to utter truth is, of course, a favorite with Browning as well. The difficulty in "A Grammarian's Funeral" is the same one presented, on a much more elaborate scale, by "Bishop Blougram's Apology": exactly where, apart from those fragments of Browningian doctrine whose apparent intention turns out to be undercut by his satirical purpose, is Browning's own voice to be discerned?

Assuming that my somewhat heretical reading has validity, it is un-likely that he intended the poem to assert that by squandering, or, more precisely, failing to make use of the gift of life on earth, the grammarian forfeited his passport to heaven. On the contrary: the serious statement, embedded in the satire, may reside in the students' implicit confidence that God did, after all, smile on him. In this respect they are right, but for the wrong reasons. Neither by works nor by clear-eyed faith—*pace* the chorus—did the grammarian prove himself entitled to eternal life. But in Browning's moral universe justice is abundantly tempered by mercy, and the very disproportion between the grammarian's deserts and his reward is a measure of God's capacity to forgive. Read in this way, the poem acquires extra dramatic force: the effect of the satire is to lengthen the odds against the grammarian's winning heaven, and thus audaciously to heighten our final sense of God's boundless charity. Even those who do not earn salvation may find it, for God's will transcends whatever rules of the game man's ethical and religious thought, including Browning's own, may attribute to him. If "A Grammarian's Funeral" is, as is commonly held, a poem of praise, the praise is directed not toward the grammarian but toward an all-loving God who, it appears, will forgive men even for their folly.

If Browning's sanguine theology compelled him to imply a happy ending to the grammarian's story, his criticism of the grammarian's waste of his life is no less genuine, and it still constitutes, it seems to me, the central interest of the poem. The grammarian is not one of the poet's "heroes" in the sense in which we ordinarily apply the word to his char-acters. Whatever posthumous salvage may be made of his career by the exercise of divine grace, the fact remains that he had the precious privilege of choice, and he chose wrongly. He grasped the stick of life by the wrong end. Instead of pursuing man's true goal, which is to extract meaning from life by living, he spent his years studying rather than being; he poured his energy into movement that carried him ever farther from fulfillment. For this not inconsiderable reason, Browning's verdict on him, as delivered through the inversion of satire, is severe. But beneath the satire lingers a poignant awareness of man's limitations: his myopic in-ability to comprehend, or in any event remain faithful to, the purpose implied in the gift of life, and, most tragic, the discrepancy between his desires and his powers. (Is it merely accidental that when it was first published, in *Men and Women*, this poem immediately followed "Two in the Campagna," whose theme is embodied in its last lines, "Infinite passion and the pain / Of finite hearts that yearn"?) Browning's condemnation thus is tempered by sympathy. The grammarian is an emblem of us all; while stubbornly refusing to concede that our ideal, however we may define it, is beyond attainment, we are in fact captives of the prison house of life and its treadmill. If Browning dissociates himself from the students' admiration of their hero, he is not lacking in compassion.

1963

2

The Symbolism of Browning's
"Master Hugues of Saxe-Gotha"

I n 1886 the critic John Churton Collins had an interview with Robert Browning during which they discussed the "allegorical"—or, in modern terminology, symbolic—interpretation of Browning's poems. Of "Master Hugues of Saxe-Gotha" in particular, Collins recorded in his commonplace book, Browning "repeated what he had told me before that he had no allegorical intent in his head when he wrote the poem; that it was composed in an organ loft and was merely the expression of a fugue—the construction of which he understood[,] he said, because he had composed fugues himself: it was an involved labyrinth of entanglement *leading to nothing*—the only allegory in it was its possible reflection of the labyrinth of human life. That was all and he warned me not to go too deep in his poetry in search of allegory."[1]

In view of the highly imaginative explanations of his poems then being delivered to him by members of the Browning Society, Browning's warning was both well timed and wholesome. But one must take exception to his specific denial of any symbolic motive in "Master Hugues" except for "its possible reflection of the labyrinth of human life." Is it possible for a poet to write a poem built upon a deftly organized and developed symbolic scheme without knowing what he is doing? Browning inferentially thought so; for Collins "asked him if he thought the famous passage in Plato's *Apology* about the unconscious inspiration of poets should be taken seriously; whether it was really true that, given genuine inspiration, a poet was so unconscious of the full meaning of what he expressed that, as Plato puts it, anyone you please could give a better explanation of what poets in their inspiration mean than the poets themselves could give. With some reservation, and making of course much allowance for the exaggerated way in which it was stated, this he said was undoubtedly and profoundly true."[2]

But this does not really meet the case as far as "Master Hugues" is concerned, for in at least two places in the poem the wording strongly suggests that Browning knew well enough what he was about. His characteristically downright statements to Collins represent, of course, neither the first nor the last occasion upon which he said things about his work

that strain his readers' credulity. He was especially sensitive on the subject
of his alleged hidden meanings, and not merely because of the excesses to
which enthusiasts had gone in interpreting some of his poems, most
notoriously "Childe Roland." Whatever the psychological explanation of
his touchiness, the fact remains that his denial of any but the most rudimentary symbolism in "Master Hugues" is contradicted by a close reading
of the poem. Using a clever combination of musical and architectural
imagery, Browning plays one more variation on a favorite theme of his:
the overwhelming superiority of intuition over intellect as a means of
reaching religious truth.

In a sense, "Master Hugues" is a companion piece to "Abt Vogler,"
though the former appeared in *Men and Women* (1855) and the latter in
Dramatis Personae (1864). The speakers in both instances are organists; but
whereas Abt Vogler is an improviser, and thus, as Browning develops his
poem, exemplifies the instinctive faith that rises on occasion to mystical
assurance, the unnamed speaker in "Master Hugues" is chained to the
notes before him, the intricate fugue handed down through the dusty
years from Master Hugues himself. It is not out of his own soul that the
present organist's music comes; it was all written down for him long ago.
Finger-taxing it may be, a formidable challenge to his powers of execution. But it affords no such freedom as Abt Vogler enjoyed for the spontaneous exploration of spiritual mysteries through sound.

The first eighteen stanzas have little overt symbolic meaning; their
true contribution to the poem can be understood only when we return to
them after a complete reading. Stanzas 1–8 set the scene, in the organ loft
of the deserted, darkening church. The shade of Master Hugues is then
summoned up, his face appearing in a half-surrealistic image suggested by
the phenomenon of retinal persistence. The organist, who has been peer-
ing long and hard at the music on the rack before him, sees the composer's

> brow ruled like a score,
> Yes, and eyes buried in pits on each cheek,
> Like two great breves, as they wrote them of yore,
> Each side that bar, your straight beak!

Stanzas 12–18 are a humorous description of the fugal structure and its
effect upon the listener, the five-line stanza corresponding to the five-voice
pattern of Hugues's own fugue. But it is already clear that the poem is
more than "merely the expression of a fugue." "What do you mean by
your mountainous fugues?" the organist has demanded in line 4, and in

lines 46–47 the problem of the meaning behind the complex pattern of sound is again alluded to, this time by the absent Hugues himself: "Good, the mere notes! / Still, couldst thou take my intent. . . ."

The description of the fugue is an effort to discover Hugues's intent; and its function in the total design of the poem is made clear by the special selection of words it contains. Long before, in line 9, the word *colloquy*, with its suggestion of formal, pedantic discourse (e.g., in the titles of learned Renaissance books), has foreshadowed the flood of words with a similar association that will occur during the fugue itself. In line 49 *sciolists*, connoting knowledge that is more showy than deep, has also served as preparation. Then, in stanzas 12–19, we have *propound, argument, dissertates, discept, distinguished, case, expounding, explaining, retorts, rejoinder, affirming, denying, holding, subjoining*: a dozen or more terms which individually are unremarkable enough, but which cumulatively produce a single, unmistakable effect. They are all words to some degree connotative of wearisome, hair-splitting disputation—of casuistry. They cluster, like semantic satellites, around Browning's assertion that the art of the fugue is, in effect, casuistry set to music: the five wrangling voices

> prick pins at a tissue
> Fine as a skein of the casuist Escobar's
> Worked on the bone of a lie. To what issue?
> Where is our gain at the Two-bars?

The fugue, like casuistry—and particularly like theological argumentation as viewed by a nineteenth-century English nonconformist—proves in the end to have gotten nowhere. What has happened to the simple, unexceptionable phrase, the self-evident truth ("Nothing . . . fit in itself for much blame or much praise") with which all the squabbling began? It has been buried beneath the musical—or argumentative—elaboration.

In thus making the fugue the symbol of intricate but sterile exercises or systems of thought, Browning was simply capitalizing on the stigma the form had acquired centuries earlier and still retains today: "the idea," as Ralph Vaughan Williams put it in his article on the fugue in the 1954 edition of *Grove's Dictionary of Music and Musicians*, "that a fugue is necessarily dull and pedantic . . . an academic exercise or an arbitrary collection of scholastic regulations." Of all possible musical forms, the fugue is best adapted, by its traditional reputation, to stand for the scholastic modes of thought that Browning devotes the poem to ridiculing.

In stanzas 19–20 Browning moves from his sustained figure of musical casuistry to one drawn from architecture, recalling perhaps, Schelling's famous dictum—echoed by Madame de Staël, Goethe, and Emerson—that "architecture is frozen music." The physical setting of the monologue, the empty church, is now put to the same metaphorical use. The fugue is like "our roof, its gilt moulding and groining / Under those spider-webs lying!" The church's gold ceiling is "music," pure melody— the initial subject of the fugue; the spider-webs are the intricate, melody-concealing elaborations.[3] The image of the web has two functions, which are connected in lines 99–100, where the "spider-web strengthens, / Blacked to the stoutest of tickens." The web made by spiders suggests the gradual obscuring of an object (the pure melody, the roof, the truth) by the passage of time; the web made on the loom of men's minds has a definite reference, as in the "tissue / Fine as a skein of the casuist Escobar's" and later in stanzas 22–23, to the steady accumulation of irrelevance and error through intellectualizing. In both cases there is the connotation of needless complexity, however caused, which hides simple truth from men's eyes.

Beginning with stanza 22 ("Is it your moral of Life?"), the organist probes for the meaning of the "master's" fugue—not Hugues's own intent (for it is quite plain by now, at least to the organist, that the fugue is devoid of useful substance), but the moral that he may draw from the fugue's very nature. The quest is not, however, presented in musical terms; the transfer of metaphor is, for the moment, complete. Man weaves his webs of "comments and glozes," and gradually the baroque church ceiling, "God's gold," "Heaven's earnest eye," with its paintings of "stars and roses, / Cherub and trophy and garland" is hidden from view. "Truth and Nature," "a glimpse of the far land"—all are shrouded by the "nothings" grown "something": the "zigzags and dodges, / Ins and outs" of the busy shuttle of cold reason. Mankind pays a totally undeserved respect to tradition:

> So many men with such various intentions,
>> Down the past ages, must know more than this age!
> Leave we the web all its dimensions!

And then, in stanza 27, as a sort of *stretto*, Browning draws together his two metaphorical threads, the musical and the architectural. The image of the fugue, absent for several stanzas, is recalled, to be equated with the web-hung roof as the symbol of artificiality, of the many-centuried increment of futile intellectualizing:

> Friend, your fugue taxes the finger.
>> Learning it once, who would lose it?
> Yet all the while a misgiving will linger—
>> Truth's golden o'er us although we refuse it—
> Nature, thro' cobwebs[4] we string her.

So: "straight I unstop the Full-Organ, / Blare out the *mode Palestrina*."[5] Back, in other words, to simple dependence upon intuition: to the melody uncluttered with fancy polyphonic embellishments. This is the "moral of Life" our speaker attributes to the monstrous fugue. But what will happen? The line "While in the roof, if I'm right there" is never completed. Does the organist expect the sheer force of exuberant sound, symbolic of a personal spiritual revelation as in "Abt Vogler," to blast away the spiderwebs and reveal once more the roof of "Truth and Nature"? In any event, the last stanza brings the poem out of its "moral of Life" and back to the actuality with which it began—a tired organist, now in utter darkness, and fearful of plunging down the "rotten-planked rat-riddled stairs." "Do I carry the moon in my pocket?"[6]

If one's conviction—to borrow line 55—needs a clinch, it can be supplied from the religious and musical history of Germany during the period when the fugue was the grandest ornament of the church service. Browning is not explicit, to be sure, concerning the time in which the poem is set. In the letter quoted in note 5 he wrote that if he had intended the long-dead composer to be "meant for the glorious Bach it were a shame to me indeed; I had in my mind one of the dry-as-dust imitators who would elaborate some such subject as [a musical quotation is here given] for a dozen pages together." If, as is probable, he meant "imitators of *Bach*," the meditation in the organ loft presumably could have occurred at any period from the middle of the eighteenth century to the middle of the nineteenth. The organist, indeed, might well be envisioned as slaving over "hard number twelve" as late as 1855.

But the precise time-setting is irrelevant. What is far more significant is the attitude of the organist; for here we unquestionably hear Browning's own voice. By enabling him implicitly to recall the religious issue that agitated middle and northern Germany in Bach's young manhood, the poem gave Browning an opportunity to protest, as he had done five years earlier in "Christmas Eve" and was to do again, at great length, in "The

Pope," against the forces of intellectualism and formalism he so fervently distrusted in religion, wherever encountered: not least in the England of Newman and Manning.

In the latter part of the seventeenth century, Lutheranism, which had originated in a rebellion against (among other things) Catholic authoritarianism and empty formalism, had itself hardened into an orthodoxy of intellect and outward show. One of Bach's biographers describes this new orthodoxy, as exemplified by the thought of the composer's friend Georg Christian Eilmar, as being "nothing but an unrefreshing and lifeless doctrine, pedantry, scholastic logic, litigious verbosity, and conspicuous coarseness."[7] Like the Catholicism it had supplanted, Lutheranism had become creed-bound, sacramentarian, dedicated to the strict observance of the letter rather than obedience to the promptings of the illuminated spirit. And now, in turn, orthodoxy was challenged by the pietistic movement within the church, led by Philipp Jacob Spener, and dedicated afresh to the proposition that religion is an affair not of the mind but of the soul.

This counter-revolution had its immediate repercussions, indeed its close analogy, in church music, which is usually prompt to respond to drastic shifts in the theological wind. When the pietistic reaction gathered force, musical *elaboratio* gave way to simplicity, and the mountainous fugues, in churches dominated by the pietistic party, were replaced by monody. Thus the new antirationalism in German religious life bred its exact counterpart in the era's church music, and to the pietistic German of (roughly) 1670 to 1720, the fugue symbolized the same evils— superficiality, formalism, impersonality, spiritual vacuity, ostentatious but futile learning—that it symbolized in Browning's poem.[8] Baroque music, as Manfred Bukofzer observed, is a language of the intellect; the new classical-romantic music, to whose emergence the pietistic movement substantially contributed, is a language of the natural feelings.[9] There can be little question where Browning's own sympathies resided. It was a fortunate accident of history that the conflict between polyphony and pietism during the last years of the baroque era supplied him, the latter-day pietist, with a metaphor ready-made to convey some of his deepest convictions relating to music and religion.

1965

3
Lovers' Finiteness: Browning's "Two in the Campagna"

"Two in the Campagna" is a prime example of Browning's gift of concentrated art.[1] Like some other poems in the *Men and Women* volumes, it is distinguished by intensity rather than diffuseness of effect, and by the tight integration of a small cluster of metaphors and symbols. In addition, it is unusual (though hardly unique) in the Browning canon in that it possesses an easily discernible substratum of physical sexuality. Blending reminiscences of both Donne and Arnold in their analyses of the completeness of lovers' union, it reaches a conclusion that wholly lacks Donne's confidence and shares little even of Arnold's heavily qualified hope. It is a poem of despair, passionate in its frustration and lovely in its eventual melancholy.

The theme is quest: quest for the ultimate meaning of life and for what is nowadays called one's "identity." Browning terms the object of the quest simply "a thought" (6), tantalizing and virtually impossible to convey in words; it is something "for rhymes / To catch at and let go" (9–10). In the manner of the great tradition reaching from Plato to Petrarch, the search leads toward, and through, the experience of human love. If a glimpse of essential truth is to be had at all, it will be achieved in such an experience. As Arnold put it in "The Buried Life," published three years before "Two in the Campagna":

> Only—but this is rare—
> When a belovèd hand is laid in ours,
> When, jaded with the rush and glare
> Of the interminable hours,
> Our eyes can in another's eyes read clear,
> When our world-deafen'd ear
> Is by the tones of a loved voice caress'd—
> A bolt is shot back somewhere in our breast,
> And a lost pulse of feeling stirs again.
> The eye sinks inward, and the heart lies plain,
> And what we mean, we say, and what we would, we know.
> A man becomes aware of his life's flow,

And hears its winding murmur; and he sees
The meadows where it glides, the sun, the breeze.[2]

This is the goal toward which the hopeful speaker of Browning's poem aspires. But the "thought" is at once elusive, almost impalpable, visible only under some conditions, breaking at the slightest touch, yet despite its unsubstantiality strangely clinging; it is gossamer in the word's fullest literal and connotative senses, "Like turns of thread the spiders throw / Mocking across our path" (8–9).

Gossamer though it is, the tantalizing thought (or, more accurately, question) threads itself across the whole landscape. The Roman campagna which provides the physical as well as the symbolic setting of the poem has two principal qualities: it is limitless, and its vegetation is, like the spider thread itself, soft and light to the point of fragility. This "endless fleece / Of feathery grasses everywhere" (21–22) is the site of nature in a perpetual state of placid, effortless fulfillment and renewal. Against this background, limitless in time as well as in space, man pursues the teasing wisp of ultimate knowledge.

> First it left
> The yellowing fennel, run to seed
> There, branching from the brickwork's cleft,
> Some old tomb's ruin.
>
> (11–14)

The question of life and its meaning, a thread at once infinitely tenuous and ceaselessly persistent, springs from twin symbols of death-in-nature and death-in-man. And it leads thence to a weed

> Where one small orange cup amassed
> Five beetles,—blind and green they grope
> Among the honey-meal.
>
> (16–18)

An image of narrow confinement, of strict limitation, is thus superimposed on the spacious background of the campagna, much as Arnold, in "To Marguerite, Continued" ("Yes! in the sea of life enisled") uses small islands and the sea for the same contrast of finitude and infinity. Inside the "small orange cup," a shape covertly suggestive of female sexuality, grope human beings, blind but instinctively insistent upon finding whatever is to be found "among the honey-meal"—pollen, stuff of the renewal of life. In an activity that is essentially sexual, enacted against the spread of eternity, men seek knowledge and happiness,

> Silence and passion, joy and peace,
>   An everlasting wash of air—
> Rome's ghost since her decease.
>
> (23–25)

The whole mood of the poem is controlled by the first of these three lines. "Silence" and "peace" suggest the calm of eternity and of natural fulfill-ment; "passion" and "joy" the disturbance and goal of human desire.

The campagna witnesses an unending cycle of birth-death-regeneration. Nature is in a constant state of renewal, and the activity leading to that renewal is as inevitable as it is innocent and delightful. The creation of new life is miracle-bearing play, and it of course bears divine sanction:

> Such life there, through such lengths of hours,
>   Such miracles performed in play,
> Such primal naked forms of flowers,
>   Such letting Nature have her way
> While Heaven looks from its towers.
>
> (26–30)

The insistence upon the absolute naturalness of life-renewal, the utter absence of shame before the vital process of sex, are more to be expected in Donne than in the Victorians, even in the one great Victorian poet who owed much to Donne; but in this poem they are visible to anyone who cares to look. The argument from nature leads to the passionate invitation,

> How say you? Let us, O my dove,
>   Let us be unashamed of soul,
> As earth lies bare to heaven above.
>   How is it under our control
> To love or not to love?
>
> (31–35)

To the sexual implication of "naked" in the lines previously quoted is now added the more explicit suggestion of the Danaë myth. "As earth lies bare to heaven above" recalls the "Now sleeps the crimson petal" lyric in *The Princess*, a song compact of erotic imagery initiated by the lines "Now lies the Earth all Danaë to the stars, / And all thy heart lies open unto me."

In Donne's love poetry, the physical and spiritual are fused: with union of body comes union of spirit. Although in "Two in the Campagna" there are undeniable fleshly elements, both in the general idea of renewal as everywhere present and necessary in nature and in the more specific imagery I have noted, Browning stresses the spiritual: "Let us be unashamed of *soul*"—not body. And after the stanzas in which the sexual suggestions have been most evident, he merges Donne and Arnold in his vision of the possible liberation of soul through the communion of love between man and woman. Man's crowning desire is to penetrate the veil of flesh that separates him both from a fellow human being—the beloved woman—and from the ultimate truth that would give orientation and meaning to his life. He yearns for simultaneous possession and illumination: through complete possession of the woman, nothing withheld, he might, he thinks, find knowledge and wisdom:

> I would that you were all to me,
>   You that are just so much, no more—
> Nor yours, nor mine,—nor slave nor free!
>   Where does the fault lie? What the core
> Of the wound, since wound must be?
>
> I would I could adopt your will,
>   See with your eyes, and set my heart
> Beating by yours, and drink my fill
>   At your soul's springs,—your part, my part
> In life, for good and ill.
>
> (36–45)

Through perfection of love, the blind beetle may be made to see; the groper for pollen in the small orange cup will be afforded the purer and more revealing draught of the woman's "soul's springs." Love can, therefore, redeem men. Its experience can enable them to breach the curtain of flesh, to cast off finiteness and find joy in full possession and full knowledge. Or can it?

> No. I yearn upward—touch you close,
>   Then stand away. I kiss your cheek,

> Catch your soul's warmth,—I pluck the rose
> And love it more than tongue can speak—
> Then the good minute goes.
>
> (46–50)

The "good minute" is an intense one; it involves emotion which, like the "thought" whose elusiveness set off this train of desire and discovery, cannot be expressed in human words. The experience of love has mounted from the low stage of a common orange flower to the exalted one of the rose, the symbol of the approach to ideal beauty. (There is an ironic but not inappropriate echo of *Othello*:

> When I have pluck'd the rose
> I cannot give it vital growth again,
> It must needs wither. . . .

Othello's is an ambivalent ecstasy—delight in the physical presence of his beloved at the moment before he murders her—but in his words, as in Browning's, lies the certainty that the moment of delight is fleeting.) The crushing truth is that even during the "good minute" toward which the whole of man's aspiration points, complete union of soul and complete knowledge of self are unattainable. They simply become more tantalizingly near—and more frustratingly beyond possibility of achievement. It is the price of being human.

The moment recedes, and the man resumes his role as a hapless, directionless "thistle-ball" driven "onward, whenever light winds blow" (53–54)—recalling the "everlasting wash of air" (24) of an earlier stanza— a creature akin to the feathery grasses of the campagna but having none of their unflawed participation in the cycle of nature. His course, "Fixed by no friendly star" (55), is unlike Shakespeare's, who found that true love

> is an ever-fixèd mark,
> That looks on tempests and is never shaken;
> It is the star to every wandering bark,
> Whose worth's unknown, although his height be taken.

In "Two in the Campagna" occurs no such comforting conclusion as one finds in the jaunty whistling-in-the-dark of "The Last Ride Together" and other poems that are more recognizably the product of Browning the sanguine. The experience has proved as fragile as the thread. Complete, satisfying, lasting union with a fellow being has been discovered to be impossible; and with this frustration returns the earlier one, the failure of self-knowledge.

> The old trick! Only I discern—
> Infinite passion and the pain
> Of finite hearts that yearn.
>
> (58–60)

The one realization that has been gained from the quest is that the quest is itself doomed to failure. To the earlier mood of "Silence and passion, joy and peace" (silence and peace the unchanging characteristics of nature, passion the possession of men, and joy their hope) has succeeded—still more passion, and instead of joy, pain. Desire without bounds, and capacity to fulfill that desire bitterly limited: the fate of men. "Eternal passion! Eternal pain!": the words are Arnold's, in "Philomela." But they are also Browning's.

1967

4
"Andrea del Sarto":
The Kingdom of Hell Is Within

Andrea del Sarto was called "The Faultless Painter." If it were not that in Browning's poem the epithet falls short of being an unqualified term of praise, one might apply it to "Andrea del Sarto," probably the poet's greatest short dramatic monologue. Certainly few of his poems approach it in sheer intensity, fidelity, and mounting horror of psychological portraiture. The received interpretation, that Andrea is simply the victim of timidity or weakness, seems to me to fall far short of the whole truth. Has anyone yet sought to express in print the full measure of Browning's achievement in this picture of a man whose capacity for self-deception is tragically insufficient for even his momentary comfort?

Andrea's condition, as this essay proposes to demonstrate, is terrible beyond the reach of irony. Ordinarily in Browning's dramatic monologues we are superior to the speaker: we are able to see him as he does not, or at least we see more than he is aware of. But Andrea has an insight into himself that approaches our own, for he recognizes as soon as we do, perhaps earlier, the illusoriness of what he calls Lucrezia's love for him, and more than that, his moral inadequacy which is manifested both in his weakness as a man and in his failure as an artist. Our response in this poem, therefore, is not governed by irony—irony such as we feel, for example, when we behold the ignorance of Pictor Ignotus, who rationalizes to his own satisfaction his refusal (actually his inability) to compete with the bright new stars of Renaissance painting, not knowing that the secret of great art lies in the artist's unfettered realization of a passionate personal vision, and that he is the slave of outmoded conventions. Although incidental ironies abound in "Andrea del Sarto," our response is chiefly one of pity, dictated not by the painter's ignorance but by his very lack of ignorance. He knows himself too well to find solace; no soothing balm of deception can alleviate his stark awareness of his nature and present situation. Browning elsewhere (as in "A Death in the Desert") celebrates God's mercy in providing clouds or eyelids by which man, a finite creature who cannot tolerate the absolute, is spared the blinding sun-rays of God's pure truth. In a similar manner, self-deception is a psychological device by which a human being is enabled to avert the whole intolerable truth about himself; it makes life, however less honest, a little more endurable. Andrea's tragedy is that he has no such refuge.

If this is the poem's implicit statement, it is worth repeating a few critical commonplaces to enlarge our realization of the extraordinarily close relationship in this poem between technique and content. In "Andrea del Sarto" Browning's artistry intensifies the ultimate psychological revealment: to a degree seldom matched in dramatic poetry, the two are inseparable. Only when we comprehend the full emotional depth of his portrait of Andrea can we appreciate the degree to which poetic means here is the vehicle of poetic meaning.

As one of the finest examples of Browning's stream-of-consciousness technique, the poem has no logical progression. The speaker's thoughts wander, double back upon themselves. The setting as evening descends on Florence, his own weariness, Lucrezia, the fatality of God, his paradoxical triumph as a draftsman and failure as an artist, the cuckolding cousin, the superior gifts and fortunes of Rafael, Leonardo, and Michelangelo, the golden year at the French court and its sordid consequence when Andrea fraudulently diverted to Lucrezia's pleasure the money the King entrusted to him to buy more art for Fontainebleau, a flicker of sexual passion not wholly spent—all these are interwoven in the natural involution of reverie. But this seeming aimlessness is actually reducible to one recurrent emotional movement. Andrea, brooding over the sterility of his life and the nullity of his prospects, clutches at a straw; he assumes confidence, attributes blame, or otherwise seeks peace in finding a reason, however untenable, or hope, however frail, only to have each comforting thought crumble as he grasps it. Only the disconsolate resignation born of weariness remains.

A second constant is the poem's pervasive tone, which has always been taken to suggest the technical perfection of Andrea's painting—even, lifeless, and dull—as well as his mood as he reflects on the failure of his life and seeks to divert responsibility from where he knows it really resides. The diction is no less colloquial than that of, say, Browning's other poems spoken by artists: but here is heard no lively (and slightly tipsy)

> I am poor brother Lippo, by your leave!
> You need not clap your torches to my face.
> Zooks, what's to blame?

The music hath a dying fall. Andrea's cadences have a sad dignity which reduces our awareness of their colloquial nature; they are spoken, for the most part, in a monotone; and the fact that they belong to a soliloquy rather than a monologue—for Lucrezia can scarcely be called an auditor in the literal sense—further drains them of animation. The very exclamations seem muted. Yet beneath the lethargy and the surface placidity, beneath the gray ashes of Andrea's resignation the fires of restlessness still smolder, and once in a while they burst into momentary flame. There is not much suggestion of physical movement to relieve the prevalent mood of enervation. Once Andrea makes a gesture of still unmastered physical desire as he reaches out his hands to "frame your face in your hair's gold, / You beautiful Lucrezia that are mine!" And at another juncture he suddenly rises to correct a false detail of anatomy in a sketch by Rafael. But the impulse soon spends itself, is quenched indeed by his ready awareness of its futility: "Ay, but the soul! he's Rafael! rub it out!"

As in Andrea's painting, so in his present mood—"I often am much wearier than you think, / This evening more than usual"—and so in the poem: "A common greyness silvers everything." There is a Tennysonian perfection of sober, melancholy ambience in the lines

> There's the bell clinking from the chapel-top;
> That length of convent-wall across the way
> Holds the trees safer, huddled more inside;
> The last monk leaves the garden; days decrease,
> And autumn grows, autumn in everything.
>
> (41–45)

(One may believe that Tennyson would particularly have admired the choice of verb in the first line: a toneless, choked-off *clink* rather than a full-voiced, resonant, freely echoing *ring*.) The dominant color throughout is the silver grayness of twilight. But it too, like the prevailing silver tone of Tennyson's "Tithonus," a poem of perpetual dawn rather than of twilight, is momentarily broken on several occasions. As in "Tithonus," gold and fire intrude, symbolic here of two influences which led Andrea to prostitute his gift—the celebrity and fortune he won as a painter at Francis I's court and the irresistible attraction of the golden-haired Lucrezia—and in addition ironically symbolic of the fire of pure internal inspiration, the divine gift which belongs to the true artist but was denied him, or perhaps, as he suspects, which he threw away. The surface calm, a "perfection" of mood corollary to the technical perfection and the neutral wash of gray and silver tones that characterize Andrea's art, thus proves to be, like his rationalizations, illusory. Underneath, in the succession of quickly extinguished bursts of passion as he recalls what was and what might have been, there is poignant disturbance. The whole poem, so quiet in superficial impression, is in fact made dramatic by the sustained tension between Andrea's wish to live out what life remains to him in a sort of drugged repose and the uncontrollable devil-pricks of his self-knowledge.

One thinks of Shakespeare's seventy-third sonnet:

> In me thou see'st the twilight of such day
> As after sunset fadeth in the west,
> Which by and by black night doth take away,
> Death's second self, that seals up all in rest.
> In me thou see'st the glowing of such fire
> That on the ashes of his youth doth lie,
> As the deathbed whereon it must expire,
> Consumed with that which it was nourish'd by.
>   This thou perceivest, which makes thy love more strong,
>   To love that well which thou must leave ere long.

But Andrea has no such comfort as is expressed in the last couplet. Accompanying his awareness of his artistic and spiritual failure, as his soliloquy continues its inexorable course, is the equally bitter knowledge that, if he ever possessed Lucrezia's love, he does not have it now. The very first lines begin with a sigh, and the true nature of their relationship as husband and wife is at once plain:

> But do not let us quarrel any more,
> No, my Lucrezia; bear with me for once:
> Sit down and all shall happen as you wish.
> You turn your face, but does it bring your heart?
>
> (1–4)

The possessive "my" of the second line, here so unremarkable a monosyllable, will acquire its own burden of irony as the situation is revealed.

Unlike most of the attending figures in Browning's dramatic monologues, Lucrezia is not a mere casual witness, a fortuitous occasion for the speaker's revealment: she is the central figure in his tragedy. None of Browning's unspeaking auditors is more silent than she, and in none is silence more eloquent. Her Gioconda smile tells more about her, about Andrea, and about their history and present situation than could pages of dialogue. It is the smile of a woman confident of her power over men, and at the same time contemptuous of the man to whom she belongs, not in fact but in name and in the transparent illusion to which he so desperately clings. She has no interest in his art; she carelessly smears with her robes a still-damp product of his brush. Nor does she listen as he pours out his soul. She merely smiles, and awaits the "cousin's" whistle.

Lucrezia's relation to her husband, as the first ten lines of the poem make clear, is limited to the interest defined by her very name, which is etymologically suggestive of profit and riches. She tolerates him, in his tired age, solely for the money he can earn her through the dogged exercise of an admired but empty art. Because of her, he suffers the ultimate degradation as both man and artist. Not only is he reduced to painting frescoes, portraits, and assorted artistic make-weights to order for a wealthy patron ("Treat his own subject after his own way, / Fix his own time, accept too his own price"): the commissions came through the "cousin," her lover, and the money he is paid will be devoted to liquidating—through the euphemism of "loans"—that same lover's gambling debts.

Except for the moments when he frames her hair and essays to correct Rafael's line, Andrea's hand presumably encloses Lucrezia's throughout most of the monologue. If so, it sustains an irony initiated in the early stages of the poem. In lines 8–9, 14, 21–22, and 49, there occurs a hand-within-hand image normally suggestive of security and comfort. But the symbolic meaning is determined by whose hand holds whose or what, and in this case God's hand encloses Andrea (49), whose hand encloses Lucrezia's (14, 21–22), which will enclose the money Andrea expects from the patron (8–9) and which she in turn will hold for the cousin. Here we have no such firm belief in God's wise beneficence as is conveyed by the use of the same figure in "Popularity"—the image of "God's glow-worm," the unrecognized poet-genius, being held tightly in "His clenched hand" until the time comes for God to "let out all the beauty." Nor does "Your soft hand is a woman of itself, / And mine the man's bared breast she curls inside" have its ordinary implication of quiet, trusting intimacy. It is belied not only by the serpent-suggestion of "curls," but by the whole emotional context.

Nor, we are invited to believe, do the lover and the patron represent the limits of Lucrezia's sphere of influence. In lines echoing Dryden's "Your Cleopatra; / Dolabella's Cleopatra; Everyman's Cleopatra" (*All for Love*, 4. 1.297–98), Andrea celebrates

My face, my moon, my everybody's moon,
Which everybody looks on and calls his,
And I suppose, is looked on by in turn,
While she looks—no one's. . . .

(29–32)

In a declension characteristic of Browning and far more devastating than Dryden's six words, the "my" gives way to the ambiguous "my everybody's," and thence to the brutal truth of the succeeding lines. Lucrezia is public property, at least so far as her superlative beauty is concerned; but she maintains the strategic distance, the cool lack of sole commitment, which is part of the desirable woman's armory of fascination. She has attributes of the *femme fatale*: her hand, inside his, represents her whole woman-self, curling snakelike against his breast; her Medusa's hair is "serpentining beauty, rounds on rounds"; and her low voice is like a "fowler's pipe" which the bird "follows to the snare." Physically she is the walking objective correlative of his art: she too is technical perfection, and as a work of art she too lacks the redeeming, crowning element of soul. She has "perfect brow, / And perfect eyes, and more than perfect mouth," and perfect ears onto which she places pearls—jewels of the same grayness which "silvers everything" in the present setting as it does in her husband's art. "There's what we painters call our harmony!" Andrea exclaims; but it is a harmony limited to the eye, one that has no counterpart in their spirits.

Andrea seeks another kind of harmony, an acceptable simple interpretation of his life which will explain as it consoles:

. . . the whole seems to fall into a shape
As if I saw alike my work and self
And all that I was born to be and do,
A twilight-piece.

(46–49)

And so begins the tortuous course of reflections on his failure. Initially he is confident of his scope as artist. He

can do with my pencil what I know,
What I see, what at bottom of my heart
I wish for, if I ever wish so deep—

(60–62)

the last clause reminding us of the similar bold and unsupported claim of Pictor Ignotus: "I could have painted pictures like that youth's / Ye praise so." But boasts are cheap, and, unlike the forgotten painter whose success lies in his ability to construct tenable rationalizations for his failure, Andrea cannot delude himself for long. What begins as an assertion of superiority ends as an admission of inferiority. He is, beyond question, a facile artist, one with dazzling skills. He can do things "easily," "perfectly," "no sketches first, no studies"—"do what many dream of, all their lives." They strive, agonize, and in the end fail; he succeeds. The truth, however, as he realizes, is that his is a lower order of accomplishment, the product of a "low-pulsed forthright craftsman's hand." The striving he attributes to the rivals who envy him his effortless command of technique is not, in the end, toward outward perfection but toward a quasi-religious vision that transcends color and line.

> Their works drop groundward, but themselves, I know,
> Reach many a time a heaven that's shut to me,
> Enter and take their place there sure enough,
> Though they come back and cannot tell the world.
> My works are nearer heaven, but I sit here.
>
> (83–87)

True fulfillment in art occurs not in the creation but in the creator. The act of striving, stirred by the "truer light of God . . . / In their vexed beating stuffed and stopped-up brain, / Heart, or whate'er else," results in no tangible evidence of success, but in an experience as supernal and ineffable as that of Lazarus or the mystics.

We have, then, the paradox that the closer a work of art comes to physical perfection, the wider the gap that separates it from true, or spiritual, perfection; and so with the artist himself. Perfection, as Browning asserts so often in his poetry, may be beyond the possibility of human achievement, but ceaselessly to struggle toward it is the impulse and deed that distinguishes man from beast, and artist from mere craftsman. "Even if the longed-for goal be never reached, even though the violence of the striving consume the soul utterly, yet it is enough that it should burn so nobly." So remarked Giordano Bruno, a philosopher of the generation just after Andrea's. In Browning's view, such struggle will strengthen, not consume, the soul. A man reaches in order "that heaven might so replenish him, / Above and through his art." But, encumbered with his special earth-bound powers, Andrea never reaches, never dares; he prefers the safety of a limited art, the perfectness, as Ruskin put it in *The Stones of Venice*, of the lower order. Unlike true artists with their fierce pride in their work, he is indifferent to praise or blame; he has no "sudden blood." His temperament is emblematized by the "length of convent-wall across the way" which "Holds the trees safer, huddled more inside"; he is, he says later, "the weak-eyed bat [a painter with weak eyes!] no sun should tempt / Out of the grange whose four walls make his world."

> In this world, who can do a thing, will not;
> And who would do it, cannot, I perceive:
> Yet the will's somewhat—somewhat, too, the power—
> And thus we half-men struggle. At the end,
> God, I conclude, compensates, punishes.
> 'Tis safer for me, if the award be strict,
> That I am something underrated here. . . .
>
> (137–43)

But can the man who values safety ever be said to struggle? The answer implicitly nullifies Andrea's momentary assurance. He is not entitled to number himself even among the "half-men" (those with the will but not the power, and those with the power but not the will), for he has not striven heroically, even in the face of certain futility, to round himself off into a whole man; therefore he will not earn God's grace. "In heaven, perhaps, new chances, one more chance," he says later—but the "perhaps" is a true measure of his confidence. The only struggle of which we have positive evidence that he is capable is the present one—the pursuit of extenuation—and it is not likely to be rewarded. Far from being attuned to divine inspiration his soul is "toned down" to the low seductive call of a callously selfish woman. On the one occasion in the poem when he looks upward, it is a physical gesture prompted by tired eyes, not a symbolic manifestation of inner desire; and the resulting vision is not of the New Jerusalem but of the walls of his "melancholy little house" cemented with the misapplied "fierce bright gold" of Francis I. He is a mercenary in a profession whose true *dévots* have a priestly vocation. At the same time—and this is the final turn of the screw—he knows that those same dedicated painters with whom he must constantly compare himself have in fact won a far greater measure of worldly fame than he has. At the end of a wasted life he has nothing to show for his ambitions but a certain ephemeral reputation for facility, while Rafael, Leonardo, and Michelangelo have enjoyed both fulfillment of spirit and ample earthly reward.

Faced with this bitter maldistribution of fortune, Andrea seeks to lay it to divine decree:

> Love, we are in God's hand.
> How strange now, looks the life he makes us lead;
> How free we seem, so fettered fast we are!
> I feel he laid the fetter: let it lie!
>
> (49–52)

But the admission that men strive, and through struggle achieve a glimpse of heaven, disposes of a foreordaining God as a scapegoat. We are not "fettered fast": man's will is free. God not serving his need, Andrea seeks some other reason for his failure—and Lucrezia is at hand. In passages laden with past conditionals (the subjunctive is the grammatical mode of regret), he considers what he might have been and done:

> I know both what I want and what might gain,
> And yet how profitless to know, to sigh
> "Had I been two, another and myself,
> Our head would have o'erlooked the world!" No doubt.
>
> (100–3)

> Had you . . . given me soul,
> We might have risen to Rafael, I and you!
> Nay, Love, you did give all I asked, I think—
> More than I merit, yes, by many times.
> But had you—oh, with the same perfect brow,
> And perfect eyes, and more than perfect mouth,
> And the low voice my soul hears, as a bird
> The fowler's pipe, and follows to the snare—
> Had you, with these the same, but brought a mind!
> Some women do so. Had the mouth there urged
> "God and the glory! never care for gain.
> The present by the future, what is that?
> Live for fame, side by side with Agnolo!
> Rafael is waiting: up to God, all three!"
> I might have done it for you.
>
> (118–32)

But this supposition is another product of a half-man. He has the power to make it, but not the power to believe it. Its frailty is summarized by "might have," and it is totally demolished by what follows: "So it seems: / Perhaps not." This bleak concession is neutralized for an instant by a return to the former theme: "All is as God over-rules." But, having been destroyed earlier, this assumption will no longer serve, and Andrea must face the truth: "incentives come from the soul's self; / The rest avail not." And the great painters he envies did not have wives, not even incomplete women like Lucrezia.

Nevertheless, this truth is not to be borne, and in his search for another incentive which would have availed him, he recalls one which indeed did once serve: "that long festal year at Fontainebleau!" This was, in retrospect, the Browningian "great moment" in Andrea's life. "I surely then could sometimes leave the ground, / Put on the glory, Rafael's daily wear." (*Could*: but did he? Rationalization is often assisted by the merciful filters of memory.) "A good time, was it not, my kingly days?" As he describes it, however, his success even then was not of the order of a Rafael's or a Michelangelo's. He basked in the "humane great monarch's golden look"; but certain details of his description of the king suggests that Francis's favor is as irrelevant to the true source of Andrea's tragedy as is Lucrezia's lack of soul and the premise that "All is as God over-rules." The king's "curl" and "smile" link him with Lucrezia, and "his gold chain" recalls God's fetters. To be sure, there was a "fire of souls / Profuse" in those halcyon days at the court; but as far as we can tell it was in other souls, those of his admiring onlookers, not his. He was not a Rafael, "flaming out his thoughts / Upon a palace-wall for Rome to see." No: he was Lucrezia's husband, and in the end the gold of her hair worked more potently upon him than the gold of the king's patronage. "You called me, and I came home to your heart."

But was her heart—if she has one—really ever his? Certainly he does not possess it now. For as Andrea talks on, Lucrezia continues to smile, and as she smiles, the utter hollowness of his confidence becomes more pronounced. It is increasingly apparent that she dominates him absolutely, and that all he wins from her presence is the grim pretense they are bound by mutual love. His only concern in life is to satisfy her, so that she will continue to play what he well knows to be merely the meaningless simulacrum of a role. Whether or not Michelangelo was right when he told Rafael that Andrea would one day "bring the sweat into that brow of yours," all he now cares for

Is, whether you're—not grateful—but more pleased.
Well, let me think so. And you smile indeed!
This hour has been an hour! Another smile?
If you would sit thus by me every night
I should work better, do you comprehend?
I mean that I should earn more, give you more.

(202–7)

Candid about his art as about his place in Lucrezia's life, he recognizes that he is deliberately prostituting the unique talents he does possess. But he persists in trying to persuade himself that the purchase is worth the sacrifice. "Come from the window, love," he pleads in phrases oddly prophetic of "Dover Beach": "Let us but love each other." It is an empty wish, and he knows it, for he undercuts it at once with "Must you go? / That Cousin here again?"

His meditations in this latter part of the poem are a commingling of rationalization, realization, and inadvertent self-revealment, all of which belie his assertion that "I am grown peaceful as old age to-night." Not all passion is spent, for beneath the surface, his feelings remain turbulent and conflicting. "Clearer grows / My better fortune, I resolve to think"—but whatever confidence is implied by the first five words is canceled by the succeeding revelation that it is generated by an act of will rather than a sincere conviction. The subjunctive "would" and "should" of lines 205–6, "If really there was such a chance" (201), and the "Well, let me think so" (203) reinforce the contrary-to-fact tone seen earlier in the use of frequent conditionals. "Well, let smiles buy me!" (223), however, ruthlessly dispels the general ambivalence. Against such a blunt admission of his helplessness before her, the succeeding platitudes—"Let each one bear his lot" (252) and "No doubt, there's something strikes a balance" (257)—are impotent.

The image of the walls of the New Jerusalem at the poem's end is the culmination of a process that began in the early lines. The "length of convent-wall" enclosing its safe huddled trees (42–3) became "the grange whose four walls" make Andrea's—the "weak-eyed bat's"—world (170), the idea of safety thus acquiring the additional suggestion of cowardice and retreat. Later, the walls turned into those of the house built with Francis's money; their drabness gone, they were "illumined" with "fierce bright gold" (216–17) and thus, by implication, tainted. Finally, the walls are transformed into those of "the New Jerusalem" upon which Leonardo, Rafael, Michelangelo, and Andrea (as he momentarily allows himself to believe) will fulfill their ultimate aspiration as artists (261–63). The concurrent expansion and alteration of the image from beginning to end of the poem is both illusory and ironic. Andrea's present confinement, symbolized by the convent wall, gives way to a vision of freedom and fulfillment. But we quickly realize, with him, that this seeming prophecy is but another futile dream.

These last ten lines of the poem contain a terrible sequence of truths, most of them ironic. There is heavy significance in the past tense of line 258: "You loved me quite enough, it seems to-night." The tense of "loved" is a slip of the tongue which adds substance to our conviction that he has a deeper subconscious awareness of the truth than his words normally express, and it renders additionally false the ensuing statement that, while Andrea's hypothesized coworkers on the celestial frescoes are without wives, "I have mine!" Neither the present tense of the verb nor the possessiveness of both verb and pronoun, we are certain by now, has any justification in fact. But the pretense persists. "There's still Lucrezia" (she is indeed still present—in the flesh) "as I choose." In this ultimate denial of the predestination he had earlier sought to embrace, he confesses that he has freely devoted himself to her, the embodiment of soulless physical perfection, rather than to the high, sacramental art to which the other three artists are dedicated. The choice may have been indefensible, as it surely was disastrous, but he alone made it.

"Again the Cousin's whistle! Go, my Love." Toward these last three monosyllables the whole poem has pointed. They are charged with the meaning of all that has gone before, as Hamlet's "Good night, Mother" is heavy with memory of the conflicting passions he has experienced in the closet scene. The verb, the possessive pronoun, and the noun: each has its bitter burden. His only comfort, and a cold one she is—the woman for whom he sacrificed his integrity as man and artist, in contemplating whom he saw mirrored at twilight the full failure of his life and character—no longer affords him even her physical presence. She leaves to keep a rendezvous with livelier company, and he resignedly watches her go ("my Love"!). He is left alone with himself, an awful fate. Like all men cursed with too much self-knowledge and lacking the saving grace of rationalizations that will stick, he carries the kingdom of hell within him.

1968

5

Carlyle's *Past and Present:*
Topicality as Technique

For indeed it is well said, "in every object there is inexhaustible
meaning; the eye sees in it what the eye brings means of seeing."
—The French Revolution (Works, 2.5)

In the summer of 1842 the "condition of England question" which had worried Carlyle for a number of years came to a crisis. He was, of course, not alone in his anxiety, nor did he exaggerate the desperate state of affairs. As more than one modern historian has observed, the year was the most ominous, the most critical, of the whole century. And so Carlyle, after beholding the idle able-bodied men who had been pauperized into the St. Ives workhouse and reading news accounts of the August riots in the cotton towns and elsewhere, put aside his research for the *Cromwell*, and in October or early November began to write what he intended to be a tract for the times: a tract, indeed, for the very moment. It was published in April 1843.

Although the rhetorical texture of *Past and Present* is dense with allusions to the Bible, to classical and Scandinavian mythology, to ancient Rome, and to the Middle Ages, this "matter of the past," as it may be called, was balanced by the "matter of the present," a system of topicalities and allusions to more or less recent history designed to underscore the urgency of the condition of England question. From one angle Carlyle looked at the crisis of English society *sub specie aeternitatis*; but from another, the one that concerns us here, he regarded it as the most pressing business before the men who read the *Times* and the newly founded *Illustrated London News* in the autumn and winter of 1842–43. In *Past and Present* the prophetic voice merges with the voice of the polemic journalist. These, Carlyle's topical references imply, are the things that affect us *today*, and must be attended to *today*.

The manifold topicalities of the book were put to numerous uses: illustration, symbolism, irony, analogy, contrast, invective. They served not only to particularize but, in Carlyle's characteristic fashion, to provide material for frequent repetition and variation. But how successful were these techniques of stimulating a sense of "presentness" in his first readers? To reconstruct with any semblance of scientific precision the impact which the topical allusions had upon the book-buyers of April 1843 would be a hopeless ambition. We do not have sufficient data, and in any case what psychologists would term the recognition- and affection-factors attached to each individual allusion inevitably varied from person to person. Despite the daunting number of imponderables, however, the mere attempt to estimate the effectiveness of Carlyle's topicalities may cast some light upon the nature of his artistry and the shrewdness of his insight into the contemporary public mind and its allusive equipment.

The term "topicality," it must be said at once, is necessarily an elastic one. As some of our most striking instances will suggest, it embraces, in addition to yesterday's headlines, allusions to events removed from the present by one or two years, or by a dozen. Unfortunately, in the psychology of literary response we possess no such neat formulation as do nuclear physicists with their concept of an isotope's half-life. It is impossible to determine how long a given topicality retained its original power, or how long it retained any at all. Some of the allusions that reached back as much as a decade had undoubtedly diminished in strength by 1843; others retained a persistent resonance, a steady and even expanding connotative aura. Which allusions faded, and which survived with unimpaired vitality, depended to some extent on the nature of each: on the depth to which it had initially rooted itself in the contemporary communal mind, on its recurrent applicability, and on what might be termed its magnetic strength, its self-renewing power of attracting kindred associations to it.

One index of an allusion's lasting vitality is the number of writers who employ it, and over how long a period. Here external evidence comes to our aid. A notable example of perennial topicality is St. John Long, the practitioner of drastic medicine whose administration of his accurately named "corrosive mixture" landed him in the dock at least twice, charged with manslaughter, some dozen years before he turned up in *Past and Present*: "This is sad news to a disconsolate discerning Public, hoping to have got off by some Morrison's Pill, some Saint-John's corrosive mixture and perhaps a little blistery friction on the back!"[1] Long's misadventures had received wide publicity at the time, not only in the newspaper press but in *Fraser's Magazine* (May and October 1830 and January 1831)— articles written by Carlyle's physician brother, John Aitken Carlyle—and in the *Lancet*, whose editor, the combative Thomas Wakley, waged against Long an editorial campaign as corrosive as his salve. This fashionable quack and his trusting patients were so well known to the public as to be satirized in prints and in a Covent Garden pantomime, *Harlequin Pat and Harlequin Bat*. The scandal of the trials was reflected in such diverse places as Greville's diary (12 December 1830) and the first of John Stuart Mill's essays on "The Spirit of the Age" (*Examiner*, 6 January 1831). Repeated allusions kept Long's memory green over the next decade; in December

1842, even as *Past and Present* was being written, an article in the *Quarterly Review* (p. 91) recalled his notoriety. Nobody needed to be reminded who St. John Long was, even though Carlyle by oversight used only his given name.

A retrospective measure of the degree to which Long was embedded in the public consciousness is afforded by his subsequent career in litera-ture. Thackeray referred to him in *The Book of Snobs* (*Punch*, 1846), and as late as the seventies he appeared in *Middlemarch* (chapter 45) and *Far from the Madding Crowd* (chapter 22: "an anticlimax somewhat resembling that of St. John Long's death by consumption in the midst of his proofs that it was not a fatal disease"). While mention of Long in *Middlemarch* may have been due in part to George Eliot's research in the files of the *Times* and the *Lancet*, both she and Hardy obviously relied upon their readers' ready recognition of a forty-year-old allusion. Probably Long's prominence in several editions of the *Newgate Calendar* had something to do with his enduring celebrity.

Another case in point is the almost legendary George Stulz (or Stultz), the fashionable tailor who appeared first in the *Post Office Directory* in 1815. (In 1842 his firm was styled "Stulz, Housley, and Wain, tailors, 10 Clifford St., Bond St.") By the time Carlyle wrote of him in *Past and Present* (pp. 215–16) he had already become the abiding symbol of masculine *haute couture*, not to say outright dandyism: "Your Stulz, with huge somerset, vaults from his high shopboard down to the depth of primal savagery,—carrying much along with him!" Hazlitt had men-tioned him (*Monthly Magazine*, 1831), as had Bulwer in *Pelham* (1828) and *England and the English* (1833), Thackeray in his *Yellowplush Correspondence* and "Epistle to the Literati" (*Fraser's*, 1838 and 1840 respectively), Carlyle himself in his essay on Scott (*London and Westminster Review*, 1838)— though, oddly, not in *Sartor Resartus*; Samuel Warren in his novel, *Ten Thousand a Year!* (*Blackwood's*, 1839); and Thomas Hood in "Miss Kil-mansegg and Her Precious Leg" (1840–41). By the time of *Past and Present* only the positively illiterate could not have known who Stulz was: Carlyle could allude to him with perfect assurance that the name would carry its intended meaning.[2]

A quack doctor, a fashionable tailor, and now a recalcitrant land-owner, the Duke of Newcastle: his name and well-established notoriety, too, served Carlyle as common coinage, but in a more complex and subtle way. The Duke first appears in *Past and Present* on page 11. Though he is unnamed there, every reader would have recognized him behind Carlyle's figure of the "Master Unworker" "coercing, bribing, cajoling: doing what he likes with his own." The latter phrase (Matthew 20:15) had been on derisive tongues ever since 1829, when the Duke had used it in defending himself against criticism in the House of Lords for having evicted two hundred of his tenants at Newark for failing to vote for the Tory candidate. "Is it not lawful," he asked, "for me to do what I please with mine own?" The Duke reappears (p. 57), this time by name, but only as owner of a Suffolk pleasure ground where the Battle of Fornham was fought in 1173. Two pages farther on, Carlyle revives the "doing what he likes with his own" theme to contrast the martyrdom of the benevolent ninth-century King (or Landlord) Edmund with nineteenth-century landowners' abnegation of their social responsibility. Again, Newcastle is not named; the reader's appreciation of Carlyle's irony—his conversion of the phrase, in Edmund's mouth, to allude to a man's inalienable freedom to sacrifice his own life—depends on his responding to the topical allusion of the echo of St. Matthew, which is repeated in later passages (p. 125, again in specific connection with Edmund; and pp. 174, 181).

At the time *Past and Present* was written, the Duke was no longer in the news. Following the burning of one of his residences, Nottingham Castle, by a Reform Bill mob which had not forgotten his ill-advised invocation of Scripture, Newcastle had retired into crusty seclusion. But his name and the indelibly associated tag from St. Matthew still served, a dozen and more years after the event, as a symbol of "landlords' coercion" (p. 80). Carlyle, in effect, did with him what he also did with St. John Long and Stulz: enlarged the character or the sentiment so that it was no longer the attribute of a single historical figure but that of a whole social class or phenomenon—quackery, dandyism, or neglect of *noblesse oblige*.[3]

Because they had been continually in the public consciousness a number of years before their appearance in *Past and Present*, these allusions had a richer resonance than did those of more immediate origin, to which we must now turn, remembering that Carlyle was writing from mid-autumn 1842 to 8 March 1843. What these references lacked in scope, they made up for in immediacy. "Honour to the name of Ashley" (p. 281) refers to the future Lord Shaftesbury's moving an address to the crown on behalf of the state-aided education of the working class, an event of 28 February. It may well be that Carlyle was writing that very page at that very moment. Ashley's speech was designed to prepare the way for the favorable reception of Sir James Graham's "Factory-Bill" (p. 261), with its crucial provisions for released-time instruction for child workers ("a right Education Bill," p. 262). This was formally introduced into the Commons in the evening of the day that Carlyle wrote the last words of *Past and Present*.

The allusions to "our new friend, the Emperor" (p. 232) and to the treaty of Nanking (p. 264) reflect the end of the Opium War and the enforced reconciliation of China with Britain, news of which had reached London late in November 1842. The focus of the " 'Black or White Surplice' Controversies" (p. 206) was an event of 10 October, the Bishop of London's widely publicized charge to his diocese on a number of questions of ritual, preeminent among which was his recommendation that the preacher wear a surplice at morning service and a black gown at the evening one.[4] Two major literary events of the year are glanced at: Dickens's ("Schnüspel" 's) tour of America from January to June (pp. 60, 246) and the publication of Tennyson's *Poems*, from which a line of "Ulysses" is quoted, in May (p. 41).

As with events, so with contemporary social phenomena. Carlyle's reference to "railway speed" (p. 267) touched a responsive point in the consciousness of the moment, because nothing more acutely induced men's awareness of the new age they were living in than did the sensation of railway velocity, an element in human experience no more than a dozen years old. Even more recent an arrival (in 1840) was the "Stamped Postman" (p. 225). And while extravagant "puffery" (pp. 144, 234) of commercial products was by no means new, it unquestionably was more ubiquitous, and to many observers more objectionable, than ever before: Mill's onslaught, in his essay on "Civilization" (*London and Westminster Review*, 1836), strikingly anticipated Carlyle's. In the literary marketplace, the flamboyant practices of publishers like Bentley and Colburn, who not only touted their books in the usual ways but arranged for favorable reviews in their own periodicals and elsewhere, gave promotion a bad name. Even more offensive, however, were the outdoor advertising devices that burgeoned at this time. The rivalry of two makers of boot blacking, Warren and Day & Martin, was responsible for the defacement by paint or poster of countless pavements and walls. It is alluded to on page 146, along with the famous "seven-feet Hat" (pp. 144, 150, 206, 267) which serves in *Past and Present* as a synecdoche to assimilate all other forms of puffery. Carlyle's readers—the Londoners through daily personal experience, those in the country through the weekly cartoons and expostulations in *Punch*—were aware that at this moment road traffic in the Strand was being choked by vehicles bearing monstrous enlargements of the products advertised. Nor would they have forgotten that in May 1842 the birth of the *Illustrated London News* itself was heralded by the proprietors' turning loose on the crowded sidewalks of central London no fewer than two hundred sign bearers. If the paper's engraving of the lineup, in its first issue (14 May), is to be credited, the signs were taller than the men.

The current fame of Morison's pill (pp. 28 ff., 41, 42, 226, 230), acquired both through its manufacturer's extravagant advertising campaigns and through several court cases resulting from fatalities allegedly caused by overdoses, needs no gloss to anyone familiar with the English scene in 1843. It would have been strange indeed if Carlyle had not seized upon Morison's pill, itself (like St. John Long's corrosive mixture) a leading exemplar of quackery in the literal sense, as a central symbol of the pervasive spiritual falsehood to which he extended the same name.[5]

Dominating the allusive fabric of *Past and Present*, of course, were the eventful 1842 session of Parliament, which was prorogued in the middle of August, and the "Manchester Insurrection" which flared in the same month. The latter, taking, in part, the form of the Plug Plot riots from which Carlyle derived the name of Plugson of Undershot, probably makes the greater impression upon the reader, supplying as it does a tempestuous background for the argument. But it actually is depicted in general terms, with little reference to particular incidents. Carlyle is much more specific in his use of the Parliament of 1842. The session had been marked by the head-on confrontation, a decade in the preparing, of the protectionist landowning class and the free-trade manufacturing bloc on the related issues of tariff revision and taxation.

In the large pattern of *Past and Present*, this conflict of vested interests is represented by a sustained interplay of allusions. On the one hand, there are the partridge-shooting, game-preserving dilettantes, of whose activities Carlyle's readers were kept well informed in the press. The *Illustrated London News* for 22 October reported that four gentlemen, shooting at Buckenham, Norfolk, had killed 433 head of game in one day. Only three rabbits were among the casualties; "the greater portion were pheasants and partridges." At the end of the year (31 December) the same paper described a "grand battu" at Dupplin Castle, the seat of the Earl and Countess of Kinnoull. Despite bad weather, the party brought down 176 pheasants, 364 hares, 27 woodcock, and 275 rabbits. With news like this constantly serving editors as column fillers, Carlyle's diatribes against the Master Unworkers needed no further documentation.

Ranged against the dilettantes were their two large bodies of enemies, the constituency of the Anti-Corn Law League and the Chartists, whose extreme wing was uneasily and fleetingly allied with the corresponding wing of the Manchester free traders. The Anti-Corn Law League, founded in Manchester in 1838, had gone national the next year, and now it was figuring in the daily news as the most powerful pressure group since Wilberforce's antislavery campaigns. While its leaders were lobbying and propagandizing against protectionism, the Chartists were receiving equal publicity as they handed in the second of their six-point petitions to Parliament (2 May).

When the newly elected Commons met at the beginning of the year, the Peelites had proposed to modify, to the patent disadvantage of the landowners, the sliding scale (pp. 34, 58, 146, 180, 190) built into the Corn Laws with the purpose of making the price of grain responsive to the shifts in supply and demand. The debate, climaxed on 5 April by the passage of the bill embodying the revised scale, inspired Carlyle to a double play on words at one point in his attack on the Idle Aristocracy: " 'sliding,' as on inclined-planes, which every new year they *soap* with new Hansard's-jargon under God's sky, and so are 'sliding' ever faster, towards a 'scale' and balance-scale whereon is written *Thou art found Wanting*" (p. 270).

The opposition to the revised sliding scale was personified by the Duke of Buckingham and Chandos, who had resigned as Lord Keeper of the Privy Seal early in the session in protest against Peel's ("his Excellenz the Titular-Herr Ritter Kauderwälsch von Pferdefuss-Quacksalber" 's, p. 215) wooing of the Manchester bloc. In May, in tribute to his services in Parliament as "a recognised Farmer's Friend" (p. 58), a group of Chandos' fellow agriculturalists had gathered at Aylesbury to present him with "a piece of plate four feet six inches high, weighing 1800 ounces, and valued at £2000" (*Illustrated London News*, 21 May). Already notorious as an employer of sweated farm labor ("Chandos daydrudges," p. 88; "Chandos Farm-Labourers," p. 188), the Duke almost inevitably joined his fellow peer, the Duke of Newcastle, in the passage (pp. 57–59) already alluded to, as a model of social irresponsibility. In a season of widespread destitution and unrest among the people, Buckingham was thrust into the news by the ill-timed action of his admirers; in an equally tumultuous year, 1831, Newcastle had achieved a doubtful celebrity through the action of his incendiary working-class enemies. Neither, it must be stressed again, is named in this skillful passage; the reader's appreciation of Carlyle's irony depended wholly upon his awareness of what lay behind the allusions to the Farmer's Friend and "doing what one likes with one's own." With that recognition, the two peers merged to exemplify the anti-Edmund, the avatar of game-preserving dilettantism.

The atmosphere and issues of this parliamentary session punctuate the text of *Past and Present* in other ways. In the very first chapter (p. 9),

"Mining-Labourer Committees" refers to the shocking report of the Commission for Inquiring into the Employment of Children which resulted in the quick passage of Ashley's act limiting the labor of women and children in collieries and mines. Elsewhere there are allusions to the proposed land property tax (pp. 29, 182) and to tariff revisions (p. 50), also anathema to the landowners, which were passed at the end of June.[6]

Streaked through many of the debates, as we find them reported in *Hansard*, was the claim of "expediency," cant which Carlyle repeatedly denounced (pp. 14, 24, 92, 152). But it is his iterated use of the word "Conservative" that probably touched his readers' politico-semantic nerve most keenly. In 1843, as applied to a party rather than a broad political philosophy and capitalized rather than set in lower case, the word was but a dozen years old, having first been used in that way by a writer—not John Wilson Croker, as used to be assumed—in the *Quarterly Review* (January 1830). From the outset it had designated the Peelite liberal wing of the Tory party. Now that the Tories were in power after having been in opposition for eleven years (with the exception of the so-called hundred days in 1834–35), the novel name attached to their now dominant Peelite bloc was on everybody's tongue. It is against this background, of a neologism in the process of taking its permanent place in the political lexicon, that Carlyle's uses of the term (pp. 15, 17, 164–66) can most profitably be read. The book's running juxtaposition of past and present is, in a way, epitomized by the recurrence of a single term, whose recently acquired extra function as the label of the party newly in power, one would imagine, caused it to stand out in discourse as if subtly italicized.[7]

This was the session celebrated for the number of constituencies (Harwich, Nottingham, Lewes, Reading, Falmouth, Penryn, Bridport) that were accused of gross electoral corruption. Carlyle's "late Bribery Committee" (pp. 180, 181, 250–54) reported at the end of July. One of the references to the committee and its concern, "Bribery could not be put down" (p. 250), is of more than ordinary interest because, like the use of the Duke of Newcastle's self-justification from Scripture, it exemplifies the Carlylean technique of the submerged allusion. Here he depended upon his readers' recognizing a catch phrase of the moment, the much-derided determination of Sir Peter Laurie, Middlesex magistrate (Alderman Cute in Dickens's *The Chimes*), to "put down suicide." Laurie is not named, but every reader of the newspapers or of *Punch*, which cherished him as a favorite butt, would have responded to the ironical implication.

Laurie's dedication to the antisuicide cause had been expressed in 1841,[8] the year in which several other allusions had their source, among them the Stockport assizes (p. 9) and Chadwick's Report on the Training of Pauper Children (p. 276). Carlyle's allusion to D. F. Strauss (p. 232) was probably more intelligible than it would otherwise have been because of the appearance in the *Foreign Quarterly Review* (July 1841) of a long review of his *Die christliche Glaubenslehre in ihrer geschichtlichen Entwicklung*, published at Tübingen. Strauss and his doctrines were already known to some British intellectuals, but this review of his new book would have served as a timely reminder. Less intelligible to the generality of readers, one feels, would have been the reference (p. 292) to Brook Farm, which was only two years old in 1843. That Carlyle and his circle were aware of it was due immediately to Bronson Alcott's visit to London in the summer of 1842 (he first called at Cheyne Row on 25 June). But the great experiment had little fame as yet, and Carlyle's allusion would seem to be an example of a topicality whose time had not yet come.

As we move further away from 1842–43 to events in the middle distance, we necessarily become less confident of the degree to which Carlyle's allusions would have had the impact he desired. Of the continuing currency of some, there can be little doubt. The public would have retained active memories of the Chartists' plan for a general strike, the "Sacred Month" (p. 269), which had been debated, and rejected, at their Birmingham convention in the summer of 1839. Thomas C. Haliburton's *The Clockmaker; or the Sayings and Doings of Sam Slick of Slicksville*, published by Bentley, 1837–38 et seq., was still being read (pp. 277–78). The Useful Knowledge Society (p. 132), though it had passed the peak of its usefulness, still served as an emblem of the utilitarians' fatuous aim (as Carlyle saw it) of improving and tranquilizing the masses through instructive books and magazines. The "taxes on knowledge" (p. 89) remained a live political issue, as they had been for more than a decade. So did the agitation for "Church-extension" (pp. 34, 168), which had been revived by the Chartist riots and was, as Carlyle wrote *Past and Present*, intensifying the Church-Dissent controversy that was to doom the education clauses in Graham's factory bill. The Ecclesiastical Commission, appointed in 1835, was still much in the public eye, and its results to date were by no means forgotten, least of all its decision, early in its career, that bishops could live respectably on the large sum, for the time, of £4500 a year (pp. 187, 195, 291).[9] Chancery (pp. 126, 133, 258) was still the somnolent symbol of legal inertia that it had been in 1827–28, when extended book-length attacks had appeared, and in 1840, when Edwin W.

Field denounced it afresh.[10] The Bridgewater Treatises (pp. 149–50), published in 1833–36, were still being read by people anxious to have fresh
verification of the truths of natural theology.

We can be less certain, however, of the continuing value, in 1843, of
several other references reaching back ten years or more. "Owen's
Labour-bank," for instance (p. 204), founded in September 1832, had
collapsed only two years later and in all likelihood was now recalled only
vaguely as an abortive episode in the early socialist movement. While "the
eupeptic Curtis" (p. 157) was unquestionably a man of considerable fame
in his lifetime as a by-word for vulgar sensuality and gluttony—Byron
had worked him into *Don Juan* (10.86) in 1823—his name probably had
vanished from many people's memory. Whatever active disrepute he possessed when he died in 1829 doubtless was soon eclipsed by the larger
notoriety of the Duke of Newcastle. And one wonders, too, how much
the reference to Hampden's exhumation in 1828 (p. 122) meant to readers
fifteen years later. This is an instance in which Carlyle was himself un-
sure, for he printed a footnote referring to reports of the episode in the
Gentleman's Magazine and the *Annual Register*.

At all events, the tensions and turbulence of the Reform Bill era were
inscribed ineffaceably upon the national memory. In Carlyle's scheme of
modern English history, as in that of most of his readers, the years 1830–
32 represented what has recently been called "the most prolonged and
dangerous crisis in the country's history since the Revolution of 1688."[11]
Two oblique references to this traumatic national experience illustrate
Carlyle's technique at its most subtle. The mentions of "heavy wet" beer
(pp. 37, 217–18) do not refer merely to the well-known fact that British
elections at that time were accompanied by much drunkenness. In addition, Carlyle must have meant to revive a specific though fortuitous association forged between democratic politics and beer in 1830, when, as
the Reform fever began to rise, Parliament removed the tax on malt
liquor. The coincidence of the Beer Bill and the agitation for the Reform
Bill was memorialized in at least two popular songs, one of which was
actually titled "Heavy Wet":

> King William and Reform, I say,
>   In such a case who can be neuter?
> Just let me blow the froth away,
>   And see how I will drain the pewter.
> Another tankard, landlord, fill,
>   And let us drink to that ere chap, Broom;

And then we'll chaunt God save King Bill,
And send the echoes thro' the tap-room.[12]

Another instance of double allusiveness is the reference to "the new Downing-Street Schedule A" (p. 251). It was timely, in that it referred to the Peel government's proposed income tax; but contemporary readers, alerted by the word "new," would have recognized that Carlyle was again reaching back to 1831–32, when there was a Downing Street Schedule A of a quite different sort—the proposed scheme of electoral redistricting.

By such indirect means Carlyle sought to link the present with the immediate past—to suggest that 1843 was witnessing a revival of the crisis conditions of a dozen years earlier. They were troubled years not only in England but in France, with its Three-Day Paris Revolution and the revolt of the Lyons silkworkers, and in Poland (all on p. 20). But looming behind the Reform Bill era was the most crucial event in all modern history; and the conclusion is inescapable that in his handling of topical material Carlyle's overriding motive was to suggest that whatever resemblances might be discovered between the events and issues of 1842–43 and those of 1830–32, the combined present-day phenomena of the Manchester Insurrection and Chartism were most ominously suggestive of the French Revolution. "Good Heavens, will not one French Revolution and Reign of Terror suffice us, but must there be two?" (p. 270).

A series of sequential associations artfully spaced throughout the book brings the events of the two epochs, separated by fifty years, into connotative alignment:

> Manchester Insurrections, French Revolutions, and thousand-fold phenomena great and small (p. 27).
>
> these stormtost seas, French Revolutions, Chartisms, Manchester Insurrections, that make the heart sick in these bad days (p. 40).
>
> no French Revolution or Manchester Insurrection, or partial or universal volcanic combustions and explosions (p. 87).
>
> Chartism, *Bare-backism*, Sansculottism so-called! (p. 125).
>
> in killing Kings, in passing Reform Bills, in French Revolutions, Manchester Insurrections, is found no remedy (p. 140).
>
> Do we wonder at French Revolutions, Chartisms, Revolts of Three Days? (p. 210).

> Hence French Revolutions, Five-point Charters, Democracies,
> and a mournful list of *Etceteras*, in these our afflicted times
> (p. 214).

To Carlyle, more than any other Englishman perhaps, the French
Revolution remained intensely topical in 1842. In *The French Revolution*
(1837) he had, in fact, anticipated several of the analogies and relationships he was to exploit, in different form, in *Past and Present*. As the fourth
in the series of quotations suggests, his clothes-conscious imagination
almost obsessively linked the sansculottism[13] of the 1790s with the bare
backs of 1842. Just as breechlessness was the condition of the wretched
men who destroyed the *ancien régime*, so shirtlessness—the frequency of its
mention (pp. 27, 135, 170, 185, 193, 266) makes it one of the book's leit-
motivs—was an omen of the impending revolt of the English masses.
Both symbolized the anarchic potential of the oppressed workers. The
economy of abundance, as Carlyle climactically showed in the opening
paragraphs of the chapter "Over-Production," had caused a glut of
both articles of clothing. "We accuse you," he imagined the Governing
Class chiding the Workers, "of making above two-hundred thousand
shirts for the bare backs of mankind. Your trousers too, which you have
made, . . . are they not manifold? . . . Millions of shirts, and empty
pairs of breeches, hang there in judgment against you" (p. 172). But the
ultimate judgment, Carlyle feared, would be delivered by the shirtless,
even as it had been delivered at the tanneries of Meudon, with "the long-
naked making for themselves breeches of human skins! May the merciful
Heavens avert the omen; may we be the wiser, that so we be less wretched"
(p. 180).

There was an implicit association, also, between the shrill, Amazo-
nian *Citoyennes* recurrently seen in *The French Revolution*—"female Jacobins, famed *Tricoteuses* with knitting-needles" (4.301)—and the harpylike
"Female Chartists" who explode into the streets of twelfth-century St.
Edmundsbury (pp. 69, 91, 95). As historical figures, the shrieking, scold-
ing old women are figments of Carlyle's analogical inventiveness; but the
name he gives them creates yet another link between past and present,
because some of the most active Chartist organizations in 1842 actually
had women's auxiliaries, and at the very moment Carlyle was writing, the
newspapers reported meetings of Female Chartists in London (17 October, 5 December). In addition, by arming his Female Chartists with dis-
taffs, the tools of spinners, rather than with the Female Jacobins' knitting
needles, Carlyle strengthened the implication that his imagined figures

were more modern then medieval. Spinning—now mechanized, to be sure—was the predominant occupation represented in the Manchester Chartist mobs.

Although it was none of Carlyle's doing that the New Poor Law workhouses had acquired the name of Bastille, the accident added a grace note to his allusive pattern. His repeated use of "Poor Law Bastilles" (pp. 7, 163–64, 170, 173, etc.) unobtrusively reinforced the association of the Revolution with the issues of the present moment. "No Bastilles!" had been the slogan of Tory and Chartist alike in the election of 1841, and it was in those hated symbols of latter-day oppression and degradation that "the all-conquering valiant Sons of Toil sit enchanted, by the million" (p. 170). History was indeed repeating itself. It is perhaps not too fanciful to read in his treatment of the Anti-Corn Law League something of the attitude Carlyle maintained toward the Girondists in *The French Revolution*: they were the respectable wing of the Revolution, in contrast to the proletarian Jacobins (1842: Chartists).

Taking Carlyle's employment of the Reform Bill crisis and of the French Revolution in *Past and Present* at its face value, we might conclude that through the public anxieties of 1842 reverberated the still vivid personal memories of 1830–32 and the residual collective memory, still alive and menacing even among a new generation, of the earlier upheaval across the Channel. Carlyle's rhetoric, it might be assumed, was addressed to a readily receptive mood in his audience, and it therefore succeeded. But this is quite possibly an oversimplification. Might it not be, instead, that the French Revolution meant considerably less to Carlyle's readers than it did to him? Is it not conceivable that he expected a more fervent response to his historical analogies than they were prepared to supply?[14] If so, we may have an additional reason, beyond those usually cited, for his superheated style: its vehemence was designed to reduce the discrepancy he felt between his personal agitation over the resemblances and what he sensed to be the comparative indifference of the public.

Wherever the truth may lie, our evidence suggests that even if he was not guilty of rhetorical overkill, he sometimes miscalculated. While the majority of his topicalities would have been fully intelligible to most of his readers, a significant number would have produced the maximum intended effect only upon those who enjoyed a prior acquaintance with Carlyle's writings. It is doubtful if the reference to "gigs and flunky 'respectabilities' " (p. 272) would have carried its proposed weight of meaning to anyone not acquainted with Carlyle's fondness for the "gigmanity"-respectability joke he had long ago drawn from a somewhat inaccurate report of testimony at Thurtell's trial and had repeated, most recently, in *The French Revolution* (4.245, 322–23). Readers similarly un-aware of the role the Female Jacobins played in that book could not have responded fully to their reappearance in *Past and Present* as Female Chartists.

So, too, with elements in *Past and Present* that echo *Sartor Resartus*. Although the pattern of references to dandyism (p. 130) and valethood/valetism (pp. 31, 86, 90, 149–50), like that involving the idle dilettantes, is self-sustaining and self-explanatory, readers who knew *Sartor* would un-questionably have discovered a richer aura of connotation in such passages. The ironies associated with the allusions to the shirtless workers of 1842 vis-à-vis the sansculottes of 1793 were enlarged by an appreciation of the symbolic role the fancy clothing of the rich played in *Sartor*.[15]

From time to time, we may assume, Carlyle's topical references fell short of the mark. But the number of such failures is small when com-pared with the number of allusions that we can be fairly sure had the effect he desired. In the wisdom of his craft, he largely eschewed private lan-guage, at least as far as topicalities were concerned. The great majority of them added substantially to the vividness, force, and immediate applica-bility that help constitute a successful and enduring tract for the times—lending *Past and Present* the qualities that made it, in Emerson's words, an "immortal newspaper."

1976

6
Education, Print, and Paper in *Our Mutual Friend*

"In these times of ours . . .": so begins *Our Mutual Friend*, in Dickens's most explicit statement of the contemporaneity of a novel's setting. "Concerning the exact year," he continues, "there is no need to be precise." Nor is there, because the setting is certainly the period just before and during that of the novel's composition, January 1864–September 1865. In each of Dickens's novels, whatever the ostensible setting, there hovers the author's sense of the *Zeitgefühl*, the elusive, intangible, often largely undefined quality of the moment. Such a sense usually is dominated by some easily apprehensible symbol, a "characteristic" of the time such as the railway in *Dombey and Son*, Chancery in *Bleak House*, the Circumlocution Office in *Little Dorrit*, and, in *Our Mutual Friend*, the dust mounds and the filth-laden Thames. These last, however, are not as precise indications of the moment as is the cluster of time-evidences—themes and incidental references—that I propose to examine here, in quest of those "finer threads" which, in Dickens's words at the end of this very novel, are related "to the whole pattern which is always before the eyes of the story-weaver at his loom" (p. 821).[1]

In a metropolis symbolically and geographically defined by the dust heaps to the north (between Battle Bridge, near King's Cross, and Holloway) and by the dirty river to the south, the spirit of the moment as Dickens felt it—or at least that element which he chose to emblematize it—was marked by a particular concern over popular education and over literacy as the leading product of that education; and the physical reflection of that concern was printed paper. Put another way, a link, additional to those already perceived by Dickens critics, which connects the dust mounds (and the illiterate Boffin) with the river (and the illiterate Gaffer Hexam) is Dickens's interpretation, in 1864–65, of the present state and consequences of the Victorian desire for education and self-improvement. The expectations are epitomized in Noddy Boffin's sanguine "Print is now opening ahead of me" as he looks forward to the advent of "a literary man—*with* a wooden leg" who "will begin to lead me a new life!" (p. 53). The realities are a leading topical subject of the novel.

Education in a wider sense is, of course, a theme of *Our Mutual Friend*, though it is not as conspicuous or as central as in, say, *David Copperfield* or *Great Expectations*. "The school of life"—moral education through experience, finding out the path to happiness the hard way—is an implicit motif. Bella Wilfer is the chief pupil, and her father sums up her gain from Boffin's benevolent tutelage in his not very original observation, "There's no royal road to learning; and what is life but learning?" (p.684). Eugene Wrayburn is redeemed from a life of aimless vacuity and made a fit husband for Lizzie almost at the cost of his life. Before his redemption, he describes his indolent habits to Mortimer Lightwood in a school analogy: "When we were at school together, I got up my lessons at the last moment, day by day and bit by bit; now we are out in life together, I get up my lessons in the same way" (p. 537).

But education enters *Our Mutual Friend* not only as a moral theme but also as a social topic. In the early sixties discussion of the perennial Victorian issue of popular education—the "democratizing" of learning to the extent of giving working-class children a minimal ability to read—acquired current relevance from the agitation for an enlarged franchise which would eventually result in the Second Reform Bill of 1867. The sardonic "We must educate our masters" had not yet been attributed to Robert Lowe, vice-president of the Committee of Council on Education, but the necessity, difficulties, and perils of universal education were already being debated in connection with the movement to double the electorate.

From the early 1840s, when he became Miss Burdett-Coutts's almoner, Dickens had taken a deep interest in the voluntary "ragged schools" which constituted the lowest rung on the educational ladder in the London slums, and in an indignant passage in *Our Mutual Friend* he returned to a favorite theme of his, the ludicrous unsuitability of the reading books used in these well-meaning but misguided institutions, one of which Charley Hexam had attended:

> Young women old in the vices of the commonest and worst life, were expected to profess themselves enthralled by the good child's book, the Adventures of Little Margery, who resided in the village cottage by the mill; severely reproved and morally squashed the miller when she was five and he was fifty; divided her porridge with singing birds; denied herself a new nankeen bonnet, on the ground that the turnips did not wear nankeen bonnets, neither did the sheep who ate them;

who plaited straw and delivered the dreariest orations to all comers, at all sorts of unseasonable times. So unwieldy young dredgers and hulking mudlarks were referred to the experiences of Thomas Twopence, who, having resolved not to rob (under circumstances of uncommon atrocity) his particular friend and benefactor, of eighteen-pence, presently came into supernatural possession of three and six-pence, and lived a shining light ever afterwards. (Note that the benefactor came to no good.) Several swaggering sinners had written their own biographies in the same strain; it always appearing from the lessons of those very boastful persons, that you were to do good, not because it *was* good, but because you were to make a good thing of it. Contrariwise, the adult pupils were taught to read (if they could learn) out of the New Testament; and by dint of stumbling over the syllables and keeping their bewildered eyes on the particular syllables coming round to their turn, were as absolutely ignorant of the sublime history, as if they had never seen or heard of it. (pp. 214–15)[2]

A degree more advanced than the ragged schools were those taught by Bradley Headstone and Miss Peecher: working-class schools, conducted by Anglican and Nonconformist educational agencies but partially subsidized by the state, and taught by men and women who had themselves come from "the million" and been prepared for their occupation in teacher training colleges. These schools were not a novelty in the period of *Our Mutual Friend* (the government subsidies, for example, had begun in a small way in 1833, and inspection in 1839), but they had become more numerous with every passing year, and their proliferation was a visible social phenomenon of the sixties. Dickens specifically associated Headstone's and Miss Peecher's schools with the building boom he and his London readers were witnessing at the moment:

> The schools—for they were twofold, as the sexes—were down in that district of the flat country tending to the Thames, where Kent and Surrey meet, and where the railways still bestride the market-gardens that will soon die under them. The schools were newly built, and there were so many like them all over the country, that one might have thought the whole were but one restless edifice with the locomotive gift of Aladdin's palace. (p. 218)

But it was with the teachers, not the buildings as features of the changing urban landscapes, that Dickens was concerned. As Philip Collins has pointed out, his "main educational interest in this novel is the sociology of the new race of trained teachers . . . The college-trained teacher of Dickens's later years [unlike his ill-paid, overworked predecessors] could not be regarded as a subject for pathos; . . . he was relatively well paid. Usually he had risen, like Headstone and Hexam, from a humble origin; his success in doing so might be regarded as admirable, and his decent salary a well-earned reward for hard work. At least as often, however, it touched off lower-class prejudices against the man who deserts his kind, and middle-class prejudices against the *parvenu*."[3] Headstone and Hexam are, in fact, poor relations of the Veneerings. The attempted upward thrust of the new breed of teachers is part of the problem of social mobility and pretension which is among the novel's chief themes. "A higher social position, . . . they felt, was their right, as men of superior education engaged in an important and respectable job, and they were the more bitterly insistent on this because generally they had risen from poor families, and wanted reassurance that they were accepted into middle-class society. . . ."[4] An additional price these teachers paid—overlooked by them, but characteristically apparent to Dickens—was the dehumanizing effect of their crudely systematized professional preparation. Miss Peecher, he noted, loved Bradley Headstone "with all the primitive and homely stock of love that had never been examined or certificated out of her" (p. 338).

The schoolmasters had brought their grievances into the public eye, which had so far been indifferent to their very existence, as a consequence of a crisis within the profession. In 1861 the Newcastle Commission, set up three years earlier to make a comprehensive study of popular education, recommended instituting regular formal examinations as a means of testing what would today be called the cost-effectiveness of the schools. Lowe readily agreed. "If education is not cheap," he declared in the accents of true Benthamism, "it should be efficient; if it is not efficient it should be cheap." In response, the Committee of Council on Education promulgated the so-called Revised Code of 1863 which made government grants to each school contingent upon the results of examinations conducted by the visiting government inspector. Each satisfactory performance won the management 6s. 6d. (in the case of an infant-school pupil) or 12s. (in that of an older one) for the coming year. Penalties were assessed for faulty performance and irregular attendance. Among the major effects of the "payment by results" system were a large increase in the membership of the two professional organizations, as angry teachers, who got all the blame if their pupils failed and none of the money if they passed, rose to arms; more stress on rote memorizing (to which we will return in a moment); and continual publicity for the state-assisted school system as the merits and iniquities of the Revised Code and the claims of the teachers were debated in Parliament. Lowe, who as deviser of the code and its most voluble and prominent apologist was one of the best-hated men of the day, was driven from office in April 1864, just before the first monthly part of *Our Mutual Friend* was published.[5]

Schools and schoolmasters, then, were very much in the news. Here as elsewhere in his fiction, Dickens deftly exploited a topicality for artistic purposes. As he developed the novel, education, and specifically literacy, a cultural value which was enjoying fresh attention as a result of the controversy over the Revised Code, directed the plot and helped delineate character; as much as the dust mounds and the river, it supplied not only scene but framework and motivation. Lizzie Hexam, whose books at the outset of the novel are the fire into which she gazes in her waterside mill-turned-hovel (pp. 28–30), at first sacrifices her own education for the sake of her brother Charley's. (The value of the boon she confers upon the ingrate Charley is quietly suggested by Dickens's comment when Charley awaits Mortimer in the Veneerings' "library of bran-new books, in bran-new bindings liberally gilded": "he glanced at the backs of the books, with an awakened curiosity that went below the binding. No one who can read, ever looks at a book, even unopened on a shelf, like one who cannot" [p. 18].) Gaffer, their illiterate father, strenuously opposes schooling for either one because it would make him their inferior. "Let him never come within sight of my eyes," he says of Charley, "nor yet within reach of my arm. His own father ain't good enough for him. He's disowned his own father. His own father, therefore, disowns him for ever and ever, as an unnatural young beggar" (p. 75). Thus the issue defines each character and the relationship of the three. Gaffer's brute nature is exemplified by his attitude, which places him in grotesque juxtaposition with those on a higher level of society who suffer the same gnawing social anxiety. Lizzie's initial self-abnegation in respect to learning is the particular mark, in this novel, of the heroine; and Charley's selfishness and social ambition are expressed by the humiliation he feels because of Lizzie's illiteracy. "It's a painful thing," he tells Headstone, "to think that if I get on as well as you hope, I shall be— I won't say disgraced, because I don't mean disgraced—but—rather put to the blush if it was known—by a sister who has been very good to me" (p. 231).

Lizzie's illiteracy, moreover, provides Dickens with a new twist for a familiar theme.[6] The social differences that form so frequent and imposing an obstacle to lovers' happiness in Victorian fiction are expressed here in the unusual terms of disparate education. Eugene Wrayburn proposes, from motives purer than those exhibited by other of Dickens's idle young men, to pay "some qualified person of your [Lizzie's] own sex and age, so many (or rather so few) contemptible shillings, to come here, certain nights in the week, and give you certain instruction which you wouldn't want if you hadn't been a self-denying daughter and sister" (p.235). Similar education for Jenny Wren is included in the arrangement. Lizzie's acceptance, after an interval of prudent hesitation, precipitates Headstone's insane jealousy, for Headstone has already decided to make the necessity of Lizzie's being educated the pretext for paying suit to her. "Some man who had worked his way," he disingenuously explains to Charley, "might come to admire—your sister—and might even in time bring himself to think of marrying—your sister—and it would be a sad drawback and a heavy penalty upon him if, overcoming in his mind other inequalities of condition and other considerations against it, this inequality and this consideration remained in full force" (p. 231). Headstone's fury when he learns that Eugene has anticipated him is shared by Charley, his *protégé*, who thereupon becomes allied with his schoolmaster against his sister. "What right," he demands, "has he [Eugene] to do it, and what does he mean by it, and how comes he to be taking such a liberty without my consent, when I am raising myself in the scale of society by my own exertions and Mr. Headstone's aid, and have no right to have any darkness cast upon my prospects, or any imputation upon my respectability, through my sister?" (p. 290).

The conflict between Headstone and Wrayburn thus originates in the disputed claim to supply her education. She is an eager pupil. Soon after her teacher (who, she assures Charley, "comes from an institution where teachers are regularly brought up" [p. 345] and therefore enjoys formal certification) has begun operations, she and Jenny are spending their holidays with pleasure and profit in "book learning." This result is agreeable enough, but one should note that it is accomplished not in the classroom but through private instruction; and, indelibly associated as they are with the popular educational system, the conduct of Charley and Headstone throughout the novel casts a deep shadow upon that system. Dickens indeed goes so far as to ascribe Headstone's villainy to his profession:

Tied up all day with his disciplined show upon him, subdued to the performance of his routine of educational tricks, encircled by a gabbling crowd, he broke loose at night like an ill-tamed wild animal. Under his daily restraint, it was his compensation, not his trouble, to give a glance towards his state at night, and to the freedom of its being indulged. (p. 546).

And as Gissing later remarked of Charley, "This youth has every fault that can attach to a half-taught cub of his particular world. He is a monstrous egotist, to begin with, and 'school' has merely put an edge on to the native vice."[7] In *Our Mutual Friend*, the contemporary school system suffers guilt by association.

Dickens was unenthusiastic, to say the least, about the methods employed in its classrooms. Mr. Podsnap's condescending didacticism as he instructs the Frenchman in the subtleties of English grammar and pronunciation and the glories of the British Constitution would qualify him, Dickens remarks, to teach in an infant school (p. 132). There was, too, the sterile Gradgrindery of the teaching routine, a favorite target in Dickens's criticism of educational method. Headstone, he says,

had acquired mechanically a great store of teacher's knowledge. He could do mental arithmetic mechanically, sing at sight mechanically, blow various wind instruments mechanically, even play the great church organ mechanically. From his early childhood up, his mind had been a place of mechanical stowage. The arrangement of his wholesale warehouse, so that it might be always ready to meet the demands of retail dealers— history here, geography there, astronomy to the right, political economy to the left—natural history, the physical sciences, figures, music, the lower mathematics, and what not, all in their several places—this care had imparted to his countenance a look of care; while the habit of questioning and being questioned had given him a suspicious manner, or a manner that would be better described as one of lying in wait. (p. 217)

"The habit of questioning and being questioned": every reader of the novel who had seen accounts of the squabble over the Revised Code, whether or not he had ever set foot inside a M'Choakumchild classroom, knew what Dickens meant. It was notorious that "payment by results"

placed a premium on sheer memory work; every pupil who glibly par-
roted the right answers to the questions the inspector set was worth as
much as 12s. per subject to the next year's grant. No wonder the question-
and-answer method was so popular with efficiency- and economy-minded
bureaucrats and so bitterly execrated, if sometimes for the wrong reasons,
by the teachers.

In *Our Mutual Friend*, a succession of widely separated scenes is given
a common point by Eugene's remark, after Headstone's and Charley's
visit to the Temple and Mortimer's subsequent questioning of Eugene
about his intentions toward Lizzie, that "the schoolmaster had left behind
him a catechizing infection" (p. 295). The origin and seat of the infection
had already been indicated in the brief scene between Miss Peecher and her
pupil-assistant Mary Anne:

> . . . "When you say *they* say, what do you mean? Part of
> speech, They?"
> Mary Anne hooked her right arm behind her in her left
> hand, as being under examination, and replied:
> "Personal pronoun."
> "Person, They?"
> "Third person."
> "Number, They?"
> "Plural number."
> "Then how many do you mean, Mary Anne? Two? Or
> more?" (p. 220)

Later, in the same setting of the schoolmistress's off-duty hours, the
catechetical method is resumed when she questions Mary Anne about
Charley's sister:

> "She is named Lizzie, ma'am."
> "She can hardly be named Lizzie, I think, Mary Anne,"
> returned Miss Peecher, in a tunefully instructive voice. "Is
> Lizzie a Christian name, Mary Anne?"
> Mary Anne laid down her work, rose, hooked herself
> behind as being under catechization, and replied: "No, it is a
> corruption, Miss Peecher."
> "Who gave her that name?" Miss Peecher was going on,
> from the mere force of habit, when she checked herself,
> on Mary Anne's evincing theological impatience to strike in

with her godfathers and her godmothers, and said: "I mean of what name is it a corruption?"

"Elizabeth or Eliza, Miss Peecher."

"Right, Mary Anne. Whether there were any Lizzies in the early Christian Church must be considered very doubtful, very doubtful." Miss Peecher was exceedingly sage here. (p. 339)

This out-of-school interrogation recurs in another context later on, in a domestic scene between Bella and John Rokesmith, which begins with a catechism on the same subject of naming:

"Now, sir! To begin at the beginning. What is your name?"

A question more decidedly rushing at the secret he was keeping from her could not have astounded him. But he kept his countenance and his secret, and answered, "John Roke-smith, my dear."

"Good boy! Who gave you that name?"

With a returning suspicion that something might have betrayed him to her, he answered, interrogatively, "My god-fathers and my godmothers, dear love?"

"Pretty good!" said Bella. "Not earnest good, because you hesitate about it. However, as you know your Catechism fairly, so far, I'll let you off the rest. . . ." (p. 686)

In a climactic variation, in which Dickens adapts a familiar classroom technique to dramatic purpose, Rogue Riderhood, assuming for the moment the role of an illiterate Matthew Arnold, becomes H.M. Inspector of Schools in Headstone's classroom, while the appointed teacher, for a reason admittedly unconnected with the annual grant, agonizes:

"Wot's the diwisions of water, my lambs? Wot sorts of water is there on the land?"

Shrill chorus: "Seas, rivers, lakes, and ponds."

"Seas, rivers, lakes, and ponds," said Riderhood. "They've got all the lot, Master! Blowed if I shouldn't have left out lakes, never having clapped eyes upon one, to my knowl-edge. Seas, rivers, lakes, and ponds. Wot is it, lambs, as they ketches in seas, rivers, lakes, and ponds?"

Shrill chorus (with some contempt for the ease of the question): "Fish!"

"Good agin!" said Riderhood. "But what else is it, my lambs, as they sometimes catches in rivers?"

Chorus at a loss. One shrill voice: "Weed!"

"Good agin!" cried Riderhood. "But it ain't weed neither. You'll never guess, my dears. Wot is it, besides fish, as they sometimes ketches in rivers? Well! I'll tell you. It's suits o'clothes."

Bradley's face changed.

"Leastways, lambs," said Riderhood, observing him out of the corners of his eyes, "that's wot I my own self sometimes ketches in rivers. For strike me blind, my lambs, if I didn't ketch in a river the wery bundle under my arm!"

The class looked at the master, as if appealing from the irregular entrapment of this mode of examination. The master looked at the examiner, as if he would have torn him to pieces. (pp. 794–95)

In such a fashion, Dickens achieved three results: he reiterated the criticism of the mechanical method of education he had made, in terms too un-comfortably close to reality to be called satire, in the famous second chapter of *Hard Times*; he enhanced the temporal immediacy of the novel; and, perhaps most important, by transferring the catechetical device to informal settings outside the schoolroom he managed a variety of comic effects in addition to the most brilliant one in the passage just quoted. Topicality, in a word, inspired technique.

The schoolmaster is assuredly abroad in this novel, as Eugene says (p. 541). In her dedication to running a respectable waterfront public house, Miss Abbey Potterson has "more of the air of a schoolmistress of the Six Jolly Fellowship-Porters" and her rough patrons are "pupils . . . who exhibited, when occasion required, the greatest docility" as she sends them home, with wholesome admonitions, at closing time (pp. 63, 65). One of them, "Captain Joey, the bottle-nosed regular customer in the glazed hat, is a pupil of the much-respected old school" (p. 443). R. Wilfer remarks to Bella that he attends "two schools. There's the Mincing Lane establishment [where he works] and there's your mother's Academy [an abortive venture, like that of Dickens's mother, where he is the only pupil]" (p. 684). Mrs. Wilfer's cheek is "a cool slate for visitors to enrol themselves upon" (p. 611), and the stiff majesty of her bearing leads the irrepressible Lavinia to describe it with her own classroom-derived figure of speech: "Why one should go out to dinner with one's own daughter or sister, as if one's under-petticoat was a blackboard, I *do not* understand" (p. 804). By inference, therefore, the "tragic Muse with a face-ache" and the strict but well-meaning proprietress of the Six Jolly Fellowship-Porters are Miss Peecher's colleagues. Betty Higden keeps a "minding school" or day nursery (p. 199), and Jenny Wren belongs to the profession by virtue of her own analogy. Old Riah is her prize pupil. "If we gave prizes at this establishment" she tells him, "(but we only keep blanks), you should have the first silver medal . . ." (p. 433). Jenny's problem pupil, by contrast, is her alcoholic father, toward whom she behaves with school-mistressly exasperation. The inverted parent/teacher-child relationship, grotesque in their case, makes a playful reappearance in the affection-ately assumed relationship between Bella and her own father (p. 684). Bella, in turn, is Noddy Boffin's pupil, as Noddy, in a certain sense, is Silas Wegg's.

Even the Limehouse police station, like Miss Abbey's nearby house of refreshment, has the air of a schoolroom. The Inspector is seen busy "with a pen and ink, and ruler, posting up his books in a whitewashed office, as studiously as if he were in a monastery on the top of a mountain" (p. 24), and his fellow-officer, similarly occupied, "might have been a writing-master setting copies" (p. 763). The ruled books of the police station—schoolroom equipment transferred to another, not wholly incon-gruous, setting—have their counterpart in the "ruled pages and printed forms" of the Registrar of Deaths (p. 14), and the Inspector in his scrip-torium has his in Riah, who at one point (p. 440), standing at the desk in a corner of the Six Jolly Fellowship-Porters, is also momentarily cast in the role of copyist, an "ancient scribe-like figure."

In a social atmosphere increasingly affected by the presence of schools for "the people," literacy and its converse acquire special significance. Illiteracy on the part of several characters figures among the many in-stances of "doubleness" for which *Our Mutual Friend* is noted. Lizzie Hexam, herself illiterate, makes it possible for Charley to learn to read, and in turn is enabled to read by Eugene; meanwhile the illiterate Boffin hires the barely literate Wegg to read to him. Boffin inherits a fortune made from salvage on land, and the equally illiterate Gaffer Hexam squeezes a tiny living from salvage, of quite another kind, on water.

Illiteracy is total in some characters and partial, or intermittent, in others. Rogue Riderhood can neither read nor write, and like many such persons, he is intensely superstitious about the art: he has a "sense of the binding powers of pen and ink and paper" (p. 149), particularly in the form of an Alfred David. The eighty-year-old Betty Higden says she "ain't . . . much of a hand at reading writing-hand, though I can read my Bible and most print" (p. 198). She is meant to be identified as a product of another age, when literacy was far less common than in the 1860s. "Letter-writing—indeed, writing of most sorts—hadn't much come up for such as me when I was young" (p. 385). Boffin's illiteracy, also an instrument of plot in that it brings Wegg into his service, is somewhat sporadic. Normally, as when Wegg reads from *The Decline and Fall of the Rooshan Empire* and the lives of celebrated misers, it prevails. But he copes, apparently with some expectation of success, with business papers (Rokesmith's function is merely to organize and interpret these disorderly and thumb-smeared notes [p. 178]), and before Rokesmith's advent he seems to have had no trouble writing proposals to parishes desiring to have their waste removed on the most favorable terms (p. 180). He is also able to read a note from Venus (p. 576) and later to slowly spell out the will which the triumphant taxidermist shows him (p. 658).

A curiously gratuitous digression by Eugene Wrayburn suggests that when Dickens wrote *Our Mutual Friend* he was for some reason—perhaps his current involvement with the platform recitals he called "readings"?—extraordinarily conscious of the word in a special sense:

> "You charm me, Mortimer, with your reading of my weaknesses. (By-the-bye, that very word, Reading, in its critical use, always charms me. An actress's Reading of a chambermaid, a dancer's Reading of a horn-pipe, a singer's Reading of a song, a marine painter's Reading of the sea, the kettledrum's Reading of an instrumental passage, are phrases ever youthful and delightful.)" (p. 542)

Whatever its origin in Dickens's free-associational storehouse, the parenthetical embroidery on the theme of the word "reading," so unusual in a writer who ordinarily relates the contents of his asides in some more immediate way to the business in hand, contributes to our sense of the importance of reading—the ability, the act—in this novel. Writing and reading dominate the Boffins' memory of the child John Harmon and his sister:

". . . I've seen him sit on these stairs, in his shy way, poor child, many a time [says Boffin]. Me and Mrs. Boffin have comforted him, sitting with his little book on these stairs often."

"Ah! And his poor sister too," said Mrs. Boffin. "And here's the sunny place on the white wall where they one day measured one another. Their own little hands wrote up their names here, only with a pencil; but the names are here still, and the poor dears gone for ever." (p. 184)

Bella, like some of Dickens's other young ladies, carries a book to read while she walks—a book, however which is not the love story Rokesmith reasonably assumes it to be, but "more about money than anything else" (p. 205). Her home study course after she becomes Mrs. Rokesmith supplies a further nexus between the novel's themes of education and print. She was "under the constant necessity of referring for advice and support to a sage volume entitled The Complete British Family Housewife . . ." (p. 682).[8] While communion with a cookbook is nothing new in the annals of the Victorian heroine, it may be taken as a sign of the times that Bella, in 1865, applies herself to the daily newspaper as a means of delighting her husband. "Wonderful was the way in which she would store up the City Intelligence, and beamingly shed it upon John in the course of the evening, incidentally mentioning the commodities that were looking up in the markets, and how much gold had been taken to the Bank . . ." (p. 682).

In Our Mutual Friend, allusions to newspaper reading as an ordinary habit of everyday life and to newspapers as a means of communication have a frequency unapproached in the social milieux of the earlier novels. Betty Higden's chief contact with print is through the newspaper, a source of information and popular entertainment which scarcely existed, as far as the masses of people were concerned, in her own girlhood before the turn of the century. "I do love a newspaper," she asserts (p. 198). "Sometimes she would hear a newspaper read out, and would learn how the Registrar General cast up the units that had within the last week died of want and of exposure to the weather" (p. 506). But her special delight, as it was of millions, was the police news. "You mightn't think it, but Sloppy is a beautiful reader of a newspaper. He do the Police in different voices" (p. 198). The newspaper is Miss Abbey's favorite study as she sits enthroned at the bar of her temperate public house (pp. 63, 437); Twemlow reads it over his dry toast and weak tea in his stable-flat in Duke Street,

St. James's, and in his Pall Mall club (pp. 115, 247); Podsnap reads it at his place of business (p. 247); and Eugene by the fire in his chambers (p. 535).

Newspapers, enjoying greatly increased circulations as a result of the repeal of the paper tax in 1861 and the consequent reduction of price, afforded Dickens a convenient device of realism at a time when readers expected to be assured that the events they read about in a novel actually happened, or at least could very well have happened. If one were skeptical, Dickens's implication went, one need only look up the files of the papers. For not only were the sensational incidents themselves reported: the newspapers were a constant vehicle of communication among the characters, and a file-searcher could turn up their messages in the agony columns. John Harmon, after he has become John Rokesmith, "examined the newspapers every day for tidings that I was missing" (p. 371); after some days, the inquest over his supposed body is "duly recorded in the newspapers" (p. 30), and the publicity given to Gaffer Hexam's grisly trade impels a "rapturous admirer subscribing himself 'A Friend to Burial' (perhaps an undertaker)" to send "eighteen postage stamps, and five 'Now Sir's' to the editor of the *Times*" (p. 31). The mysterious stranger, Julius Handford, is advertised for, without result, "every day for six weeks . . . at the head of all the newspapers" (p. 195). The eventual disclosure of the real and living John Harmon is announced to Wegg through the papers (p. 787). Meanwhile, Mrs. Boffin has proposed advertising in the newspapers for suitable orphans (p. 102). At a later stage of the plot, Lizzie, in the country, is "afraid to see a newspaper, or to hear a word spoken of what is done in London, lest he [Headstone] should have done some violence" (p. 525), and still later Rogue Riderhood tells Headstone, no doubt facetiously, that he had contemplated the same means of locating *him*: "I had as good as half a mind for to advertise you in the newspapers to come for'ard" (p. 703). Remembering the remark, after his return to London from his brutal assault on Eugene, Headstone "examined the advertisements in the newspapers for any sign that Riderhood acted on his hinted threat of . . . summoning him to renew their acquaintance, but found none" (p. 792).

Side by side with the newspapers, however, remained handbills and placards, much older forms of printed announcement. The freshly printed police notice concerning John Harmon, headed BODY FOUND, another copy of which Rokesmith will carefully preserve (p. 451), takes its place among the other mementos of similar discoveries that serve Gaffer Hexam's room as wallpaper: descriptions of bodies with money still in pocket, bodies without money, "a sailor, with two anchors and a flag and G.F.T. on his arm," a young woman in grey boots and linen marked with a cross, a body with a nasty cut over the eye, "two young sisters what tied themselves together with a handkecher,"[9] and "the drunken old chap, in a pair of list slippers and a nightcap, wot had offered—it afterwards come out—to make a hole in the water for a quartern of rum stood aforehand, and kept to his word for the first and last time in his life" (p. 22).[10] These same placards are Charley's shame. His reaction to Lizzie's mention of them is an early clue to his character: "Confound the bills upon the walls at home! I want to forget the bills upon the walls at home, and it would be better for you to do the same" (p. 227).

And just as handbills advertising violent deaths and inquiring for missing men—sometimes proclaiming a reward of £100 for information leading to a murderer (p. 31)—dominate the opening of the novel, so they recur at its close, when the guilty Headstone haunts the railway station to read the printed notices on the walls (pp. 749, 791). Handbills were an old accessory of English daily life, and they may well have decorated an occasional riverman's dwelling centuries earlier; but the locale in which they are now found, a railway station, is a novel one. This suggestion of the ancient lineage and continuity of print is also conveyed by Wegg's ballads. Hexam's walls have their outdoor counterpart in the clotheshorse-turned-screen upon which Wegg displays his stock. The ballads, which Wegg liberally (in a double sense) quotes in the course of the novel, link the new world of sensational daily newspapers with the old one of Autolycus.

In view of the ubiquity of print in *Our Mutual Friend*, it is fitting that Dickens should use dicta on reading to illustrate the philistinism, assumed or real, of two characters. The beginning of Boffin's playacting as a tyrannical employer is signalized when he tells Rokesmith with self-canceling magnanimity, "it ain't that I want to occupy your whole time; you can take up a book for a minute or two when you've nothing better to do, though I think you'll a'most always find something useful to do" (p. 463). And the essence of Podsnappery is that estimable moralist's view of Literature, among the other arts, as "large print, respectively descriptive of getting up at eight, shaving close at a quarter-past, breakfasting at nine, going to the City at ten, coming home at half-past five, and dining at seven" (p. 128), as well as being devoid of anything that would bring a blush to the cheek of the young person.

It is appropriate, too, that when Dickens sends Lizzie to work in the country, he rejects the more obvious choices of occupation and places her instead in a paper mill, representative of an industry that seldom appears in fiction despite the affinity of the two commodities.[11] As part of his amends to Mrs. Eliza Davis, who had protested his treatment of Jews, Dickens designated Jews as the proprietors of this mill, which he depicts as an ideal establishment, benevolently managed, with good labor relations and a pleasant workers' village to which was attached a "Christian school"—a tribute to the millowners' broadmindedness but also an implicit contrast, in its wholesome traditionalism and piety, with the dismal urban schools that produced and harbored Charley Hexams and Bradley Headstones.

The prevalence of paper in many contexts is one physical detail that sets *Our Mutual Friend* apart from its predecessors. It is true that in *Bleak House* the paper which has the most significant function, as both symbol and accessory detail, is what might be called "institutional" or "private" paper, the mass of dusty detritus—parchment as well as paper properly speaking—generated by Chancery and ending up either in the despondent archives of the litigants or in Krook's junk shop. It is upon the existence and interpretation of certain written legal documents that the plot hinges.[12] In *Our Mutual Friend*, by contrast, the paper that is thematically and dramatically important is both printed and public: newspapers, police notices, election bills (pp. 251–52) rather than pleas and judgments. It circulates not in the limited sphere of Chancery, its victims and parasites, but in the wide ambience of a metropolis, open to everyone's gaze. Its thematic reference, finally, is not to law but to literacy.[13]

Just as the railway defines the contemporaneity of *Dombey and Son*, therefore, so the more diffuse and variegated references to education, print, and paper are Dickens's expression of the special tone of urban England twenty years later. This was the condition of the country five years before the passage of Forster's Education Act, whose consequences Dickens did not live to see, but of whose basic principle he presumably would have approved.[14] His allusions to printed matter and the ability to read are, on the whole, period color rather than commentary; their function is sociological, not symbolic except insofar as they are connected with the theme of education. Yet (though the association is not expressed in the novel) it is impossible not to think of the dust heaps in this connection, for waste paper was one of their many components; and it is waste paper, swirling through the streets on the wind that is blowing throughout the novel, which seems to define the physical and social milieu:

> That mysterious paper currency which circulates in London when the wind blows, gyrated here and there and everywhere.

Whence can it come, whither can it go? It hangs on every
bush, flutters in every tree, is caught flying by the electric
wire, haunts every enclosure, drinks at every pump, cowers at
every grating, shudders upon every plot of grass, seeks rest in
vain behind the legions of iron rails. (p. 144)[15]

1974

7
Bleak House: The Reach
of Chapter One

In this Bleak House *beginning we have the feeling that it is not only a beginning; we have the feeling that the author sees the conclusion and the whole. The beginning is alpha and omega: the beginning and the end.*

—G. K. Chesterton

Many forms of praise have been applied to that *tour de force*, the first chapter of *Bleak House*. Its atmospheric, impressionistic, symbolic, and cinematic qualities have been described in many places. But full justice has not yet been done to it as one of the means by which Dickens imposed coherence on his complex and teeming masterpiece. Its manifold strains of imagery and theme, its very language, induce echoes that are repeatedly heard, often elaborated or modified, down to the very last chapters.[1]

The very title of the chapter, "In Chancery," is resonant. Instead of setting up vibrations, as the paragraphs beneath it will do, it vibrates to language found outside the novel. For at least twenty years before Dickens wrote *Bleak House*, the jargon of prizefighting had included the phrase "suit in Chancery," the first word often being dropped in customary usage.[2] A purveyor of advice to boxers in 1841—this, of course, was long before the Queensberry rules were adopted—described the device: "If by chance you are lucky enough to get your left or right arm over your adversary's neck, with his head under your arm, while his arm is round your waist, do not fail with the other hand to give him an upper-cut. If you can secure his disengaged arm by crooking your own, which is over his neck, under it the punishment to him will be awful."[3] In *Past and Present*, a book to which *Bleak House* owed a considerable ideological debt, Carlyle had specifically reapplied the law-derived pugilistic figure to the law. In the course of a diatribe against "owl-eyed Pedantry . . . owlish and vulturish and many other forms of Folly . . . mountains of wiggeries and folly . . . a huge mountain of greased parchment, of unclean horsehair" (all images that would appear in *Bleak House*) Carlyle declared: "From the time of Cain's slaying Abel by swift head-breakage, to this time of killing your man in Chancery by inches, and slow heartbreak for forty years,—there too is an interval!"[4] The term's applicability to the innumerable victims of Chancery, Tom Jarndyce, Miss Flite, Gridley, Richard Carstone, and the rest, is obvious.[5]

An especially noteworthy device adopted in the first six paragraphs of the chapter will reappear later in the novel. Dickens's restless camera focuses first on the muddy street crossing in the vicinity of Holborn and Lincoln's Inn, then moves for quick glimpses of a variety of scenes up and down the river (paragraph 2), and finally zooms in on the foggy interior of Lincoln's Inn Hall, where the Court of Chancery is sitting. The same technique, now elaborated, is used in the whole of chapter 16 ("Tom-all-Alone's"), which is probably as close to a film shooting-script as any pre-twentieth-century novelist ever came. In its fluid course the camera records the scene and activities in no fewer than eight locales: Chesney Wold, the Dedlock town house, Jo's crossing (three times), Tom-all-Alone's, the doorstep of the Gospel Society, Tulkinghorn's chambers, Cook's Court, and the graveyard. The effect of moving from one locale to another, in both cases, is to stress the novel's great theme, the fateful mutual dependence of human relationships that underlies the seeming separateness of the numerous social communities and groups of characters.

1. *London. Michaelmas Term lately over, and the Lord Chancellor sitting in Lincoln's Inn Hall. Implacable November weather. As much mud in the streets, as if the waters had but newly retired from the face of the earth, and it would not be wonderful to meet a Megalosaurus, forty feet long or so, waddling like an elephantine lizard up Holborn Hill. Smoke lowering down from chimney-pots, making a soft black drizzle, with flakes of soot in it as big as full-grown snow-flakes—gone into mourning, one might imagine, for the death of the sun. Dogs, undistinguishable in mire. Horses, scarcely better; splashed to their very blinkers. Foot passengers, jostling one another's umbrellas, in a general infection of ill-temper, and losing their foot-hold at street-corners, where tens of thousands of other foot passengers have been slipping and sliding since the day broke (if the day ever broke), adding new deposits to the crust upon crust of mud, sticking at those points tenaciously to the pavement, and accumulating at compound interest.*

The setting of chapter 1, the premature twilight of a gloomy London afternoon, not only defines the dominant tone of the novel but provides it with a fundamental rhythm. Day is waning, lamps in shops and streets are being lighted, and fog, rain, or snow is usually depressing spirits in several of the book's crucial movements. When Tulkinghorn is about to enlist Snagsby to locate Nemo, "the day is closing in and the gas is lighted, but is not yet fully effective, for it is not quite dark. Mr. Snagsby standing at his shopdoor looking up at the clouds, sees a crow, who is out late, skim westward over the leaden slice of sky belonging to Cook's Court" (10.119). (One hears, however faintly, one of the several passages from *Macbeth* that hovered in Dickens's mind as he wrote:

    Light thickens, and the crow
Makes wing to th' rooky wood.
Good things of day begin to droop and drowse,
Whiles night's black agents to their preys do rouse.
                                    [III.ii. 50–52].)

The passing of time is marked precisely; by the time Tulkinghorn and
Snagsby are on the streets, "it is quite dark now, and the gas-lamps have
acquired their full effect" (10.123).

When Lady Dedlock enlists Jo to point out Nemo's grave, "twilight
comes on; gas begins to start up in the shops; the lamplighter, with his
ladder, runs along the margin of the pavement. A wretched evening is
beginning to close in" (16.199). In the aftermath of Lady Dedlock's disclosure to Esther Summerson that she is her mother, "the day waned into
a gloomy evening, overcast and sad" (36.453). When Tulkinghorn has his
last interview with Lady Dedlock, before he goes to his death, "inter-
posed between her and the fading light of day in the now quiet street, his
shadow falls upon her, and he darkens all before her" (48.575). When Sir
Leicester keeps vigil for his wife after her disappearance, "the day is now
beginning to decline. The mist, and the sleet into which the snow has all
resolved itself, are darker. . . . The gloom augments. . . ."(58.698). As
we shall see, the foul winter weather that attends the flight and pursuit of
Lady Dedlock has been prepared for by the November fog and mud
of chapter 1.

The major imagistic, verbal, and thematic connections *within*
the chapter are apparent enough—the manner in which, for example, the
iteration of the mud and fog motifs prepares for the extensive description
of Chancery beginning with paragraph 4. There are also less conspicuous
internal ties: the conversion of the tens of thousands of sliding and slipping
pedestrians in paragraph 1 to "ten thousand stages of an endless cause,
tripping one another up on slippery precedents" (paragraph 6) and then
into "tens of thousands of Chancery-folio-pages" (paragraph 10); and
the balancing of the "large advocate with great whiskers, a little voice, and
an interminable brief" (paragraph 6) with, near the end of the chapter, "a
very little counsel, with a terrific bass voice."

The allusion to "the waters [which] had but newly retired from the
face of the earth" has what will prove to be multiple significance. It refers
not only to the story of the Flood and to contemporary geological theory
("adding new deposits to the crust upon crust of mud" suggests Lyell's
"uniformitarian" hypothesis) but also to the floods in Lincolnshire that

make Chesney Wold so dank and depressing an estate,[6] and to the Biblical flood as a symbolical representation of the end of the good old days when the aristocracy ruled England. To Sir Leicester Dedlock, "the marvellous part of the matter is, that England has not appeared to care very much about it, but has gone on eating and drinking and marrying and giving in marriage, as the old world did in the days before the flood" (40.495–96). The idea of *après nous, le déluge* is implied, also, by Sir Leicester's heartfelt repetition, several times, of the newspaper leader writer's cliché ". . . a remarkable example of the confusion into which the present age has fallen; of the obliteration of landmarks, the opening of floodgates, and the up-rooting of distinctions" (28.350, 354, 356; 29.358; 40.504). Near the end of the novel, Esther uses the same image for a different purpose. In her deathly fatigue, as she hears Guster telling of her encounter with the disguised Lady Dedlock, "great water-gates seemed to be opening and closing in my head, or in the air; and . . . the unreal things were more substantial than the real" (59.712–13).

The forty-foot-long megalosaurus waddling up Holborn Hill "like an elephantine lizard" is a survivor from antediluvian times. As a symbol of the remotest past, the animal had come to figure conspicuously in the popular imagination at the time *Bleak House* was being published.[7] It will reappear, generalized, transformed, or reduced (but still recognizable), on several occasions, the first of which is in chapter 1 itself—". . . but Jarndyce and Jarndyce still drags its dreary length before the Court," followed shortly by the image of "reams of dusty warrants" transformed into serpents, grimly writhing into many shapes (paragraphs 8 and 10). Whether the effect is enhanced by recalling the wounded snake implicit in the amended quotation from Pope, as well as a faint suggestion of the Medusa's head, is doubtless a matter of taste. But a similar, rather unfocused image occurs in the powerful passage in which the "ruined human wretch" who inhabits Tom-all-Alone's is multiplied into a snakelike "crowd of foul existence that crawls in and out of gaps in walls and boards; and coils itself to sleep, in maggot numbers, where the rain drips in" (16.197).

The original megalosaurus is recalled late in the novel, when Lady Dedlock's hauteur and coldness suggest that "all passion, feeling, and interest, had been worn out in the earlier ages of the world, and had perished from its surface with its other departed monsters" (48.574). Several times the megalosaurus (a real creature, though long extinct) reappears in the form of a dragon (a mythical one). In the immediately contemporary mind, the two were often identified. Only two years before the serialization of *Bleak House* began, Tennyson (*In Memoriam*, 56) wrote of "Dragons of the prime, / That tare each other in their slime"—a clear reference to one breed or another of prehistoric animal. The megalosaurus-as-dragon first appears, suitably enough, on Holborn Hill itself, where the traffic roars past the late Mr. Peffer's grave in St. Andrew's churchyard "like one great dragon" (10.116). Krook's malignant cat, Lady Jane, "went leaping and bounding and tearing about . . . like a Dragon" on the night of her master's demise (39.493). The boredom that besets the fair Volumnia Dedlock also is figured as a dragon (58.694).

The novel's pattern of interwoven allusions to geological-paleontological time, to past cataclysms that prefigure apocalyptic events to come, is additionally commenced in the first paragraph by the reference to "the death of the sun."[8] More or less peripherally related to the cluster of cosmic images having to do with the Dedlocks' presumed position at the very center of the solar system and the inclusion of Lady Dedlock's picture in the Galaxy Gallery of British Beauty, the concept of "the death of the sun" is revived in other contexts suggesting the disruption of the natural order as an accompaniment to or consequence of the ramified evil that pervades the novel's social milieu.

Scene after scene is wrapped in unnatural darkness, early as well as late. To the gloomy city, daylight comes reluctantly. Esther's first impression of London is of "its being night in the day-time" (3.29). Lodging overnight at the Jellybys', she awakens to find "the purblind day . . . feebly struggling with the fog" (4.45), and at the same time "the windows were so encrusted with dirt, that they would have made Midsummer sunshine dim" and hence prevented her from seeing the heavy fog (5.45). Thus the surrounding world is doubly obscured, as is the interior of Krook's shop when Esther, Richard, and Ada visit it that morning. "As it was still foggy and dark, and as the shop was blinded besides by the wall of Lincoln's Inn, intercepting the light within a couple of yards, we should not have seen so much but for a lighted lantern" that Krook carried about (5.49). Much later, Esther, weary and confused after her long pursuit of her mother, is aware "that it was neither night nor day; that morning was dawning, but the street-lamps were not yet put out" (59.712).[9]

The smoke of paragraph 1, "lowering down from chimney-pots, making a soft black drizzle, with flakes of soot in it as big as full-grown snow-flakes," serves an immediately practical purpose, as it identifies this day as the same on which, a mile or two away, Esther arrives in London and mistakes the "dense brown smoke" for a great fire. "Oh dear no, miss," says Guppy. "This is a London particular" (3.29). The smoke also foreshadows, at longer remove, the sooty, greasy precipitate that will strike horror into Guppy and Weevle during that harrowing evening above Krook's shop (32.398, 400). (The "soft black drizzle" has a rhyming echo later in chapter 1, when Chizzle, Mizzle, and Drizzle are names Dickens bestows on Chancery lawyers.)

The nexus between Chancery and the mud-spattered, irritable crowd at the street crossing, amplified later in the chapter, is rendered more sharply in chapter 10, when again the dismal day is ending and the law is closing up shop:

> Jostling against clerks going to post the day's letters, and against counsel and attorneys going home to dinner, and against plaintiffs and defendants, and suitors of all sorts, and against the general crowd, in whose way the forensic wisdom of ages has interposed a million of obstacles to the transaction of the commonest business of life—driving through law and equity, and through that kindred mystery, the street mud, which is made of nobody knows what, and collects about us nobody knows whence or how . . . (10.123)

Given the significance of mud in the novel's symbolic pattern, it is not surprising that two characters echo the word as they complain of the difficulties and confusions of life. "We both grub on in a muddle," says Krook of himself and Lady Jane (5.51; "grubbed and muddled" a page later). "We live in such a state of muddle that it's impossible" to learn to keep house, says Caddy Jellyby (14.177).

The "infection" that spreads ill temper among the jostling pedestrians, like the characterization of Chancery (in paragraph 5) as "most pestilent of hoary sinners," points forward to the theme of physical and moral infection which takes so many forms in *Bleak House*, from the fever that links Jo, Charley Neckett, and Esther, to Tom-all-Alone's inexorable power to spread corruption throughout society. "There is not a drop of Tom's corrupted blood but propagates infection and contagion somewhere. . . . There is not an atom of Tom's slime, not a cubic inch of any pestilential gas in which he lives, . . . but shall work its retribution, through every order of society, up to the proudest of the proud, and to the highest of the high" (46.553).

The leading imagistic motifs of the first paragraph later are orchestrated to provide the background of incessant, hampering winter weather that attends Bucket's and Esther's pursuit of Lady Dedlock in chapters 57–59. It is winter again, and the "flakes of soot . . . as big as full-grown snow-flakes" are now replaced by real snowflakes, falling thickly—so densely, in fact, that they have the same blinding effect as fog. Once again, horses and pedestrians slip and flounder and splash one another, and the roadway and sidewalks are in worse condition than that described in the initial paragraph. As the snow and sleet melt, they turn to slush and deepen the mud that was already there:

> The air was so thick with the darkness of the day, and the density of the fall, that we could see but a very little way in any direction. Although it was extremely cold, the snow was but partially frozen, and it churned . . . under the hoofs of the horses, into mire and water. They sometimes slipped and floundered for a mile together, and we were obliged to come to a standstill to rest them. (57.686)
>
> The sleet fell all that day unceasingly, a thick mist came on early, and it never rose or lightened for a moment. Such roads I had never seen. I sometimes feared we had missed the way and got into the ploughed grounds, or the marshes. (57.687)

At the climax of the search, early in the morning that hesitates between night and day, when "the sleet was still falling, and. . . . all the ways were deep with it," Esther and Bucket pick their way across the "mounds of blackened ice and snow" (59.712)—"It ain't so easy to keep your feet," Bucket had said (59.704)—and find themselves back at the corner of Holborn and Chancery Lane. The first locale of the novel has been regained, after many excursions by many characters. Thus *Bleak House*, all but the last forty pages or so, is framed between the immediate neighborhood of Holborn and Lincoln's Inn in a foggy, drizzly November twilight and the corner of Holborn and Chancery Lane on a sleety, snowy, half-frozen, half-melting early morning. Since the beginning of chapter 1, the mire has become deeper, the footing more treacherous: a fact to be borne in mind in any attempt to interpret the weather symbolism of the novel.

2. *Fog everywhere. Fog up the river, where it flows among green aits and meadows; fog down the river, where it rolls defiled among the tiers of shipping, and the waterside pollutions of a great (and dirty) city. Fog on the Essex marshes, fog on the Kentish heights. Fog creeping into the cabooses of collier-brigs, fog lying out on the yards, and hovering in the rigging of great ships; fog drooping on the*

gunwales of barges and small boats. Fog in the eyes and throats of ancient Green-
wich pensioners, wheezing by the firesides of their wards; fog in the stem and bowl
of the afternoon pipe of the wrathful skipper, down in his close cabin; fog cruelly
pinching the toes and fingers of his shivering little 'prentice boy on deck. Chance
people on the bridges peeping over the parapets into a nether sky of fog, with fog
all round them, as if they were up in a balloon, and hanging in the misty clouds.

The filthy air is present in the first paragraph, but the fog is first
explicitly described in the second, which is wholly devoted to it. Its ubiquity is rhetorically illustrated by Dickens's insistent repetition of the word,
twelve times in a passage of some 160 words, and each isolated, each from
all the rest, as the human beings of the story later will seem to be, until
the enveloping effect of the fog is matched by the unseen but ineluctable
ties of social community. The fleeting mention of the "green aits [small
islands] and meadows" is the only intimation we will have, for some time,
that beyond the dreary city with its "waterside pollutions" lies a sunlit and
pastoral England in which Esther and her adoring circle will find comfort
and pleasure. The first echo of the image, in the next chapter, wipes out
that suggestion, relating flood conditions in Lincolnshire to the polluted
Thames of the present afternoon. At Chesney Wold, the "low-lying
ground, for half a mile in breadth, is a stagnant river, with melancholy
trees for islands in it" (2.11). Only much later will we learn, in an almost
lyric description of a moonlit panorama that has a certain resemblance in
technique to the opening of chapter 1, that upriver "the water-meadows
are fresh and green, and the stream sparkles on among pleasant islands,
murmuring weirs, and whispering rushes" (48.584). Still later, Esther and
John Jarndyce will visit a similar place, "with such a rich and smiling
country spread around it; with water sparkling away into the distance"
(64.751). The setting of the new cottage to be called Bleak House, it is all
the more idyllic because it contrasts so strongly with the remembered
initial picture of the fogbound Thames.

We shall visit the dark, sinister waterside again in the course of
the search for Lady Dedlock. We shall see the shipping again, not fog-
wrapped but in the brightness of summer, first as a symbol—including
an appearance of the clients in Chancery as the crew of the Flying
Dutchman—and then, more prosaically, as a simile founded on mud
at ebbtide:

> It is the long vacation in the regions of Chancery Lane.
> The good ships Law and Equity, those teak-built, copper-
> bottomed, iron-fastened, brazened-faced, and not by any

means fast-sailing Clippers, are laid up in ordinary. The Flying Dutchman, with a crew of ghostly clients imploring all whom they may encounter to peruse their papers, has drifted, for the time being, Heaven knows where. . . . The Temple, Chancery Lane, Serjeants' Inn, and Lincoln's Inn even unto the Fields, are like tidal harbours at low water; where stranded proceedings, offices at anchor, idle clerks lounging on lopsided stools that will not recover their perpendicular until the current of Term sets in, lie high and dry upon the ooze of the long vacation. (19.231–32)

Later, too, we shall see the fog and the ships again, this time on an unpromising morning at Deal; but on this occasion we are with Esther, who records that "the fog began to rise like a curtain; and numbers of ships, that we had no idea were near, appeared" (45.544). The flotilla, which includes the East Indiaman in which Woodcourt has returned, is at least as large as the one dimly seen in chapter 1.

The inn room from which Esther sees the fog lift is "like a ship's cabin," the counterpart of the "close cabin" in paragraph 2 which initiates the novel's theme of confinement. Walled-in space, dead air, and the unpleasant smells they contain combine to produce a recurrent effect of claustrophobia and near-asphyxiation. The pipe smoke of the "wrathful skipper," to be sure, offers a tiny momentary suggestion of comfortable normality, even of coziness, in this generally upset and uncomfortable world. Pipes will serve the same artistic purpose twice in Cook's Court. The coroner's jurymen, having rendered their verdict in the matter of Nemo, deceased, "are caught up in a cloud of pipe-smoke that pervades the parlour of the Sol's Arms" (11.135): after Nemo's death, the world wags on. Later the "smell as of the smoking of pipes" provides the last hint of domestic placidity (despite the earlier mention of Nemo's opium smoking and even though the "smell" ominously foreshadows the disturbing supposed odor of tainted chops cooking at the Sol's Arms) before the horror of Krook's greasy-smoky demise begins (32.393). Trooper George's pipe-smoking with old Smallweed when he renews the promissory note, superficially a companionable enough ceremony, has no such overtones in such a context (21.267).

These small exceptions apart, the captain's close cabin typifies the stifling plight of many of the novel's individuals and groups. The Dedlocks' social universe is "a deadened world, and its growth is sometimes unhealthy for want of air" (2.11). In the long drawing room at Chesney

Wold, Lady Dedlock, spiritually almost suffocated by the secret she bears, must sit by an open window (40.502). In Tulkinghorn's room later that night, as he prepares to spring his mine, she insists, " I wish to hear it at the window, then. I can't breathe where I am" (41.510). Even the Dedlock fortune and name cannot buy fresh air; in the town house also the "air is . . . shut in and shut out" (29.364).

Tulkinghorn is more fortunate. In the sultry summer evening, he can throw open both windows of his house facing Lincoln's Inn Fields (22.272). And the sturdy John Jarndyce, in defiance of current medical opinion, "slept, all the year round, with his window open" (6.63). He has no guilty secret, and he is a good and happy man. But it is only the truly lucky people in *Bleak House* who enjoy fresh air. At the opposite pole from affluence and social eminence, the air is even more oppressive than at the Dedlocks'. Tom-all-Alone's is "unventilated . . . and reeking with such smells and sights that he [Mr. Snagsby], who has lived in London all his life, can scarce believe his senses." The ruinous tenements are "stinking" and the air is "dreadful" (22.277–78). In the rural equivalent of Tom-all-Alone's, the brickmakers' slum, "a stifling vapour" sets towards the visitors from the kiln, and the hovel itself has "an unhealthy, and a very peculiar smell" (31.380).

Close, noisome air pervades many of the places that lie between manor and slum. Virtually every locale where law business is done smells unpleasantly, beginning with the Court of Chancery itself, where "a quantity of bad air" is finally released when Jarndyce and Jarndyce ends (66.758). In Vholes's office, "a smell as of unwholesome sheep, blending with the smell of must and dust, is referable to the nightly (and often daily) consumption of mutton fat in candles, and to the fretting of parchment forms and skins in greasy drawers. The atmosphere is otherwise stale and close" (39.482). Snagsby's combination warehouse, counting room, and copying office is a "confined room, strong of parchment-grease" (10.121), an odor it will retain when Esther visits it on the morning she catches up with Lady Dedlock (59.707). The air in Krook's chaotic premises is "almost bad enough to have extinguished" his candle (10.124). At Krook's, indeed, the "unwholesome" air comes in different flavors. Downstairs, in the shop, it is "stained" with the odor of gin (20.253); upstairs, in Nemo's room, "foul and filthy as the room is, foul and filthy as the air, it is not easy to perceive what fumes those are which most oppress the senses in it; but through the general sickness and faintness, and the odour of stale tobacco, there comes into the lawyer's mouth the bitter, vapid taste of opium" (10.124). Miss Flite, the other lodger, "cannot admit the air freely" to her room for fear of Lady Jane's designs upon her birds (5.54). As Cook's Court prepares to retire on the night of Krook's vanishing, "it is a close night, . . . a fine steaming night," which adds to Weevle's unease as he chats with Snagsby: "Why, there's not much air to be got here; and what there is, is not very freshening" (32.393–94).

The Jellybys' drawing room tastes "strongly of hot tallow" from the snuffed candles (4.38), and after the dead fire is blown to life "it smoked to that degree . . . that we all sat coughing and crying with the windows open for half an hour" (4.40). Turveydrop's "great room," where his son Prince gives dancing lessons, smells of stables (14.170). The Smallweeds' house, says Trooper George, "wants a bit of youth as much as it wants fresh air" (21.266).

The foggy-snowy weather and the smell of confined space are at the center of the novel's cluster of images relating to dampness and decay—images rendered all the more effective by the repeated glimpses of fires blazing at Bleak House, in the Dedlocks' mansions,[10] and even, once, at the Smallweeds', where, however, the heat strikes Trooper George as being unhealthy and anticipatory of an eternal fire to come: "Whew! You are hot here. Always a fire, eh? Well! Perhaps you do right to get used to one" (21.264). The dampness exuded in the first two paragraphs will recur time and again, most notably, perhaps, in the extended descriptions of the dank manor of Chesney Wold (2.11–12; 7.76–77; 28.346–47). The family church on the estate has, even to Esther's well-disposed senses, a smell "as earthy as a grave" (18.224), one which, we learn elsewhere, communicates itself to the house itself, though it is "something dryer: suggesting that the dead and buried Dedlocks walk there, in the long nights, and leave the flavour of their graves behind them" (29.357). The "earthy atmosphere" of the wine cellar to which Tulkinghorn, clad as always in his rusty[11] old-fashioned clothing, repairs to fetch a bottle of old port (22.273), links it with the Chesney Wold church. The "marshy smell" Esther notices at the Jellybys' (4.39) links those London rooms too with the sodden fens of Lincolnshire, which may well be the "spongey fields" referred to in the third paragraph. (The only glimpse of country that Phil Squod ever had was of flat and misty "marshes" [26.326].) Even Vholes's aged parent and his three "raw-visaged" daughters share the London dampness, living as they do, not in the Arcadian Vale of Taunton as the lawyer alleges, but "in an earthy cottage situated in a damp garden at Kennington" (39.489).

Most repulsive of all is the moisture that envelops the London grave-yard and its adjoining filthy houses, "on whose walls a thick humidity broke out like a disease." Esther finally overtakes her mother "on the step at the gate, drenched in the fearful wet of such a place, which oozed and splashed down everywhere" (59.713). The earthiness in the church at Chesney Wold, repository of the Dedlock dead, is at least decorous, as befits its occupants. Here the dampness of decay, generated by the multitudes of anonymous Londoners who have been cast hugger-mugger into the wet soil, becomes an obscenity.

The living, too, are unhealthily damp. The equally anonymous umbrella-wielding foot passengers of the first paragraph and, in the second, the Greenwich pensioners, skippers, 'prentice boys, and "chance people on the bridge peeping over the parapets into a nether sky of fog" have their individual counterparts later, who not only carry the fog and drizzle with them but actually emit moisture. Vholes's "black dye was so deep from head to foot that it . . . quite steamed before the fire, diffusing a very unpleasant perfume" (45.543). Krook has "perspiration standing on his forehead" (5.55); Mr. Gusher, one of Mrs. Jellyby's satellites, is "a flabby gentleman with a moist surface" (15.183); Snagsby, occupationally greasy from his daily dealing with sheepskins, "faintly wipes his forehead with his handkerchief" during an unhappy interview with his wife (33.407); and Guppy, at the conclusion of an equally uncomfortable session with Tulkinghorn, walks away "in a great perspiration" (39.494). Trooper George, enraged by the very mention of the lawyer's name, "finds it necessary to wipe his forehead on his shirt-sleeve" (47.567), and later, accused by Bucket of murdering Tulkinghorn, "sinks upon a seat behind him, and great drops start out upon his forehead, and a deadly pallor overspreads his face" (49.597).

Chadband, though, is the wettest of all. His unctuousness is both literal and metaphorical, and, along with his gormandizing and his peculiar homiletic style, is his most prominent characteristic. He is always "very much in a perspiration about the head" (19.235), not least when he is working away at the Snagsbys' tea table, and in the figurative pulpit from which he sermonizes Jo, his fat head "smokes to such an extent that he seems to light his pocket-handkerchief at it, which smokes, too, after every dab" (25.321).[12]

So too do Bucket's horses steam in the heat of their wintry chase (56.672). And it is in this culminating movement of the novel that, as the snow and sleet fall pitilessly down and turn to muddy slush, human beings are most weather-soaked. The Gaffer Hexam-like river rat who shows Bucket a retrieved corpse that turns out not to be Lady Dedlock— "a man yet dank and muddy, in long swollen sodden boots and a hat like them" (57.676)—typifies all Londoners who are abroad on so foul a night. Bucket is soaked to the skin, "the wet snow encrusted upon him, and dropping off him" (57.686), "a pile of wet" "with his wet hat and shawls in his hand" (59.708). Esther, having "got out two or three times when a fallen horse was plunging, and had to be got up," finds that "the wet had penetrated my dress." The drivers "were as completely covered with splashes as if they had been dragged along the roads like the carriage itself" (59.703). Lady Dedlock, too, we learn from Guster, had turned up in Cook's Court "all wet and muddy" (59.711).

The fires to which Bucket runs to warm himself at intervals during that desperate ride through town and country have been foreshadowed by the firesides near which the wheezing Greenwich pensioners huddle in their wards. Other small touches in the rapid montage of paragraph 2 anticipate later characters and events. The wretched "shivering little 'prentice boy on deck," with his frost-pinched toes and fingers, is the prototype of the victimized and deprived children of the novel. Jo the crossing sweeper is once seen "shivering in a doorway near his crossing" (11.135), and the Neckett children's noses are "red and pinched"; they are "wrapped in some poor shawls and tippets" as a substitute for a fire and warm clothing (15.188). The people looking over the bridge parapets into the nether sky of fog are recalled by the "solitaries" Bucket sees in his mind's eye, "in nooks of bridges, looking over" in the snowy night (56.673). The image of bridge and river is elaborated shortly thereafter. Although the fog is not present, the river is again almost hidden. It "had a fearful look," Esther says, "so overcast and secret, creeping away so fast between the low flat lines of shore: so heavy with indistinct and awful shapes, both of substance and shadow: so deathlike and mysterious. . . . In my memory, the lights upon the bridge are always burning dim" (57.678).

3. *Gas looming through the fog in divers places in the streets, much as the sun may, from the spongey fields, be seen to loom by husbandman and ploughboy. Most of the shops lighted two hours before their time—as the gas seems to know, for it has a haggard and unwilling look.*

The dim lighting that is the sole topic of the third paragraph will prove to be one of the most recurrent and effective atmospheric motifs of the novel. Perhaps the passage which best sums up the symbolism contained in the many gas and oil lamps and candles is the one which begins chapter 46:

Darkness rests upon Tom-all-Alone's. Dilating and dilating since the sun went down last night, it has gradually swelled until it fills every void in the place. For a time there were some dungeon lights burning, as the lamp of Life burns in Tom-all-Alone's, heavily, heavily, in the nauseous air, and winking—as that lamp, too, winks in Tom-all-Alone's—at many horrible things. (46.551)

As night falls on Cook's Court, at the same hour as in the first chapter but on a different day (that of Nemo's death), "the gas is lighted, but is not yet fully effective" (10.119). The next night, in the aftermath of the coroner's inquest, which has brought welcome business to the establishment, the gas flares brightly from the windows of the Sol's Arms, where news of the death of the sun has not penetrated (11.136). But the brightness of the gas on the former occasion serves only to enhance the sinister darkness of the brief scene that follows no more than six paragraphs later, when Jo pauses at the gate of the awful graveyard where Nemo is buried. In another passage recalling *Macbeth*, the omniscient narrator apostrophizes the powers of darkness, including the "haggard and unwilling" gas light:

> Come night, come darkness, for you cannot come too soon, or stay too long, by such a place as this! Come, *straggling* lights into the windows of the ugly houses; and you who do iniquity therein, do it at least with this dread scene shut out! Come, flame of gas, burning so *sullenly* above the iron gate, on which the poisoned air deposits its witch-ointment slimy to the touch! (11.137; emphasis added)

That same solitary gas lamp will dimly light the end of Esther's search (59.713). Situated as it is at the graveyard gate, it is inferentially associated with another kind of gas, the "pestilential" sort mentioned above—the mephitic death-bearing vapor from rotting corpses.

In the street where the Dedlocks live, the "upstart gas," contrasted with the "extinguishers for obsolete flambeaux," is yet one more emblem of the changing times which the Dedlock-ruled society resists with all its impotent might. Almost as antiquated as the torch snuffers is another source of public lighting in the same street, the "oil . . . yet lingering at long intervals in a little absurd glass pot, with a knob in the bottom like an oyster, [which] blinks and sulks at newer lights every night, like its high and dry master in the House of Lords" (48.575). The same combination, its symbolism intact and, by this later stage, enhanced, figures in yet another twilight as Sir Leicester awaits word of his wife. "The gloom augments; the bright gas springs up in the streets; and the pertinacious oil lamps which yet hold their ground here, with their source of life half frozen and half thawed, twinkle graspingly, like fiery fish out of water—as they are" (58.698–99).

Just as the gas in the streets and shops fails to dispel the fog in chapter 1, so the "wasting candles" inside the Court of Chancery bedim, rather than illuminate, that august chamber (paragraph 6). Tiny simulacra of the dying sun, agents that barely contend with the enveloping darkness let alone give off heat, they too appear time and again. In the aggregate, their effect suggests not only the absence of life-giving oxygen but the deathly smouldering produced by spontaneous combustion. Esther sees the candles at Kenge and Carboy's "burning with a white flame, and looking raw and cold . . . flickering and guttering, and there were no snuffers— until the young gentleman by-and-bye brought a very dirty pair; for two hours" (3.29–30). At Tulkinghorn's, the secretive old lawyer "sits, attended by two candles in old-fashioned silver candlesticks, that give a very insufficient light to his large room" (10.119). When, on the same evening, he goes to Krook's shop, he finds it "dim enough with a blot-headed candle or so in the windows" and another in the proprietor's hand, which he gives to Tulkinghorn to light his way to Nemo's room. They behold Nemo's body "in the spectral darkness of a candle that has guttered down, until the whole length of its wick (still burning) has doubled over, and left a tower of winding-sheet above it" (10.123–124).

The squalid houses adjoining the graveyard have "a few dull lights in their windows" (59.713). In the room at Tom-all-Alone's in which the brickmakers and their wives huddle, "even the gross candle burns pale and sickly in the polluted air" (22.279). Back at their hovel near St. Albans, when Esther and Charley overtake the ailing Jo, "there was a feeble candle in the patched window" (31.380). On the same night, in the dirty upper casements of Lincoln's Inn "hazy little patches of candle-light reveal where some wise draughtsman and conveyancer yet toils" (32.392). A few yards away in Cook's Court, the jumpy Guppy and Weevle, stationed in Nemo's old room, have their "horrors" intensified by the unnatural behavior of their own candle.

". . . *There's* a blessed-looking candle!" says Tony, point-ing to the heavily burning taper on his table with a great cabbage head and a long winding-sheet.

"That's easily improved," Mr. Guppy observes, as he takes the snuffers in hand.

"*Is* it?" returns his friend. "Not so easily as you think. It has been smouldering like that ever since it was lighted." (32.396).

The oil lamps that flicker side by side with the older candles and the newer gas, as in the Dedlocks' street, are no more satisfactory. They add gloom to staircases in particular. At the Jellybys', a mug labeled "A Present from Tunbridge Wells" with a wick floating in it serves as a makeshift oil lamp (4.40). In the staircases of Lincoln's Inn "clogged lamps like the eyes of Equity, bleared Argus with a fathomless pocket for every eye and an eye upon it, dimly blink at the stars" (32.392). When Esther steals upstairs at Symond's Inn to see Richard, she is, as she puts it with uncharacteristic dryness, "not distressed by any glare from the feeble oil lanterns on the way" (51.615). (Richard, incidentally, is repeatedly characterized by the word "haggard," first used to describe the "unwilling" gas that has been lighted two hours early [45.545; 51.609; 61.730].)[13]

4. *The raw afternoon is rawest, and the dense fog is densest, and the muddy streets are muddiest, near that leaden-headed old obstruction, appropriate ornament for the threshold of a leaden-headed old corporation: Temple Bar. And hard by Temple Bar, in Lincoln's Inn Hall, at the very heart of the fog, sits the Lord High Chancellor in his High Court of Chancery.*

5. *Never can there come fog too thick, never can there come mud and mire too deep, to assort with the groping and floundering condition which this High Court of Chancery, most pestilent of hoary sinners, holds, this day, in the sight of heaven and earth.*

The cadence that opens the fourth paragraph is echoed much later: "Where the throng is thickest, where the lights are brightest, where all the senses are ministered to with the greatest delicacy and refinement . . ." (48.572). The contrasting focuses are upon, in the first instance, Temple Bar, "leaden-headed old obstruction" that is "threshold of a leaden-headed old corporation," and, in the second, the "shining heights" of fashionable society. By rhetorical matching, Dickens suggests the affinity of outmoded, tradition-bound government (the corporation of the City of London) to the world of the Dedlocks, both being old and formidable obstructions to progress; to which, since Temple Bar was flanked on one side by the Temple and the other by the legal neighborhood of Chancery Lane and Lincoln's Inn, Dickens probably meant implicitly to add a third, the law.

The detailed, heavily ironical description of Chancery that these paragraphs introduce has its counterpart in chapter 24, when Esther provides a simple, objective view of the Court of Chancery, sitting now at Westminster Hall, followed by a paragraph of controlled indignation in marked contrast to the omniscient narrator's furious sarcasm. Esther's criticism of Chancery, expressed in a long sentence composed of formally balanced infinitive phrases, covers the same ground as does that in chapter 1, but in a quite different manner (24.307–8). When the sunny Esther deplores, something must be wrong indeed.

The long sixth paragraph—henceforth, the reader must be relied upon to have a copy of *Bleak House* at hand for textual references—completes the analogy between the slippery streets outside and the court where also energy is expended without result. Now it is the lawyers in "an endless cause" who find the going as treacherous indoors as outside, "tripping one another up on slippery precedents, groping knee-deep in technicalities, running their goat-hair and horse-hair warded heads against walls of words." So too, as the novel progresses, will other men act as they are confronted with frustration and futility. The hopeless Mr. Jellyby is repeatedly seen laying his head against a wall, "as if he were subject to low spirits" (4.41; 30.373, 374; 38.473). He does not actually bang his head only because he lacks the necessary energy. In fact, he foretells the coming exhaustion of Jarndyce *v.* Jarndyce, as well as (if we adopt the thermodynamic interpretation of Dickens' symbolism) the eventual running-down of cosmic energy. "He seemed," says Esther, "to have been completely exhausted long before I knew him" (30.374).

The "blinded oxen" being driven to Smithfield, "over-goaded, over-driven, never guided, . . . plunge, red-eyed and foaming, at stone walls"—"Very like Jo and his order; very, very like!" comments Dickens (16.199). Not only Jo and his order, but all the victims of Chancery, and even those only peripherally affected by it, such as Mrs. Snagsby, whom Bucket chides for her gratuitous involvement: "And yet a married woman, possessing your attractions, shuts her eyes (and sparklers too), and goes and runs her delicate-formed head against a wall" (59.709). Trooper

George sums up the futility of the law, indeed the actual danger of an innocent man's becoming entangled in it: "I don't see how an innocent man is to make up his mind to this kind of thing [his false arrest for the murder of Tulkinghorn] without knocking his head against the walls" (52.619).

Availing himself of the double meaning of "lantern"—the common definition and the specialized architectural one—Dickens represents the Lord Chancellor as looking upward into "the lantern in the roof, where he can see nothing but fog," a lantern therefore "that has no light in it." Other lanterns in the novel are somewhat more effective—Krook's, which dispels the foggy darkness in his shop (5.49), and the one in the loft at Bleak House after Jo has been spirited away (31.387).

The "foggy glory" (halo) around the Lord Chancellor's head has been anticipated, by inference at least, in paragraph 3, for gas looming through fog creates a corona. This corona, surrounding the Lord Chancellor's head, initiates a stream of imagery that will wind through the whole novel, appearing in various forms in several different contexts. In the very next chapter, Tulkinghorn is said to be "surrounded by a mysterious halo of family confidences" (2.13). In the second scene at the brickmaker's hut, Esther "seemed to see a halo shine around the [dead] child through Ada's drooping hair as her pity bent her head" (8.102). The religious suggestion is made explicit the next time the image appears, again in connection with the brickmakers, but now in their temporary lodgings in Tom-all-Alone's, and with a living child. As Bucket "turns his light gently on the infant, Mr. Snagsby is strangely reminded of another infant, encircled with light, that he has seen in pictures" (22.279). Immediately thereafter, by what can only be called a theatrical trick, the halo, enlarged, is transferred to another wretched child: "Jo stands amazed in the disc of light, like a ragged figure in a magic-lanthorn" (22.280). There is an ironical reprise of the religious allusion in the sunset scene in the Chesney Wold picture gallery, when "one ancestress of Volumnia, in high-heeled shoes, very like her—casting the shadow of that virgin event before her full two centuries—shoots out into a halo and becomes a saint" (40.498). The police lantern will reappear during the night of the pursuit, when Bucket walks up to Snagsby's door "in the little round of light produced for the purpose" (59.706). The remaining occurrences of the halo and the radiance associated with it are also in Esther's narrative. In her memory of the seedy quarters in which Ada lived with Richard during his last illness "there is a mournful glory shining on the place, which will shine forever" (61.725). And when John Jarndyce, in his noblest moment, renounces his claim to Esther, as "the sun's rays descended, softly shining through the leaves, upon his bare head, I felt as if the brightness on him must be like the brightness of the Angels" (64.752).

It is not too fanciful to find the "foggy glory," originally surrounding the Lord Chancellor's head, reflected both in Chadband's "smoking head" as he rises to address his captive parishioners (19.242) and, only a page farther on, in the image of the cross on St. Paul's summit "glittering above a red and violet-tinted cloud of smoke" (19.243). Although the cathedral's dome is not specifically mentioned, it was the predominant part of every reader's mental picture of the building, inseparable from the cross, and the image he retained of Chadband's dome shining amidst a cloud of smoke was readily assimilated into the succeeding image of the cathedral. The ironies of such an association are worth considering.

Mention of the "two or three" solicitors in the cause of Jarndyce and Jarndyce who "have inherited it from their fathers" anticipates, of course, the later stress on the long Dedlock ancestry and Sir Leicester's heritage of land, portraits, gout, family pride and honor, and outmoded political views. The solicitors are ranged, says Dickens, "in a long matted well (but you might look in vain for Truth at the bottom of it). . . ." The word "well" thus is introduced with a double meaning, as the word "lantern" had been just above. In the present context, it refers literally to the railed-in rectangular space, reserved for counsel, between the bench and the bar of the court. But the parenthesis refers to "well" in the wider, or, more precisely, deeper sense, and the reverberation of the word—it is repeated four times in the next eight lines—seems to enforce the latter meaning, as if to emphasize the hollowness of the well, and, no doubt, of the whole institution surrounding it. Henceforth the two meanings proceed side by side. The next image in the series partakes of both: Thavies Inn, the narrow street where the Jellybys first live, is "an oblong cistern to hold the fog" (4.36). The specialized law-court meaning predominates, as it should, when Krook's shop, a grotesque distorting mirror of the Court of Chancery, is seen to have "a kind of well in the floor," where he stows still more waste paper (5.55) and where the avaricious Smallweeds will grope, like beetles or vermin, after they have taken possession (39.492). The matted well is also recalled in the "old mat, trodden to shreds of rope-yarn" on the hearth of Nemo's room upstairs (10.124).

In the Smallweed reference, the paralytic old usurer, replacing the Lord Chancellor and, more recently, Krook, the shadow Lord Chancellor, is said to be "seated in his chair upon the brink of a well *or grave* of waste paper" (emphasis added), an association which perhaps deepens the

implication of "well" in the other occurrences and lends an extra resonance to a later allusion to Tulkinghorn and the "narrow house" that is
the grave: "Away in the moonlight lie the woodland fields at rest, and the
wide house [Chesney Wold] is as quiet as the narrow one. The narrow
one! Where are the digger and the spade, this peaceful night, destined
to add the last great secret to the many secrets of the Tulkinghorn
existence?" (41.509). Later, Dickens seizes upon still another meaning of
"well" and indulges in a further mild play on the word. Snagsby, inspect-
ing a long legal instrument just back from the engrosser's, finds it
"an immense desert of law-hand and parchment, with here and there a
resting-place of a few large letters, to break the awful monotony, and
save the traveller from despair." These resting places—oases—are "inky
wells" (47.567).

"Well may the fog hang heavy in it, as if it would never get out":
the announcement of the captivity theme, to be ramified throughout the
novel. Trooper George's is the only case of actual imprisonment, but
claimants in Chancery, to say nothing of the inhabitants of Tom-all-
Alone's and the St. Albans slum, will never find release except by death.
Conversely, daylight cannot enter the courtroom; "the stained glass windows lose their colour, and admit no light of day into the place." Things
are only marginally better in the Dedlock town house, where "the stained
glass is reflected in pale and faded hues upon the floors" (40.498). Except
in the summer days, color is noticeably lacking in the London scenes in
Bleak House. Almost every urban locale is wrapped in a drab, neutral gray.
Most days are what Esther calls "those colourless days when everything
looks heavy and harsh" (51.611). The morning following "the blank
wintry night" when Sir Leicester hopes to see Lady Dedlock's return
"comes like a phantom. Cold, colourless, and vague" (58.702).

The Chancery windows through which no light and little color penetrate have their gloomy counterparts throughout the novel. Several have
already been mentioned, at the Jellybys', at St. Albans, and in the conveyancer's room at Lincoln's Inn. When it rains at Chesney Wold, "the view
from my Lady Dedlock's own windows is alternately a lead-coloured
view, and a view in India ink" (2.11). (Mrs. Rouncewell sees no more
clearly as the rain continues to fall. She "has several times taken off her
spectacles"—miniature windows—"and cleaned them, to make certain
that the drops were not upon the glasses" [7.77].) The night of Krook's
combustion, Guppy and Weevle find momentary comfort of a sort in the
"lights in frowsy windows here and there" which are a sign of the presence of ordinary life (32.401). In Vholes's chambers, "the dull cracked

windows in their heavy frames have but one piece of character in them, which is a determination to be always dirty, and always shut, unless coerced" (39.482). Later, Esther describes Vholes, in Richard's room, "smearing the glass with his black glove to make it clearer for me. 'There is not much to see here,' said I" (60.719). Tulkinghorn, musing over his wine, thinks of the "vast blank shut-up houses"—shuttered, and therefore windowless—whose families' secrets he knows (22.273). And amidst the "shabby luxury" of the Skimpoles' flat in Somers Town "a broken pane of glass in one of the dirty windows was papered and wafered over" (43.523).

The "owlish aspect"—one recalls Carlyle's use of the adjective in connection with Chancery—which the court presents to those who "peep in through the glass panes in the door" communicates itself to young Smallweed, who "stands precociously possessed of centuries of owlish wisdom" (20.246), and at Chesney Wold, after Lady Dedlock has been laid in the mausoleum, "the owl is heard at night making the woods ring" (66.763).

As more than one student of *Bleak House* has noted, the "drawl languidly echoing to the roof from the padded dais" where the Lord Chancellor sits probably determines the pronunciation of "Jarndyce," for whatever that may be worth. It is responsible, certainly, for the conversion of the initial "mud" into the solicitor's form of address to the bench: "Mlud" and "Begludship." The sound is thickly viscous. Far into the book, it takes another form as Miss Volumnia follows her habitual three little screams with "O Lud!" in true Dedlockian revulsion at the very notion of an iron-master (28.351).[14] The drawl first heard in the court-room is heard again the same day, from a lawyer addressing the Lord Chancellor as Esther, Ada, and Richard await their audience with that dignitary (3.31). It connects the world of the law with the fashionable world, for part of Society's obligation is to affect "the last new drawl" (58.691). The Dedlock cousins cultivate it, particularly the debilitated one, who "observes from his couch, that—man told him ya'as'dy that Tulkinghorn had gone down t' that iron place t' give legal 'pinion 'bout something; and that, contest being over t'day, 'twould be highly jawlly thing if Tulkinghorn should pear with news that Coodle man was floored" (40.502). Later the drawl has become so aggravated that the sounds run together: "The debilitated cousin says of her [Lady Dedlock] that she's beauty nough—tsetup Shopofwomen—but rather larming kind—remindingmanfact—inconvenient woman—who *will* getoutofbedand-bawthstablishment'—Shakspeare" (48.572).

Sir Leicester's stroke, in addition to other leveling effects, aligns him with the cousin. He too has "an unusual slowness in his speech, with now and then a curious trouble in beginning, which occasions him to utter inarticulate sounds" (54.640). Now "he can only whisper; and what he whispers sounds like what it is—mere jumble and jargon" (56.668). Although sometimes (one feels mainly for the reader's convenience) Dickens has him speak plainly and in good form, more often he utters "a thick crowd of sounds, but still intelligibly enough to be understood" (58.696). Trooper George "needs to look at him, and to separate this sound from that sound, before he knows what he has said" (58.696). What began, in chapter 1, as a hallmark of a debilitated institution of society— law and the legal profession—ends as the mumbled penance of a proud man brought low.

The languor that issues in the lawyers' drawl has its own course to run in *Bleak House*. It is the social and personal analogue of the diminution of cosmic energy. For the fashionable ladies and gentlemen "who have found out the perpetual stoppage," "everything must be languid and pretty" (12.145). Lady Dedlock is the reclining embodiment of languor; the narrator calls attention to this unremitting affectation—a mask, of course, and one that initially intensifies the mystery—at least six times, beginning at 12.149. The debilitated cousin is "languid," whether from affectation or genuine deep-seated inertia is uncertain (40.502). In the later stages of his doomed contest with Chancery, the haggard Richard Carstone becomes "thin and languid, . . . forcing his spirits now and then, and at other intervals relapsing into a dull thoughtfulness" (60.722).

Among the humbler characters, the lovesick Guppy treats Esther to numerous undesired sights of "his languishing eyes" (13.155), and later, suffering from unquenchable thirst in the hot London summer, "reclines his head upon the window-sill in a state of hopeless languor" (20.245). Mr. Snagsby finds Weevle "languishing over tea and toast; with a considerable expression on him of exhausted excitement" (33.406). Even Chadband indulges this affectation. When Guster brings news of the cabman's discontent with the fare proffered, we see him "languidly folding up his chin into his fat smile" as he commands, "Let us hear the maiden! Speak, maiden!" (19.236). Inspector Bucket adopts the manner of a *flâneur* as he goes about his detecting. "Mr. Bucket pervades a vast number of houses, and strolls about an infinity of streets: to outward appearance rather languishing for want of an object" (53.626). But with Jo, who is incapable of any pose, the "languid unconcern" Esther notices when he is brought to Bleak House is a symptom of the disease that will soon ravage her as well (31.386). Like the moral and social disease that sweeps relentlessly through the novel, the entropy of languor, whatever its cause or intention, communicates itself indiscriminately to the lofty and the low.

The typical suitor's "slipshod heels" (the adjective is possibly connected with the slipperiness of the footing at the muddy street crossing) will be recalled in the first appearance of Caddy Jellyby, whose "pretty feet . . . were disfigured with frayed and broken satin slippers trodden down at heel" (4.38) and subsequently in the "trodden down pair of shoes" that one of Caddy's husband's dancing pupils puts on after her lesson (38.475). (The fact that Miss Flite walks all the way to St. Albans "in a pair of dancing shoes" [35.437] may, by a circuitous operation of the shoe allusion, freshly associate her with the ruined suitor with whom it was introduced.) Meanwhile, Prince Turveydrop, who wears "little dancing-shoes" when he teaches (14.170), has been described by Esther as wearing a suit which, like that of the ruined man in Chancery, was "plain—threadbare—almost shabby" in contrast to his father's plumage as a decayed Regency buck (14.173). Eventually, however, this strain of imagery shifts from the Turveydrops to find its culmination in Lady Dedlock's last hours, when she turns up through the snowstorm at the brickmaker's hovel. "Her shoes," the brickmaker tells Esther, "was the worse, and her clothes was the worse, but she warn't—not as I see" (57.684). It is slipshod, and in Jenny's clothes, that Lady Dedlock goes to her death. The descent of this image of outworn clothing, from suitors in Chancery to the proudest woman of all—clothing threadbare to begin with, now nothing but hand-me-down rags—has its own symbolic potential.[15]

Although Dickens initially asserts, in paragraph 7, that "no crumb of amusement ever falls from JARNDYCE AND JARNDYCE," he devotes a full paragraph below (the ninth) to elaborating the idea that "Jarndyce and Jarndyce has passed into a joke." The explanation of the seeming contradiction perhaps is that while nothing funny happens during the wearisome day-to-day proceedings apart from an occasional sally from the bench (end of paragraph 9), the case itself, *in toto* and in name, is the cause of laughter—a joke—among those who have been, and remain, profitably associated with it. It also gives them a chance to hone their legal wit. The newspaper reporters find it only a bore, providing them with never a single line of copy; in contrast, the legal people, from eminent counsel down to solicitors' boys, enjoy it because of the lavish costs they extract from it. Thus, when Esther and Richard visit the court nothing happens until the Lord Chancellor "threw down a bundle of papers from his desk to the gentlemen below him" (note the verb) "and someone said, 'JARNDYCE AND JARNDYCE.' Upon this there was a buzz, and a laugh, and a general withdrawal of the bystanders, and a bringing in of great heaps, and piles, and bags and bags-full of papers" (26.308). In chapter 1, there were eighteen lawyers all in a row, plus Mr. Tangle; now, in accordance with Parkinson's law, there are twenty-three.

The hope persists, especially on a dismal November day, that Gridley, the man from Shropshire—a victim of Chancery, but not of Jarndyce *v.* Jarndyce—will call out "My Lord!" the moment the court rises. In fact he does rise on cue and call out. He is aware of his value as comic relief. "Go into the Court of Chancery yonder," he urges John Jarndyce, "and ask what is one of the standing jokes that brighten up their business sometimes, and they will tell you that the best joke they have is the man from Shropshire" (15.192). When Gridley is dying at the shooting gallery, Bucket tries to raise his spirits by assuring him that "you're half the fun of the fair, in the Court of Chancery" (24.315). This probably is the last straw for Gridley, who dies a dozen lines later. The court, we may assume, becomes a duller place when the risible claimant from Shropshire is no longer present. But when Jarndyce *v.* Jarndyce finally ends, it does so not with one more sprightly little professional joke but as the occasion for a general guffaw (65.758–59). The "costs, a mere bud on the forest tree of the parent suit," have, to adopt the image used in another connection, become an "affectionate parasite [which] quite overpowered the parent tree" (10.116). The old adage, that he who laughs last laughs best, conspicuously does *not* apply: the laughter has been on one side all along, and at the end it is deafening. The lawyers and their supporting troops have prospered mightily and lost nothing. Into the vacuum left by the exhaustion of the Jarndyce cause will rush other equally protracted and lucrative lawsuits.

Before chapter 1 ends, we meet both individuals and groups who will figure largely or incidentally in the narrative to come. In the latter class is old Tom Jarndyce—or his memory, at least—who, we will learn, was John Jarndyce's great uncle and owner of Bleak House, one of the early fatalities in the case (8.89). Krook will relate Tom's warning against getting involved in Chancery and his eventual suicide (5.52), and there is some hint that he gave his name to Tom-all-Alone's (16.198). Among the still living victims of Chancery there is poor mad little Miss Flite, with her "documents" that consist of paper matches and dry lavender.[16]

The pomposity with which the Lord Chancellor is introduced is somewhat neutralized by his restlessness, slight smile, and the cutting exchange he has with the lawyer Tangle. We are prepared to meet, at his next appearance—the same day, in chapter 3—a decent human being rather than a gorgeously attired figurehead. This impression will be substantiated by the report that during the long vacation he or his deputy, the only judge in town, sits in chambers in white trousers and hat, with a bronzed complexion, "a strip of bark peeled by the solar rays from the judicial nose," and a human thirst for iced ginger-beer (19.232). Among the professionals and para-professionals in attendance, we see the eighteen lawyers who bob up and down like pianoforte hammers, an image later recalled in the description of the "hideous old General, with a mouth of false teeth like a pianoforte too full of keys," upon whom Volumnia fatuously dreams of bestowing a dower of fifty thousand pounds (41.513–14). Conversation Kenge and Vholes are not among the lawyers mentioned by name, but they are surely present. The clerks and office boys, "who have kept the wretched suitors at bay, by protesting time out of mind that Mr. Chizzle, Mizzle, or otherwise, was particularly engaged and had appointments until dinner," in due course will be individualized into the Guppys and Bart Smallweeds of the *Bleak House* world. The nameless "copying-clerk in the Six Clerks' Office," mentioned in the same paragraph, represents Nemo (himself a solitary worker) and all the other piecework scriveners employed by Snagsby. And the newspaper reporters who "invariably decamp with the rest of the regulars when Jarndyce and Jarndyce comes on" will reappear, now happily covering a sensational story for a change, when the inquest is held over the body of Nemo (11.133) and, even more sensational, the fiery deliquescence of Krook (33.403–4).

The first chapter of *Bleak House*, then, in addition to its universally admired function of setting the atmosphere for the whole novel, serves as an elaborate verbal complement to the cover design, with which it has only one motif in common, that of Chancery.[17] It sets afloat in the reader's consciousness a large and variegated stream of words and images which, wherever they are later encountered, in whatever modified forms and in whatever new contexts, recall the rich complexity of chapter 1, and so acquire additional connotative significance. Sometimes, to be sure, the links are tenuous and indistinct, and no great case could be made for their belonging to a symbolic pattern. Other motifs exhibit a stronger continuity. And at several points, especially the Tom-all-Alone's chapter (16), "The Appointed Time" (Krook's death: 32), and the series of chapters describing the snowy pursuit of Lady Dedlock (57–59), there are nodes of juxtaposed or iterated motifs which deepen the poetic texture of those crucial or climactic sections. The chapter is a great overture, one of the greatest in fiction—not only in itself but in the way its reach extends across the whole of this marvelously crafted novel.

1980

8

The Sociology of Authorship:
The Social Origins, Education, and Occupations
of 1,100 British Writers, 1800–1935

In his book *The Long Revolution* (London, 1961) Raymond Williams made a point that was something of a commonplace to students of the relation between literature and society: "We argue a good deal about the effects on literature of the social origins of writers, their kind of education, their ways of getting a living, and the kinds of audience they expect and get. Theoretical questions, often very difficult, are of course involved in this argument, but the most obvious difficulty is the lack of any outline of facts by which some of the theoretical principles could be tested" (p. 230). Williams then presented "an outline of such facts based on a standard list, . . . the index of the *Oxford Introduction to English Literature*, and with the *Dictionary of National Biography* as main authority." In all, he analyzed the social origins, education, and nonliterary occupations of about 350 writers born between 1470 and 1920.

For no other period of English literary and cultural history is the need for such information more urgent than the epoch beginning about 1800 and covering roughly four generations: the age when readers of books and periodicals came to be reckoned no longer in tens of thousands but instead in millions. During it, the role of literature in the nation's total culture was profoundly altered, and writers became the suppliers of a valuable commercial product. It was the long age immediately preceding our own, in which the problems of so-called mass culture and the plight of the author in a mass-culture society have attained both crucial and heatedly controversial significance.

We know that the dramatic change in the size and composition of the English reading audience in the nineteenth and the early twentieth centuries wrought a veritable revolution in popular and semi-popular literature. Was there an accompanying change in the class origins and other relevant aspects of the life histories of the people who made the nation's literature? Several years before Williams's book appeared I supervised the gathering of a mass of data which was intended to help answer this question and thus illuminate one of the innumerable dark spots that make the theorizing of the sociologists of literature less well informed than it should be. The results of that statistical survey of British authorship, much more comprehensive than Williams's for the nineteenth and early twentieth centuries, are the subject of this essay.

The data relate to the lives of 1,100 British and Irish writers, born between 1750 and 1909, whose reputations were established between 1800 and 1935. For the nineteenth century, the authors studied were those listed in the following sections of the *Cambridge Bibliography of English Literature*, volume 3: section 2 ("The Poetry"), section 3 ("Prose Fiction"), section 4 ("The Drama"), and section 5 ("Critical and Miscellaneous Prose"). These sections are broken down chronologically into three subdivisions, marked "Early Nineteenth Century," "Mid-Nineteenth Century," and "Later Nineteenth Century" in the case of the major figures, and into corresponding periods ("1800–35," "1835–70," and "1870–1900") in that of the minor ones. Forty-two writers were added from the section devoted to "Anglo-Irish Literature." Since the chronological divisions are merely convenient designations of the *floruit* era for each author, a certain amount of approximation is bound to diminish the statistical rigor of our proceedings. But in a study of this kind, arbitrary groupings are inevitable, as Williams's own use of even longer periods—half-centuries—suggests; and at all events, the tripartite division of the nineteenth century is useful for the study of broad trends.

The three periods, 1800–35, 1835–70, and 1870–1900, will be designated as 1, 2, and 3 respectively. In order to continue the analysis as close to the present as the availability of standard lists of modern authors permits, I have added a fourth period (4), which reaches from 1900 to 1935. The authors examined for this epoch were drawn from Millett's *Contemporary British Literature* (New York, 1935), supplemented by a large selection from Kunitz and Haycraft's *Twentieth Century Authors* (New York, 1942). The twenty-three authors who are listed in both *CBEL* and Millett were assigned to Period 3 (late nineteenth century) rather than 4 (early twentieth) in conformity with the view of the *CBEL*'s editor that they had begun to produce their significant work before the end of the nineteenth century. Writers whose family background and the major part of whose education were non-British (e.g., Joseph Conrad) were excluded, as were those on whom no relevant data were obtained.

In the categories from which the list of nineteenth-century writers was drawn, the *CBEL* has entries for 849 men and women. For 112 of these, however, no biographical information was found in the two principal sources consulted, the *Dictionary of National Biography* and Allibone's *Critical Dictionary of English Literature*.[1] Thus the net number of nineteenth-century authors on whom some relevant data were available was 737. The early twentieth-century writers on whom information was obtained totaled 363.

Any discussion of authorship and its social bearings which confines itself to the celebrated names and neglects the journeymen inevitably has its limitations. Concentration on the élite is less culpable, to be sure, when the reading public itself is composed chiefly of the intelligent, well-educated minority. But when the audience for the printed word has a broader base, as it has had in the past century and a half, the study of the people who produced its reading matter must be similarly broadened. We must keep in mind always the fact that, just as the public for subliterature has dwarfed the one which reads what we prefer to call genuine literature, so the suppliers of subliterature have also become far more numerous. These second- and third-rate authors are as meaningful for cultural analysis, in a period when the audience for their wares was swelling year by year, as the first-rate ones are for the predemocratic centuries of reading.

The present compilation has the advantage of including a much wider range of literary producers than Williams's. Far from being limited to those whose fame is preserved in the standard histories of English literature, it gathers into its net, as a glance through the names in the preliminary pages of the *CBEL*'s volume 3 will show, hundreds of writers of importance—or popularity—in their own day, whose celebrity has proved ephemeral. In fact, the tabulations that follow include all but the very lowest stratum of hacks, who are not commemorated in the *CBEL* or any other reference work.[2]

Who, then, made up the British author-class, and what shifts were there in its composition from Wordsworth's time to Dylan Thomas's? Our data allow us to examine four aspects of the problem: the proportion of men to women, the social origins of writers, their educations, and their extra-literary occupations.

In all periods the proportion of women writers to men remained fairly constant. The range of less than six percentage points is insignificant in terms of the numbers involved:

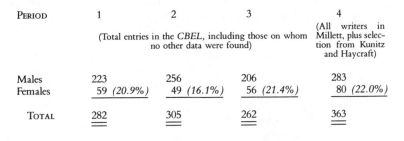

PERIOD	1	2	3	4
		(Total entries in the *CBEL*, including those on whom no other data were found)		(All writers in Millett, plus selection from Kunitz and Haycraft)
Males	223	256	206	283
Females	59 *(20.9%)*	49 *(16.1%)*	56 *(21.4%)*	80 *(22.0%)*
TOTAL	282	305	262	363

Clearly the broadening opportunities in the field of letters had little effect on women during the nineteenth century, because of the inadequate educational provisions and the persisting prejudice against careers for females. The woman's place in the home was not at the writing desk. Even so, from the 1880s onward the distribution shown in figures obtained from sources that imply literary value judgments is markedly different from that derived from the coldly objective census returns. The former does not reflect the impact that the late Victorian and Edwardian "emancipation" of women had on the profession of authorship as on so many other aspects of society. The latter, on the other hand (see footnote 6), reveals a slow but uninterrupted increase in the number of women who counted themselves professional writers, from 8 percent of the total in 1881 to 16.6 percent in 1931. In the nineteenth century, female writers were either strictly amateurs, who would never have dreamed of enrolling themselves in the census returns as professional authors, or women who, like Mrs. Trollope and Mrs. Oliphant, were forced by circumstances to support themselves and their relatives by the pen. In the twentieth century, as the census figures show, journalism enlisted the talents of more and more women as editors and contributors to popular periodicals—at no cost to their respectability and often with considerable financial success. The increasing percentage of "working" women writers, however, had no effect on that of women who attained a certain reference-book status in the profession.

But a much more important topic on which statistical analysis can help shed light is this: Were the gradual disintegration of the old social structure and the increasing social mobility of the period after 1800 responsible for a greater democratizing of the profession of letters? Put in another way, to what extent, if at all, did men and women of humble origin enter a profession that had hitherto, as a general rule, been closed to them? While the occupation of the father is not always an accurate indication of social position, it is the best guide we have, and the nineteenth century, and to hardly less an extent the twentieth, set great store by it. The divisions adopted here, while inescapably arbitrary, reflect prevailing nineteenth-century standards. The fathers of both male and female authors are included in this tabulation:

PERIOD	1	2	3	4	TOTAL 1/4
UPPER CLASS					
Nobleman	12	10	5	8	
Baronet, knight, squire	6	5	5	—	
Gentleman	8	11	3	16	
TOTAL	26	26	13	24	89
Percentage	*12.7*	*11.3*	*7.9*	*10.0*	*10.6*
MIDDLE CLASS					
Upper division					
Merchant, shipowner	31	15	17	5	
Banker, broker	5	10	3	5	
Middle division					
Arts and professions:					
Physician	6	12	7	13	
Journalist, writer, scholar	6	15	9	14	
Tutor, schoolmaster, professor	9	11	8	29	
Clergyman	18	39	31	36	
Solicitor, barrister, law-court official	11 ⎫74	25 ⎫128	18 ⎫83	21 ⎫137	
Government official, civil servant, diplomat	9	14	5	13	
Composer, painter, engraver, actor, architect, theatre manager	15	12	5	11	
Manufacturer, shipbuilder	9	6	2	5	
Engineer	—	—	4	4	
Dock owner	—	1	2	1	
Farmer (mainly yeoman)	15	8	8	4	
Builder	—	2	2	1	
Officer in army, navy, merchant marine	9	13	9	16	
Workhouse master, estate agent, auctioneer, club manager	1	2	—	3	
Miscellaneous businessman (including commercial traveler, insurance agent)	—	—	—	11	
Irish politician	—	—	—	2	
Jewish ritual orator, social worker	—	—	—	2	
Lower division					
Tradesman	17	9	12	4	
Artisan	7	9	5	2	
Domestic servant	2	—	—	—	
Riding master, carrier, bookkeeper	2	—	1	—	
TOTAL	172	203	148	202	725
Percentage	*83.9*	*87.8*	*90.3*	*84.2*	*86.3*
LOWER CLASS					
Laborers of all descriptions	7	2	3	14	26
Percentage	*3.4*	*.9*	*1.8*	*5.8*	*3.1*

Thus for the four periods as a whole, of 840 authors whose fathers' occupation and social status have been identified, 10.6 percent were born into the nobility and gentry, 86.3 percent into the middle class, and only 3.1 percent into the working class. The percentages would be slightly altered, of course, were we to translate a few wealthy merchants, bankers, and the like to the upper class and, by an equally permissible exercise of discretion, to demote some small tradesmen and artisans to the lower, or working, class. The Victorians were never sure to which station of life people in such occupations belonged. But even if adjustments of this sort were made, the great majority of English writers from 1800 to near our own day could still be said to have come from the middle class. Yet, according to a rule of thumb favored by writers on social and economic topics throughout the nineteenth century, the upper and middle classes together constituted only about a quarter of the total population.[3] All but 3 percent of the writers, in other words, came from a numerically minor portion of the people. The chief reason is that the schooling available to children of the working classes (75 percent or more of the population) was so meager and ineffectual that the odds against a working-class child's becoming a writer, or for that matter the practitioner of any other art or humane discipline, were overwhelming. That this remained true long after the Forster Act of 1870 spread, and subsequent laws made compulsory, the benefits of elementary education is proved by the fact that only fourteen out of 240 writers of the period 1900–35 had working-class origins; and the number would be even smaller if Irish writers were eliminated from the list. Thus, whatever progress British popular education has made in the past sixty or seventy years, the results, as I shall have occasion to note below, have only just begun to be evident in the increase of writers with proletarian backgrounds.

Several other points of interest may be observed in connection with the preceding table. In spite of the widely discussed decline in the cultural authority of the upper class during the nineteenth century—its degeneration into Carlyle's "idle dilettantes" and Arnold's "barbarians"—the percentage of writers it produced remained fairly constant. A more perceptible decline is that in the number of writers who came from the aristocracy of wealth (merchants, shipowners, bankers, brokers): thirty-six in period 1, twenty-five in period 2, twenty in period 3, and only ten in period 4. At the same time, notwithstanding its immense numerical growth, the commercial portion of the middle class never bred more than a handful of writers. In period 1, there were seventeen; in 2, nine; in 3, twelve; and in 4 (if we lump "tradesmen" and "miscellaneous businessmen" together), fifteen. Throughout the era studied, by far the largest proportion of writers came from the professional and artistic grades of the middle class. Indeed, of the total of 840 writers represented, 422, or almost exactly half, were children of physicians, teachers, lawyers, government officials, and persons associated with the various arts; and in every period, writers whose fathers were clergymen outnumbered the children of men in any other single profession. Thus the assumption that the professional and artistic classes tend to perpetuate themselves seems well supported. Literary ambitions, it appears, were more likely to be nurtured in a social group traditionally favorable to literature than in one—such as the commercial class—whose members had only recently begun to have books about them.

Some information was found on the schooling of 946 authors of both sexes (197 in period 1, 233 in period 2, 186 in period 3, 330 in period 4). For the men, the figures are as follows:

Period	1	2	3	4
Little or no schooling	20 (11.3%)	13 (5.9%)	7 (4.1%)	19 (7.2%)
Education ended on secondary level	64 (36.2%)	62 (27.9%)	43 (25.0%)	54 (20.5%)
Education continued into university or comparable institution	93 (52.5%)	147 (66.2%)	122 (70.9%)	191 (72.3%)
Total	177	222	172	264

The records afford little definite information on where our authors received their elementary education. On only a few writers, in each of the first three periods, are such data forthcoming:

Period	1	2	3
"Self-educated"	5	8	2
Educated at home	11	17	13
Charity, parish, burgh or private school	22	15	10

If specific evidence were available on the early schooling of all the authors under study, it is unlikely that the proportions suggested by the above figures would hold good. The fact that a writer was "self-educated" was so noteworthy as to call for mention in even the briefest biographical sketch, whereas in the middle class from which the great majority of authors came, some amount of formal education could reasonably be assumed. Probably, therefore, the majority of nineteenth-century writers received their early education in parish, burgh, or private venture school. (Few authors attended the charity schools of the National or British and Foreign School Society, because these drew their pupils almost exclusively from the working class. Similarly, only a small handful of twentieth-century authors were products of the board and council schools that sprang up after 1870.) Throughout the first two-thirds of the nineteenth century, of course, a number of prospective writers were taught the rudiments by parents, governesses, or tutors. But this practice virtually ceased, except on the highest social level or in special circumstances, notably illness, when school attendance was made compulsory.

The biographical sources are much more specific on the matter of secondary education:

PERIOD	1	2	3	4
Grammar schools				
The nine "ancient" ones:				
Eton	11	18	9	19
Harrow	9	6	7	6
Rugby	2	5	2	9
Shrewsbury	—	2	2	3
Winchester	2	3	1	5
Westminster	7	3	—	3
Charterhouse	3	4	—	5
St. Paul's	2	—	2	6
Merchant Taylors	—	3	2	2
TOTAL	36	44	25	58
Nineteenth-century foundations				
King's College School (1829)	—	4	3	—
University College School (1833)	1	2	2	—
Cheltenham (1841)	—	1	4	2
Marlborough (1843)	—	1	3	6
Edinburgh High School	3	6	—	—
Other (local) grammar schools	36	41	37	95
TOTAL OF ALL GRAMMAR SCHOOLS	76	99	74	161
Dissenting academies	10	7	12	3
Edinburgh Academy	—	2	2	2
Private venture schools	58	61	45	8
"Privately educated" (by tutor)	9	23	12	15
Catholic schools (especially Stonyhurst)	4	2	8	8
Foreign schools	5	9	9	6
Miscellaneous (teacher training schools, Birkbeck Institute, etc.)	—	—	—	12

Perhaps the most interesting set of trends to be noted here is the changing relative importance, as seedbeds of literary talent, of the three major types of secondary schools: the old-established "public" (national grammar) schools, the lesser (local) grammar schools—both endowed and proprietary—and the private venture schools, many of which offered an education modeled after that of the grammar schools while others specialized in a nonclassical, "modern" curriculum. In period 1, of all writers who had gone to some kind of grammar school, nearly half (thirty-six out of seventy-six) had been to one or another of the public schools.[4] This proportion then decreased to forty-four out of ninety-nine in period 2, twenty-five out of seventy-four in period 3, and only fifty-eight out of 161 in period 4. In the latter part of the Victorian era, therefore, the rehabilitated endowed and proprietary grammar schools overshadowed the ancient public schools as producers of literary men. This marked change may be interpreted in either of two ways: as more positive evidence of the decline in cultural authority of the top social classes, whose schools these traditionally had been, or as evidence that the upper- and upper-middle-class talents which formerly had been nourished almost exclusively in the great public schools, were now more widely distributed among the nation's grammar schools.

Unquestionably the growing importance of the less famous schools was due to the educational reforms inspired by the Taunton Commission inquiry of 1864–68, which exposed the decay into which numerous schools on old foundations had fallen. Their reemergence as reputable institutions of learning is probably the reason why the private venture schools so prominent in the educational histories of nineteenth-century writers—and in their fiction: both Mr. Creakle's and Mr. Squeers' establishments belonged to the type—virtually disappeared as an educational force by the end of the century. They had been set up in the first place to supply the needs of the enlarging middle class, needs which were most inadequately met by the ancient public schools and their hundreds of local satellites. When the grammar school system was revitalized, above all by the gradual modernization of the curriculum, the private schools, good, bad, and indifferent, to which many scores of nineteenth-century writers had gone, passed into eclipse.

It will be observed, incidentally, that at no time did the dissenting academies, which had had so conspicuous a role in eighteenth-century English education, produce many men of letters. They were characteristically more utilitarian in their educational philosophy than the grammar schools and many of the private schools; their boys were trained for commercial, not literary, careers. The secondary education of the great majority of English authors was classical in spirit and substance. Whatever its virtues and defects (and it was of course bitterly attacked throughout the utilitarian-minded nineteenth century), it played no small part in determining the ideas, attitudes, and even the literary style of the epoch's writers, and through them, in turn, the opinions and tastes of their readers.

As for higher education, we have already seen a steady increase in the percentage of literary men who attended a university or other post-secondary school, from 52.5 percent in period 1 to 72.3 percent in period 4. Analyzed in more detail, this was the pattern:

PERIOD	1	2	3	4	TOTAL 1/4
Oxford	33	40	58	78	209
Cambridge	22	45	25	51	143
London (i.e., King's College, University College)	—	14	7	8	29
Edinburgh	8	18	9	4	39
Trinity College, Dublin	13	10	6	5	34
Glasgow	9	5	8	3	25
Other universities	2	1	1	13	17
Art schools (especially Slade)	3	11	6	10	30
Miscellaneous (including Woolwich, Sandhurst, medical college)	3	3	2	19	27

In all but one period (and the reason for this mild reversal of form is not apparent) Oxford held a substantial edge over Cambridge in the number of former undergraduates engaged in letters. Its overall superiority of 209 to 143 conforms to the tradition that Oxford is the seat of the humanities and Cambridge that of the sciences. (One wonders if a similar analysis of the educational careers of 1,100 nineteenth-century scientists would support the belief.[5]) Although no strict count was made, the single Oxford college to which the greatest number of future writers belonged unquestionably was Balliol; its Cambridge counterpart was Trinity. The rise of provincial universities in the late Victorian era and the early twentieth century is reflected in the number of writers in period 4 who went to universities other than Oxford and Cambridge—a trend that has been accelerating in the present "redbrick" era. Somewhat puzzling, however, is the discovery that the two early teaching colleges of London University (University College, opened in 1828, and King's, 1831) contributed twice as many writers to England in the generation immediately after their founding as in either of the subsequent epochs.

Much less information is available on the schooling of the women authors than of the men. In each of the three nineteenth-century periods, approximately ten or eleven women writers were specifically reported to have received their education at home, and the same number to have had formal schooling on both the elementary and secondary levels. In period

3, in addition, seven had gone on to some kind of advanced study—an indication of the slow progress of higher education for women. However, among the sixty-six women writers of the early twentieth century on whom educational data were found, the pattern is notably different. Twenty-five were educated at home; but thirty-seven attended private secondary schools in England, in addition to a few who "finished" on the continent. The single institution that produced more than two writers was Cheltenham Ladies' College, five of whose alumnae are included in our list. In view of Cheltenham's distinction as a pioneer in late Victorian education for girls, this is pleasantly appropriate. Probably the most noteworthy feature in the educational histories of women writers in period 4 is the fact that twenty-five studied in higher institutions—among them seven at London University, six at Somerville College, Oxford, and three at Cambridge (two at Newnham, one at Girton). Thus the typical twentieth-century woman author, unlike her predecessors in the generations of Harriet Martineau and Ouida, brought to her profession a considerable amount of formal education, and of education that in general was more liberal than had been possible under Victorian conditions.

Our final concern is with the degree to which the authors studied constituted a true *profession* of letters. How many earned their livelihood exclusively or chiefly as writers, how many wrote as a sideline to some other occupation, and how many had independent incomes? In the nature of the case, no clear-cut answers are possible. The biographical sources are unsatisfactory on the subject of a man's private income, and the occupational restlessness and versatility of many, if not most, nineteenth-century writers defeat the categorizer. An author who at one time or another followed as many as half a dozen nonliterary vocations cannot easily be identified as a professional writer, nor is classification simplified when an author pursued another career simultaneously with his literary one.

Between 1800 and 1935 the number of professional writers—men and women, that is, who derived their chief if not their sole livelihood from the pen—steadily grew. According to Sir Walter Besant, "it was estimated that in 1836 there were no fewer than four thousand persons living by literary work. Most of them, of course, must have been simple publishers' hacks. But seven hundred of them in London were journalists. At the present day [1888] there are said to be in London alone fourteen thousand men and women who live by writing. And of this number I should think that thirteen thousand are in some way or other connected with journalism."[6] Certainly it is true that with the widening of the reading audience and the intensified commercialization of literature, it became increasingly possible to make a living by the pen. Journalism, as distinct from book-writing, was the principal support of numerous writers in each of our four periods. A very conservative count, including only those who for a considerable period of their lives were editors, reporters, and staff members of newspapers, magazines, and reviews, shows that seventeen authors were professional journalists in period 1, forty in period 2, twenty-seven in period 3, and thirty-seven in period 4. If we were to take into account those who frequently contributed to periodicals but were usually not salaried employees, the number of authors connected with journalism would be much larger for each period, and probably would represent a larger proportion of the whole for each successive period.

These were the main extra-literary professions of our authors:

Period	1	2	3	4
Clergyman	29	38	16	3
Practicing solicitor or barrister	5	10	2	4
Government official, civil servant, diplomat	17	27	17	13
Artist, architect, musician, actor	11	21	10	13
Teacher, professor	4	17	25	37
Practicing physician	5	10	2	4

The church, the arts, and government obviously were the three institutions that helped subsidize the production of literature in the nineteenth century. It is noteworthy that after reaching a peak of influence in the middle of the century, the church declined into insignificance as a habitat of writers, at least of belles lettres, in the twentieth century; and simultaneously the academic profession, to which few poets, novelists, critics, or dramatists belonged in the earlier decades of the nineteenth century, grew in importance through the succeeding periods. The law, government service, and the arts had a more or less steady role in the support of literature in all four periods.

In addition to the authors who were also medical practitioners or lawyers for a substantial part of their lives, a number entered literature with some training in these professions:

Period	1	2	3	4
Read law but never practiced	14	27	14	9
Studied medicine but never practiced	2	4	4	3

Literature has often been a profession to which a man turned after discovering himself unsuited for some other. The traffic flow in the other direction has been at least as heavy, but of it we have no record.

In every period there were, of course, numerous men whose work-aday occupations, either before or during their literary careers, were remote from literature and the other learned or artistic professions. We find, for example, a dozen or two bankers, manufacturers, insurance agents, and other kinds of businessmen; a scattering of army and navy officers, nearly all of whom retired before beginning to write; a few engineers; clerks of various descriptions, accountants, commercial travelers. And in every period, too, we find record of some authors who were artisans or common laborers. Among our nineteenth-century writers are two miners, five weavers, two shoemakers, two peddlers, a shepherd, a railroad platelayer, a cooper, an upholsterer, a millwright, two stonemasons, a calico printer, a wool sorter, a silk miller, a basketmaker, a wood turner, and a reed maker. Their appearance in literary annals reminds us that an occasional, highly exceptional member of the working classes could and did find his way into print. Few if any contributed much to literature, but the drama of their struggle against adversity won them a fair amount of publicity and prestige in their own time.

Nevertheless, the self-made writer of working-class background has until recently been the sport, the anomaly, of the literary scene. But the postwar reforms by which workers' children have been given a somewhat better chance for secondary and university education may well have altered substantially the class distribution of writers. The recent prominence of young authors like Colin Wilson (son of a boot-and-shoe machine operator, himself a former laborer, mortuary attendant, café waiter, and junior tax collector), Alan Sillitoe (son of a bicycle-factory worker, himself a former mill-hand and lathe operator), Brendan Behan (the slum-bred scion of a family of housepainters), Arnold Wesker (ex-kitchenhand), and Harold Pinter (son of an East End tailor) is clearly not a mere recrudescence of the sentimental interest in self-made authors—shepherds and milkmaids—that was a minor symptom of early nineteenth-century romanticism.

The predominant conclusion we are forced to reach through a review of our data is that from the beginning of the nineteenth century down to the dawn of the Welfare State, the readers of Great Britain were supplied by authors the great majority of whom had sprung from the "solid" middle class. They had, for the most part, whatever intellectual advantages the formal education of their time offered them; and socially and politically they were, with conspicuous exceptions that come immediately to mind, in sympathy with the attitudes of their class and era.

Between 1800 and 1935, therefore, the author-class remained relatively constant in its makeup; but the reader-class did not. As literacy and leisure increased, and cheap production of books, magazines, and news-papers made the printed word infinitely more accessible than ever before in British history, the essence of the literary situation was no longer, as it had been ever since Caxton's time, a dialogue of equals—well-educated, socially superior writers addressing well-educated, socially superior read-ers. Instead, many nineteenth-century writers found themselves in the un-precedented position of having to adapt their techniques and messages to the limited capacities and special expectations of a newly formed mass audience. This literary lag, this lengthening discrepancy between an author-class that was slow to mirror the social changes of the time and a reader-class that was in a state of constant flux and expansion, had all kinds of ramifications. The circumstance that the multitude of new readers were ill educated and only half literate posed a staggering problem of communication. But to attempt to solve it was eminently worthwhile, since the middle-class domination of the press made possible the spread-ing and (hopefully) the perpetuation of the middle-class ethos and of middle-class literary taste. The genuinely dedicated literary artist, how-ever, found himself in a predicament that has deep reverberations in our own time. To what extent was he obliged, as a member of his age's ruling class and supported, sometimes handsomely, by the pounds and shillings of his cultural inferiors, to debase his art, either for the sake of sheer intelligibility or for the more specific one of imparting desirable social, political, moral, and aesthetic attitudes? Amidst all the complaint, then and now, that the advent of a huge new audience meant the corrupting of literary tastes, it might be pertinent to inquire who did the corrupting.

Such generalizations as I have made from the data assembled in the preceding pages have, I think, their validity and value. Others will occur to everyone who has read this far. But a social profile of British authorship in a given epoch provides only a first tentative step toward a solution of the manifold riddles that have been posed since the problem of author-audience relationship became a subject of heated debate. These, we can say (granting that we need to collect much more information about them), were the people who *wrote*; what about the equally important people who *read*? Before we can go much further into the cultural and literary impli-cations of the data we possess on authors, we need a comparable analysis, or, actually, a whole series or complex of analyses, of the quantitative growth, social composition, and above all the tastes of the public for whom our 1,100 authors wrote over the course of a century and a third. In my book *The English Common Reader* (Chicago, 1957) I attempted a preliminary exploration of the social history of the nineteenth-century reading public, though deliberately and explicitly disclaiming any concern with its tastes. There have subsequently been a very few discussions of the latter topic, among them Margaret Dalziel's *Popular Fiction a Hundred Years Ago* (London, 1957). But we simply cannot talk intelligently about the interaction of social and literary processes in any age, including the present one, without having more facts—and, I venture to add, without divesting ourselves of our preconceptions and prejudices.

Reviewing Williams's *The Long Revolution* in the *Universities Quarterly* (September 1961), A. H. Gomme observed that "a more secure sense of history might have resulted in rather more progress and rather less iteration." The remark might well be applied to the whole record, to date, of the literature-and-culture controversy. The abundance of sociological double-talk, which even past masters of the art found oppressive in Williams's book, has not satisfactorily concealed the paucity of information. If we are to get anywhere with such topics as the many-faceted one of the relationship between author and audience, we will somehow have to bring ourselves to vacate the steamy arena of speculation, theory, and tendentiousness, and move to a platform supported by at least a few concrete blocks of historical evidence. In a debate as important and complicated as this one is, it is always useful to have some dependable facts, however prosaic, to refer to. The foregoing essay in statistical analysis is offered as a modest step toward that most desirable goal.

1962

READERS

9
Varieties of Readers' Response:
The Case of *Dombey and Son*

Any attempt to recreate the expectations which the purchasers of a serialized Dickens novel brought to it, and, even more, their reactions to those freshly opened pages, is an enterprise fraught with opportunities, difficulties, and hazards. Despite the imposing bulk of Victorian comment on "the Dickens phenomenon," we know very little directly about the responses of his first readers apart from reviewers. Because they bear intimately on any form of modern Dickens criticism that is historically oriented, they are worth speculating about in some detail. This essay is intended to outline the direction and scope of such an inquiry and to indicate the methodology and types of evidence involved.

Dombey and Son, published in monthly parts from October 1846 to April 1848, offers an especially good experimental model, for several reasons: (1) It was read by an established audience which had been with Dickens from the beginning. For ten years, since the appearance of *Pickwick Papers* in 1836–37, the public had acquired much experience in reading Dickens and came to each new novel with more decided expectations of what it would find there. (2) Dickens, for his part, had had ten years' experience in writing for a mass audience. *Dombey and Son* was, as John Forster said and as most modern critics agree, "the turning point of his career." Just as his readers were now accustomed to reading the unique kind of fiction he produced for them, so too he had become accustomed to writing for them: both audience and novelist had "matured." The text of *Dombey and Son* reflects the conception of his steady audience that Dickens had formed over a decade of successfully writing for it. Significantly, it was the first novel he meticulously planned from beginning to end. Thus we can, with all due caution, infer from his artistic choices what he thought his readers were like and what they wanted. (3) The readership Dickens had acquired in those ten years was *relatively* (the qualifier must be stressed) homogeneous. Complications arise in the case of the later novels, which were read not only by members of his first audience but by a new, younger generation whose tastes were in some respects quite different from those of veteran readers. (4) Much of the background material for a study of the first readers of *Dombey and Son* has already been conveniently assembled. The status of fiction in the 1840s, and the popular taste, literary conventions, and publishing practices of the day are authoritatively canvassed in Kathleen Tillotson's *Novels of the Eighteen-Forties* (London, 1954), and the early reception of the novel in Philip Collins's article, "*Dombey and Son*—Then and Now" (*Dickensian* 63 [1967]: 82–94). Collins's *Dickens: The Critical Heritage* (London, 1971) collects (pp. 212–41) generous excerpts from contemporary reviews.[1]

Who, then, were the first readers of *Dombey and Son*? The 25,000 copies initially printed of part 1 sold out within hours, and 5,000 more were run off immediately, with an additional 4,000 during November. Part 2 had a press run of 30,000 with 2,000 more printed soon after. Thenceforward, between 32,000 and 34,000 copies of each number were produced.[2] If one adopts Edgar Johnson's rule of thumb, admittedly arbitrary, that each copy of a Dickens number was read (or listened to) by perhaps fifteen people, it is possible that the total audience for *Dombey and Son* in 1846–48 amounted to half a million persons.[3] The fact that sales remained constant to the end of the serialization does not necessarily imply that everyone was happy with the novel. Many readers are said to have lost interest after the prematurely climactic episode of Paul Dombey's death in part 5, and some even disliked the novel before that; Henry Hallam, the historian's son, after reading that number, growled, "Dombey if possible, viler than usual."[4]

The book was a topic of the day from the moment serialization began. Within weeks after part 1 appeared, a *Punch* skit (24 October 1846) depicted a meeting of "working playwrights" debating how many numbers should appear before they began to dramatize it (the decision was to await the publication of the fourth number). By the time part 8 was out, *Punch* (8 May 1847) was sufficiently confident that its readers were following the novel to make it the subject of an editorial allusion on a topic close to Dickens's heart: "We have every confidence that eventually American booksellers will—like *Mrs Chick*—'make an effort' to be decent, and cease to become the *Fagins* of letters—the 'very respectable' dealers in stolen goods." A few months later (28 August) it printed a political cartoon by Leech, showing Sir Robert Peel as Mr. Dombey and Lord John Russell as Paul, and a year after that, a few months after serialization was completed (9 September 1848), another Leech cartoon, "The Parliamentary Toots," cast Lord John Russell as Toots, with Disraeli as Mrs. Blimber.

The sales figures shed no light on the social distribution of Dickens's audience. From the time of *Pickwick*'s sensational reception to the end of Dickens's career, impressionistic evidence, couched in hyperbole, abounds: everybody, the deathless cliché had it, read him, from the Queen, peers of the realm, and grave judges down to butcher boys, maidservants, and chimney sweeps; "all classes, in fact," said George Henry Lewes in 1837, "read *'Boz'*." "Right or wrong," declared Theodore Martin ("Bon Gaultier") the year before *Dombey and Son* began to appear, "he has discovered the secret of ingratiating himself with the million." Four months before part 1 was published, William Howitt wrote in the *People's Journal*, whose lower middle-class and possibly working-class readers would have been in a position to check his assertion, that "his public has consisted of every rank and grade; he has found entrance into every circle . . . The Lords Verisopht themselves have not felt comfortable without their weekly [actually, monthly] Nickleby."[5]

It is true that the Verisophts and their fellow aristocrats were Dickens fans, albeit it not unanimously. The intellectual élite, again with exceptions, shared the general enthusiasm. But members of the upper class and the intelligentsia constituted only a minor portion of Dickens's total audience, and though he was aware of their approval he did not write primarily for them. They were not typical of his audience at large.

One of the most picturesque anecdotes that have served to support the notion that Dickens's appeal was universal has to do with *Dombey and Son*. Dickens's mother-in-law, Mrs. Hogarth, had an illiterate charwoman who "attended on the first Monday of every month a tea held by subscription at a snuff-shop above which she lodged, where the landlord read the month's number aloud."[6] But anecdotes are not necessarily reliable history, and while there may well have been a number of such clubs, for *Dombey and Son* as well as the other early novels, their existence does not, by itself, prove very much. To be sure, there are other fragments of evidence that Dickens somehow reached an audience typified in the novel itself by Toodle, the railway stoker, whose children taught him to read. A year and a half after the serialization ended, Henry Mayhew interviewed a poor seamstress in a slum attic near Drury Lane. Her nine-year-old son, who went to a charity school, was reading a story in *Lloyd's Weekly Miscellany*, and commented to his brother, "That's something after Dickens' style." Mayhew also implies that *Dombey and Son* had the good fortune to appear during relatively flush times for the working class. A shoemaker told him:

> In the years '45, '46 and '47 . . . I was able to take my periodicals in. I used to have near a shilling's worth of them every

"Dombey and Son" (Sir Robert Peel and Lord John Russell)
(*Punch*, 28 August 1847)

week, sir. I took in *Chambers's Journal*. I took in 'Knight's
Encyclopaedia', and others of the same kind. I used to have my
weekly newspaper, too. But since '48 I have not had the most
of them, and I now take in none at all—I can't afford it.[7]

But surely this man was exceptional, both in his appetite for improving
literature and in his ability to buy it. Few members of the "industrious
classes" could regularly afford to pay a shilling a month for one-twentieth
(thirty-two pages) of an ongoing novel. They could more easily buy one
of the weekly papers aimed at their class: the Chartist *Northern Star*, which
reviewed *The Chimes* in 1844 (an indication that its readers would at least

"The Parliamentary Toots" (Lord John Russell and Disraeli)
(*Punch*, 6 September 1848)

have heard of Dickens),[8] or *Cleave's Weekly Gazette*, which had printed long extracts from *Nicholas Nickleby*.[9] But this was not the same thing as reading a complete novel.

While reviewers decade after decade spoke, glibly and repetitiously, of Dickens's unique appeal to "the million," there were, therefore, other millions who were disqualified from reading him on the twin counts of illiteracy and poverty.[10] A writer in the *English Review* (10 [December 1848]: 275) echoed the usual platitude: "Dickens, affectionate, earnest, at times sublime, speaks to rich and poor, high and low; to all, perhaps, save some of the middle classes, who think him 'vulgar.' His sphere of operation is almost boundless; he may be said to write for all, and work for all." But a writer in another periodical earlier in the year significantly qualified that sweeping sentiment. Dickens's works, he said, had "a peculiar appeal in language and subject to the middle classes—*we had almost written,* the masses of society."[11]

This was closer to the mark. The fact was that Dickens's main audience, overwhelmingly the most numerous one, was the middle class. But this in itself does not take us very far towards understanding his readers' responses to a novel. The Victorians used the term "middle class" so broadly and flexibly that it is virtually useless as an indicator of the level of education, attitudes, and tastes that governed such responses. It embraced the whole social spectrum from university graduates to self-taught small tradesmen, with their widely disparate stores of knowledge and degrees of literary sophistication; political conservatives and liberals; Churchmen and Nonconformists; city dwellers and country people.

These last two considerations, religion and place of residence, are especially pertinent when the nature of Dickens's first audience is in question. Churchmen and Nonconformists shared certain fundamental moral values and biases which transcended religious affiliation and can simply be called "Victorian." Beyond that, however, they differed in their attitudes toward fiction and the demands they placed on the novelists of the time. Some, for example, insisted more than did others that the fiction they read be strongly didactic rather than a mere source of amusement. Other sectarian differences will be touched on below.

Unfortunately there is no means of knowing how many copies of *Dombey and Son* were shipped to the country, to be read there either by townspeople or by the literate portion of the rural population. This is a category of demographic information one would especially wish to possess in drawing a profile of the original audience. In 1838 the *Spectator* touched on the point:

> We suspect that the circulation of Boz takes certain channels, beyond which he is not greatly relished or read. It would be curious, were it attainable, to know respectively the demand for his publications in the metropolis, in large provincial towns, and in the country. In the latter we suspect it would be small, of course supposing the district removed beyond town impulses.[12]

That Dickens (understandably enough, given his lifelong fascination with the London scene) assumed that most of his readers had a thorough knowledge of the metropolitan topography is evident from his innumerable references to specific London places and the manifold artistic uses to which he put them. Some of the London readers of *Dombey and Son* would have had a more intimate acquaintance with the city than did others, and to these, naturally, the references to locale would have connoted more: the precise neighborhood of the Dombey house, between Portland Place and Bryanston Square (along with the fact that its corner location made it somewhat less desirable than other houses in the same vicinity), the urban ambience of Miss Tox's and Major Bagstock's pinched accommodations, the topography of the City (dominated by the Dombey office and Sol Gills's shop), and the location of Mrs. MacStinger's dwelling on the Isle of Dogs. The famous description of Staggs's Gardens would have meant more to a Londoner who actually beheld the upheaval in Camden Town when the railway was built than it would have done to country readers. Some of the latter, brought up to believe that London was as distant and exotic as Constantinople and that, moreover, it was a Babylon of sin and seduction, would have reacted stereotypically to the Good Mrs. Brown slum episodes. Down to the time of *Dombey and Son*, in any event, most country readers would have possessed only a vicarious acquaintance with London gained through the printed word and pictures, greatly assisted after 1841–42 by the portrayal of London scenes in *Punch* and the *Illustrated London News*. With the spread of the railway network at the very time *Dombey and Son* was published, more and more of Dickens's rural audience acquired a certain amount of first-hand knowledge of the metropolis. From that time onward, he could increasingly depend on his readers' reacting as he desired to mentions of London localities.

The unknown factors relating to the distribution of Dickens's first readers thus make confident generalizations almost impossible. And every individual man, woman, and adolescent among the hypothetical half million had his or her own personal reading habits; there was no such person as a "typical" reader of a Dickens novel. We can, however, be reasonably certain that a fair number of them were what Kathleen Tillotson calls "novel addicts," persons who habitually read voraciously, but superficially and indiscriminately.[13] The minds they brought to a time-killing perusal of, say, *Dombey and Son* were at once smooth (offering no traction for ideas) and soft (offering no defense against artistic manipulation). Novel addicts, therefore, offer a special and probably insoluble problem: on the one hand, simply because they read with their minds more or less in a state of suspension, they may have been the members of the audience who were most unaffected by whatever stratagems Dickens adopted to move them; on the other, they may have been the most affected, because they were incapable of resisting. Unless their sensibilities were jaded beyond hope of cure, we may no doubt assume that they reacted in a crude, predictable manner to Dickens's large, obvious effects. But the quieter touches would have gone unnoticed.

Much of what can be inferred about readers' response is found in contemporary reviews. But while these are, necessarily, the principal source of our knowledge, it must be borne in mind that *vox critici* is by no means *vox populi*. As *Tait's Edinburgh Magazine* remarked in January 1847, "the facts" (that is, the discrepancy between the critical consensus and the testimony of the sales figures) "merely show that book-buyers and reviewers do not always entertain similar opinions."[14] Dickens was much more roughly handled in the reviews than the manifold evidences of his popularity would suggest. The obvious reason is that the critics and ordinary book buyers often read a novel in different ways. Some reviewers, it is true, may have expressed quite faithfully the reactions of thousands of readers who never publicly articulated them. Some were more representative of the common experience than were others who wrote for more decidedly partisan periodicals and audiences (for example, High Church, Evangelical, Nonconformist, Roman Catholic, Tory, Benthamite). But, in general, the reviewers were exceptional readers, whose literary criteria and intellectual equipment qualified them to speak for one section of the reading public but not for anything like a majority. Moreover, it is at least arguable that only a portion of the total contemporary response to a novel (conscious response, that is) ever found its way into print. There may well have been significant reactions among the generality of readers which never figured in critical discussions because they were so widespread as to be taken for granted, or because the prevailing critical system made no provision for them.

Reviewers not infrequently ventured to associate certain tastes and kinds of responses with specific levels of audience. Some were confident that discriminations could be made between, say, the appreciation of pathos and high moral sentiments that was supposedly a characteristic of the "higher orders" of society and the enjoyment of "vulgarity," broad comedy, overt theatricality, and so on that was fundamental in the response of the lower orders. It was doubtless possible to make some such distinctions, but at the time whatever beliefs there were on the subject were clouded by irrelevant social prejudice.

Further sources of information on reader response are the diaries, letters, memoirs, and recorded verbal remarks of the readers themselves.

Many of these have been gathered, in their fragmentary abundance, in Amy Cruse's *The Victorians and Their Books*.[15] Originating as they did in informal private circumstances, they probably come closer to the spontaneous experience of the common reader than does most printed criticism. But, almost without exception, they are casual, brief, and simplistic. Witness the vagueness of the comment of Harriett Mozley, John Henry Newman's sister (not quoted by Cruse), after reading extracts from the first number of *Dombey and Son* in *The Guardian*:

> it is impossible to express my disgust—for it—*The Guardian*—and all its readers, who could tolerate either. It is the worst of the worst of Boz. At the same time I knew it would *take*, and this made me more disgusted still. He is a man who knows *nothing at all* of what he undertakes to write upon and I am more ashamed of the admirers than himself. I am sure if one goes by literature it is a sad look-out, for never was there such a dearth of decently clever and good books.[16]

One, more satisfactory, kind of evidence is unfortunately not available in Dickens's case: the countless letters his readers wrote to him, from motives ranging from adulation and gratitude to mendicity. Dickens probably received more fan letters than did any other nineteenth-century English writer, including Scott, Byron, and Tennyson, but he destroyed virtually all of them, and the only record we have is a second-hand one, in such few of his replies as have been preserved.

Another source of information is widely applicable to Dickens but not, as it happens, to *Dombey and Son*. From contemporary dramatizations it is possible to infer what stage-adaptable aspects of most of his novels were most agreeable to readers, at least those sharing to some extent the taste of habitués of cheap theatres. The numerous stage versions of *Pickwick Papers, Oliver Twist, Nicholas Nickleby, The Old Curiosity Shop,* and *Martin Chuzzlewit* are useful collateral evidence of readers' tastes, for in them Dickens's art was cut down to a few of its bare, but marketable, essentials. "In this process of transmutation," as a writer in the *North British Review* said in May 1845, "the better and more sober parts necessarily disappear, and the striking figures, amusing low life, smart vulgar conversation, and broad farce, are naturally preserved with care."[17] At the beginning of 1846, nine months before the serialization of *Dombey and Son* began, no fewer than fourteen versions of *The Cricket on the Hearth* were playing. But only two English dramatizations of *Dombey and Son* appeared at the time of its publication, and neither is of much help for our purposes. The first, Tom Taylor's, was produced on 2 August 1847, when the serialization was only half finished. Containing eighteen scenes, with fifteen tableaux inspired by Phiz's illustrations, this had a clumsy supplied ending, with Edith somehow being reconciled with Dombey and Dombey himself developing a sudden unmotivated liking for Florence. The second contemporary dramatization, by W. Sydney, appeared a year after the book was completed (4 June 1849). Neither was a success, probably because, as a critic observed at the time, "a more difficult story for the purposes of the playwright could scarcely have been selected."[18] The tight construction, lack of melodramatic action, and emphasis on moral and psychological problems and development all militated against the successful staging of *Dombey and Son* in the popular theatre.[19]

In the ten years between *Pickwick Papers* and *Dombey and Son*, Dickens became increasingly aware of his peculiarly intimate relationship with his audience. It is, of course, impossible to differentiate between artistic decisions dictated simply by his instincts of craftsmanlike rightness and those induced by an immediate sense of the prospective reader with book in hand. But the fact that it was for *Dombey and Son* that he first made elaborate "mems," as he called his working papers, may imply a more acute concern than before for his readers' satisfaction and comfort. In the "mems" there is, admittedly, only one overt reflection of this concern (plan for part 5: "Not to make too much of the scene with the father, or it may be *too painful*");[20] but in his letters to Forster it became explicit. "Do you think it [that is, arranging for Walter Gay to disappoint all the expectations initially raised for him] may be done, without making people angry?" he asked as he was finishing part 1; and again, in connection with part 3: "Do you think the people so likely to be pleased with Florence, and Walter, as to relish another number of them at their present age?"[21]

Dickens's phenomenal popularity is proof enough that his instincts usually were sound, and that his estimate of his readers' capabilities and interests was accurate. But (to repeat a point made earlier) this is not to say that the broad public's response to a given novel was exclusively one of delighted acquiescence and acceptance, as the vast printed record of Bozolatry implies. Readers at large may well have shared some, if not all of the reviewers' reservations concerning the success of his exuberant art.

Nevertheless, Dickens's unremitting efforts to induce what was literally a unique rapport, unmatched before and after his time, between himself and his readers tended to disarm such resistance. Forster wrote in his belated review of the completed *Dombey and Son*:

> We doubt if any writer that ever lived has inspired such strong feelings of personal attachment, in his impersonal character of author. He counts his readers by tens of thousands, and all of them 'unknown friends' with perhaps few exceptions. . . . There was probably not a family in this country where fictitious literature is read, that did not feel the death of Paul Dombey as something little short of a family sorrow.[22]

Dickens's preface to the final number of the novel exemplified his consciousness of his role as a welcome guest in English households: "I cannot forego my usual opportunity of saying farewell to my readers in this greeting-place, though I have only to acknowledge the unbounded warmth and earnestness of their sympathy in every stage of the journey we have just concluded." Dickens's presence was as strongly felt throughout the serialization of *Dombey and Son* as it had been in any previous novel. He was, in effect, a spellbinding performer-showman, whose powerful personality actually was a compound of two: the undefined fictive author whose "voice" was always heard, and the living man behind him, the age's most celebrated author, Charles Dickens, Boz.[23]

The fact that it was a serialized spectacle which readers watched was crucial to the nature of their literary experience. It heightened their sense of familiar (one may also say familial) involvement with the author. It was as if they received a monthly budget of news about various sets of characters who, after the first number or two, had become parts of their daily imaginative lives. Each number, as the *Spectator* said in 1838, "contained something striking and readable for all ranks": an additional indication of the feeling that people of different social classes expected different things in a Dickens novel. Number publishing, the *Spectator* observed on another occasion, accommodated the limited attention span of most readers: it "gives just enough to serve as a meal to the mob of readers; and this quantity, or a little more, is perhaps as much of him as can be well borne at a time."[24] But it was a meal that kept on providing. In the interval between installments, many readers must have passed the time by rereading the latest one. They thereby noticed touches they missed the first headlong time through. And each repeated reading impressed the characters, settings, motifs, and small particulars more deeply in their memories. Their powers of retention were strengthened also by the necessity of keeping the various characters and plots in mind across a span of nineteen months. Dickens, of course, came to their assistance by proliferating the speech tags, physical idiosyncrasies, and other devices which refreshed the reader's memory. The result of this dual kind of "reinforcement," to use the present-day psychological term, was, in addition to the vicarious experience the novel provided of a wonderfully lively and variegated world, a steadily growing store of permanently available memories. Dickens gave his readers more to furnish their minds with than did any other novelist.

According to some reviewers, the lack of unity in the serialized novels preceding *Dombey and Son* was one reason for Dickens's popularity among the unperceptive, undiscriminating masses. "He would be subjected to a severer criticism," the *Edinburgh Review* had said in 1838, "if his fiction could be read continuedly—if his power of maintaining a sustained interest could be tested—if his work could be viewed as a connected whole, and its object, plan, consistency, and arrangement brought to the notice of the reader at once."[25] In *Dombey and Son* Dickens made a great effort to unify his novel. His former fondness, to which his unsophisticated readers raised no objection, for "passages that lead to nothing"[26] (self-contained descriptions and scenes and other indulgent excursions) now was curbed. If writing the novel called for new discipline on his part, it required no less unaccustomed discipline on the part of the reader. The "swift and cursory reading which is one of the effects of serial publications," as Forster put it in his review, did not suffice now, as it had for the succession of novels through *Martin Chuzzlewit.* Now that Dickens produced a work that "could be viewed as a connected whole," serialization placed readers at a disadvantage. The devices that, in the long run, contributed to the novel's unity (the parallel scenes, atmospheric contrasts, and thematic and metaphorical motifs) were scattered across, or divided by, many months. Forster seems to have recognized the difficulty:

> Much that the ordinary reader may pass carelessly in the book, will seize upon the fancy alive to poetical expression, and accustomed to poetical art. The recurrence of particular thoughts and phrases is an instance of the kind, running like the leading colour through a picture, or the predominant phrase in a piece of music, because subtly connected with the emotion which it is the design of the story to create.[27]

It may be, as Robert Garis maintains, that the failure of Dickens's contemporary readers to speak of his "symbolic structures" does not mean they were not conscious of them.[28] But this would have been true only of those who could read the long novel continuously, the bound volume making it conveniently possible to trace a motif across many chapters or to compare widely separated passages, such as the several scenes in church, or the descriptions of the Dombey house at successive stages of the narrative. Rereading a number in the course of a single month was easy and pleasant enough, but few readers, one suspects, would have been moved to go back several months or a year in their collection of the parts to locate the unifying elements that are so manifest to modern readers. The sheer fact that the novel was physically broken up into what eventually amounted to nineteen pamphlets (one was a double number) would have served as a psychological deterrent to its being looked upon as an artistic whole. Serialization, then, undoubtedly dissipated and diffused readers' consciousness of the novel's enveloping structure.

In any event, most readers' primary interest was less in architectonics than in immediate effects, as was only natural when the narrative was conducted in as emphatically dramatic a style as was Dickens's practice. Specifically literary effects, such as Forster referred to, were less noticeable when the reading experience took the form of attendance at a silent monthly performance of theatre-at-home, during which the star performer, the novelist who was master of the show, brought off point after point, in the histrionic jargon of the day. Richard Ford wrote that

> *Boz* furnishes subjects to playwrights and farce-writers; he is the play himself, now that brutes feed where Garrick trod; he brings home to us tragedy, comedy, and farce; the mountain comes to Mahomet, to us in our easy chairs, by our fires, and wives' sides, unpoisoned by the gas and galleries, unheadached by the music and bill of the play.[29]

It would be instructive—indeed, the issue is vital when one tries to define the impact of Dickens's theatricality on his readers—to know what proportion of his audience went to the theatre and what proportion did not. To the former, first-hand experience of the early Victorian drama, especially farce and melodrama, would have enriched their response to the innumerable instances in which Dickens brought theatrical scenes and theatrically inspired characters to the printed page. To the latter, the novels would have been a surrogate for the theatre, converting an impermissible or inaccessible form of entertainment into a respectable one to be enjoyed with clear conscience in the home. But their experience would not have been as vivid.

The accompanying illustrations, sometimes imitating stage tableaux, would have reminded theatre-going readers of scenes in popular plays, and a number of the characters in *Dombey and Son* (Edith the tragedy queen, Carker the stage villain, Major Bagstock the choleric old soldier, Captain Cuttle the bluff comic sailor, Walter Gay the romantic lead, Toodle the honest working man) were identifiable stage types. Readers meeting them on the printed page would have filled in Dickens's portraits by absorption and association, so to speak, from their numerous prototypes on the contemporary stage. Often, too, such readers would, in their imaginations, cast their favorite actors and actresses in the Dickensian roles to which they were best suited.[30] In fiction as theatrical as Dickens's, the involvement of readers in the sympathetic characters was as intense as the identification across the footlights that constitutes a certain part of the dramatic experience. Witness (though it is too long to quote here) Lord Jeffrey's famous letter to Dickens in which he expatiated on his emotional involvement in the lives and fortunes of Florence, Walter, Susan Nipper, Paul (not yet dead), Captain Cuttle, and John Carker.[31]

It was the combined theatrical and oral quality of Dickens's novels, too, which so admirably fitted them to be read aloud. His characteristic style, the *Times* noted four months before the serialization of *Dombey and Son* commenced, "may be called, for want of a better term, the *literary ventriloquial*, for it aims at producing in words to the eye precisely the same effects as ventriloquism achieves in sounds in the ear."[32] To realize these effects by translating them from print to speech was the fortunate privilege of drawing-room performers; it was not only Sloppy, in *Our Mutual Friend*, who did the Police (or any Dickens scene) in different voices. Sometimes the father of the family, armed with the latest number and by no means reluctant to serve as Dickens's stand-in, gave a one-man show; sometimes the respective roles were parceled out around the fireside. One wonders, incidentally, whether *Dombey and Son* was more discernibly ear-oriented than the earlier novels.[33] Dickens himself may have thought so; it may not be entirely accidental that his first notion of reading selections from his works on the platform came when he read part I aloud in Lausanne in September 1846. When, twelve years later, he finally took the plunge, it was with a two-hour program entitled "Little Dombey."

To understand fully the frame and furniture of mind with which Dickens's readers came to a new novel of his, it would be necessary to read all that they were reading simultaneously with the monthly parts as well as all they had read so recently as to affect their reaction to the novel. But this would be virtually impossible, and so one can only suggest in general terms the literary factors that influenced their response.

It is likely that some people who bought Dickens's fiction as first issued, though they habitually read newspapers, magazines, and various other forms of small-scale and ephemeral reading matter, had not read any other novels. As for those who had, their experience of reading Dickens would have been enlarged by what might be called generic recollection: a prior acquaintance with fiction belonging to the same genre. Unlike *Oliver Twist*, however, with its numerous affinities to the Newgate novel, and *Barnaby Rudge* with its roots in the historical novel, *Dombey and Son* did not have many characteristics traceable to specific current "schools" of fiction. There is a hint of the Newgate novel in Good Mrs. Brown and Alice Marwood, and of silver fork fiction in the Sir Barnet Skettleses. Some readers, too, may have brought to their acquaintance with Captain Cuttle, the Wooden Midshipman, and the seagoing atmosphere and plot of *Dombey and Son* memories of the popular nautical novel of the 1830s, typified by Michael Scott's *Tom Cringle's Log* (1833) and Captain Marryat's *Peter Simple* (1834) and *Mr. Midshipman Easy* (1836). Further afield, the responses of some readers would have been affected by their prior knowledge of Dickens's two great eighteenth-century models, Fielding and Smollett.

How many readers were thus equipped, we cannot tell. But most of them had certainly read at least some of Dickens's own preceding novels, and their expectations and reactions were most immediately influenced by their having become attuned to his characteristic voice and their awareness of his special brand of characters and what had by now become established as his uniquely "Dickensian" social world. The nature of their experience as they read *Dombey and Son* was determined in part by the place it had in the sequence of his novels, and particularly by its position (excluding the Christmas books) just after *Martin Chuzzlewit*. They had, in short, learned to read Dickens, to single out for appreciation his "inimitable" qualities. But what they found in *Dombey and Son* was a mixture of the old familiar Dickens and a new one. Five months into serialization, he gave them a death scene to match that in *The Old Curiosity Shop*, which had unquestionably been responsible for the great sale of that novel and which, unfortunately for sales, had had no counterpart in *Martin Chuzzlewit*. *Dombey and Son* also had the expected quota of amiable or eccentric "Dickensian" characters: not only Cuttle but Bunsby, the Toodles, Mr. Toots, Susan Nipper, and Sol Gills. There were recognizable traces of Ruth Pinch in Harriet Carker, and of Sairey Gamp in Mrs. MacStinger.[34]

With *Dombey and Son*, however, new and important ingredients were introduced into the Dickens formula, and readers had to adjust their sights accordingly. There was, for example, a greater emphasis on the immediacy of the time setting. There were new techniques to respond to, such as the bravura trick of seeing the puzzling world through the eyes of the sensitive and prematurely grave Paul Dombey. There was a renewed concentration, successful this time as it had not been in *Martin Chuzzlewit*, on a dominant moral theme. And, as we have noted, Dickens's meticulous planning, his avoidance of loose ends and culs-de-sac, his attention to relating even the most minor characters and small episodes to the overall design, called for unprecedented attention on the part of the reader if Dickens's artistic purpose was not to be defeated by serialization. While Dickens's comic inventiveness did not flag, in *Dombey and Son* there was less of Boz's plenty, the overflowing cornucopia of incidental delight.

Whatever the public of 1846–48 read alongside *Dombey and Son* had the greatest influence on its response to the novel. Thackeray's *Snob* papers, running in *Punch* from 28 February 1846 to 27 February 1847, more than once anticipated Dickens's themes and characters, so that when, for example, they met Major Bagstock, readers would have filled in his portrait with their memories of the "military snob" Lieut. Gen. Sir Granby Tufto, and when they read of the disastrous dinner party at the Dombeys' they would have recalled Thackeray's descriptions of similar events in his chapters on "Dining-out Snobs" and "Dinner-Giving Snobs." In effect, the *Punch* series prepared readers for those passages in *Dombey and Son* in which Dickens did his own anatomizing of the snob mentality as Thackeray broadly defined it. His rival's type characters and his moralizing did a good deal of work for Dickens in advance.

We cannot know how many readers of *Dombey and Son* thus superimposed their impressions of Thackeray's snobs on their experience of Dickens's novel, nor can we know how many also bought the monthly parts of *Vanity Fair*, the serialization of which (January 1847–July 1848) was largely concurrent with that of *Dombey and Son*. There surely was some overlapping of audiences for these two novels, although their simultaneous publication was often used as a means of distinguishing Dickens's public from Thackeray's. Whereas, as the *English Review* said, Dickens's "sphere of operation is almost boundless . . . Thackeray writes, on the contrary, for the elect of mankind; for keen intellects and lofty

minds" (10 [1848]: 275). The elect of mankind, to judge from comparative sales figures, was a decided minority. *Vanity Fair* "never sold a quarter
as many copies as *Dombey*."[35]

Dickens, of course, did not foresee that two of Thackeray's books, in
serialized form, would appear immediately before or alongside his own
and so, to some extent, influence his audience. What kind of prior literary
experience did he, in fact, ascribe to his readers? It was sometimes said
that one reason for his popularity was the fact that readers could come to
his novels with little if any store of book knowledge; the ignorant could
read him with as much delight as the learned. This is an exaggeration. The
frequency and variety of his allusions and (often hidden) quotations indicate that he assumed, not surprisingly, that his readers had a background
of reading and a stock of general information coextensive with his own.
They would, therefore, have read all the books he read as a youth, prominently represented, in the case of *Dombey and Son*, by the *Arabian Nights*,
Tales of the Genii, the large adjacent variety of fairy tales and nursery
rhymes, Goldsmith, and the edifying poetry of Isaac Watts. The score or
so of biblical allusions presumably would have been recognized by nearly
all readers, along with the occasional comedy involved in misquotation or
misapplication. Dickens also expected that his readers, though few had
had a formal classical education, would at least have identified the elementary mythological references and known the names of the various Greek
and Latin authors mentioned in the scenes at Dr. Blimber's academy. The
nautical songs Captain Cuttle quotes in mangled snatches probably were
more available to Dickens, who had picked them up during his childhood
among the old salts at Chatham and in the Dibdinesque naval dramas at
the popular theatres, than to his readers at large. Like the classical allusions, they had no intrinsic function in the novel but were merely
employed to embellish a certain theme, in this instance Captain Cuttle's
occupation. Those readers who did know the words and detected Cuttle's
misquotations had a satisfaction denied to the rest. Some, too, would have
noticed that his supposed quotation from Proverbs, "May we never
want a friend in need, nor a bottle to give him!" was actually from a
Dibdin song.[36]

One feels that Dickens, devoted as he was to the stage, may have
overestimated his readers' familiarity with some of the plays to which he
refers. There is little doubt that his Shakespearian allusions would have
been fully intelligible to them, for they knew Shakespeare from books if
not from performances. Many would have recognized the Cordelia-Lear
situation in that of Florence and Mr. Dombey, as well as the grotesque

ironies permeating the characterization of Mrs. Skewton as the fatal Cleopatra. But were echoes of, say, Thomas Morton's *A Cure for the Heartache*
(1797) (1.4) or Sheridan's *The Duenna* (1775) (14.199) instantaneously
recognizable, even granting that such plays were occasionally revived in
Dickens's time?[37]

Similarly with other allusions that seemingly went beyond the audience's treasury of miscellaneous knowledge: it would have taken an unusually learned reader to realize that Cuttle's "Science which is the mother
of Inwention, and knows no law" (23.325) was an amalgam of the old
proverb "Necessity is the mother of invention" and Publius Syrus's "Necessity knows no law except to conquer" (A.D. 42).[38] When all due allowance is made for the vast difference between the store of information
common to the early Victorian reading public and that which we possess
today, a gap which is among the most formidable of the obstacles in the
way of historical reconstruction of a past generation's mind, it seems
unlikely that either Captain Cuttle or Dickens's readers would have
run across such out-of-the-way tags as the latter, let alone made a note of
them.

Dombey and Son is sprinkled with topicalities which, by juxtaposing
the actual with the fictional, provide on occasion a kind of deepening
stereoscopic effect. Mr. Dombey's reference to little Paul's aching bones,
"He is not a living skeleton, I suppose" (8.97: the time context is the
late 1830s), acquired poignancy when the term evoked memories of
the emaciated Frenchman Claude Seurat, who, to the indignant disgust
of humanitarians, was the subject of a callously mercenary exhibition
in London in 1825. (There probably were other freak shows, with the
same name, later on, and in any event Seurat was pictured and described
in William Hone's widely distributed *Every-Day Book* (1826–27).) To the
brief mention in Dickens's text (6.70) of the "mad bull" scare in
the streets near Smithfield Market which delivered Florence into Good
Mrs. Brown's hands, readers could have added their recollection of the
numerous news stories in 1846 and 1847 that described the dangerous
nuisance caused by the practice of herding cattle through central London.

Banal though it was, the plot of Walter Gay's disappearance at sea and
Sol Gills's setting out to find him acquired fresh emotional connotations
from its timeliness. At the very moment that the mystery of Walter Gay
and the *Son and Heir* engrossed readers of *Dombey and Son*, the mystery of
the vanished Sir John Franklin and his crew was engrossing Mr. Chick
and his fellow newspaper readers. Continuing lack of word from the polar
expedition, which had set out from England in the spring of 1845 to

the accompaniment of much patriotic publicity, began to stir anxiety in January 1847, and in the course of that year the Admiralty dispatched three simultaneous expeditions to search for the missing explorers. Dickens's readers transferred the emotions stirred by the Franklin mystery to the question of what had happened to Walter Gay (with whom, along with Cuttle, Gills, and Florence, they identified far more closely than they could have with Sir John Franklin and his anguished wife). The eventual return of the shipwrecked Walter represented a fulfillment of hopes which, in the case of Franklin, were destined to be dashed.

Mention of the electric telegraph (60.808) was another immediately topical touch. It was at this time that the invention, originally a railroading device, was beginning to be adopted commercially; in 1847 some 2,000 miles of line were already in operation. But, it need hardly be said, the presiding topicality in *Dombey and Son* is the railroad, which Dickens converted into a massive and reverberant symbol of the spirit of the age. The description of Staggs's Gardens and the set pieces of Dombey's train ride and of Carker's death led contemporary readers to focus the various impressions and ideas that this new and revolutionary mode of transport, a portentous social phenomenon, had so far generated in them: its dazzling speed, its physical alteration of the countryside and urban neighborhoods, and its breeding of new kinds of workmen. The several famous passages in *Dombey and Son* would have meant quite different things, and different combinations of things, to readers who had already ridden the railways and those who had not, those who had watched the engineering operations that drastically changed the landscape and cityscape, and those who had invested in railway shares. Readers who saw J. M. W. Turner's *Rain, Steam, and Speed* at the Royal Academy exhibition in 1844 may have superimposed their memories of that painting's bold colors and indistinct forms on the imagery they found in Dickens's prose flights.

The very name "Staggs" then had a significance that is lost to us. It was current slang, evidently coined by Thackeray, for speculators, especially speculators in railway shares, and, because of its suggestion of impending financial disaster (the famous promoter George Hudson was much in the news, and Dickens, we learn from a newly published letter, disliked him intensely)[39] somewhat prepared the reader for the eventual fall of the house of Dombey.[40] But the topical name that evoked the most complex set of associations among the earliest readers of *Dombey and Son* was "Charitable Grinders." In addition to the perhaps dominant allusion to oppressive drudgeful education as provided by an aptly named imaginary London livery company (with a side glance at Dr. Blimber's academy, where Mr. Feeder ground the handle of a barrel organ loaded with Latin exercises), "Grinders" referred also to a familiar cockney gesture (a form of nose thumbing), Carker's teeth, sweated labor, and the current notoriety of the strike- and violence-plagued Sheffield grinding (cutlery) industry.[41]

Among the first readers of *Dombey and Son* there were many, quite probably a majority, who were moved by what the envious Thackeray had to admit was the "stupendous" pathos not only of Paul Dombey's death-bed but of the whole Paul-Florence story. Macaulay, too (though his testimony is less valuable because, as a novel addict, he was a soft touch for sentimental writing), said that in the first number there was "one passage which made me cry as if my heart would break. It is the description of a little girl who had lost an affectionate mother, and is unkindly treated by everybody."[42] The seventy-five-year-old Lord Jeffrey reported to Dickens that on receipt of part 5 he "so cried and sobbed over it last night, and again this morning; and felt my heart purified by those tears."[43] Like many other readers, he declared (and no one was prepared to contradict him) that there had been nothing like it since the death of Little Nell. The men and women who wept over Paul did so in part because they clung to sacred memories of children's deathbeds in their own lives as parents or siblings, and in part because they had been conditioned to do so by countless similar scenes in popular literature, including pious and sentimental poems.[44] If we are to believe Charlotte Yonge (*The Heir of Redclyffe* [1853], chapter 3), if a young lady was able to read the deathbed scene, "the part of Dombey that hurts women's feelings most," without crying, she was proved to be "stony hearted" and, inferentially, a discredit to her sex.

An older novelist of the time, Mrs. Anne Marsh, declared that Paul's "death flung a nation into mourning."[45] But this, like so many observations bearing on the presumed universality of Dickens's public and the uniformity of its response, is sheer hyperbole.[46] A sizable number of people, it appears, failed to participate in the lachrymose furor. Dickens's pathos was by no means unanimously approved or totally effective. Reviewers had repeatedly warned him that, in the words of Richard Ford in the *Quarterly Review* in 1839, "he should . . . avoid, in future, all attempts at pure pathos,—on which he never ventures without reminding us of Sterne, and of his own immense inferiority to that master."[47] As for the Paul Dombey death scene itself, a writer in the *North British Review*, perhaps Coventry Patmore, admitted that a case could be made against Dickens's handling of it:

We might indeed, were we so minded, find some flaws in the beautiful sentimentalism of Paul's death-bed scene; some affectations of style, some little mawkishness of feeling, more than a little want of a healthy spirit in contemplating death. We might object to the whole description, its too close resemblance, in touch and colouring, and light and tone, to the well-remembered chapters which told the death of Little Nell. We might say, it is not the sign of strength to reproduce old creations. But we forbear.[48]

Other not wholly reverential readers exercised no such ironic restraint. Henry Hallam wrote to Mrs. Brookfield: "Everybody is pretending that the death of Paul Dombey is the most beautiful thing ever written. Milnes, Thackeray, and your Uncle [Hallam's father, the historian] own to tears. I am so hardened as to be unable to look on it in any light but pure 'business.' "[49] And at the very moment when the nation presumably was in deepest mourning, purchasers of the March 1847 number of *The Man in the Moon*, an impudent satirical magazine edited by Albert Smith, formerly of *Punch*, found a burlesque "Inquest on the Late Master Paul Dombey" (held at a public house) followed by a description of his funeral cortège and a "Requiem" set to a popular tune of the day.[50] The whole was not especially funny, but its existence, and doubtless its popularity among the magazine's buyers, are evidence that readers responded in more than one way to Dickens's sentimentality. Given the early Victorians' mercurial temperament, it is not impossible that some of the same people who cried over Dickens's pages subsequently laughed over their parody in *The Man in the Moon*.

If conditioned responses accounted for a portion of the public's grief over Paul, similar ones were excited elsewhere in the novel, notably in relation to the deep-seated Victorian dread of losing one's money. The casually introduced and repeated allusions to Mrs. Pipchin's husband's disastrous investment in Peruvian gold mines touched a sensitive nerve in middle-class readers' psyches. So too, even more, did the extended passages describing the selling-up of the Dombey mansion after the failure of the firm. This typified a traumatic event in the experience of many early Victorian families, and it was dreaded by many more. Thackeray portrayed the sale of John Sedley's home and household effects in the May 1847 number of *Vanity Fair*; Dickens showed the equivalent event in *his* novel in April 1848. Even though the Dombey house itself had never been the scene of domestic bliss, every such calamity symbolized the violation of the sanctity of the home. So deep-seated, in fact, were the values associated with affectionate parent-child relationships and all that the idea of home and hearth connoted that their transgression throughout the novel struck at the moral center of the reader's response.

The language of *Dombey and Son* conformed to the expectations that previous acquaintance with Dickens's novels had formed. In general, it was a natural, fluent style, intelligible and graphic. "He calls upon his reader for no exertion," the *Spectator* had said in 1838, "—requires from him no mental elevation: he who runs may read Boz—'he is plain to the meanest capacity.' "[51] The more cultivated public, however, may have agreed more or less with the several charges that the critics laid against Dickens as a stylist: that he deviated too far from the neoclassic mode that was the norm for literary discourse; that he committed numerous lexical and syntactical solecisms; that he was given to mawkishness and, even worse, low colloquialism. "Indeed," remarked the *North British Review*, "Mr. Dickens seems often purposely to cast his language into the mould of the vulgar characters he represents, and as it were, to fondle their phrases, idioms, and ideas."[52] But might not this have ingratiated Dickens even more with his many nonpurist readers, writing as he did in a language flecked with their own "barbarisms"?

Once in a while, it is true, Dickens used a term that may not have been widely familiar, for example "non-Dominical holidays" (9.112). How many readers' active vocabularies extended to pugilistic slang is hard to determine, but the terms in which the Game Chicken's "visage . . . in a state of . . . great dilapidation" was described would have presented no more difficulty than the many flash terms in *Oliver Twist*. In context, they were largely self-explanatory:

> The Chicken himself attributed this punishment to his having had the misfortune to get into Chancery early in the proceedings, when he was severely fibbed by the Larkey one, and heavily grassed. But it appeared from the published records of that great contest that the Larkey Boy had had it all his own way from the beginning, and that the Chicken had been tapped, and bunged, and had received pepper, and had been made groggy, and had come up piping, and had endured a complication of similar strange inconveniences, until he had been gone into and finished. (44.597)[53]

As for the style at the other end of the spectrum, the florid rhetoric that sometimes bordered on metrical prose, one can only conclude that it was acceptable to most readers. To one correspondent who ventured to question its propriety in his earlier works, Dickens replied in 1844:

> considering that it is a very melodious and agreeable march of words, usually; and may be perfectly plain and free; I cannot agree with you that it is likely to be considered by discreet readers as turgid or bombastic, unless the sentiments expressed in it, be of that character. Then indeed it matters very little how they are attired, as they cannot fail to be disagreeable in any garb.[54]

But some readers, typified by the reviewer of *Dombey and Son* in *Sharpe's London Magazine* (6 [1848]: 201), objected to the book's being "full to overflowing of waves whispering and wandering; of dark rivers rolling to the sea; of winds, and golden ripples, and such like matters, which are sometimes very pretty, generally very untrue, and have become, at all events, excessively stale."

The social criticism in the novel, dealing as it did with broad tendencies in contemporary society rather than with specific abuses, as in *Oliver Twist* and *Nicholas Nickleby*, seems to have made little impression one way or another among the generality of readers. In the audience, however, there were those who objected to Dickens's democratic sentiments. The readers of *Blackwood's Magazine* who subscribed to its Tory views would have echoed its complaint that Dickens's "mischievous" purpose was "to decry, and bring into contempt as unfeeling, the higher classes."[55] The severest critics of Dickens's social bearings were his Roman Catholic readers, if they followed the line taken by the new periodical, the *Rambler*, in its first issue (January 1848). After announcing its distinctly unorthodox opinion that Florence's story, "stripped of the adventitious charm with which it is invested," would not "stand the test of propriety and feminine modesty," it went on to attack the same story as evidence that Dickens

> mistakes confusion of all distinctions in the social scale and contempt of the world's conventionalities for the triumph of charity and love. How can we otherwise account for the total insensibility which he makes his heroine display for all those lines of distinction which the feelings and opinions of mankind have sanctioned? . . . This levelling principle, frequently

peeping out in Mr. Dickens's works is also imported from France, where that spirit is so rife. (p. 64)

Probably a more frequent source of offense was the several varieties of "unpleasantness" some critics detected in the novel. Chief among these was "vulgarity," a vaguely defined but far from negligible quality, the response to which was determined by a mixture of class feeling and literary "taste." And while, apart from Good Mrs. Brown, Alice Marwood, and Rob Toodle, there was no criminal element in *Dombey and Son* as there had been in *Oliver Twist*, there were numerous "low" characters. A certain portion of the novel's audience would have found them as inadmissible to their world as they had Oliver's associates. "I don't *like* these things," Lord Melbourne had said of the latter: "I wish to avoid them; I don't like them in *reality*, and therefore I don't wish them represented."[56]

An even more sensitive point was the possibility of irreligion. Momentarily forgetting that here he trod on dangerous ground, Dickens included in the christening scene in *Dombey and Son* a passage that he thought better of before returning proofs. The font, he wrote, was "a cold and rigid marble basin which seemed to have been playing a churchyard game at cup and ball with its matter-of-fact pedestal, and to have been just at that moment caught on the top of it."[57] The excision was well advised. Dickens, if he saw the parsonical *English Review* notice of the book, must have smiled at the reviewer's "pleasure" at his "reverential tone as to the holy mystery of Baptism."[58]

Few readers of *Dombey and Son* would have taken umbrage at its comedy, because Dickens's humor, after all, was what people prized most in his fiction. The new bottle contained an abundance of the old wine: Captain Cuttle's salty-sentimental quotations and bonhomie, Bunsby's oracular stupidity, Susan Nipper's tart remarks, Mr. Toots's callow self-abnegating lovesickness. But did Dickens's readers laugh as heartily as he expected them to laugh at the repeated references to Mrs. Perch's pregnancies and breast feeding or, for that matter, at Toots's elaborate solicitude for his new wife in her gravid condition? Or may this not have been a more or less private joke, by which a husband whose wife seemingly was in a permanent state of either pregnancy or lactation sought to deflect his exasperation into humor? One questions, too, whether the several slapstick instances of knocked-about children tickled Dickens's readers as much as he expected—notably Alexander MacStinger's routine of being shaken, buffeted, and slapped or spanked and then turning black in the face as he holds his breath (23.320; 39.532; 60.816).[59]

We turn, finally, to the problem of how attentively Dickens's audience read. In *Dombey and Son*, perhaps more than any of the other novels, Dickens took pains to spell things out and to add authorial commentary, sometimes brief passages of sermonizing, to the narrative. This, despite his assertion to Lewes ten years earlier that "if readers cannot detect the point of a passage without having their attention called to it by the writer, I would much rather they lost it and looked out for something else."[60] Evidently (perhaps as a result of inquiring letters from readers?) he had decided that his audience was not as quick to see his point as he had thought.

Some readers, if they were like some reviewers, found glaring improbabilities and inconsistencies as the novel progressed. They refused to believe, for example, that Edith would have run away from Dombey, or that Florence, whose inexorable devotion to her stiff-necked father was itself incredible to some, could eventually have had so beneficent an influence on him. To some, also, it was unlikely that she should have been so free to ramble about London, that a girl of her upbringing should have kissed Captain Cuttle or asked Bunsby for his views on Walter's possible safety; or that Dombey would have made Carker his confidant and agent in so delicate and momentous a business as his wife's conduct.[61] Other readers would have boggled at smaller points. Why did John Carker stay with the firm of Dombey and Son when, after his youthful disgrace, he might have made a fresh start elsewhere? Why did Bunsby not bring back Sol Gills's letters when he brought back Captain Cuttle's box? Why was the returning Walter frightened away from his uncle's shop by a mere dog? When did Edith give Carker reason to believe she would become his mistress? Why, after many years when their paths would naturally have crossed, was Harriet Carker not acquainted with Mr. Morfin? Why was Captain Cuttle, the veteran sailor, unable to identify the instruments in Sol Gills's shop?[62] A few readers, with sharp eyes and long memories across the span of the monthly numbers, would have noticed such small inconsistencies as Dickens's uncertainty whether the London streets were lighted by gas (3.24; 59.804) or linkmen's torches (36.498). A larger number would have picked up such howlers as Cuttle's "putting a hand to each side of his mouth" (23.324).

Dickens's devotees read also with their eyes divided between the printed text and the illustrations. Writing of his early acquaintance with the novels, Henry James associated the pictures and the dramatizations inferentially as two means by which the sense of the text was, in the one case, enlarged, and in the other, simplified; in either case, impressed more vividly and lastingly on the memory.[63] The year before *Dombey and Son* began publication, a patronizing but discerning reviewer noted that

> the vast popularity of [Dickens's] works may, perhaps, in some degree be owing to the indolence of the reading public, and that the very clever 'illustrations' which accompany them all, may have contributed greatly to their success. No reader need ever task his mind's eye to form a picture corresponding to the full description; he has but to turn the page, and there stands the Pickwick, Pecksniff, or Tom Pinch, embodied to his hand, and kindly saving him the labour of thought.[64]

Placed as each was at the point of the number of *Dombey and Son* where it would not only duplicate but expand on Dickens's description, Phiz's engravings were an integral part of the reader's total experience. Michael Steig has summarized the engravings' triple function: "the paralleling, through visually and/or conceptually analogous details, of one part of the novel, or one character, with another; the complex use of emblematic details to interpret some part of the text; and finally, the use of allusion to earlier graphic art."[65] A close examination of the *Dombey and Son* illustrations reveals emblematic and allegorical allusions to *Tristram Shandy*, Massinger's *The City Madam*, Atalanta, Clytemnestra, the sacrifice of Iphigenia, Judith slaying Holofernes, the Amazons, and numerous other thematic references and clarifications.[66]

But how much of this intricate interplay of text and picture was evident to Dickens's first readers? Steig admits that there is no easy answer to the question. What he says of the problem of the *Bleak House* illustrations is fully applicable also to *Dombey and Son*, and not to the illustrations alone but to the whole Dickens text:

> what we like to think of as a full recapturing of the total experience of the text-plus-illustrations often requires so much research, knowledge of various graphic and emblematic traditions, and putting together of evidence—in short, so much hard study and heavy ratiocination—that one may wonder whether we are really recapturing something that was ever there for even the best readers among Dickens's contemporaries. The only possible answer to such an objection seems to be that it is time to acknowledge that Dickens is an extremely complex artist, and that in some respects our historical per-

spective may make us better readers of his works than were his own contemporaries. . . . What is perhaps most interesting about Phiz's illustrations and their sources is that some of the connections which critics have had to infer from the novel were actually emphasized quite directly in the original plates. . . . Yet the lack of contemporary testimony to this effect makes one wonder if Dickens and Browne ['Phiz'] were collaborating in a mixed genre whose full force was in reality lost on contemporary readers. . . . Perhaps it is only now, with the historical distance of another century, that we can begin to experience the full effect of [a novel] as its creators intended.[67]

This is one conclusion, daunting but I think defensible, to which the existing evidence directs us. Even assuming, as we certainly may, that a considerable portion of what modern exegetes find in a Dickens novel would have been invisible to Victorian eyes accustomed to reading fiction in other ways than ours, there is much, one feels, that those eyes, in Victorian circumstances, should have seen. Yet there is little or no record that they did so. Dickens's true complexity, to say nothing of his subtleties, seems to have gone largely unnoticed in his own time.

So runs the argument from silence, which, although not infallible, is compelling. But it is a silence that issues, in part, from the sheer limitations of historical evidence, which is confined to the conscious level of response. No doubt the Victorians missed much that they were equipped to see; but perhaps they saw more than they knew they saw, and were subconsciously affected in ways that only twentieth-century psychology—and, more recently, the influential school of reader-response criticism—has come to describe and define. They did not analyze their experience of literature in any really penetrating manner, and so they did not leave any psychological documents (as, for example, Coleridge had done) to aid us in our effort to discover how they read. Nothing that they set down on paper can answer such questions as whether, beneath the obvious staginess of Edith Dombey as a stereotyped tragedy queen and in spite of their own inhibitions in such matters, the Victorians detected a woman of powerful, though repressed, sexuality; or whether, even as on the conscious level they regarded the Florence–Edith relationship as an innocent sisterhood, they were subliminally (and uncomfortably?) aware of the strong suggestions of lesbianism. The materials of biography and literary and social history can take us part way toward understanding how the

Victorians read Dickens. We have an approximate idea of what constituted their superficial conscious experience. But, apart from whatever specula-tion we may wish to devote to the question, the deeper psychological elements of their response, not only to the subject matter but to the nuances of language as well, are past retrieval.

1980

10

English Publishing and
the Mass Audience in 1852

From the very beginnings of publishing as a profit-making enterprise, the publisher's estimate of the size of a book's potential audience, its willingness to pay the price he will ask, and above all its current tastes, has been the major consideration in his decision whether or not to send the manuscript on to the typesetter. The whole history of literature in the past few centuries is, in a sense, the aggregate history of such decisions. But we know very little about how publishers of various periods regarded their market. What was their conception of its numerical size? of its social composition and educational level? of its ability to pay the asking prices of books? of the manifold elements in the cultural and social background of the age which influenced the book-buying habit?[1]

Today's publishers have at their disposal the results of hundreds of studies, made chiefly by students of library science and market analysis specialists, of twentieth-century reading habits and the conditions that influence them. The latest results of this continuing survey are constantly drawn upon by the publishers of mass-circulation periodicals and paperbound books. To that degree the contemporary reading public, as delineated by modern techniques of opinion- and behavior-sampling, exerts a direct and relatively measurable influence upon what is published. Elsewhere in the trade, it is true, that influence is less direct, but it is still potent, for modern commercial publishers stake their very existence, fully as much as do the makers of detergents or deep-freeze units, upon an accurate estimate of the potential market for their product and its current likes and dislikes.

When some future scholar sets out to assess the influence of the audience upon what was published in our own age, he will have a large body of information to work upon, make of it what he will. But the present-day scholar who attempts to answer the same question for the Victorian age must deal with two quantities which are still largely unknown: x, the true nature of the Victorian reading public, and y, the average publisher's conception of it and the degree to which that conception influenced his editorial decisions.

With y we shall have little to do here, except to remark that the evidence that comes down to us on the point is scanty. Shrewd though some Victorian publishers were, few, at least until the later decades of the century, seem to have bothered very much about the reading public as a whole. Most of them, with the conspicuous exception of the newcomers in the trade who unabashedly angled for the pennies and shillings of the masses, were untouched by the revolution that was going on about them. Such ideas as they had about the new audience were clouded by indifference, prejudice, and misinformation. The Victorians were statistics-conscious, even statistics-mad; they had a passion for collecting and codifying data on all sorts of other subjects—education, sanitary conditions, crime, wages, trade—but they seem never to have thought of making a thorough study of the contemporary reading public and of the place of the reading habit in the whole social scene.

In this essay our business is with x. We are only beginning to understand what the Victorian audience was really like; only now are we beginning to subject to the test of original research the facile assumptions that have been so long current. In the pages that follow, I shall make a retrospective audience survey for an English publisher of the year 1852. My purpose is not to measure the publishers' actual awareness of the swiftly changing audience—a task for which, as I say, our present knowledge is inadequate—but to suggest how research, aided by the perspective of a hundred years, allows us to see the mid-Victorian reading public as it might have appeared to a publisher as market-conscious as his modern counterpart.

I have chosen the year 1852 not just because there is something satisfactorily tidy in going back precisely a century. It was in the fifties, I think, that the reading public could first be called a mass public in anything like modern terms. Admittedly, people as far back as Dr. Johnson's time had been exclaiming over the increase in the number of readers, and the March of Mind was one of the most publicized phenomena of the period stretching from the 1820s to mid-century. But it was only around the fifties that the familiar phrase of "literature for the millions" ceased to be mere hyperbole and came to have a basis in sober fact. The spread of elementary education had raised the literacy rate. Popular interest in reading, generated initially by the radical press of the Reform Bill and Chartist periods, had been exploited by the proprietors of cheap sensational weekly newspapers, men like Edward Lloyd and G. W. M. Reynolds, who also produced enormous quantities of melodramatic fiction in penny numbers—the famous "penny bloods." On the more decorous side, the activities of the religious denominations in spreading tracts and other edifying reading matter broadcast among the population encouraged the reading habit.

It is significant that in this decade of the 1850s one finds the first recurrent journalistic interest in the new mass market for the printed word. In 1858, for example, Wilkie Collins wrote of his discovery of "The Unknown Public" as dramatically as if he had come upon the sources of the Nile.[2] The mass audience for cheap periodicals he described had been in existence for some years before he announced his discovery of it; but the point is that it had by now become large enough and important enough to constitute an interesting and provocative subject for an article in the middle-class press, and that Collins could tell the readers of *Household Words*, itself a twopenny periodical for the middle classes, that there had come into being a much larger reading public lower down on the social and cultural scale. This was the era when reading first became genuinely democratized.

How large was the greatest possible audience to which a publisher could appeal? By the census of 1851, the total population of England, Scotland, and Wales above the age of twenty was eleven and a half million—an increase of more than four million adults in thirty years.[3] Of these, 31 percent of the males and 45 percent of the females were unable to sign their names to the marriage register.[4] A literacy rate based upon this test is not, of course, a reliable indication of the number who could *read*. Undoubtedly many men and women who could not sign their names could nevertheless master simple reading matter. On the other hand, many who could scrawl their signatures, as a purely mechanical accomplishment, could not read at all. The two considerations may cancel each other out; in any case, evidence from other sources suggests that while a literacy rate of somewhere around 60 percent may be a bit low for the fifties, it is not too far off the mark. We may, therefore, write off 40 percent of the total adult population as not conceivably forming any market for printed matter. In addition, we must eliminate the by no means inconsiderable number of people who were on the sheer fringes of literacy and who therefore would be no more likely to buy a book or a paper than would their coevals who were in total darkness. On the other hand, we should throw in perhaps a half-million youths under twenty who might buy adult reading matter. All these calculations are so speculative that a final figure is nothing more than a guess crowning a precarious pile of other guesses, but for the sake of hanging up some sort of goal for the ambitious Victorian publisher to strive for, let us say that, omitting the market for juvenile literature and school texts, the gross potential British reading public in 1852 was between five and six million.

This optimum audience (to use a notably un-Victorian phrase) and the practicing one were, of course, very different things. The only guide we have to the number of people who actually read in 1852 is sales figures, and these must always be handled with caution. For one thing, few of them are authentic beyond question; the great majority come down to us as second-hand reports or as frank guesses. For another, they include quantities of books exported to the colonies and elsewhere. But since there is no way of knowing what reduction should be made on this account, we shall have to follow the usual practice, however mistaken it may be, and let gross sales figures represent home consumption only. It must be understood, therefore, that whatever statistical conclusions are reached on this basis are bound to be on the liberal side.

In 1852 occurred one of those events which periodically, perhaps every generation or so, give publishers and other students of the contemporary literary scene a fresh glimpse of the farthest limits of the reading audience. This was the amazing vogue of *Uncle Tom's Cabin*, the biggest sensation the English book trade had ever known. In a single fortnight in October 1852, at least ten different editions came out, and Routledge alone was selling 10,000 copies a day. Some eighteen publishers climbed on the bandwagon; within six months of publication, the book had sold 150,000 copies, and within a year, according to one account, the total sales had reached a million and a half, a figure that includes both home and colonial distribution.[5]

If we lop off an arbitrary fraction which represents export sales, and in addition exercise a measure of scholarly conservatism, we are still left with a figure of, say, a million immediate buyers. But it is obvious that a great many of those who purchased whatever edition of *Uncle Tom's Cabin* was suited to their particular purses seldom, if ever, bought any other book. These scores, if not hundreds, of thousands of nonce-readers could not by any stretch of the imagination be counted as part of a dependable audience; the figure of a million purchasers represents the ultimate extreme to which the book market could, on a very rare occasion, expand.

The sales of less spectacular best-sellers of the period give us a surer indication of the size to which the market could expand at relatively more frequent intervals, the number of constant book buyers—the irreducible minimum in the publisher's calculations—being swelled several times over by the interest of those who buy only that occasional book which is all the talk. *In Memoriam* is said to have sold 60,000 copies within a short time after its publication in 1850.[6] In 1852–53 Dickens's *Bleak House*, appearing in shilling parts, soon reached 35,000 and climbed to 40,000 before publication was completed.[7] In 1855 the third and fourth volumes of Macaulay's *History of England* sold 25,000 on the day of publication alone.[8] These figures suggest that the short-term sale of a highly popular book, at the original published price, could run as high as 50,000, and within a very few years, as was the case with W. H. Russell's two-volume account of the Crimean War, published in 1855–56, it could go as high as 200,000.[9] Reckoning four or five readers per copy, that again gives us an audience of, at the very most, a million—*for books only of the very greatest immediate appeal.* The *normal* book-buying audience was, of course, infinitely smaller, probably somewhere in the high tens of thousands; and of this number only a small proportion could be expected to buy a given title unless it was a best-seller. For the ordinary book, an edition of from 500 to 1,000 copies sufficed.

We must remember, though, that there was, and is, an important distinction between the book-buying public and the public that reads books but does not buy them. In 1852 the *Edinburgh Review* was remarking that although the demand for books had "increased tenfold upon what it was seventy years ago," "few people now buy books." The reason was, of course, that "the mass of the reading world are supplied from the subscription-library or the book-club."[10] Hence multiplying the number of copies sold by four or five to obtain the total number of readers fails to take into account the larger number through whose hands the circulating-library copies passed. Of the number initially printed of volumes 3 and 4 of Macaulay's *History*, 2,400 copies went to Mudie's Library alone;[11] and in the decade beginning in 1853, Mudie's were to buy a total of almost a million volumes.[12] Mudie himself is said to have estimated that every book in his library found "on an average, thirty readers—considerably more, in the majority of instances, as regards novels, and considerably less in the case of scientific and philosophical works."[13] So long, therefore, as a substantial proportion of an edition was sold not to individual buyers but to the libraries and to the more or less informal book clubs which then abounded, especially in the provinces, the size of the actual book-reading public could be but partially reflected by sales figures.

Just as in our own day, the portion of the total reading public which habitually bought periodicals was immensely larger than that which bought books or borrowed them from the subscription libraries. As the century began its second half, the most popular periodicals were achieving circulations that greatly surpassed the record set by the *Penny Magazine*, which had sold 200,000 for a brief time in the early 1830s.[14] The *Family Herald* was in the process of more than doubling its circulation, from 125,000 in 1849 to 300,000 in 1855.[15] The *London Journal* was approaching a circulation of 450,000, and *Reynolds' Miscellany* 200,000.[16] *Chambers's Journal*, one of the earliest successful cheap periodicals, was selling between 60,000 and 70,000.[17] In addition, there were the threepenny weekly newspapers, which were sold both to the readers of the mass-circulation periodicals and to a large class of readers who looked at nothing else. The *Illustrated London News* sold 140,000 a week, while the *News of the World* and *Lloyd's Weekly Newspaper* each sold in the neighborhood of 110,000 copies, and several other popular papers circulated between 40,000 and 75,000 weekly.[18] It was on the basis of such sales figures as these, conservatively reckoning three readers to a copy, that Wilkie Collins decided that the "unknown public"—the public unknown, that is, to the book publishers, the public "which lies right out of the pale of literary civilisation"—amounted to three million persons.[19] The estimate on the whole is sound, and if anything, considering the size of the typical Victorian family, too low. All in all, there is no doubt whatever that in the 1850s Britain had an audience for printed matter immensely larger than it had ever known before.

So much for the quantitative extent of the 1852 market. But what of the economic considerations which play so vital a part in consumer analysis? In 1852 books were not quite the luxury items they had been for most of the century, but they were not, on the other hand, as readily obtainable as the reformers wished. Three years earlier one such friend of the people, the lecturer George Dawson, had told a committee of Commons, "The fact is, we give the people in this country an appetite to read, and supply them with nothing. For the last many years in England everybody has been educating the people, but they have forgotten to find them any books. In plain language, you have made them hungry, but you have given them nothing to eat; it is almost a misfortune to a man to have a great taste for reading, and not to have the power of satisfying it."[20] The circulation figures I have just cited would seem to discredit Dawson so far as cheap periodicals are concerned, but on the score of books he was right. Original editions were priced beyond the reach of all but the distinctly prosperous. The sacrosanct three-decker novel held obstinately firm at a guinea and a half, and other types of newly published literature were priced more or less to match. For the ordinary London clerk, say, who was lucky to make the thirty bob a week of which John Davidson was to sing later in the century, to buy a newly published novel would have meant the sacrifice of a week's salary. Two of the best novelists of the time, Dickens and Thackeray, were bringing out their newest fictions in monthly parts at a shilling apiece, and while this practice did bring the total cost of a new novel down to, say, twenty shillings, it still left the purchaser with the expense of binding up the parts. Its principal advantage was that it spread the cost over a year or two, thus making new novels available to the man who had one shilling to spend every month, but seldom twenty or thirty at a time.

However, many successful works of both fiction and nonfiction were reprinted, within a few years or even a few months of original publication, in five- or six-shilling editions. Lower in the price scale was the extensive class of railway novels or yellow-backs, the forms which are so admirably displayed in the showcase of Michael Sadleir's affectionate bibliography.[21] In 1852 this genre was just five years old, having originated in the Parlour Library of Simms and McIntyre, whose volumes were priced at a shilling or a shilling sixpence. The immediate success of this series had forced Bentley and Colburn, the proprietors of five-shilling reprint "libraries," to come down to 2s.6d. and had inspired other firms, notably that of Routledge, to compete with their own reprints at one or two shillings.[22] Though this represented the greatest movement toward cheap books since the exciting false dawn between 1828 and 1832, only current literature as a rule was published in this form, and many valuable publishers' properties—valuable both commercially and from the point of view of literature—were not made available for cheap reprints. Reprints of standard classics, best exemplified in this period by the proliferating Bohn Libraries, were 5s. or 3s.6d.

These prices are list. But the year 1852 witnessed a development which for the next four decades would make the advertised prices somewhat misleading. For many years an association of publishers and certain booksellers had enforced what we today call, somewhat euphemistically, a fair-trade practices agreement, by which anyone selling the books of those publishers under the list price was boycotted. In 1852, however, the publisher John Chapman, with the powerful assistance of most of the celebrated authors of the day as well as of the *Times*, the *Athenaeum*, and Gladstone, forced the Booksellers' Association to submit their case for literary protectionism to a board of arbitration headed by Lord Campbell. The decision was that the principle of free trade, by then so firmly established in other phases of Britain's economic life, should be observed in the book trade as well.[23] As a result, down to the nineties, one could, with a little shopping about, buy a new book at a reduction of two or three pence on the shilling.[24] Hence books were not quite as expensive as the advertised prices would indicate.

But how many people could afford to buy books even at this discount? It may well be that the amazing success of *Uncle Tom's Cabin* and the great leaps in periodical circulation were due in part to the favorable economic conditions prevailing in the early fifties. Employment was high, money was plentiful, and prices were generally low. Thus the economic barrier to book-buying was less formidable than it had been in the hungry forties or was to be in the later fifties and sixties. But it was still sufficiently high to bar great segments of the population. In 1852 about 110,000 persons had a taxable income of more than £150 a year, but of these, 75 percent, or about 83,000, received less than £400,[25] and one suspects that for most of them the purchase of an occasional five-shilling reprint, more frequently of a shilling railway novel, and of one or two cheap periodicals or Sunday newspapers a week would have been the extent of their spending for reading matter. (There were no penny daily papers until after the abolition of the stamp tax in 1855.) Those who simply had to have new books about the house found it more economical to spend a guinea for a year's privileges at Mudie's than to buy books outright. In a household whose weekly income ranged from three to eight pounds little money remained after the necessities had been provided for: not even when beef was selling at 8d. a pound. Furthermore, most of the population were worse off than those who had a taxable income. The average family of a skilled artisan had an annual income of only £90, or 34s. a week,[26] and the hundreds of thousands of working-class families could count on far less than that. The average weekly wage in Lancashire and Cheshire was only 9s.6d. a week.[27] For the great bulk of the population, then, book-buying was out of the question except for the very cheap part-issues of Salisbury Square fiction or the shilling yellow-back; what reading was done, was done in cheap periodicals, whether of the *Reynolds' Miscellany* or *Family Herald* type, and weekly newspapers, which cost only 2d. or 3d. As a very general conclusion, we may conjecture that the market for ordinary trade books, at the prices then prevailing, was limited to the 27,000 or so families with an annual income of more than £400, and that for the one- or two-shilling reprints, the cheapest books published, to the 110,000 families with more than £150 a year. All the rest of the readers in Britain in 1852 formed a market for cheap periodicals alone.

Even among those who were financially able to be occasional patrons of the bookshop or the library, however, there were many thousands who seldom if ever stepped inside either one. In the educational experience of the great majority of the people there had been absolutely nothing to encourage a taste for reading as an adult pastime. Even among the substantial middle class, most men, and even more women, had been to school for only a few years, and while they had learned to perform the mechanical operation of reading, the books they had practiced upon, books of dull, pious edification, were not calculated to give them any enduring affection for printed matter in hard covers. No incentive came from the teachers, who were themselves wretchedly educated. In the classroom all forces seemingly conspired to breed an everlasting distaste for reading, and anyone who knows what elementary education was like in nineteenth-century England must consider it miraculous that under the circumstances, the reading habit was as widespread as it was.[28] Nor was this true only of the schools to which the masses of children went. The witnesses before a Parliamentary commission in the early sixties were virtually unanimous in declaring that in the great public schools of the nation no effort whatsoever was made to encourage the boys to read for pleasure or general culture, and that as a result few did.[29] Nor was the situation very much better in the universities. No doubt many readers of the *Times* and holders of baccalaureate degrees shared the feeling of the forthright Colonel Sibthorp, M.P. for Lincoln, when he confided to Commons in 1850 that "he did not like reading at all, and he hated it when at Oxford."[30] I am persuaded that English educational practices—which were dominated either by the Gradgrind philosophy of the age or by the decayed classical tradition—were more instrumental than any other single element in limiting the size of the nineteenth-century book-reading public. I have no illusions about the educational accomplishments of our own day, but in this respect, at least, I am certain that we do no worse than the Victorians did.

In 1852, it is true, the newspapers contained what appeared to be a hopeful sign. This was the year when the first free library to be established under Ewart's Act was opened at Manchester. The orators there, as at other library dedications in the next few years, exhausted much rhetoric in hailing the public-library movement as a symbol of the spread of the reading habit among the people. But actually the movement was in no sense a popular one. Ewart's bill was pushed through Parliament by a small band of reformers, behind whom was no strong force of opinion on the part either of the working class or of the middle class. And once local corporations were empowered to levy a small tax for library buildings, relatively few did so. Never during the rest of the century did public libraries enjoy really popular support. In town after town general apathy and, on the part of the ratepayers, vehement opposition, defeated the efforts of a minority to provide free reading facilities for the public at large.[31]

Conditions of life in the Victorian era were not necessarily conducive to reading. We hear much about the way in which the sacred institution of family reading-aloud encouraged a taste for books, and undoubtedly it did. But even more powerful influences operated on the other side. The minority of working-class men and women who could read found little time to do so. Only in the textile industry had the ten-hour day been won; elsewhere the usual work week was seventy-two hours or more. Shop assistants worked eighty-five to ninety hours a week, their places of employment remaining open long into the evening. The only day of theoretical rest was Sunday, but a good part of it, at least among the respectable middle class, was spent at church, and in what hours remained, one's choice of reading-matter was severely limited, in middle-class Victorian households, by the Sabbatarian ban on any but religious books. We need not wonder, as has been pointed out more than once, that the Victorians were so well versed in *Paradise Lost* and *The Pilgrim's Progress*: they were two of the least deadly books on the list approved for Sunday reading.

In fact, what with the pressure of work and the ban on secular reading on Sunday, the only extended leisure many Victorians had for reading was when they made a railway journey. It is no accident that in the early fifties the new class of cheap light literature was referred to as "railway reading," and that the biggest volume of bookselling was beginning to be accomplished at railway stations, where, in 1852, the stalls of W. H. Smith and Son were becoming familiar landmarks.[32] A long slow trip in a second-class carriage was one occasion upon which the earnest Victorian felt that a bit of self-indulgence was justified—indeed it was almost indispensable.

In the railway carriage, too, the traveler might, if he was lucky, find a degree of peace not often enjoyed at home. Throughout the nineteenth century the average British family—by which I mean one of the lower middle class, probably below the income-tax level—was living in quarters far too small for it. The crowding in the homes of the working class was, of course, constantly a matter for Parliamentary remark; a missionary to the Spitalfields silkmakers told a committee at Westminster in 1849 that "I frequently find as many as seven or eight persons living all in one room; in that room, perhaps, there will be two looms at work, so that the noise and discomfort render it almost impossible that a working man, if he were ever so well inclined to read, could sit down and read quietly."[33] But overcrowded conditions existed among a large section of the middle class as well, because Victorian fertility notoriously had a way of outrunning Victorian income. It was a fortunate reader indeed, in any but the fairly prosperous segment of the population, who could command the solitude he needed whenever he needed it.

Nor may we neglect the effect of Evangelicalism upon the size of the Victorian publisher's potential market. This most influential form of religion, which set the whole tone of life in Victorian times, immensely stimulated the reading habit, because it stressed the spiritually salutary effect of contact with the right kind of moral and religious literature at the same time that it forbade many kinds of nonliterary recreation. The perusal of the printed word was as vital a part of one's journey to salvation as was listening to public sermons. The result was a great increase in the sale of edifying works of every description. But Evangelicalism had revived and even intensified the old Puritan distrust of secular literature, and so thoroughly did this distrust permeate the middle class, and the church-going portion of the lower, that it remained in 1852 a strong deterrent to the reading of ordinary literature, above all fiction.[34] No Victorian publisher of ordinary trade books, in surveying his prospective market, could afford to overlook the existence of multitudes of men and women who may well have been devoted readers, but who would never think of buying the majority of titles he had on his list. These people were in the main the patrons of the specialized religious-book houses and of those general publishers who maintained strong religious lists.[35] They were, therefore, a special public, and they decreased by just so much the potential audience for general reading matter.

In some well-known discussions of English literary trends at the end of the nineteenth century and in the beginning of our own we are told that a great deal of whatever is saddening in post-Victorian literary history can be attributed to the fragmentation of what had been until recently a homogeneous public. In other words, whereas the Victorian man of letters addressed himself to the reading audience at large, his grandson had to be content with addressing a small splinter of that audience—what Arnold called, in another connection, "the saving remnant." Now as a matter of fact, no Victorian writer, no matter how popular, was read by the whole contemporary audience.[36] If any lament is to be made over the change that had occurred in the reading public during the past century, it is that the cultured minority, which normally forms the special audience of the great men of letters, has not grown apace with the growth of the total public, and indeed has actually shrunk. But the facts forbid us to assume that the extreme social and cultural diversification of the English reading audience began, say, at the time of the Education Act of 1870, and that until then the audience was the ideal homogeneous one recalled, with a kind of wishful hindsight, in some of our literary histories. Dickens and Eliot and Thackeray and Tennyson, and for that matter G. P. R. James and Martin Tupper, wrote for only one or two publics out of the numerous ones already in existence by mid-century. Actually, however convenient the practice may be, it is inaccurate to refer to the "reading public"—singular—in any century after the fifteenth. A few moments' contemplation of the variety of Elizabethan literature, from Spenser, say, down to the lowliest chapbook, should dispose once and for all of the myth that the reading public began to break down into separate audiences only late in the nineteenth century. What the Victorian age witnessed was not the beginning of multiple publics but simply the spectacular growth in both size and influence of certain publics which had hitherto been either small or not much thought about. In 1858 Wilkie Collins distinguished four separate audiences: ". . . the religious public . . . the public which reads for information . . . the public which reads for amusement, and patronizes the circulating libraries and the railway bookstalls . . . [and] the public which reads nothing but newspapers."[37] All of these, except the last, had existed for centuries. The great difference was that all except the first were growing prodigiously.

In 1852 publishers generally had not accommodated their policies to the various realities I have mentioned. I am not speaking of those few firms which were busily cashing in on the development of a mass public by issuing yellow-backs, penny bloods, and other popular-priced literature. I refer to the old-line firms, the stalwarts of Paternoster Row, whose conservatism was something of a scandal in their own time, and who looked down their patrician noses at the upstart Cassells, Routledges, Reynoldses, Lloyds, and the rest. They continued to assume that the only public worth publishing for was the public that bought books at the prevailing prices or subscribed to the circulating libraries. In 1852 Gladstone told Parliament that hardly 5 percent of the books published in England every year sold more than 500 copies.[38] If his estimate is anywhere near correct, it means that, in the face of an enormously expanded interest in reading, most publishers remained content with selling as many copies of a given title as were normally sold in Pope's day.

This means, in turn, that the editorial decisions in the old-established houses were based upon the anticipated reaction of that same small public of well-heeled buyers who had governed decisions in the past. The whole economic rationale of publishing was still what it had been a hundred years before: to make this small initial clientele pay for the cost of publishing a book. There was, of course, this difference: whereas earlier the clientele had been composed of individual purchasers, in Victorian times it was largely represented by the circulating libraries. This circumstance worked to the advantage of the publisher, and to the disadvantage of every man who wanted books for his own shelves. The publisher could, and, it is notorious, did rely upon Mudie and his confrères to take a substantial part of the initial edition of any work intended for the general reader, and the library operators, who in any event got a large discount, were not disposed to quibble about prices. So the publisher could afford to be quite indifferent to the fact he was pricing his wares out of the reach of the ordinary purchaser. If the book subsequently had a success in a cheap reprint, well and good; that meant so much extra profit for the publisher. But, in contrast to the situation in the second half of the twentieth century, the reprint audience did not figure in the original calculations which attended the editorial decision. The silent guest at the table around which such decisions were made, therefore, was not so much the individual reader (whether a man with a guinea and a half to spend, or only two shillings) but his surrogate, Mr. Mudie. And though Mudie had great influence on what was published, there is no proof that he was an infallibly shrewd diviner of current taste. He did not have to be; so long as the circulating library was the chief means by which the public got to read newly published books, he had the power, at least as much as did the publishers, to decide what it should be given to read. He may have been wrong quite frequently, but there was little the public could do about it. Under these circumstances, the tastes of the audience influenced editorial decisions only at second hand.

Now and again there were protests against this state of affairs—both against the stranglehold of the libraries and against the whole resulting policy of small original editions at high prices. In 1854, for instance, a writer in the *Times* urged that "instead of commencing with editions of a guinea, and gradually coming down in the course of years to cheap editions of 5s., all good books on their first appearance shall appeal to the needy multitude, while the requirements of the fortunate and lazier few are postponed to a more convenient season."[39] If that reversal of traditional policy had come about, the whole basis of editorial decisions, and therefore eventually the whole nature of contemporary literature, would have been considerably altered. It is fascinating to speculate what would have happened to the reading public, and to literature in general, if the firms that published most of the age's great writers—the Smith and Elders, the Chapman and Halls, the Macmillans and Murrays and Longmans—had seriously attempted a policy of cheap original editions. What concessions would they have asked their writers to make in order to appeal to the much larger audience they then would have had? Would Carlyle, Ruskin, and Trollope have written any differently if they had had in view an immediate audience of hundreds of thousands instead of tens of thousands?[40]

As it was, however, the reading of the masses was allowed to be chiefly the concern of the handful of publishers who had discovered that publishing in cheap form and large volume, however lacking in respectability it might be, was not necessarily ruinous. But because in the nature of things they could not pay large prices to authors for original work, they were limited to the productions of hacks, or to copyright works which other publishers were willing to part with, or to translations, or, finally, to American works, which were unprotected by international copyright. It is quite true that the cheap publishers occasionally made available at three-and-six or even at a shilling books of serious content and genuine literary merit, but these were almost lost in the flood of vapid or sensational trash. Under such circumstances, the word "cheap" did not have an exclusively economic reference; it had an aesthetic, and often a moral, one as well. In this way the publishing situation contributed to the division of the total reading public into two worlds, the small one of the intellectual élite, who could pay either the publisher or Mudie for what they wanted, and the infinitely greater one of those who perforce had to want what they could pay for.

It would be absurd, of course, to argue that the masses of people read what they did just because it was forced upon them by publishing conditions beyond their control, and because there was nothing better for them to read at a price they could pay. They bought hundreds of thousands of copies of cheap papers every week simply because they liked what they found therein, and most of them, even if the whole rich store of current book publications had been laid before them at sixpence or a shilling a title, would have kept on reading *Reynolds' Miscellany* and the *News of the World* to the exclusion of nearly everything else. Nevertheless, it would be unrealistic to assume that in a mass audience of this size, in an era when self-improvement was so much in the air, there were not many people who were ready and eager for reading matter of a better sort and who suffered from what was in effect a literary disfranchisement.

Such people had little opportunity to make their wants known even when they were conscious of them. The self-appointed spokesmen for the common reader were almost wholly unconcerned with the *literary* improvement of popular reading matter. This is well illustrated by the whole tone of the testimony before the committee of Commons which was appointed in 1851, as the result of pressure from a few liberal members, to look into the advisability of abolishing the newspaper stamp. Opposition to the proposal was based chiefly upon the historic identification of the cheap press with radicalism. The task of the men who agitated for removal of the penny newspaper duty was to show that the reading tastes of the masses had improved so far that there was now no danger of a revival of the "scurrilous" and "immoral" publications, such as the *Penny Satirist* and *Cleave's Penny Gazette*, which had enjoyed favor a decade or so before.

A star witness before the committee was Abel Heywood, the leading wholesale newsagent of Manchester, who analyzed his business in this way: The more respectable of the mass-circulation periodicals had a weekly sale of from 9,000 (for the *Family Herald* and the *London Journal*) down to 600 (for *Eliza Cook's Journal* and *Household Words*). Two principal weekly newspapers, the *News of the World* and the *Weekly Times*, sold 3,500 and 4,000 respectively. At the bottom of the scale came the frankly sensational number-publications, the equivalents of today's pulps. G. W. M. Reynolds's *Mysteries of the Court of London* sold 1,500 a week, while the current Lloyd penny dreadfuls—*Three-Fingered Jack, The Adventures of Captain Hawk, Mazeppa, Love and Mystery*, almost twenty different titles in all—sold *in the aggregate* 3,400. As a not wholly irrelevant footnote, it must be added that Heywood sold penny numbers of Shakespeare at a rate of 150 a week.[41]

Heywood, who spoke with the authority of long experience in his trade and the prejudice of a veteran backer of popular causes, construed his own figures as showing that there had been a remarkable improvement in popular taste, and other witnesses testified to the same effect. The papers whose circulation had most benefited from the growth of the reading habit in recent years were those of a "good tendency"; the immoral and seditious ones had been driven from the market. This was, they maintained, proof of a sort of literary inversion of Gresham's law: good reading matter, if given half a chance, would inevitably drive out bad.[42]

But their definition of "good reading-matter" was determined not by any literary or cultural standards but by existing political and social conditions. When the great concern was whether cheap publications would or would not contribute to a fresh unsettling of the populace, the specifically literary qualities of the *Family Herald* and the *London Journal* were of no relevance. The criterion of acceptable popular reading matter was, to put it bluntly, innocuousness. The ideal of the advocates of a cheap press was simply that the humble reader should be enabled to purchase a few hours of innocent recreation, without being troubled by any thoughts dangerous to his own moral welfare or the peace of the nation. There was no thought of trying to improve the general cultural tone of the people's reading; enough if it were "safe."

With attention centered upon the mass reading public from this angle, it was only natural that the need for issuing works of true literary merit in cheap form in order to encourage the elevation of popular taste, and the actual existence of a market for such publications, should have been largely neglected. During the decade with which we are concerned, however, there were several signs that gave promise that the man of some intellectual ambition but little pocket-money, whose tastes were not irrevocably fixed upon the sensational newspaper and the shilling shocker, was slowly making his presence felt.

Two significant events occurred in the periodical field. In 1850 Dickens began his twopenny *Household Words*, which immediately attracted an audience for which the half-crown monthlies were too expensive and the popular weekly papers too frivolous and crude. Among the cheap weeklies both of the two major predecessors of *Household Words* had failed to satisfy this audience. The *Penny Magazine*, whose connection with the Society for the Diffusion of Useful Knowledge limited its contents to instructional articles and discouraged the introduction of fiction, had gone under in 1845. *Chambers's Journal*, although it did print fiction, and for that reason still enjoyed favor among a certain clientele, was studiously following its original policy of cultivating inoffensiveness to the point of what contemporary observers called "namby-pambyness." *Household Words*, under Dickens's vigorous direction, escaped both pitfalls: it printed plenty of fiction, and it was not afraid, in its serious articles, to speak out on current issues. Furthermore, its contributors included many highly competent writers. The gratitude with which it was received is measured by its circulation, which ran as high as 40,000 weekly.[43]

But that figure, exciting as it was for the time, was eclipsed when George Smith launched the *Cornhill Magazine* early in 1860, with a staff of contributors that reads today like a Who's Who of Victorian literature. No fewer than 120,000 men and women bought the first issue, and though the initial circulation did not hold up, during the first two years the *Cornhill's* average monthly sale, at a shilling, was 84,000 copies.[44]

The success of these two innovations in periodical literature, at prices within the reach of at least all middle-class readers, was evidence of a steadily expanding market for serious reading matter. In the book trade, additional evidence was supplied by the spectacular prosperity of John Cassell's publishing enterprises. Beginning in 1852 with his *Popular Educator*, a sort of high-school-at-home course, Cassell adapted the old technique of number-publishing to new conditions and brought out in installments scores of excellent standard works in history, literature, and other fields. It is significant that the man who made the discovery that supplying the people with truly solid books could become a big and lucrative business had no background in publishing at all; he had entered the trade only three or four years earlier, after a career as a temperance lecturer and packer of tea and coffee. Seemingly it took a rank outsider to succeed where old professionals like Charles Knight had failed.[45]

Cheaper and better books did become available to the additional millions who were made literate by the extension of education during the second half of the century. But by that time the great opportunity had passed. In 1852 the habits and tastes of the new mass audience were not yet crystallized. The people were wretchedly educated, to be sure, and their tastes were crude; but they could still have been taught to like better things. The accidents of publishing, however, as much as any other single factor, caused the new audience to associate the reading habit with a certain type of reading-matter, a type deplored by all contemporary observers and no less by those at a distance of a century. This in turn—increasingly so as the mass audience began to influence editorial decisions—set the permanent course of publishing for the millions, with its implied dismal assumptions regarding the level of popular taste, and so a vicious circle was created, which has never been broken. Perhaps it is too late now to break it. But while we browse in the files of old periodicals and read the Victorians' ceaseless complaints of the unutterable vulgarity of "the million's" reading tastes—complaints so feelingful and comprehensive that our own seem but tired echoes—we may perhaps speculate whether, under happier circumstances, the history of English popular culture might not have taken a different turn. If a few influential publishers had had more vision, more willingness to experiment, more missionary spirit; if somehow the art of sound popularization had been learned while there was still time; if the railway bookstalls and the hole-in-the-wall newsvendors had had Penguins and Pocket Books in stock—

But the realities of the Victorian situation were quite another thing.

1954

The Literature of an
Imminent Democracy, 1859

*Grant that the old Adam in these persons may be so
buried, that the new man may be raised up in them.*
—The Book of Common Prayer

The English people in 1859 were entering a new age of popular culture, and they were fully aware of it.[1] "An immense number of new and powerful processes," wrote a contributor to the January *Blackwood's Magazine* as he led into one of the year's most repeated platitudes, were "converging to one great end."[2] Popular education, despite grievous inefficiency, low aims, and lack of funds, was making headway. Books were, from a practical standpoint, more than ever necessary: to ply his trade, the eighteenth-century cobbler needed no alphabet, but now the man who made shoes in Northampton had to be literate to survive. The oppressive newspaper stamp tax had been abolished four years earlier. The electric telegraph had given newspapers the fascination of immediacy, and other revolutionizing inventions had made possible the cheap large-scale production of all kinds of reading matter, as well as the means of reproducing illustrations, so that he who ran, even if he could not read, could enjoy the pictures. This, proclaimed the oracles, was the age of "the universality of print, the omnipotence of ink."

In 1859 there existed a many-leveled reading public with divisions and tastes strikingly similar to those of the mass public a century later. Catering to it was a book trade which, despite the eradication one evil winter night in 1940 of the Paternoster Row the Victorians had known, survives today, essentially unaltered in structure or method. And even in 1859 there was a chorus of protest or pessimism—or, at best, gentle melancholy—over the developing democracy of print. Thoughtful men were already lamenting the debasement of traditional literary culture.

But here the resemblance between 1859 and 1959 abruptly ends; for in the earlier year lament was still tempered by hope. Belief in progress was never stronger than in the year of Darwin. In the orthodox Victorian creed, progress was an undoubted metaphysical force which it was the duty and privilege of a reforming society to assist in every possible way. Education, cheap books and papers, and free libraries could refine the taste and enlarge the intellectual capacities of the common man, making him a thoughtful, well-informed, socially responsible citizen, receptive to good literature and impatient with all inferior varieties. Substantial progress had lately been made in respect to certain of his social habits: drunkenness was declining, the deposits in savings societies were increasing, domestic sanitation was gradually improving. Why, then, should he not also, in those other realms of mind and taste, "Move upward, working out the beast, / And let the ape and tiger die"?

It was an article of faith that man could move upward. What in fact were the signs of the times? One at least (looking back after a hundred years) was most hopeful. The reading public of 1859, unknowingly put on its mettle by the appearance in a single year of a remarkable group of books destined to become "classics," responded in a fashion that posterity is bound to applaud. The great books of 1859 were immediately recognized as great, with two exceptions, *The Ordeal of Richard Feverel*, which had an indifferent press and a small sale, and *The Rubáiyát of Omar Khayyám*, which had to await discovery in a penny-remainder box, two years later, by a prospector who thereupon carried the book to Dante Gabriel Rossetti. But *Adam Bede*, published on 1 February, went through eight printings before the year ended, for a total of almost 16,000 copies: a remarkable record in that day of small, relatively expensive editions.[3] The first *Idylls of the King* appeared late in June, and sold 10,000 copies in a single week, a feat that raised the Laureate to a commercial eminence hitherto occupied only by Martin Tupper.[4] *The Origin of Species*, which had the popular appeal of neither fiction nor narrative poetry, was a bestseller in its own class. Its first edition of 1,250 copies was exhausted on publication day, 24 November. "I sometimes fancied," Darwin wrote, "that my book would be successful, but I never even built a castle in the air of such success as it has met with." With incredulous underscoring and exclamation points, he recorded hearing of "a man enquiring for it at the *Railway Station!!!* at Waterloo Bridge; and the bookseller said that he had none till the new edition was out."[5] Within eighteen months John Murray had printed 6,250 copies:[6] a figure small enough of itself, but, seen in the frame of reference of contemporary publishing, an impressive testimony to the book's initial impact on thoughtful Victorians.

Not all the best-sellers of 1859, of course, were destined to be remembered. Conspicuous among the ephemeral titles was Harriet Beecher Stowe's *A Minister's Wooing*, issued in monthly parts beginning in January and in book form in October. Its total sale, down to mid-November, amounted to 42,000 copies,[7] two and a half times the sale of *Adam Bede* for the same period; but one must bear in mind that this was a book by the lady whose *Uncle Tom's Cabin* had broken all British sales records only seven years before, and that it was issued in a variety of forms and at a price considerably less than that of *Adam Bede*, which originally appeared in the conventional three-volume form.

No better index can be obtained to the tastes of the middle-class audience in 1859 than the traffic of Mr. Mudie, then at the height of his prosperity and influence. As the year opened, his inventory included 1,000 copies of Bulwer-Lytton's *What Will He Do With It?* and 1,400 of the first two volumes of Carlyle's *Frederick the Great*. As 1859 wore on, he supplied his readers with 2,500 copies of *Adam Bede*, 1,000 of the *Idylls of the King*, 2,500 of Dinah Mulock's *A Life for a Life*, 1,200 of Thomas Hughes's *The Scouring of the White Horse*, and 3,000 of one of the autumn's publishing sensations, Sir Francis McClintock's story of his voyage to discover the fate of Sir John Franklin.[8] These in addition to lesser quantities of hundreds of other titles; for "the insatiable Mudie," as the publisher of *Adam Bede* appreciatively called him,[9] then boasted that he was adding 120,000 volumes a year to his stock. Among the new titles fiction predominated, accounting for about 44 percent of the total, with history and biography in second place (28 percent) and travel and adventure in third (13 percent).[10] So long as Mudie purchased on this scale, his subscribers could be sure that whatever of current literature they were inclined to read, he could provide—if he was at ease about its morality.

The middle-class men and women who borrowed from Mudie's, and to a limited extent bought copies of first editions for their personal libraries, constituted the central level of the reading audience, just below the small pinnacle occupied by the intellectual élite. As the figures I have mentioned suggest, it was a sizable public, and it was steadily broadening as prosperity, increased opportunities for education, the expansion of the professions and the new civil service, and other forces of social change enlarged the boundaries of the middle class itself. Publishers tended, understandably, to regard it with affection. "If the public is sometimes a stupid beast," wrote a complacent John Blackwood to his best-selling author George Eliot on 30 March, "I am happy to say I have found him a most excellent beast in the main."[11] To this audience belonged the reputation-makers, the people whom the leading novelists of the day (but not Meredith, who detested Mudie's constituency[12]) sought to please. Now that the financial rewards of authorship were becoming ever larger, professional writers wished nothing more than to help that public grow and encourage it to buy more books. Dickens did so, quite deliberately, through the many public readings he gave up and down the island in the season of 1858–59. "Your present correspondent," he observed in a letter of 1 February, "is more popular than he ever has been. I rather think that the readings in the country have opened up a new public who were outside before; but however that may be, his books have a wider range than they ever had, and his public welcomes are prodigious."[13]

The pleasure and profit of catering to this widening audience were not left to Mudie and his confreres alone. For the past decade, certain alert and aggressive publishers had recognized that however large the gross potential of the democratic market was, its individual members, especially the newcomers, had not much money to spend. Hence the yellow-back or railway novel, which sold for a shilling or two at a time when circulating-library novels retailed at 31s. 6d. These highly popular books were mostly reprints. In 1859 the firm of Routledge, a leader in the field, brought out their series of Select Standard Novels—a volume a month, 2s. 6d. in cloth binding, selected from the works of such successful novelists as Marryat, Disraeli, Cooper, Lover, and Mrs. Trollope. And simultaneously (one result of a famous publishing coup by which, for the sum of £20,000, they had secured ten years' exclusive reprint rights to nineteen of the author's novels) Routledge launched a "cheap and complete" edition of Bulwer-Lytton.

This Bulwer enterprise involved, not complete volumes, but parts: weekly numbers at a penny, monthly installments at 5d. Here was another favorite means by which the democratic audience was supplied with what it wanted to read. Certain new works and old ones alike appeared in weekly or monthly segments, priced to suit the contents of the average man's odd-change purse. Although the practice was declining in favor of magazine serialization, in 1859 some high-quality fiction still made its first appearance in parts; the last ten installments of Thackeray's *The Virginians*, for example, were published during the year. The form was widely adopted for serious nonfiction, including encyclopedic works of one sort or another, ranging from George Henry Lewes's *The Physiology of Common Life* through *Chambers's Encyclopaedia* (advertised as "the crowning contribution of its Editors to CHEAP LITERATURE—a work designed in a special manner, equally in its construction and in its price, FOR THE PEOPLE": weekly sheets at 1½d., monthly parts at 7d.[14]) to Mrs. Beeton's *Book of Household Management*, which began its famous career in the autumn with the issue of the first threepenny part. Older, "standard" literature was reissued in similar form. Longmans, for example, were issuing "People's Editions" of Thomas Moore's *Poetical Works* and *Irish Melodies* (with the music), Sydney Smith's works, and Macaulay's essays, all in monthly shilling numbers. Meanwhile Routledge brought out fortnightly or monthly installments of Prescott's *Ferdinand and Isabella*,

Boswell's *Johnson*, Staunton's edition of Shakespeare, and Charles Knight's popular anthology, *Half-Hours with the Best Authors*.

But the most talked-of aspect of the publishing scene in 1859 was the tremendous increase in the number and variety of periodicals. Among the papers which were born in this year (and for the most part died soon after, for the mortality rate among Victorian periodicals was shocking) were the *Temperance Messenger and Domestic Journal, Good News for the Little Ones*, the *Journal of the Workhouse Visiting Society*, the *Family Treasury of Sunday Reading*, and, at the other end of the moral spectrum, a pornographic sheet called *Fast Life*. In addition there were political journals, such as the one whose title was almost as long as its text, *The Friends of Labour Association's Monthly Educator of General Information and Working Man's Advocate* (it survived under this burden until 1863), and innumerable trade papers. In 1859 alone, new specialized journals claimed the attention of carriage builders, drapers, chemists, stationers, ironmongers, railwaymen, shipping merchants, and dentists.[15]

The birth on 30 April of *All the Year Round*, edited by Dickens, enjoyed ample advance publicity, thanks to his squabble with his publishers over, among other things, the management of its predecessor, *Household Words*. The new weekly started off with the serialization of *A Tale of Two Cities*, to be succeeded in November by Wilkie Collins's *A Woman in White*, and by its fifth number it reached a circulation of perhaps 120,000 copies[16]—an immense sale for a periodical, which in addition to its serial fiction published light essays, "personal experience" pieces, and other forms of chatty journalism.

It was undoubtedly Dickens's policy of placing first-rate serial fiction in the front of each issue that made *All the Year Round* so successful. Stories, everybody agreed, were what the new mass audience hungered for beyond all else. But not all editors, even if they were themselves novelists, were happy about this appetite. When he was planning the *Cornhill Magazine* in the autumn of 1859, Thackeray wrote to Anthony Trollope: "One of our chief objects in this magazine is the getting out of novel spinning, and back into the world. Don't understand me to disparage our craft, especially *your* wares. I often say I am like the pastry-cook, and don't care for tarts, but prefer bread and cheese; but the public love the tarts (luckily for us), and we must bake and sell them."[17] And in his form letter to prospective contributors he desired "as much reality as possible—discussion and narrative of events interesting to the public, personal adventures and observations, familiar reports of scientific discovery, description of Social Institutions—*quicquid agunt homines*—a 'Great East-

"Familiar in their Mouths as HOUSEHOLD WORDS."—Shakespeare.

HOUSEHOLD WORDS.

A WEEKLY JOURNAL.

CONDUCTED BY CHARLES DICKENS.

N⁰· 479.] SATURDAY, MAY 28, 1859. { Price 2*d*. Stamped 3*d*.

ALL THE YEAR ROUND.

AFTER the appearance of the present concluding Number of HOUSEHOLD WORDS, this publication will merge into the new weekly publication, ALL THE YEAR ROUND, and the title, HOUSEHOLD WORDS, will form a part of the title-page of ALL THE YEAR ROUND.

The Prospectus of the latter Journal described it in these words :

"ADDRESS.

"Nine years of HOUSEHOLD WORDS, are the best practical assurance that can be offered to the public, of the spirit and objects of ALL THE YEAR ROUND.

"In transferring myself, and my strongest energies, from the publication that is about to be discontinued, to the publication that is about to be begun, I have the happiness of taking with me the staff of writers with whom I have laboured, and all the literary and business co-operation that can make my work a pleasure. In some important respects, I am now free greatly to advance on past arrangements. Those, I leave to testify for themselves in due course.

"That fusion of the graces of the imagination with the realities of life, which is vital to the welfare of any community, and for which I have striven from week to week as honestly as I could during the last nine years, will continue to be striven for 'all the year round.' The old weekly cares and duties become things of the Past, merely to be assumed, with an increased love for them and brighter hopes springing out of them, in the Present and the Future.

"I look, and plan, for a very much wider circle of readers, and yet again for a steadily expanding circle of readers, in the projects I hope to carry through 'all the year round.' And I feel confident that this expectation will be realised, if it deserve realisation.

"The task of my new journal is set, and it will steadily try to work the task out. Its pages shall show to what good purpose their motto is remembered in them, and with how much of fidelity and earnestness they tell

"THE STORY OF OUR LIVES FROM YEAR TO YEAR.

"CHARLES DICKENS."

Since this was issued, the Journal itself has come into existence, and has spoken for itself five weeks. Its fifth Number is published to-day, and its circulation, moderately stated, trebles that now relinquished in HOUSEHOLD WORDS.

In referring our readers, henceforth, to ALL THE YEAR ROUND, we can but assure them afresh, of our unwearying and faithful service, in what is at once the work and the chief pleasure of our life. Through all that we are doing, and through all that we design to do, our aim is to do our best in sincerity of purpose, and true devotion of spirit.

We do not for a moment suppose that we may lean on the character of these pages, and rest contented at the point where they stop. We see in that point but a starting-place for our new journey ; and on that journey, with new prospects opening out before us everywhere, we joyfully proceed, entreating our readers—without any of the pain of leave-taking incidental to most journeys—to bear us company All the year round.

Household Words gives way to All the Year Round

"Lord Lufton and Lucy Robarts" (one of Millais's illustrations for
Trollope's *Framley Parsonage, Cornhill Magazine,* April 1860)

ern,' a battle in China, a Race-Course, a popular Preacher—there is hardly
any subject we don't want to hear about, from lettered and instructed men
who are competent to speak on it."[18] Luckily Thackeray found a way to
deck his table with both tarts and bread-and-cheese. The *Cornhill's* first
number, dated January 1860 but published on 23 December to catch the
Christmas trade, contained the opening chapters of Trollope's *Framley
Parsonage*, Thackeray's own *Lovel the Widower* and his first *Roundabout
Paper*, along with a good selection of serious articles. It sold 120,000
copies,[19] and the euphoric Thackeray, in a happy delirium, treated himself
to a spendthrift holiday in Paris.

have left him. In fact, when I went out in the evening, he was sitting up and able to walk—for he came down and bolted the front door after me, as was his wont——"

"Ah! I remember that the door *was* bolted inside, when I first entered the house," exclaimed Page. "But how did you obtain admittance——"

"Rather let me ask how *you* got into this place in the first instance?" cried the girl, now surveying the commercial traveller with looks indicative of mistrust.

"I will satisfy you on that head, Julia," was his immediate answer. "It was by the back way that I came hither——"

"Ah! then you are one of the gentlemen who escaped from the cellar in the next house?" exclaimed the young woman, her countenance clearing up. "Well—don't be afraid—I am not going to betray you. But you asked me how I got into the place, sir; there was no one—*living*," she added, with a

cold shudder, "to open the door. Why—I did not come back until about eight o'clock this morning," she continued; "and then I was accosted in the court by Briggs——"

"Who's Briggs?" demanded the commercial traveller.

"The man that keeps the house next door," was the answer."

"Is he a great stout fellow, with an immense wen upon the crown of his bald head?" inquired Page.

"Just so," replied the girl; and the commercial traveller learnt accordingly that the individual alluded to was the same who had made him write the letter to Mr. Hodson, and who had given him the glass of gin. "Well," resumed Julia, "this man Briggs called me into his room next door—told me that a couple of gentlemen had escaped out of his cellar during the night—and begged me not to say a word about it in the neighbourhood. Of course it was no business of mine; and as I wanted to get into

The Skeleton in the Closet (illustration for G. W. M. Reynolds's *Mysteries of the Court of London*, 1849–55)

Overshadowed by the *Cornhill's* success, but symptomatic too of the bright hopes entertained for thoughtful middle-class journalism, was *Macmillan's Magazine*, which began in November with a reported circulation of 10,000.[20] In its two 1859 issues it ran the early chapters of Thomas Hughes's *Tom Brown at Oxford*, an essay by Alexander Smith, articles on the *Idylls of the King* and on Victor Hugo's *Legend of the Ages*, and one of Huxley's discussions of *The Origin of Species*. On the whole, it was too stodgy, lacking the delicate balance between instruction and entertainment that was the early *Cornhill's* special distinction.

Thackeray had envisaged the *Cornhill* audience as encompassing learned professors, curates, artisans, and schoolmasters: a mixed clientele, but still essentially middle-class. Dickens's audience for *All the Year Round* overlapped the *Cornhill's* to some extent, but it probably reached lower in the social scale, into the class whose income allowed spending twopence a week but not a shilling a month. Large as they were, these publics were eclipsed by the "unknown public" Wilkie Collins had described in *Household Words* in August 1858: readers—three million of them, he estimated—who seldom if ever bought a book, but who formed an insatiable market for cheap weeklies of a quality distinctly below that of Dickens's.[21] To most observers, the low literary and intellectual level of these fiction papers, read by servants, unskilled workers, shop assistants, and their families, more than neutralized whatever optimistic conclusions could be reached after contemplating the *Cornhill's* success. The ominous implications of democracy's encroachment on English literary culture could be read most disturbingly in the pages of periodicals like the *Family Herald*, the *London Journal*, and *Cassell's Illustrated Family Paper*, a class of publications whose five leaders, Collins guessed, had a combined circulation of a million copies.

Below these, in turn, was the true "literature of the streets," the sensational serials typified by G. W. M. Reynolds's *Mysteries of the Court of London*, which had wound up in 1855 after a prosperous penny-weekly run of six years. Unfortunately, since these weeklies were both disreputable and flimsy they have left but a meager record. We have no reliable statistics on the quantity in which they were produced, nor do we know how many titles there were; though it is said that about 1859 "sixty publications of a notoriously objectionable character [were] issued by one printing establishment alone."[22] At least we can be certain that the "Salisbury Square" trade was flourishing, unabashed by its exclusion from the company of respectable publishers and by the drum-fire of high-minded criticism.

The fictional "rubbish" of 1859—a contemporary description of not only penny serials but cheap sensational and "family" papers of all descriptions, as well as much railway reading—caused alarm by its crudeness, its disregard of all the canons of decent literary art in its anxiety to make sense to the barely literate. Its characters were all flat stereotypes of the most rudimentary sort; heroes were bold, selfless, masculine, yet capable of immense tenderness if the occasion arose; heroines were fragile, easily stirred to tears, dependent, ordinarily incapable of action but blessed with miraculous reserves of fortitude when required; villains were—well, the word used in a Victorian context is self-defining. And all parties, regardless of their moral roles, were sedulously unintellectual. The ordinary reader of 1859 wanted people to whom things happened, and he cared nothing for people who merely thought. A certain amount of sensibility was acceptable, but only if indulged in to pass the time while a new crisis was brewing. Furthermore, in 1859 national and racial stereotypes—the amiable, language-mangling Negro, the lisping, usurious Jew, the phlegmatic Dutchman, the libidinous Latin, and the rest— were far more blatant and pervasive than they now are.

This literature was almost wholly escapist. Not only were the plots contrived to remove the reader as far as possible from the deadly monotony of back-street existence among people as drab as himself, to participate vicariously in adventure and romance; the characters and settings had the least possible resemblance to people and places he himself knew. "What has to be read in the workshop and kitchen," remarked a writer in 1858, "must be enacted at club and boudoir; there must be lackeys at the door, splendid as any macaw of the Zoological Gardens, and stately gentlemen in white neckcloths to usher the visitor upstairs." Not even genteel poverty could be admitted to this dream world. "Even poor superior high-minded governesses, and refined poverty in elegant distress, those staple commodities of fiction, do not flourish in the penny periodicals; *that* public does not care to know how careful gentility makes both ends meet, or how the gentlewoman who has seen better days suffers delicate martyrdom."[23]

Freud was only three years old in 1859, a fact that doubtless explains why people in that year were not disturbed by a quality of sensational literature which figures so prominently in our modern consciousness. Even the severest critics of popular fiction admitted that in sexual matters it was decorous enough. Their test was primarily verbal, and in that regard the critics were quite correct. Seldom, even in the lowest reaches of literature for the multitude, was language used that could bring a blush to the young person's cheek. It is also true that, as Margaret Dalziel has noted,[24] apart from G. W. M. Reynolds there were virtually no fictionists whose stock in trade was the uninhibited exploitation of sex, especially sexual violence, and even Reynolds had calmed down considerably by 1859.

But had the Victorians been armed with the instruments of psychoanalysis—a fascinating notion—and concerned themselves not so much with what the printed lines contained but with what might be read between them, they would have been appalled. For if the popular fiction of 1859 was lacking in explicitness, it abounded (as we can see today) in covert symbolism and suggestion. Though its tones were muted and its surface morality unassailable, it was, like ours, a mirror, stimulator, sublimator, and gratifier of its readers' obscure psychological needs. A modern content-analyst could explore its broad tracts with profit to our understanding both of the nature of popular literature itself and of the frustrations and conflicts that were at work in the ordinary Victorian's subconscious. An analysis of the stories in, say, *Reynolds' Miscellany* for 1859, or of a second-rate "society" novel from Mudie's shelves, would be as revealing as any that have been performed on our own mass-circulation fiction.

Neither authors nor publishers were aware, of course, of what their product contained in this respect. But they were very conscious of the power they possessed for affecting their readers' attitudes on economic, social, religious, and political issues, and writers saw nothing unethical, and indeed much that was admirable, in insinuating their own views into novels and periodicals. This attempt at benevolent thought-control took the form not only of overt and frank propaganda, as in Charles Kingsley's novels, but also of unobtrusive slanting and selection. In July 1859 Alexander Macmillan told Kingsley, apropos of the magazine the publisher was planning, that "these things have considerable influence, and ought not to be left wholly in hands that use the influence unworthily"[25]—a reference to the fact that cheap periodicals had a deplorable tendency to issue from the hands of people like Reynolds and Edward Lloyd, whose anticlerical, even republican, sentiments haunted them from the 1840s. Thus, although press lords on the grand scale of Harmsworth and Beaverbrook were still in the future, in 1859 popular periodicals, however disinterested their outward appearance, were often made to serve as the would-be legislators of mass opinion.

Symbolically one of the most significant events of 1859 was the publication, in November, of Samuel Smiles's *Self-Help*, which sold 20,000 copies the first year.[26] Everywhere we look in the popular reading fare of the period, we note a persistent strain of earnestness. Even on the fringes of the literate public, the proportion of readers who wanted, or flattered themselves that they wanted, information and guidance was larger than it is today. Few readers had any illusion that in their brief and largely profitless period at school they had learned enough to last them through life. Hence the diversity and quantity of self-culture publications was enormous. All periodicals, down to the cheapest and crudest, paid at least lip-service to the age's ideal of democratized learning. Sensational fiction papers like the *Family Herald* sought to cultivate an air of respectability by printing short informational articles, snippets of odd facts, interesting statistics, and sayings of the poets and philosophers. By 1859, however, the incidence of these fillers was declining, and the half-pennyworth of bread was about to be totally lost in the intolerable deal of sack.

This was what worried contemporary observers. It was heartening to find on the bookstalls scores of newly published books bearing titles like *A Sketch Book of Popular Geology, Art and How to Enjoy It, Evenings at the Microscope* (by Philip Gosse), and *A Popular History of the United States*. But these assumed a concentration of purpose that relatively few readers, among the millions who made up the total public, possessed. The books and papers that sold best were the most superficial and the most miscellaneous. It was not surprising that in 1859 John Timbs's *Things Not Generally Known*, a compilation of wildly assorted curious facts, was in its twenty-third thousand, with a sequel doing well also.[27] Samuel Smiles himself complained that knowledge was "spread so widely, and in such thin layers, that it only serves to reveal the mass of ignorance lying beneath. Never perhaps were books more extensively read, or less studied; and the number is rapidly increasing of those who know a little of everything, but nothing well." The profusion of print, he continued, "doubtless furnishes unprecedented facilities for learning many things easily and without effort; but at the same time it probably tends rather towards superficialism than depth or vigour of thinking."[28]

The popularization of knowledge was well under way, with all its mixed blessings. Superficiality, short cuts, oversimplification were accompanied by persistent and nearly always ill-advised efforts to amuse. "Comic histories" and "comic grammars" were sold on the premise that they made learning pleasant—even, one is tempted to add, imperceptible. "We may yet possibly," remarked Smiles, "reach the heights of a Comic Euclid and a Comic Prayer-book," or even, as Douglas Jerrold had suggested, a Comic Sermon on the Mount.[29] While no comic Sermons on the

Mount seem in fact to have been composed, the necessity for livening up grave material was felt even (not, of course, for the first time) in religious circles. A writer in the *Athenaeum* at the end of the year decried the meretriciousness of the titles given current tracts: "The Cabman's Dying Cry," "The Bullet in the Bible," "Christ Knocking at the Door of the Soul" (supposedly an effort to trade on the popularity of a Negro song, "Who's That Knocking at the Door?"), and "Pearls from the Ocean" (the name also of a well-known quadrille).[30] The line between legitimate popularization and mere vulgarization is never very clearly defined, and in 1859 it was disregarded as blithely as it has been ever since.

This increasing neglect of the canons of good taste was aided by the fact that not only were more people—ordinary people—reading; more were writing, too. They were encouraged to do so by periodical publishers like John Cassell, who offered prizes of £2 to £5 for essays by working-class men and women on such topics as "Sanitary Reform," "The Advantages of Sunday," "Indiscreet Marriages," and "Labour and Relaxation." In 1859, too, the Crystal Palace Company's contest for an ode to mark the centenary of the birth of Burns, the Victorians' ideal "poet of the people," attracted over six hundred entries. The winner was one Isa Craig, whom a weekly paper dubbed "the Sappho of Sydenham."[31] But most significant of all, the multiplication of specialized periodicals created a wholly unprecedented demand for the services of untrained but purposeful writers, who, however indifferently they managed the pen, were zealous in one cause or another, or had the advantage of knowing gardening or sailing or the cotton trade at first hand.

Thus the common writer came into his own, along with the common reader, with results not wholly beneficial to popular enlightenment. Nothing was more conducive to leveling, to vulgarization, to spreading mediocrity, than this development, which, while it ensured adequate communication between writer and reader, scarcely elevated the reader's mind. The typical literature of a democracy became, in a way appropriately, a conversation between equals. And where the writers were actually more intelligent and better educated than their readers, it was essential that they hide the fact behind a matey tone whose cultivation was one of mid-Victorian journalism's proudest achievements. The mass audience's favorite "literary personalities," writers like John Frederick Smith in *Cassell's Family Paper* and G. A. Sala in the *Welcome Guest*, specialized in the discursive confiding of their whims and prejudices and (in Sala's case) the parading of a pseudosophisticated cosmopolitanism that sat very well with the stay-at-homes in Birmingham and Bethnal Green. The very titles of the popular papers, *Welcome Guest, Family Herald, Sunday at Home*, as well as the ubiquitous "Answers to Correspondents" departments that served as confidants and counselors, reflect the great tendency of the time to make the printed word a natural, indeed indispensable, companion in millions of crowd-lonely lives. So long as popular journalism had for one of its principal functions the providing of vicarious friends (at a penny for a weekly chat), it could hardly fulfill the nobler purposes of literature.

And so, in 1859, popular books and papers had a multiple social role: cinema and television set, pulpit and street meeting, schoolroom and neighborhood club. Because they served so many purposes, it was only to be expected that their significance for the future of English culture could not be clearly discerned. Everybody seemed to agree, at least, that the spread of the reading habit was not an unalloyed boon to the nation. But how was one to read the year's specific portents—and which portents, of the many available, were to be heeded? On the one hand there was the brisk sale of serious instructional works like *Chambers's Encyclopedia* and Cassell's various schoolroom-at-home publications; on the other, the far greater demand for the *London Journal*, which, while serializing *Kenilworth* and *The Fortunes of Nigel* for reasons of economy (Scott's novels were then falling out of copyright), protected its circulation by printing the younger Pierce Egan's novels, *The Love Test* and *Love Me, Leave Me Not*. A Victorian reader could select from a wide offering of classics in Bohn's convenient, well-produced volumes at 3s. 6d. or 5s. each. He could also buy a new card game called "Poetry and Literature," which was advertised as combining "the Fun and Laughter of Mischance and Forgetfulness with the higher delights that belong to the gratification of Literary Taste and the enjoyment of Poetry."[32]

To maintain, with Mrs. Leavis and most other modern critics, that there has been an almost catastrophic decline in the quality of popular literature in the past hundred years is to confess both an ignorance of what the mid-Victorians really read and an excessively dour view of our modern mass reading tastes. It is no less unrealistic than the Victorians' oft-ridiculed idealization of the Middle Ages. Actually generalization is hardly possible. It seems likely that the literature of an imminent democracy does not change very much either in character or in general quality when the democracy has ceased to be merely imminent. There is simply a great deal more of it, and a great many more people are reading it. For the most conspicuous difference between 1859 and 1959 is less qualitative than quantitative: it is the altered structural proportion of the total audience. Year by year, the pyramid-shaped reading public, for centuries far taller than broad, has bulged wider and wider near the base. The process was well under way in 1859. Since then, the gross population of Great Britain has almost doubled, and the percentage of people able, in some fashion, to read has increased from about seventy to ninety-eight. In sheer numbers, the philistines and the populace have overwhelmed the saving remnant, whose concern is no longer the altruistic one of 1859—throwing out the cultural lifeline to the masses—but rather that of saving itself from being pulled under as well.

In 1859 there were already serious doubts whether the millions of new readers really wanted to be rescued. The various agencies of popular enlightenment had been at work long enough, it was felt, for some effect to be noticeable—and there was none. The farther literature spread, and the cheaper and more accessible and more various it became, the more confirmed the popular audience seemed to be in its old tastes. It wanted to be delighted, but only in obvious, simple ways; it wanted to learn, but at no expense to the intellect. It had its bursts of virtue, as when it bought 120,000 copies of the first *Cornhill* as a Christmas present to itself, but it soon relapsed into its familiar habits[33] and picked up Sala, Mrs. Southworth, and Mayne Reid instead. Seemingly the human constitution contained a strong, instinctual love of mediocrity and worse that was proof against every form of prodding and enticement. Beholding the mass audience's stubborn attachment to reading matter of "a vulgar, exciting, and injurious character,"[34] people could indeed wonder whether progress was a universal principle of British life.

Still, they felt, there was hope; this reading public of millions was very new and very ignorant, and it took time for inveterate preferences to be corrected. Surely as education spread, and as opportunities for self-improvement multiplied, the level of popular culture would rise? But it did not; or at least it failed to do so in anything like the degree expected. We are torn, as the men of 1859 were, between two opposing convictions: a residual democratic faith in the possibility of the common man's eventual improvement, and a haunting suspicion that the old Adam can never, in any cultural sense, be buried.

1959

12

From Aldine to Everyman:
Cheap Reprint Series of the English Classics
1830–1906

"A prominent bookseller," reported an English book trade journal at the end of the last century, "lately affirmed that the dead are today taking the bread out of the mouths of the living at a rate unparalleled in the history of literature. Even the popular novelist, he said, feels the competition of those who 'rule our spirits from their urn.' "[1]

Not that Marie Corelli, Hall Caine, Rider Haggard, and the other best-selling writers of the 1890s were in any danger of starvation. Financially the profession of authorship had never before been as rewarding. But it was also true that the flood of reprinted classics, which had been steadily mounting for several decades, had reached a new peak. The full history of this important branch of Victorian publishing, a task that a leader-writer in the *Times Literary Supplement* once urged some "industrious bibliographer" to undertake,[2] will not be attempted here. Instead, we shall be concerned mainly with two aspects of cheap-reprint publishing: its relation to the contemporary social and cultural background, and the way in which it illustrates in microcosm some of the theories and practices of the Victorian book trade generally.

From one viewpoint, Victorian England was not a very fertile ground on which to sow reprints of the national classics. In some educated quarters, the work of English writers was still looked upon, as it had been in Elizabethan times, as a second-class literature. This attitude is implied in a letter Sir Alexander Grant wrote from Bombay to F. T. Palgrave in 1862, discussing the possibility of adopting Palgrave's *Golden Treasury* as a classbook for Indian students: "I hope you won't think this a degradation. English poetry is to these people what Homer is to us."[3] Down almost to the end of the century, the old universities were officially unaware of English literature as a subject for serious study. Again, the lofty or complex style that characterized many English classics, their far-ranging allusiveness, and the sophistication of their thought placed them beyond the grasp of readers with limited education. The mass audience of Victorian times was ill equipped to understand, let alone find pleasure in, books that had been addressed to the intellectual élite of preceding centuries. In that era, as in any other, it was contemporary writers, speaking their audience's own language, and reflecting their audience's own preoccupations, who had the greatest appeal. Finally, the anti-imaginative bias of evangelicalism and utilitarianism was everywhere felt, especially in the first half of the century. Reading belles lettres, it was alleged, was both irreligious and wasteful of time that could be put to far better advantage in "practical" pursuits.

But even more numerous and stronger counterforces were at work. One was a backwash of romanticism: the growing charm of the antique, exemplified in the bibliophily of men like Lamb, Hunt, and the elder Disraeli. The sense that books, and particularly old ones, have a magical glamour spread as the high place of imaginative and emotional experience in men's lives was reaffirmed. Closely associated with this reaction against rationalism and gritty utilitarianism was the increased importance literature acquired as a social institution. As Lionel Trilling pointed out, literature "came to be the medium and the repository of the ethical values and the feelings that had once been peculiar to religion. And literature became even more. Carlyle, under the influence of Goethe, formulated the notion of the Man of Letters not only as a priest but as a hero and a seer and thus made him coequal with the political leader and the rival of the scientist. In short, literature took upon itself the very greatest responsibilities and arrogated to itself the most effective powers."[4]

Furthermore, as democracy slowly spread, the age-old notion that literature was the concern only of the cultural and social aristocracy faded. As early as 1819, Francis Jeffrey announced that "the fame of a poet is popular, or nothing. He does not address himself, like the man of science, to the learned, or those who desire to learn, but to all mankind; and his purpose being to delight and be praised, necessarily extends to all who can receive pleasure, or join in applause."[5] Literature of both the past and the present gradually came to be looked upon as part of the cultural heritage of all the people.

As the limitations of the utilitarian philosophy became more apparent, the Victorians became uncomfortably aware that in their society humanistic values had been more and more neglected; and in an attempt to redress the balance, their journalists and public men joined to praise books as the great medium of cultural enrichment. The innumerable essays and speeches they composed on "The Blessedness of Books," "Little Books with Large Aims," "What a Single Book May Do for a Youth," and similar topics were part of a continuous campaign to encourage the habit of serious, profitable reading among the multitude. With opportunities for formal education severely limited, the idea of self-help was part of the Victorian creed; hence books were revered as fireside universities. Polite literature was prized not so much for its capacity to give pleasure as for its extraliterary, or nonaesthetic, values. It was through reading masterpieces of literature that the student could, for instance, enhance his understanding of history. Such an approach was used by F. D. Maurice in his lectures on English literature at King's College in the forties,[6] and by the author of the articles on literature in Cassell's influential *Popular Educator*.

These were some of the reasons why noncontemporary English literature was constantly brought to the attention of ordinary readers, through excerpts and appreciative comment, in the pages of early mass-circulation periodicals such as *Penny Magazine* and *Chambers's Journal*. Indeed, all the way down to the era of George Newnes's *Tit-Bits*, some of the most popular cheap weeklies unapologetically used extracts from classical English literature as fillers. Middle-class newspapers gave generous space to reviews of current books and other literary topics. Literature was a favorite subject for the mechanics' institute lectures which had so prominent a part in middle-class cultural life in early and mid-Victorian England. And, with the adoption of Mundella's code in 1883, elementary schools began to require pupils in the upper standards to read, parse, and memorize selected English classics. Full-length works, or substantial parts thereof, replaced the old "beauties" anthologies which for many decades had represented virtually the only chance children had to gain a glimpse of the standard classics, at least in the schoolroom.

This, in brief, was the background against which the rise of the cheap classic reprint series took place. Historically, the first important inexpensive reprints, made possible by the momentous decision in Donaldson *v.* Beckett (1774), which killed the legal fiction of perpetual copyright, were those of John Bell, John Cooke, and James Harrison, each of whom produced two or more series devoted to poetry, plays, and essays that had thus entered the public domain. The delight they brought to impecunious book lovers in the last quarter of the eighteenth century and the early years of the nineteenth was celebrated by Leigh Hunt, Hazlitt, Henry Kirke White, and William Hone, among others. Of Cooke in particular, Augustine Birrell wrote a century later: "You never see on a stall one of Cooke's books but it is soiled by honest usage, its odour . . . speaks of the thousand thumbs that have turned over its pages with delight. . . . He believed both in genius and his country. He gave people cheap books, and they bought them gladly."[7]

Between 1790 and 1830 there was a scattering of relatively cheap series, appealing to a class of readers who could not afford the better-remembered, but higher-priced, collections of Alexander Chalmers (English Poets and British Essayists), Robert Anderson (British Poets), Robert Lynam (British Essayists), and Sir Walter Scott (Ballantyne's Novelist's Library). The bookseller John Sharpe brought out a long series of English poets, another of the eighteenth-century essayists, and a third of the dramatists. John Fowler Dove's miniature (24mo.) reprints of the English classics, ranging from *The Compleat Angler* to Pope's *Poetical Works*, ran to well over 100 titles. The Chiswick printer Charles Whittingham, producer of a typographically distinguished 100-volume set of British poets for the carriage trade, served the humbler public with his Cabinet Library and Novelists Library (or, as it was also called, Whittingham's Pocket Novelists). The price range of all these series was rather wide—in the case of Whittingham's, from 2s. to 4s. 6d. per volume. The cheapest series of all during this period seems to have been that of John Limbird, publisher of the 2d. weekly *Mirror of Literature*, who brought out a series of British novels at prices running from 6d. to 3s. 6d., and another of miscellaneous British classics from 8d. a volume upward. In addition to reprints dignified by a series title, individual cheap editions of classic authors were also issued by various publishers, nearly all of whom were despised by the genteel firms of Paternoster Row. Conspicuous among them was Thomas Tegg, the energetic scavenger of remainders and expired copyrights, whose products were noted for their low prices, miserly format, and slovenly, not to say slashed, texts.

The period 1827–32 saw the first important burst of interest in cheap books among "respectable" publishers. The appearance of Constable's Miscellany, the Society for the Diffusion of Useful Knowledge's twin Libraries of Useful and Entertaining Knowledge, Murray's Family Library, Cadell's reissue of Scott's novels at 5s., and Colburn and Bentley's Standard Novels touched off a virtual mania in the trade. No firm was without at least one hastily contrived "library" in its bid for the shillings of the suddenly discovered mass reading public, whose size was now as much exaggerated as it had previously been underestimated. Cheap reprints of literary classics inevitably figured in the boom. In 1830 appeared the first volumes of the Aldine Edition of the British Poets, the result of the collaboration of the bookseller William Pickering and the printer Charles Whittingham. The most memorable classic-reprint series of the period, it held an honorable place in an increasingly competitive field down into the present century. For these reasons, it is convenient and fitting to settle upon the year 1830 as the beginning of the era when publishers developed cheap classic libraries as an integral—not merely incidental—part of their lists.

The next ten pages of this article are based, for the most part, upon a list I have compiled, from all available sources, of cheap reprint series of English classics from 1830 to 1906. At the outset, the criteria of eligibility I have used should be made clear: (1) No hard-and-fast test of "cheapness" has been adopted; but series designed chiefly for the specialist or scholar (such as the Fuller Worthies Library and W. E. Henley's Tudor Translations), or published at a price that was clearly beyond the reach of any but the well-to-do, have been omitted. (2) What is a "classic"? Since value judgments are irrelevant to our present purposes, perhaps the best definition is the one implied in the statement, attributed to the publisher Stanley Unwin, that "it takes two generations to make a classic."[8] Obviously some books become established classics even within the lifetime of their authors, as did the novels of Scott and Dickens and the poetry of Byron and Tennyson, so that the demarcation between classics and recent books of evidently lasting popularity is vague indeed. But since a line must be drawn somewhere, series composed mainly of nineteenth-century titles have been excluded, except for series late in the century, by which time works surviving from the generation of Wordsworth, Shelley, and Lamb had achieved, by any definition, the status of classic. (3) Series expressly designed for schoolroom use have been excluded. (4) Series which were virtually abortive, running to only a few titles and then vanishing, have also been omitted.

The remarkable thing is that even with these severe restrictions, the list of cheap classic reprint series for the period 1830–1906 runs to between ninety and one hundred. Even if we make liberal allowance for series that appear more than once, under different names—for the bibliographer, a source of exasperation which will be commented on in a little while—the number would in any event exceed seventy-five: an average of one new classic reprint series for every year in the period covered.

Some of the main cultural reasons for the proliferation of cheap classics after 1830 have already been mentioned. In addition, a powerful economic factor encouraged publishers to launch such series: the simple circumstance that most standard classics were in the public domain and therefore were cheaper to reprint than works still in copyright. As the literacy rate increased and the reading habit became more widespread, the demand for cheap books grew. For various reasons, among them the tyranny of the circulating-library system, books by contemporary writers

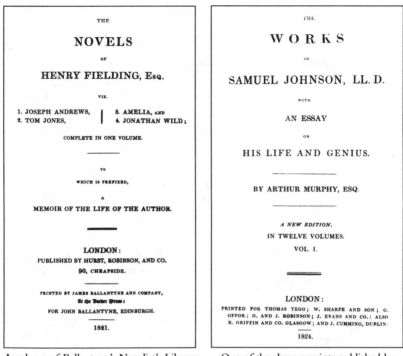

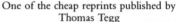

A volume of Ballantyne's Novelist's Library

One of the cheap reprints published by Thomas Tegg

were expensive and, despite the developing practice of issuing 6s. reprints of successful works some time after first publication, they remained so until the 1890s. In 1894 Augustine Birrell observed that "you may buy twenty books by dead men at the price of one work by a living man."[9]

The prices charged for volumes by "dead men" more or less followed the broad tendencies in the publishing trade as a whole. Technological improvements—the use of steam-driven presses; the cheapening of paper by the introduction of papermaking machines, the substitution of esparto and chemical woodpulp for expensive rags, and the reduction and eventual repeal of the paper tax; the invention of machine-made casings to replace hand-sewed bindings and, above all, the introduction of stereotyping— made the production of cheap books more and more rewarding. The low profit per copy was compensated for by the enlarged quantity sold.

Down into the fifties and sixties, the usual price of a classic reprint was between 3s. 6d. and 5s. The lower figure was that charged, for instance, for a volume in Bohn's Standard Library and British Classics (series begun in 1846 and 1853 respectively); the higher was the price of most of the other Bohn libraries, which in the aggregate comprised one of the century's two or three most famous reprint lists. Into this price range fell also the other leading series of the period—Routledge's British Poets and Chandos Library, Nelson's Illustrated Series of the Poets, Nimmo's Cheap Edition of the Poets, and Macmillan's Globe Library. But already, because the 3s. 6d. price for noncopyright reprints compared unfavorably with the shilling or two charged for "railway library" reprints of copyright works, certain firms experimented with lower prices. The highly diversified Cottage Library of Milner and Sowerby, a firm originally of Halifax but later of Paternoster Row, sold for a shilling a volume. Robert Bell's Annotated Series of the English Poets came out at 2s. 6d. in 1854–57 and was reissued in 1864 in monthly volumes, 1s. in paper and 1s. 6d. in cloth. In the sixties Griffin's Universal Library and Warne's Chandos Classics sold at 2s. or less.

This trend toward lower prices was hastened by two spectacular free-for-alls in the reprint trade. One was occasioned by the Waverley novels, the "Author's Edition" of which, issued in 1829, had initiated the 5s. or 6s. copyright reprint. Cadell's "People's Edition," issued in weekly numbers (i.e., parts of volumes) in 1844, sold over 7,000,000 numbers of the novels alone, and 674,000 of the poems. After Cadell's death in 1849, his Scott copyrights were bought by the firm of A. and C. Black, who felt that there still was life left in the fabulous old property. For their "Railway Edition" in 1858–60 the price per volume was reduced to 1s. 6d., and in 1862–63 it was further cut, to a straight shilling. At this point the novels began to fall out of copyright, and other firms scrambled to pick them up. One publisher, John Camden Hotten, brought out 6d. monthly volumes, each containing a complete novel. Black responded with a competitively priced series, which had the extra attraction of Scott's own revisions and notes—material that was still in copyright. But within a few years (1873) even this sensationally low price was halved when John Dicks, a reprint publisher whose activities deserve more study than the extant records permit, brought out complete Waverley novels at 3d.[10]

There was also the episode of the shilling Shakespeares. In 1864, the year of the poet's tercentenary, John Dicks brought out the plays at two for a penny, and sold about 150,000 copies. Collecting them into a 2s. cloth-bound volume, he sold 50,000 more. Then, hearing that Hotten was planning a complete Shakespeare to sell at 1s., Dicks cut the price of his own edition in half, substituting wrappers for cloth, and sold 700,000 copies in the next three or four years. For his shilling the Shakespeare

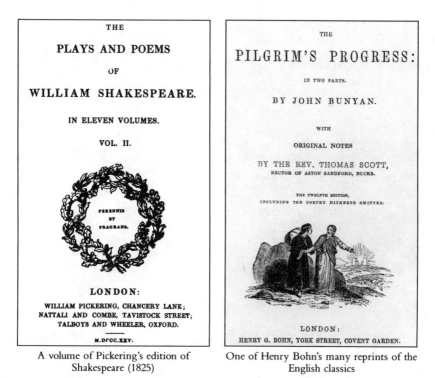

THE

PLAYS AND POEMS

OF

WILLIAM SHAKESPEARE.

IN ELEVEN VOLUMES.

VOL. II.

PERENNIS
ET
FRAGRANS.

LONDON:

WILLIAM PICKERING, CHANCERY LANE;
NATTALI AND COMBE, TAVISTOCK STREET;
TALBOYS AND WHEELER, OXFORD.

M.DCCC.XXV.

A volume of Pickering's edition of
Shakespeare (1825)

THE

PILGRIM'S PROGRESS:

IN TWO PARTS.

BY JOHN BUNYAN.

WITH

ORIGINAL NOTES

BY THE REV. THOMAS SCOTT,
RECTOR OF ASTON SANDFORD, BUCKS.

THE TWELFTH EDITION,
INCLUDING THE POETRY HITHERTO OMITTED.

LONDON:
HENRY G. BOHN, YORK STREET, COVENT GARDEN.

One of Henry Bohn's many reprints of the
English classics

lover got 1,020 pages of closely packed text and thirty-seven woodcuts. In 1868 both Routledge and Warne issued editions at the same price.[11]

In the seventies, the increased demand created by the schools, further economies in production, and, we may suppose, the example of the irrepressible Dicks, who had followed up his shilling Shakespeare with a 473-page illustrated Byron at 7*d*., a Thomson at 6*d*., and about a dozen other classic authors at similar reductions, pushed prices down still further. The Aldine Poets were reissued at 1*s*. 6*d*., and in response Bell's Annotated Edition was cut to 1*s*. 3*d*. Later in the decade the Moxon Library Poets, originally priced at 5*s*., were taken over by Ward, Lock and Co., and, renamed the Standard Poets, sold at 1*s*. 6*d*. in paper and 2*s*. in cloth.

In the eighties, houses like Routledge and Cassell, by then the titans of the reprint trade, waged an all-out price war. Routledge's Universal Library, edited by Henry Morley, began in 1883 at a shilling a volume. Two years later Cassell hired Morley to edit the firm's new National Library, issued weekly at 3*d*. in paper and 6*d*. in cloth. This proved the most popular classic series yet produced, and in quick retaliation

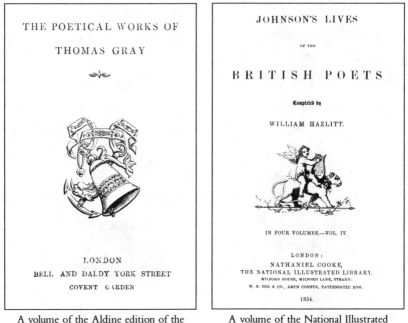

A volume of the Aldine edition of the British Poets

A volume of the National Illustrated Library (1854)

Routledge brought out their World Library at the same price. The bitterness of the rivalry between these houses can be judged from a squabble they conducted in the correspondence columns of the *Times* for 20, 22, and 23 March 1886. Cassell vigorously objected to Routledge's issuing, in their World Library, the same titles that had been announced for Cassell's National Library; Routledge retorted that they had been forced to do so by similar "illegitimate competition" on the part of Cassell. Morley managed to smooth the ruffled feathers of both of his employers, but among other questions left unanswered was that of the ethics involved in an editor's managing two rival series at once.[12]

The gradual but steady reduction in price during the second half of the century is exemplified by the fact that Sampson Low's Choice Editions of Choice Books, originally published in the late 1850s at 5s. a volume, were reprinted in the seventies at 2s. 6d., and again in the nineties at 1s. (There was also a progressive shrinkage in size, from "small quarto" to "small octavo" to "royal 16mo.") By the end of the century, one or two shillings or a half-crown was the standard price for a full-length pocket classic bound in cloth. The enterprising W. T. Stead, to be sure, undercut even the 3d. National and World Libraries with his Masterpiece Library

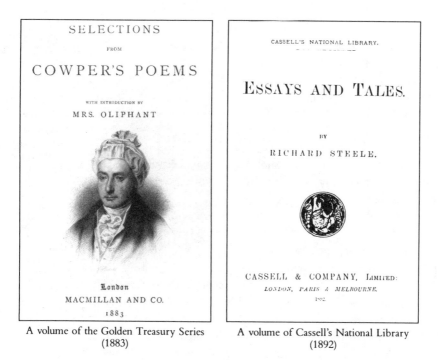

A volume of the Golden Treasury Series (1883)

A volume of Cassell's National Library (1892)

(1895), composed of weekly leaflets in two series, the Penny Novelists and Penny Poets. But this venture, though initially successful, was short-lived and set no precedent.

Our modern era of cheap-reprint publishing may be dated from 1906, the year with which the present study ends. It was then that J. M. Dent, who had gained experience as the publisher of the Temple Shakespeare, the Temple Dramatists, and the Temple Classics, fulfilled a long-standing ambition by issuing Everyman's Library at 1s. a volume: not one title at a time, but fifty. The frenzied editorial and production activity and financial maneuvering necessary to issue a classic library on so grandiose a scale—a "small army" of "British Museum foragers" and introduction-writers was employed, extended credit was wheedled from papermakers—is a vividly recorded episode in British book trade history.[13] But the larger significance of the Everyman series (and in this connection, the World's Classics, begun a few years earlier by Grant Richards but soon transferred to Henry Frowde, must also receive honorable mention) is twofold: it reintroduced into reprint publishing the concern for attractive format which had been largely neglected since the days of Whittingham and the Chiswick Press, and it boldly departed from the conventionalized lists of classics, reprinting for the first time scores upon scores of good books which had never before been available in inexpensive editions.

The practices adopted in producing and marketing the cheap classic series often throw interesting light upon contemporary publishing theory and book-buying habits. The "library" idea—selling a frequently miscellaneous list of books under a generic title—reflects three familiar merchandising premises, now known as "package psychology," "brand name psychology," and "snob appeal" respectively. The first assumes that when a buyer owns a few volumes in a given series (the "package"), he is likely to want to acquire the rest. The second assumes that a reader who is already pleased with one or two books belonging to a particular "library" will regard the name of that series as a guarantee of excellence. The third depends on the connotation of "library," a term which in the nineteenth century was frequently preceded by "gentleman's." Possession of a shelf or two of books prominently labeled "library" gave a man a pleasant feeling of added status, however humble his actual circumstances.

Closely associated with the series concept—they developed side by side in the eighteenth century—was the practice of publishing a book in installments. From the publisher's standpoint, part-issue not only had the advantages just attributed to the series but in addition, by spreading the book's cost to the purchaser over a period of time, made it seem lower than it actually was. Many classic reprint series during the first two-thirds of the century—Cassell's various illustrated editions of literary masterpieces offer examples from the 1860s—were initially issued in weekly or monthly numbers at a few pennies each, with the completed volume becoming available immediately upon publication of the last part. This, of course, was exactly the procedure followed in the case of well-known Victorian novels from *Pickwick Papers* on into the early seventies.

Frequently, too, the principle of publishing at stated intervals was applied to complete volumes without the preliminary step of issuing in several separate numbers. Thus book publishers exploited the habit of regular purchase, which became increasingly prevalent as cheap periodicals won the allegiance of the mass public. If a reader was used to buying a favorite paper each Saturday, why should he not acquire the custom of buying the latest title in a certain reprint series at the same time? This was the reasoning behind the weekly or monthly issue of series like Walter Scott's Camelot Classics (see note 17) and Canterbury Poets, Routledge's Universal Library, and Cassell's National Library. Like the yellow-backs that had won great popularity a generation earlier, the classic reprint series of the nineties, priced at 3*d*., and 1*s*., used the newsagents' stalls to reach a large public that never ventured inside a regular bookshop. Then as now (at least in certain outlets) classic reprints were displayed alongside soft-bound copyright reprints and mass-circulation weeklies.

In their eagerness to squeeze every possible farthing of profit from the plates and sheets of their classic titles, publishers used almost every conceivable merchandising device. Frequently an old series whose component titles had not originally appeared at regular intervals—the Aldine Poets, Bell's English Poets, and Kent's (later Cassell's) Miniature Library of Poets are cases in point—was reissued in periodic volumes, fortnightly or monthly. Sometimes, as was true of Moxon's Old Dramatists, a series previously issued in complete volumes was reintroduced in numbers. Almost every successful series was reissued, sometimes more than once, in a cheaper format. Occasionally the process was reversed, and a cheap series (for instance, Bell and Daldy's Pocket Volumes) was transmuted into a more expensive one (the Elzevir Series) "so as to be more suitable for Presents and School Prizes."[14]

Some series had relatively brief lives, at least in the catalogues of their original publishers. They strutted their brief moment on the stage, heralded by blaring publicity, and then were heard no more. In 1866, for example, Frederick Warne proclaimed the debut of the Clydesdale Classics, "Marvels of Standard Cheap Literature, without a parallel as yet in English Publishing"; their first number, a *Pilgrim's Progress*, offered original colored designs, new type, and fine paper—all for 6*d*. "One Hundred Thousand of this elegant Pocket Edition is all that can be produced this year," Warne advertised.[15] But the supply must have exceeded the demand, for nothing more is recorded of the series.

Series with longer lives often were transferred from firm to firm. Sometimes they retained their baptismal name, as did the Aldine Poets, acquired after Pickering's death in 1854 by Bell and Daldy and later inherited (1873) by their successors, George Bell and Sons. Still others suffered a name-change every time they passed to a new house, and a few appeared simultaneously, under different names, in the catalogues of two or more firms—the result of the practice, not infrequent in that era, of a "publisher-jobber [selling] other firms' sheets over his own imprint."[16] Even libraries retained by the original publisher were not exempt from rechristening whenever sales needed a boost. The firms that purveyed serial shockers to the pavement market often did the same thing when they started a fresh issue of an old favorite, and the practice is hardly extinct today, when individual softbound reprints some-times bear titles different from those under which the hardcover edition appeared.[17]

Renamed series and series that led double or triple lives under the auspices of different firms are the bibliographer's despair. As he attempts to establish their provenance and history from the published records of the trade, he feels as if he were reviewing a stage army; the same lists of titles turn up again and again under different series designations. For example, unless the firm's archives were painstakingly examined, it would be an almost hopeless task to disentangle and properly label the various series of reprints that the Edinburgh house of Nimmo advertised over two or three decades. Nimmo seems to have specialized in buying up odds and ends; and he displayed remarkable energy and ingenuity in dressing his wares in new bindings and marshaling them under new series titles. There is a striking family resemblance between his Cheap Edition of the Poets, Red Line Editions (later retitled Popular Edition of the Works of the Poets), and Crown Library, all published in the sixties. Nimmo's Library Edition of the British Poets was a reissue of George Gilfillan's British Poets, an expensive series originally published by Nimmo's townsman, J. Nichol. In 1870 the sheets of this edition were remaindered to a third owner, Cassell, who sent them forth again in 6d. parts as Cassell's Library Edition, and in cloth-bound volumes as Cassell's Three-and-Sixpenny Edition.[18]

Or take the case of Moxon's Popular Poets, first issued about 1870 at 3s. 6d., then presented in more expensive formats as Moxon's Royal Poets (7s. 6d.) and Moxon's Library Poets (5s.). As if membership in three separate series were not enough, the collection was subsequently acquired by Ward, Lock, who reissued it in cheaper form as Ward, Lock's Standard Poets, and in turn by Collins, who converted it into the Grosvenor Poets.

After coping with genealogies like these, one is grateful for the com-parative simplicity of concurrent series within a single house. There is no problem, for instance, with Warne's five series of the 1860s and '70s: the Chandos Classics, which eventually extended to over 120 titles, were a cheaper edition of works printed earlier in the Chandos Library of prose writers and the Chandos Poets; and the Lansdowne and Arundel Poets were simply alternative formats, the one cheap, the other expensive, for certain titles in the Chandos Poets. In 1882 Warne published Longfellow's *Poems* in no fewer than four series—the Chandos Poets, the Chandos Classics, the Arundel Poets, and the Lansdowne Poets. Warne, indeed, was one of the most resourceful of all Victorian publishers when it came to getting the maximum mileage out of his stock of standard authors. In addition to the series already named, in the eighties he offered a dozen or so titles (all of them long familiar to readers of his advertisements) in the Imperial Poets, and at the same time a virtually identical list in the Albion Poets. The latter genus was divided into several species according to binding: cloth gilt 3s. 6d, imitation half-roxburghe 5s, limp French morocco 7s. 6d., full calf 10s. 6d.

This diversification of binding styles, either under a single series heading or under a new name for each style, was common Victorian practice. Many, if not most, series were offered in both paper and cloth, and some also were available in at least one kind of leather. In an age when middle-class taste favored ornate household objects, more than a few publishers regarded the printed sheets of a classic work primarily as something around which to sew or glue a pretty binding. Nimmo, for instance, devised new bindings every season; between 1870 and 1873 his Popular Edition of the Works of the Poets could be had in (among others) "Cloth Extra, Gold and Colours," "Morocco Extra, with novel prismatic effect and floral silk centre," and "entirely new cloth binding, with beautifully illuminated imitation ivory tablet on side."

Elaborate bindings and lavish internal "embellishments" of course tended to remove such books from the cheap-reprint category. But even among reprints whose price was unquestionably low, the quality of physical makeup varied widely. The Aldine Poets set a high standard of typography and general design that was seldom equaled until the advent of J. M. Dent and his Temple and Everyman series. It would be hard to say which series, of the several scores published, marked the nadir of cheap book production. The 6d. plays and novels of John Dicks would be a strong contender for the distinction, but numerous other series would be in the running. Strenuously small (and often badly worn) type; thin margins, sometimes crowded with legends advertising tea, baking powder, or patent medicines; poor paper; paper wrappers; flimsy sewing—these were too often the result of the pressure to cut prices. Whatever aesthetic satisfaction the impecunious reader derived from his purchase came from the text alone, not from the volume's appearance.

Though some series were designed for parlor display and thus were of a size that would catch the eye, the majority were in small octavo or 12mo., or even as tiny as 32mo.—true "pocket books."[19] Not only were these smaller sizes, requiring less paper and binding material per volume, more economical to produce; they were best adapted to the living habits of the period. Popular books had to be portable, for an ever-increasing amount of reading was done in railway carriages and buses, and they had to be small enough to find room in the cramped households of the lower-middle and working classes.

The quantity and quality of text in these series varied as greatly as did the format. Some series provided complete texts of the works described on the title page, while others provided only selections or truncated texts, a fact that was often suppressed in advertisements and on title pages. A buyer of Spenser's "works" in one volume, for example, was not likely to acquire the whole of the Spenser canon thereby. A reprint publisher especially notorious for his cavalier handling of texts was Thomas Tegg, who, according to some of his contemporaries, included only as much of a given classic in a volume as the paper set aside for the job permitted. Tegg was scarcely unique in this respect. While most publishers may not have been so completely lacking in concern for textual accuracy and completeness as to give rise to trade legends, they were content to reprint whatever version of a masterpiece came to hand, however corrupt or fragmentary the text might be. Even if accuracy had been prized as highly in Victorian times as it is today—at least among scholars—the economics of the cheap-reprint business made careful scrutiny of the printer's copy, and subsequently of proofs, a dispensable luxury. Editorial supervision in the modern sense was rare, except in the interests of bowdlerization. Money laid out to oblige Mrs. Grundy was a thoroughly justifiable business expense.

The contents of the various series, if subjected to close statistical analysis, would provide an interesting, if not always dependable, index of Victorian literary taste and of the comparative reputations of classic authors in Victorian times. The relative frequency with which various standard works were reprinted, as well as the decline in availability of certain classics and the rise of others, can be documented by studying the advertisements in the trade journals and the lists of reprints-in-series in the *Reference Catalogue of Current Literature* and appendix B of the cumulated volumes of the *English Catalogue*. But one cannot assume that the reprint libraries were an unerringly faithful barometer of the literary climate, the publishers readily responding to changes in the critical and popular standings of classic authors. Practical considerations, such as the publishers' desire to squeeze their full money's worth out of their investment in plates and stock, may well have caused certain old standbys, such as Dryden, Pope, Goldsmith, Johnson, and Cowper, to overstay their welcome. Accessibility, in short, must not be equated with popularity. The fact that old author A was represented in 75 percent of the reprint series current at a certain date, while author B was in only 10 percent, does not prove that author A actually stood that much higher in contemporary esteem. Thus it is quite possible that by artificially prolonging the dominance of certain classic writers in the reprint libraries, publishers not only impeded the normal fluctuations of taste but left us a record of popular preference which is easily misinterpreted. However, until much more information on the inner workings of the English book trade is available, the problem of how far the reprint publisher was responsive to public taste, and how far he influenced it, must remain a matter for speculation.

The selection of titles for a classic reprint series and the preparation of introductory matter often gave employment to well-known men of letters, just as they do today. Robert Bell consulted Leigh Hunt when planning his Annotated Edition of the English Poets; it was Hunt who encouraged Bell to stray from the beaten path and include some little-known poets in his collection.[20] After Bell and Daldy acquired the Aldine Poets, they called upon men like Lord Houghton, William Michael Rossetti, Buxton Forman, and Edward Dowden to prepare new titles for the series. The individual volumes in Macmillan's Globe Edition, one of the few relatively authoritative series in respect to text, were edited by men of the stature of David Masson, F. T. Palgrave, and A. W. Ward. Rossetti was the general editor of Moxon's Popular Poets during the brief period before Ward and Lock took over the series. He specifically stated in his autobiography, however, that revision or emendation of the text was not part of his job.[21] The Camelot and Canterbury series, issued by Walter Scott, a wealthy Newcastle dock and railway contractor and colliery owner who turned publisher in his late fifties, were edited in part by the self-taught collier-poet Joseph Skipsey, the novelist William Sharp, and Ernest Rhys. But perhaps the brightest galaxy of "name" editors was the one associated with Kegan Paul's Parchment Library, begun in 1880. It included Dowden, Edmund Gosse, Andrew Lang, Richard Garnett, Mark Pattison, Austin Dobson, and George Saintsbury.

Until Ernest Rhys became the living symbol of Everyman's Library, the single figure most conspicuously associated with cheap classic reprints in the public mind was the critic and lecturer Henry Morley. His son-in-law and biographer, Henry Solly, implies that his fame as editor of various reprint series somewhat embarrassed his family. "There seemed real danger," wrote Solly, "that he would be remembered after his death only in connection with his services for the diffusion of cheap literature."[22] *Punch* praised him thus, in lines whose sentiment is more to be admired than their execution:

JOHN BULL is not sweet on the type of "Professor,"
But good HENRY MORLEY was happy possessor
Of JOHN BULL's respect, JOHN BULL, Junior's, love.
He *made Good Letters Cheap!* 'Tis a title above
Many Dryasdust dignities told in strung letters.
Ah! many who felt Iron Fortune's stern fetters
In days ante-Morleyish, look on the rows
Of cheap Classics, in musical verse and sound prose,
Which bear the well-known editorial "H.M.,"
And sigh, "If *my* youth-time had only known *them,*
These threepenny treasures, and sixpenny glories,
These histories, treatises, poems, and stories,
Which cost in my time a small fortune, what thanks
And what joys would have swelled o'er their neat-rangèd ranks!"
Ah! studious boys must feel gratitude, surely,
To have lived in the times of the good HENRY MORLEY![23]

Comment in trade journals suggests that the National Library, which Morley edited for Cassell, had the greatest success of any classic-reprint series down to that time. As Solly said, "At a cost not exceeding the gas or water rate, a constant supply of good literature could be 'laid on' to any house in town or country, and a circulation varying from 50,000 to 100,000 copies for each volume attests the popular appreciation of the enterprise. Letters, which Professor Morley greatly prized, came from the far West in America, and from other lands on the borders of civilization, expressing gratitude for these cheap and handy volumes, which seemed almost as ubiquitous as Palmer's biscuits."[24]

Which raises the question, Just how influential were these reprint series in stimulating an interest in English masterpieces among the expanding reading public? In a period when cheap weeklies like the *Family Herald* and *Tit-Bits* achieved individual circulations of from 500,000 to a million, what place had older works of established literary merit in the reading diet of the multitude? One view of the matter was reported at the beginning of this article. But what were the facts?

We have the boasts of certain reprint publishers, for whatever they may be worth. Of Macmillan's Globe Edition, "upwards of 140,000 volumes" were sold to the end of 1870; presumably this figure includes the sales of the first and most famous member of the series, the Shakespeare, which had found 95,000 buyers since publication in December 1864.[25] Between the spring of 1870 and May 1872, Moxon's sold 150,000 volumes

of their Popular Poets.[26] Over a quarter-million copies of the Miniature
Library of the Poets were disposed of in the period 1879–84, according to
the publishers, William Kent and Co.[27] In 1884 Warne and Co. advertised
that their Chandos Classics, then numbering over 100 titles, had sold
3,500,000 volumes since publication had begun in 1868.[28] Through what
seems to have been either unaccountable dereliction or heroic restraint on
the part of their advertising writer, this figure remained unchanged for
several years. In 1894, however, Warne revised their copy, and the total to
date for the Chandos Classics was announced as six million.[29] The Canterbury Poets were reported to have sold "about a million volumes"
within ten years of their beginning in 1884.[30] Ward and Lock's Minerva
Library sold over 150,000 between 1889 and 1894.[31] For some years after
first publication in 1894–96, the Temple Shakespeare, a forty-volume
series, sold 250,000 volumes annually (and the total between 1894 and
1934 was five million).[32] Of W. T. Stead's Penny Poets, almost five million
copies were published in a year, a figure exceeded by Stead's condensed
Popular Novels, which were said to have sold "about six and a half
million."[33]

These are staggering totals indeed; but in estimating their significance, one must remember several things. One is that since some, if not
most of the series mentioned included some copyright works, or at least
works whose copyright had only recently lapsed, the figures are not a
good indication of the current appetite for older literature. Another is that
the figures are for the total sale of a whole series, which might comprise
twenty, fifty, or a hundred volumes. Unfortunately, with one or two
exceptions, such as the Globe one-volume Shakespeare, sales figures for
individual titles in the various series are unavailable.[34] A further consideration is that the totals often, if not always, include export sales. Of the
annual total for the Temple Shakespeare, for example, 100,000 copies went
to America;[35] and the Empire itself provided a large market for books
published in the British Isles.

Although the books we are concerned with here were designed for
the general trade, not for classroom use, they were in great demand as
school prizes. And, as the advertisements also show, they were among
the items most favored for family Christmas giving, or for a decorous
exchange of presents between swain and sweetheart. The extent to which
school prizes or sentimental gifts were actually read, let alone understood,
is, however, something else again. As George Gissing observed, "Hardly
will a prudent statistician venture to declare that one in every score of
those who actually read sterling books do so with comprehension of

their author. These dainty series of noble and delightful works, which have so seemingly wide an acceptance, think you they vouch for true appreciation in all who buy them? Remember those who purchase to follow the fashion, to impose upon their neighbor, or even to flatter themselves; think of those who wish to make cheap presents, and those who are merely pleased by the outer aspect of the volume."[36]

Gissing's pessimism was widely shared by observers of the cultural scene throughout the Victorian period; more widely than ever at the end of the epoch, when the reading preferences of the masses had been fully expressed at public libraries and newsagents', and the verdict was overwhelmingly in favor of light novels and penny papers. "The constant flow of new editions of Great Authors," observed a writer in the *Academy* in 1903, "is deceptive. They are regarded as part of the necessary furniture of the house—not of the mind; and having been duly and dutifully bought they are taught to know their place on the appointed shelf. They are taken as read. . . . There are few men now who, when a new book is published, read an old one."[37]

In such views—and examples could be multiplied from the annals of the nineteenth-century reading public—there is more than a hint of snobbery. The phenomenon of a semiliterate reading audience numbering in the millions stirred the residual social prejudices of the class who wrote for, and read, the leading literary journals, and it was only to be expected that they would exaggerate the situation they deplored. On the other hand, there were sturdy believers in the common man's capacity for literary culture and his active interest in acquiring it. The best known of these was Charles Dickens, who told the Birmingham Society of Artists in 1853, "I believe there are in Birmingham at this moment many working men infinitely better versed in Shakespeare and in Milton than the average of fine gentlemen in the days of bought-and-sold dedications and dear books."[38] Every public man who had faith in mechanics' institutes and free libraries as effective disseminators of culture among the middle and lower classes, everyone who advocated the repeal of the newspaper tax, the amendment of the copyright law, and other schemes connected with spreading the blessings of cheap print, asserted that the multitude was ready and eager for good literature.[39]

As events proved, there was just as much exaggeration on this side of the issue. The bright words of hope uttered at mid-century, when the "taxes on knowledge" and the absence of free libraries were alleged to be the only barriers to the development of a broadly cultured populace, were seldom echoed a generation later. It was indisputable that the widening of educational opportunity had not been accompanied by the same degree of literary enlightenment. In 1886 a writer in the *Nineteenth Century* said: "Cheap editions have brought standard works within their [the workers'] reach, and though the privilege is not largely availed of, it is not altogether neglected. . . . Lots of working men have studied with great care one or two of Shakespeare's plays; others know one or two of Dickens's works almost by heart. . . . At the same time there are working men who will devour every book they can buy or can secure from friends, and a curious undigested, if not indigestible, mass they do sometimes get hold of Hundreds, on the other hand, have never read a line of a book." But having achieved this precarious balance on the fence, the writer continued: "The chief difficulty about literature for the working classes is to reach them. If the literature were lying on their table they would often read, but they seldom sally forth into the highways and byways of the literary world to discover what they shall purchase."[40] Since it was at this very time that paperbound classic reprints were finding wider distribution through newsagents and other channels, one would expect to hear no more complaint that cheap reprints were difficult to obtain. Yet fifteen years later— in 1901—another writer, committed to the assumption that "hordes of men and women . . . are waiting to respond to an offer of really good and really cheap books," alleged that the trouble still lay in distribution (more specifically, the high postal rate charged for books as against the negligible cost of mailing sensational papers) and price. The solution he put forth was the issue of weekly volumes in a "General Library" subdivided into series, to be sold by subscription: 104 volumes in two years, total cost £4 in paper, £6 in cloth.[41]

There was nothing really new in this proposal; but the very fact that it was reiterated defines the position of the idealist confronted with a situation in whose permanence he refuses to believe. The hard fact seemed to be that the constant activity in cheap reprint series for the past seventy years had not made the common man a devotee of great literature; no combination of merchandising devices, no amount of cheapening, had achieved that goal. But men who shared Dickens's, Sir John Herschel's, and Wilkie Collins's faith in the common man's latent hunger for literary experience clung to the familiar Victorian reliance on "the proper measures."

However short the cheap reprint series fell of the most optimistic expectations in Victorian times, they were responsible for a wider popular interest in classic English literature than would otherwise have prevailed. Concurrently with them, designed especially for students facing the various examinations for university admission and civil service posts, but undoubtedly finding an additional market beyond the crammers, were published a score or more of concise manuals, outlines, and other study-guides of English literature. *Chambers's Cyclopaedia of English Literature*, originally published (1842–43) in weekly numbers, and in two volumes (1844), within a few years sold 130,000 copies in England alone.[42] During the Victorian period, too, there was a revival, to which the proliferation of cheap classic reprints undoubtedly contributed, of appreciative literary journalism. In both periodicals and collected volumes, the bookish commentaries of men like Gosse, Lang, Birrell, Dowden, and Saintsbury delighted readers who, in another era, would have read Lamb, Hazlitt, and Hunt. Demand increased for popular biographies of literary figures. Macmillan's English Men of Letters series, a pioneer in its field, sold over 300,000 copies between 1878, when the first volumes, priced at 2s. 6d. were published, and 1887, when a reissue in monthly volumes, at 1s. in paper, 1s. 6d. in cloth, was begun. Some of the titles were reprinted from three to six times in the first ten years, while others had only a single reprinting.[43] The popularity of the various volumes evidently depended on the contemporary interest in the author treated and on the reputation of the man who wrote the biography itself.

Few of the boys and girls and men and women into whose hands fell copies of cheap classic reprints left any explicit record of their pleasure. Only occasionally did the mute, inglorious common reader take pen in hand, in the manner of the Lancashire workman who wrote to Cassell's that the first twenty-three volumes of the National Library "have done a great deal of good even in my own neighbourhood, for several of my own friends have given up drinking for the sake of taking and reading your beautiful little books."[44] But a systematic combing of the memoirs of eventually well-known people who grew up in the Victorian period would reveal how many cultivated and expanded their literary taste by reading these inexpensive volumes. Thomas Hardy's first copy of Shelley was an edition of *Queen Mab and Other Poems* published in the Cottage Library.[45] Havelock Ellis's interest in the Elizabethan drama, which was to bear fruit in his editorship of the Mermaid series, was nurtured by his buying, as a schoolboy at Mitcham in the early 1870s, successive penny numbers of Dicks's Standard Plays.[46] Dicks's penny-number edition of Shakespeare was affectionately remembered by Thomas Burt, the Labour politician: "No matter that the print was small and the paper poor; no matter that there were neither theatre nor stage, neither actors nor orchestra. All the more scope was given to fancy and imagination."[47] Perhaps the final word may be that of the journalist Sir John Hammerton, looking back on his early days in Glasgow, about the time he left school and went to work as a correspondence clerk. In his reminiscences he exclaimed of Cassell's National Library: "What an Aladdin's cave that proved to me! Addison, Goldsmith, Bacon, Steele, DeQuincey . . . Charles Lamb, Macaulay and many scores of others whom old Professor Morley introduced to me— what a joy of life I obtained from these, and how greatly they made life worth living!"[48]

1958

13

Cope's Tobacco Plant:
An Episode in Victorian Journalism

Some day someone is going to write a book about nineteenth-century English trade journals, a deed which may well enrich our knowledge of Victorian social history. There was much more in those papers than commercial gossip and dry details about current trade conditions and technological advances. We should not expect such a history, however, to be of great interest to the student of literary taste. Books and commerce mixed scarcely more easily then than they do now. But to that generalization there is at least one notable exception—a Liverpool tobacco firm's trade- and customers'-organ which was also a very respectable literary review. If the contents of *Cope's Tobacco Plant*, "A Monthly Periodical Interesting," as its subtitle said, "to the Manufacturer, the Dealer, and the Smoker," are a reliable index of the cultural level of later Victorian tobacco-users, they were a select lot indeed. Although its editor possibly overestimated the tastes of his readers, the periodical had a successful run of eleven years, and in its time it was as much discussed as those of its contemporaries whose names are more familiar to us today.[1]

Cope's Tobacco Plant was published by Cope Brothers and Company, of Lord Nelson Street, Liverpool. Volume 1, number 1 appeared on 30 March 1870, and the periodical came out monthly thereafter. The first volume was completed with number 83 in February 1877, the total number of pages (including occasional supplements) running to 1,012. Volume 2 ended with the number for January 1881, which also marked the sudden and unexplained demise of the paper. Each issue comprised twelve double-columned pages, thirteen inches tall and printed on good coated paper, with frequent illustrations. Produced on Cope's own premises by John Fraser, it was distributed through tobacconists, newsagents, and railway bookstalls, for a brief period at the price of a penny but during most of its career for twopence. Subscribers received it by mail for two shillings a year. The circulation of the first number "largely exceeded" 10,000 copies; unfortunately we do not know what the later figures were.[2] The printer, John Fraser, was also the editor of the *Tobacco Plant*. That he was an unusually shrewd and enterprising journalist, as well as a man of catholic literary tastes, can be inferred from the contents of his periodical, and it is too bad that we know so little about him. All that I have been able to discover is that he was in earlier life the captain of an ocean-going Liverpool steamer who took over the printing business of his father when the latter was permanently incapacitated by illness.

The names of some of his contributors may be recognized by students of very minor Victorian letters. One was Tom Hood the younger, whose death was lamented in a black-bordered obituary box in the December 1874 issue. Another was William Maccall, who had been a Unitarian minister in Lancashire in the 1830s and then moved to London, where he was for decades a busy hack journalist and the author of a number of now-forgotten books.[3] A third was William Gordon Stables, M.D., R.N., the author, according to the *British Museum Catalogue* and his obituary in the *Athenaeum* (14 May 1910), of many scores of books for boys and a number on popular science, medicine, and cycling. And a fourth was Llewellynn F. W. Jewitt, a leading antiquary, illustrator, and editor for a time of the *Derby Telegraph*, who published a long list of books, mainly on antiquarian subjects, and whose many contributions to the *Tobacco Plant* were largely on the antiquarian lore of pipes, snuffboxes, and tobacconists' signs.

The one contributor who won an enduring place in literary history was James Thomson ("B.V."). It is not at all impossible that but for the periodical's acceptance of his work, Thomson would have starved. In 1875 he broke away from Bradlaugh's *National Reformer*, for which he had been writing for several years—"The City of Dreadful Night" had appeared there in the spring of 1874—and found himself with no means of support. A few months later, introduced to Fraser by his friend Maccall, he began his contributions to the *Tobacco Plant*, which, as Thomson's latest biographer says, was "his steadiest and best market," paying punctually for his work. Several times during the six years of his connection with the magazine, when he was more hard up than usual, he asked for and received advances from Fraser.[4]

Sometimes anonymously, sometimes over the signature "Sigvat," sometimes over his initials, but never over his full name (perhaps because his notoriety as a freethinker would have embarrassed the magazine?), Thomson supplied the *Tobacco Plant* with essays, articles, and reviews. On the strictly nicotian side there were such articles, obviously the result of hard work in his favorite haunt, the British Museum, as "Tobacco Smuggling in the Last Generation" (seven installments), "Tobacco Legislation in the Three Kingdoms" (a long series of articles, in great part nothing but dreary summaries extracted from the State Papers), and "The Tobacco

Duties." One need not imagine that such work was done *con amore*, although Thomson did conform to the one article of faith required of the *Tobacco Plant*'s contributors, a steady devotion to the weed. But since, as will become clear before we have finished, John Fraser was extraordinarily hospitable to material of literary interest, Thomson supplied him with some of his best critical writing: a fourteen-part essay on Ben Jonson, shorter ones on St. Amant, Rabelais, John Wilson and the *Noctes Ambrosianae*, James Hogg, and George Meredith. In addition, he reviewed a number of volumes in the English Men of Letters series.[5]

But it is the *Tobacco Plant* itself, rather than Thomson's connection with it, that concerns us here. In its first years it gave most of its space to news of interest to tobacco manufacturers and dealers—announcements of patents, classified advertisements, articles on the hated excise tax, descriptions of improvements in tobacco culture, and so forth. Later such material became less and less prominent; the advertisements (except for those of Cope's own products, which, understandably, persisted to the last), the lists of patents, and the other more specialized information disappeared quite early, and the columns which remained dedicated to the trade featured articles like Thomson's on the history of tobacco smuggling and legislation.

The chief purpose of the paper was made plain in the very first issue: "As we desire to interest the SMOKER, as well as the TRADER, we have arranged for lighter contributions—as Stories, Verse, and Anecdote,—which we trust will furnish the CONSUMER with a VADE MECUM and a PASTIME-BOOK for those hours of ease in which he enjoys his favourite luxury." In those days, smokers were something of a class apart. Following the august examples of Tennyson and Carlyle, they took their smoking seriously; they were, in a way, cultists. And, like all cultists, they wanted to read everything that was even remotely connected with the object of their devotion. From the very inception of the paper, therefore, the editor cast a wide net for passages in books old and new, newspaper and magazine pieces, and original contributions—anything that would make the *Tobacco Plant* live up to its ideal of being "the organ of Tobacco use and Tobacco sentiment." Tobacco was considered in its historical, geographical, ethnological, societal, physiological, literary, and every other conceivable relation; the periodical became, indeed, a monthly encyclopedia of nicotian learning. It discussed the history of tobacconists' signboards and advertisements; it gave a recipe for tooth powder made of cigar ashes; it uttered severe strictures on tobacconists' practice of selling explosive cigars; it advised on the care of pipes and the social manners of smokers; it ran descriptive essays on various restaurants, such as Simpson's in London, where smoking was an amenity to be enjoyed along with good food and drink; it thundered its disapproval of the use of tobacco shops as fronts for places of gaudier entertainment—a practice first reported from New York, but later admitted to be not unknown in Liverpool, where also "Coquettes and Cigarettes" were occasionally available under the same roof.

More than eighty years before a battery of scientific studies brought to public attention the carcinogenic and other deleterious properties of tobacco, the *Tobacco Plant* was troubled by occasional allegations that smoking was bad for the health. Its duty to its readers, of course, was clear. The American exchanges which poured onto the editor's desk with the arrival of every Atlantic steamer provided him with plenty of reports of centenarians who attributed their longevity to a practically immemorial addiction to tobacco. And whenever an English medical man published a treatise in which he proved the harmlessness of the habit, he was assured of ample attention in the *Tobacco Plant*. Sometimes, it is true, in its zeal to preserve at least a semblance of impartiality, the periodical had to give space to physicians who came to the opposite conclusion; but it always appended an editorial note attempting to expose the weaknesses in such arguments, and, when the weapons of logic and scientific knowledge failed, taking refuge in the claim that "we can't make head or tail of what Dr. So-and-so is trying to say."[6]

A great deal of the miscellaneous material which filled up the odd space in every issue came from America, with which, as a homeland of the precious commodity, the *Tobacco Plant* was always on cordial terms. The American newspapers and magazines, and above all the *Tobacco Plant*'s opposite number, the New York *Tobacco Leaf*, furnished the editor with all the curious news items, anecdotes, and jokes he needed. A talented hen in Pittsfield, Massachusetts, which specialized in laying eggs shaped like an Irishman's clay pipe, was good for a paragraph. So were the difficulties which were reported to have ensued when a trolley line in New York put on special smoking cars. And in both England and America tobacco seems to have been, in the 1870s, an inexhaustible peg upon which to hang a witticism. The following examples, taken at random, are, I am afraid, entirely typical of the thousands Cope's printed: "OUTRAGING THE SEX.—A lady who has a great horror of tobacco got into a railroad car the other day, and inquired of a male neighbour, 'Do you chew tobacco, sir?' 'No, madam, I don't,' was the reply, 'but I can get you a chew if you want one.' " And: "HOW TO PUT ON HIGH AIRS.—Become accustomed to 'see garrets' (cigarettes)."

The *Tobacco Plant* thus was devoted to a cause—that of encouraging a communal spirit among smokers by reminding them not only of the mellow delights of the habit they shared but also of the way in which tobacco permeated history (at least in the post-Raleighan centuries) and was ubiquitous, the unfailing subject of rhapsodic comment and pleasant mirth, in the present day. But the magazine's role as propagandist did not end there. For there was abroad in the land a band of sanctimonious busybodies known as the Anti-Tobacco Society, intent upon carrying on the work initiated in 1604 by a crowned king of England in a work called *A Counter Blaste to Tobacco*. The *Tobacco Plant* deemed it proper that the vociferations of the reformers against tobacco should be met with "a few animated words . . . in its vindication." The "few animated words" ran to at least a thousand in every issue. With heavy humor the men of Cope's provided their readers with a running account of the doings of the Anti-Tobacco Society—taking up a subscription to ease the declining years of the society's underpaid agent, offering to atone for the perennially expected demise of the society's paper by giving over a column of each *Tobacco Plant* to the Anti-Tobaccoites' purposes, and publishing detailed (and not wholly trustworthy!) narratives of the society's meetings written by "our special correspondent." The paper's satire ranged from an interminable series of labored fictional pieces signed "Didimus Goggs" to a full-page prospectus of the "Anti-Teapot Association," including a long "Address to the Public" which detailed all the horrors that attended the habit of tea drinking. That the battle was not won in the *Tobacco Plant*'s lifetime is attested by the fact that in the 1890s its successor, *Cope's Smoke Room Booklets*, still had to fire away at the obstinate enemy. The frontispiece of number 9 (1893) showed a stained-glass triptych, in each of whose panels appeared the figure of the anti-nicotinist who had long since become familiar to the Cope audience through the exertions of the *Tobacco Plant* artist: a clergyman with umbrella, long ulster, gaiters, big feet, and pious mien—the direct forebear of the lugubrious prohibitionists drawn by Rollin Kirby in the 1920s. The three versions of the same figure were labeled "Chadband," "Pecksniff," and "Stiggins." Above them was unfolded a scroll bearing what the Cope people, at least, maintained was the Anti-Tobacco Society's motto: "The Pig Smoketh Not, Neither Doth the Ass"—and to make the representation explicit beyond doubt, there duly appeared portraits of the nonsmoking pig and the antinicotian ass, whose features had something in common with those of the human beings depicted below.

But it was not this crusade against cant, instructive as it sometimes may be to the student of Victorian satire, that gave the *Tobacco Plant* its distinctive flavor. If it was, as Thomson said, "one of the most daring and original publications of the day," it was so for the reason he assigned: "It actually loves literature, though it has to make this subordinate to the Herb Divine." Its love of literature was somewhat more inclusive than discriminating, but there can be no question that it was genuine. The same may be said, doubtless, for the tastes of its readers. In the first two or three years of its existence, the *Tobacco Plant* went in heavily for verse, devoting two or three columns in every issue to an anthology of metrical praise of tobacco, half of it lifted from printed sources from the late sixteenth century onward, the other half the work of the magazine's own contributors and readers. The entire issue for January 1872 was devoted to what the *New Yorker* would call poesy—the result of a prize competition for "epigrams for tobacco jars." Nearly seven hundred entries were received, and from them the editors selected enough to fill nineteen tall columns. The quality of the effusions need not be commented upon here. In fairness, however, it should be added that the editors deliberately printed "a few of the worst only for their eccentricity, or extreme badness, as a caution to persons afflicted with *cacoëthes scribendi*; whilst others still are presented as specimens of our enemies' rabid outpourings of bigotry and bile." After this debauch the *Tobacco Plant* quietly reduced the incidence of verse in its pages, although to the very end few issues appeared without at least one poem.

But John Fraser had higher ambitions. Not satisfied with printing crumbs of tobacco-connected lore from old and current publications and from the pens of his readers, he determined to commission and print serious articles on books and their writers, his only condition being that somehow, however obscure or forced the connection might be, some allusion should be made to smoking. If the writer under discussion lived before tobacco was introduced into Europe, the article could be blandly rationalized by a preliminary comment lamenting that he never knew the joys of smoking.

Leafing through the two stout bound volumes of the *Tobacco Plant* one is charmed by the ingenuity of the paper's contributors in finding nicotian tie-ups almost at random in English literature. An article on "Charles Lamb as a Smoker" in the issue for July 1870 and a follow-up piece by Tom Hood, Jr., on "Lamb's Farewell to Tobacco" were sufficient to establish Lamb's orthodoxy, and no further allusion to his smoking habits was necessary; thereafter nothing Elian was foreign to the paper. It was no strain on the *Tobacco Plant*'s policy, therefore, to print (June and July 1875) "The Sayings of Charles Lamb," a collection intended to supplement R. H. Shepherd's newly issued edition of Lamb's works, as well as some additions by Alexander Ireland. In the numbers for April and July 1871 we find "Famous Smokers: I. Thomas Carlyle" and "II. Alfred Tennyson, Poet Laureate"—which, despite the general title and a few passing comments to justify it, were really literary appreciations. The Christmas number for the same year contained "The Sentimental Snuff-Box," an extract from *The Sentimental Journey*. During the summer of 1872 appeared three articles on Thackeray and tobacco, which were succeeded by three on "The Poet Cowper and Tobacco." When Samuel Butler's *Erewhon* was published in 1872, its author's addiction entitled him to a review, headed, naturally, "A Smoking Satirist." From August to December of 1873, the *Tobacco Plant* ran a five-part survey of "Tobacco in the Waverley Novels." In the same fashion Dickens was discussed ("Dickens as a Nicotian"—four full columns in the issue for May 1874), and Parson Adams and even Dr. Syntax. The roster of James Thomson's contributions includes his essays "Charles Baudelaire on Hasheesh" and "Théophile Gautier as Hasheesh-Eater," and no fewer than seven of the fourteen installments of his critical account of Ben Jonson are devoted to "Tobacco and Jonson."[7]

As time went on, even a token insistence upon some mention of tobacco in the literary material was dispensed with, and a pleasant allusion to smoking was no more *de rigueur* in an article contributed to the *Tobacco Plant* than it was in one intended for the *Athenaeum*. Although each issue continued to have much material specifically referring to tobacco, its history, its sentiment, and its current place on the social scene, the remaining columns were indistinguishable from those appearing in avowedly literary journals. In 1875–76, for instance, there was a long series of articles on Ruskin's *Fors Clavigera*—a noteworthy evidence of the *Tobacco Plant*'s toleration, as Ruskin was well known to despise tobacco.[8] In March 1874 appeared a four-column review of Forster's *Life of Dickens*, in which the reviewer, "An Old University Man," characterized the work as "a desert of Dame Quickly garrulities . . . twaddle . . . toadyism . . . ridiculous trumpery." A regular department, "The Smoke Room Table," instituted in March 1876, reviewed current books, especially those of literary importance. Every volume in the English Men of Letters series published between 1876 and 1880 received notice here. At least six of the volumes—

Forster's *Swift*, Morison's *Gibbon*, Shairp's *Burns*, Church's *Spenser*, Symonds's *Shelley*, and Morley's *Burke*—were reviewed by Thomson, and it is possible that he was responsible for notices of other titles in the same series.

Probably the most startling announcement in the whole file of the *Tobacco Plant* appeared in its January 1874 issue. Since there was an obvious affinity, said the editor, "between the lovers of old books, irreverently called Bibliomaniacs, and Tobacco," the magazine would institute the practice of reviewing reprints of old and scarce books as they issued from the press. The practice was not actually begun until the June issue, but once started, it lasted until the end of 1878, when (it is just possible) the editor reluctantly concluded that he had misjudged his clientele. But during those four and a half years the tenth page of each monthly issue contained notices of books of interest to collectors and literary antiquarians. Among many other items, we discover reviews of Arber's edition of the Stationers' Register, the Roxburghe Library, the Arber English Reprints, and the Fuller Worthies Library; the publications of the Hunterian Club, the Holbein Society, the Philobiblon Society, the English Dialect Society, the New Shakespeare Society, and the Early English Text Society. Such notices were not limited to books recently published; in many instances, such as those of the publications of printing societies, the whole run of volumes was retrospectively summarized.

The *Tobacco Plant* shared fully the current English excitement over American writers. It gave generous space to reviews of American books, two full columns, for instance, to the "Danbury News Man's" *Life in Danbury* (1873) and even more to the 1871 edition of the Hans Breitmann ballads.[9] Mark Twain was represented (December 1870) by a sketch called "Mark Twain Tells About A Pipe"—reprinted, without acknowledgment, from the New York *Galaxy*, October 1870, where it was called "A Curious Relic for Sale"—and (December 1871) by "The Anti-Tobaccoite: a Sketch from Life," which had earlier appeared, though the *Tobacco Plant* failed to say so, as one of the "Answers to Correspondents" ("Moral Statistician") in the *Jumping Frog* volume. John Hay's "Jim Bludso" was picked up from the New York *Tribune* in the *Tobacco Plant* issue for April 1871.[10] In June 1871, a full page, adorned with original drawings, was devoted to "Breitmann's Rauch-Lied," signed "Charles Godfrey Leland, London, March 16, 1871"—a fragment of the Breitmann canon not included in the standard editions. In the same issue appeared "The Fate of a Fighting Dog" by Bret Harte, a five-stanza poem which I have been unable to locate elsewhere.

34 John Ruskin, Political Economist.
35 One of our Poor Relations.
36 Dr. Kenealy, Queen's Counsellor.
37 Miss Braddon, Novelist.
38 H. W. Beecher, Brooklyn Divine. Fun.
39 Marshal MacMahon, Imperial Warning
40 Marshal Bazaine, Fugitive.
30 Holman Hunt, Figure Painter.
31 Prince Imperial, Baptised in the Purple.
32 John Hollingshead, Comic Diseuse.
33 James Greenwood, Amateur Casual.
34 Alfred Domett, Philander Snuff.
36 Mathew Arnold, Sweetness and Light.
37 Goldwin Smith, Political Lecturer.
38 A. W. Kinglake, Invasion of the Crimea.
39 John L. Motley, Rise of the Dutch Republic.
40 Orlando Dawson, Faddist.
41 Sir Henry Thompson, Cremationist.
42 Herbert Spencer, Evolutionist.
43 W. B. Carpenter, Unconscious Cerebration.
44 G. H. Lewes, Life of Goethe.
45 W. E. H. Lecky, Spirit of Rationalism.
46 John Tyndall, Scientific Imagination.
47 Charles Voysey, Heterodox Revivalist.
48 Ned Wright, Orthodox Revivalist.

33 Sir John Gilbert, Artist.
32 John Foster, Flag of Truce.
31 G. Dore, Illustrator of Rabelais.
30 Jean-Léon Gérome, Gladiator.
29 Miss Thompson, Roll Call.
28 A. B. Walker, ex-Mayor of Liverpool, Art-Gallery.
27 Dr. John Brown, Rab and his Friends.
16 Dean Stanley, Evangelical and Apostolical Teaching.
15 Dean Close, Anti-Tobacconist.
14 Charles Kingsley: Alton Locke.
13 James Smith, Printer Poet.
12 Thomas Brassey, Millionaire.
11 G. J. Holyoake, Journalist.
10 Bishop of Manchester, Working-man's Friend.
9 Tom Hughes, Tom Brown's School Days.
8 Lord John Manners, Poet and Postmaster-General.
7 F. C. Burnand, Captain Crostrees.
6 George Cruikshank, Inventor of Fagin.
5 J. H. Freswell, Modern Men of Letters.
4 Charles Bradlaugh, Political Energy.
3 E. H. Knatchbull-Hugessen, Moonshine.
2 Martin Farquhar Tupper, D.C.L., Words, Words, Words.
1 Sir Garnet J. Wolseley, Bart., K.C.B., Umbrella Coaser. Kiss Koffee Koffee-potted.

It has always been known, of course, that the second of James Thomson's discerning critical discussions of Walt Whitman was written for the *Tobacco Plant*. Bertram Dobell recorded that this essay is incomplete "owing to the fact that the *Tobacco Plant* was discontinued after the fifth section of 'Walt Whitman' had appeared in it. Two other sections were written, but these unfortunately cannot now be recovered."[11] But it is not often remembered that it was in the *Tobacco Plant* that two bits of Whitman's own writing first appeared. One was "Three Young Men's Deaths," printed in the April 1879 issue. Composed of three sections—one a letter to his mother, dated 28 July 1863, which properly belongs in the *Wound Dresser* series, the second an obituary of a fireman which had already been printed in the Camden *New Republic* for 14 November 1874, and the third a letter from John Burroughs—"Three Young Men's Deaths" found its way three years later into the *Specimen Days* volume.[12] Whitman's other contribution was the poem "The Dalliance of the Eagles," printed by Cope's in November 1880, and later absorbed into the seventh edition of *Leaves of Grass*. John Fraser seems to have been an early Whitman enthusiast; it was he who gave Thomson "the latest two-volume edition" of the poet in 1879 and "requested some articles on him."[13] No doubt he himself asked Whitman for those contributions; at least, we know that the two men corresponded. Thomson told William Michael Rossetti in a letter dated 7 April 1880 that "Whitman wrote to Fraser . . . that he never smokes; but added that he likes to carry good cigars for his friends."[14]

An annual feature of the *Tobacco Plant*, to which its readers must have looked forward eagerly, was its highly topical and mildly satirical "Christmas card," a reprint, in a special supplement to the February number, of a lithographed advertisement issued and distributed separately to tobacconists at the holiday season. The Christmas card was patently inspired by the lampoons of the Prince of Wales which began appearing in *Beeton's Christmas Annual* in 1872, but its tone was inoffensive indeed in comparison with the scurrility of the "Coming K——" series.[15] The first of the Cope series, issued at Christmas 1873, and appearing in the *Tobacco Plant* two months later, was "The Panorama of the Pipe Fumes," a crowded drawing containing caricatures of the men most talked about in England during 1873—most of them smoking pipes or cigars with obvious relish. Among the celebrities remembered today are the Tichborne Claimant, D. D. Home (the American spiritualist anathematized by Browning in "Mr. Sludge, the Medium"), Victor Emmanuel, Disraeli, Mark Twain, Ruskin (addressing a gathering of "cheap-shaggy" workmen, with an overturned locomotive in the background to attest the effectiveness of his discourse), Trollope, Longfellow, Froude, Dion Boucicault, Browning, Swinburne, and Tennyson ("the most sweetly favoured poet of the time and best of smokers"). And—since Cope's could never let their friends forget the existence of the insidious Anti-Tobacco Society, threatening their most cherished pastime—into the design was worked a portrayal of the latest victory of the Crusader and the Jester over the antinicotian Pecksniffs, Chadbands, and Stigginses.

The card for 1874, reprinted in February 1875 ("Cope," the editor commented, "celebrates Christmas *after* its time, which nobody ever thought of doing before"), introduced a new set of *literati*, among them "Wreathless" Tupper, George Cruikshank (astride a barrel and holding a tankard—a wry allusion to his years of activity in behalf of total abstinence), F. C. Burnand, Charles Kingsley, Dean Stanley, Miss Braddon, Herbert Spencer, Matthew Arnold, George Henry Lewes, and W. E. H. Lecky. The happiest hit in this drawing was the conjunction of Byron with Henry Ward Beecher, whose involvement in the Tilton scandal had been titillating newspaper readers on both sides of the Atlantic. "The real Nemesis of prosaic life," commented the gloss, "avenges the libel perpetrated upon Lord Byron by Mrs. Harriet Beecher Stowe, by accumulating upon her brother's head charges as heinous as those with which it pleased her to kick the carcass of the deceased lion."

The literary flavor of the next supplement, "Prophetic Calendar for 1876," whose central topic was the Prince of Wales's visit to India, was less marked. Again there appeared the caricatures of half-a-hundred men and women who "made the news," and among them, signifying the great popular literary events of the year, were Ouida, John Hay, Hans Breitmann, Bret Harte, and George du Maurier—along with the American revivalists Moody and Sankey, Barnum, and three composers: "The first is the Musician of the Past, for it was of him the Ghost of Hamlet's Father spoke, when he exclaimed—Liszt! Liszt! O Liszt!' The second is the Musician of the Present; for, though he be banished daily, he is Offenbach. And the third is Wagner, the Musician of the Future, whom the Liszteners would willingly relegate, with his compositions, to Posterity."

The supplement for 1877, "Cope's Arctic Card," representing the arrival of the North Pole in England, while as richly topical as its predecessors, has no literary interest. But two of the remaining Christmas cards—which are not included in the files of the *Tobacco Plant* I have examined, having been offered to subscribers separately—are of some importance because the letterpress was the work of James Thomson. The one for 1878 was "The Pilgrimage of St. Nicotine of the Holy Herb," a twenty-nine-page pamphlet of topical verse in Chaucerian style, and that for 1879 was "The Pursuit of Diva Nicotina," a burlesque of Sir Noel Paton's *Pursuit of Pleasure*.[16]

The *Tobacco Plant* expired in January 1881. A decade later, however, Cope's thriftily put some of the best of its contents to new use, in a series of fourteen *Smoke Room Booklets* issued from 1889 to 1893. A generous selection of verse and prose in praise of tobacco, some written especially for the periodical and the rest drawn from the works of various recognized authors from Isaac Hawkins Browne onward, was given in "The Smoker's Text-Book" and three pamphlets collectively called "The Smoker's Garland." "Amber: All About It," by J. G. Haddow, was based on materials collected by William Maccall and printed in the *Tobacco Plant*. "Cope's Mixture" was an anthology of excerpts from the column of that name which had run in the magazine during most of its career and which on occasion had been written by Thomson—a *causerie* on nicotian matters suggested in most cases by some bit of recent news or newspaper comment. Three other *Smoke Room Booklets* collected the curious material the *Tobacco Plant* had printed on pipes in America, Asia, Africa, Europe, and England. And, true to the bold tradition of the original publication, the series devoted several numbers to literary subjects. Number 3 was a selection from the contributions of Thomson himself. Number 4 presented "Charles Lamb in Pipefuls," generous extracts from Elia's letters and table talk; number 5 was "Thomas Carlyle: Table Talk," with a prefatory poem by Richard LeGallienne; and number 13 was the ill-fated garland of quotations from Ruskin alluded to above.

In sum, the publishing activities of the Cope firm form an honorable little chapter in the history of Victorian journalism. At a time when, in the view of many observers, England was "shooting Niagara" culturally as well as politically, with the proliferation of cheap newspapers and magazines frankly designed to strike the lowest common denominator of popular taste, the *Tobacco Plant* did its substantial bit to maintain a lively interest in literary topics among ordinary middle-class readers. Seldom, before or since, could an Englishman get as much good reading matter for his twopence. Presumably Cope's regarded their publications as a sound advertising investment; otherwise they would not have supported the *Tobacco Plant* for eleven years. What would happen in our day if a leading cigarette company diverted even a small fraction of its annual multi-million-dollar advertising budget to the support of a cheap literary review? That way, the monarchs of commercial propaganda would cry in unison, madness lies; and they would surely be right. Our depleted cultural soil is not one in which *Tobacco Plants* can flourish.[17]

1951

14

The Reading Public in England
and America in 1900

t the turn of the century, more people were reading, and a
larger quantity of printed matter was being produced, than
ever before in the history of the English-speaking world. In
Lord Salisbury's Britain and President McKinley's America,
the continuing steady growth of the mass reading audience and the refinement of the various instruments designed to serve it were witness to the
power the printed word had acquired in the course of the nineteenth
century. In terms of popular culture, if not of politics, the dictum of Finley
Peter Dunne's Chicago saloon-keeper, Mr. Dooley, was wholly accurate:
"Yes sir, th' hand that rocks th' fountain pen is th' hand that rules th'
wurruld."

The similarities between the British mass audience and that of the
United States in 1900 were more numerous than the differences: a
circumstance the more striking because they were the products of quite
dissimilar developments. In Britain, the existence of millions of habitual readers represented the long-delayed triumph of the idea of social and
cultural democracy over the powerful forces that for centuries had
opposed the spread of reading for any but narrowly religious purposes
throughout the lower stratum of the enlarging middle class and into the
very ranks of the workers. It had been a hard-won victory, with effects on
the national culture that were then, as they have remained, the topic of
endless controversy and concern. In America there had been no such
struggle. The "right to read" had always been implicit in the premises of
American society; no body of clergy, no aristocracy, no political faction
had ever, in any important way, ventured to deny it. In the one nation,
therefore, the reading public was the product of many decades of social
friction, anxiety, and attempted repression; in the other, it was the un-
scarred fruit of social evolution.

Britons of the era agreed that the state of reading in the United States
was markedly superior to that at home. The historian E. A. Freeman,
writing in 1883, called America "the land of the 'general reader' "; five
years later James Bryce, in his classic work *The American Commonwealth*,
declared that "Nowhere in the world is there growing up such a vast

multitude of intelligent, cultivated, and curious readers." Most Americans were of the same mind. One, writing in the *Forum* (December 1894), enumerated the various factors that, he believed, made his nation more of a reading one than the English, and concluded that "the great bulk of the English read nothing, literally nothing." That this was mere exuberant American hyperbole is proved by sales figures of the sort that are presented below. But it is probably true that, relative to the total population, America had a larger body of readers than did Britain. It may also be true that, as Freeman maintained, "the class of those who read widely, who read, as far as they go, intelligently, but who do not read deeply—the class of those who, without being professed scholars, read enough and know enough to be quite worth talking to—form a larger proportion of mankind in America than they do in England."

According to the same *Forum* writer, the reason for England's inferiority in this respect was that "a very large number of intelligent people . . . are altogether opposed to free general education . . . [They] hold that the children, as of old, in each parish, should be taught to read and write and to say their catechism in the schools under the supervision of the clergy, and then earn a living as did their forefathers." Here he was clearly misinformed: in the 1890s nobody, except perhaps the few extreme reactionaries who survive in every age, held such opinions. But in the earlier part of the century they had been influential enough, and popular education was still paying the price at its end. As national life had been transformed by the simultaneous shift from an agrarian to an industrial economy and from a rural to a predominantly urban population, the practical necessity of literacy had steadily increased. In factories and mills, in city shops and streets, illiterate men and women were at an ever greater disadvantage both in their occupation and in the everyday routine of living. In the earlier part of the century these pressures had been met by equally strong counterforces, chiefly stemming from the fear of a potentially revolutionary populace (a chronic English anxiety from the time of the French Revolution to the Chartist fiasco of 1848), that opposed any but the most rudimentary education for the masses. Responsibility for providing this had been assumed by the rival educational organizations of Church and dissent, whose "voluntary" schools did what they could within the stringent limitations of their funds and of their aims, which remained prudently modest. Successive attempts to shift a major portion of the financing and management of elementary schools to the state had foundered on the venerable and still formidable religious issue: Church and dissent, though they agreed on nothing else in connection with their educational mission, concurred in resisting any inroads of secularization. Until 1870, the state's role in education had been confined to small annual grants made to the voluntary schools, a loose system of inspection that had been imposed as a condition of the grants, and a much deplored scheme of "payment by results," which determined the annual amount of a school's subsidy on the basis of the number of pupils who passed the standards set in the various subjects. As a result, the schools attended by working-class children were poorly housed and equipped, incompetently taught, and generally so inefficient that the millions who—to use a grossly inapplicable word—enjoyed such education were hardly better off than the thousands who never went to school at all, as was the case in some parts of the countryside and in the slums of the new mill and factory cities.

While it is true, therefore, that in absolute terms educational opportunity did spread throughout the century, it lagged far behind the need, in respect both to the numbers to be taught and to the changing conditions that made literacy increasingly indispensable. Only in 1870 did an act of Parliament provide for the state education of children unreached by voluntary schools. Only in 1880 did another law make attendance compulsory for children between the ages of five and ten. But the law was full of loopholes and unevenly enforced, and in any case the quality of instruction remained very poor. Not until the very last years of the century, moreover, were there enough places for all the children who by law should have been in school.

On the whole, America was better off, but such superiority as it possessed should not be exaggerated. The principle of tax-supported education had been accepted in the North as early as the middle of the century, but the schools made available on this principle had been slow in appearing, and in the South, whose school system was shattered by the Civil War, they were almost nonexistent. By 1900, some thirty states had enacted compulsory laws, typically requiring children between eight and fourteen to attend school from twelve to sixteen weeks a year. As in England, however, the degree of enforcement varied from place to place, and children in the country attended school for much shorter periods than did their city cousins. Although the nation was experiencing what one historian would later call "the educational revival" at the turn of the century, the marked improvements in American elementary education—longer terms of attendance, provision of free textbooks in a score of states, gradual substitution of consolidated rural schools for the picturesque but primitive one-room establishments—had come too late to affect the millions who comprised the adult audience of 1900. The average adult American of that year had the equivalent of no more than four or five years of formal schooling.

Literacy figures, inseparable though they are from any discussion of the reading public, are (here as always) undependable indexes of size or quality. On the English side one thing, at least, is certain: despite the common assumption that persists even today, the Forster Education Act of 1870 did not dramatically hasten the spread of literacy. In the two preceding decades, the literacy rate for males had increased by 11.3 percent and for females by 18.4; in the next two decades, the rate of increase was 13.0 and 19.5 respectively. The chief effect of the 1870 law was that it underwrote elementary education in those areas of the nation that had previously been the most neglected; it was there, supposedly, that the greatest gains in literacy occurred between 1871 and 1891, the year of the first census that fully reflected the results of the state's decisive intervention in educational affairs.

In 1900 the literacy rate in England and Wales was approximately 97 percent. This figure, however, represents only those young men and women who, upon being married in that year, were able to sign their names. It does not reveal how many could actually read—a quite different accomplishment from the mechanical one of scrawling a signature—and it is useless as an indication of the understanding with which the brides and bridegrooms could read, if they read at all. Moreover, it takes no account of the millions of older persons who, having had less chance to learn to read in their own youth, greatly reduced the real percentage of literacy in the population as a whole. These older persons formed no market whatever for reading matter, a fact too often obscured by the size of the population that did, but one that must be remembered if the mass reading public is to be seen in its proper perspective.

No simple comparison is possible with America, whose own literacy rate—a little above 89 percent in the census of 1900—was based on the ability of persons ten years of age or older to read their own language. The greatest incidence of illiteracy was found, not surprisingly, among the large immigrant population and in the South. If the American criterion had been applied in Britain, it is likely that the British literacy rate would have proved to be no higher than the American one, if indeed as high. However that may be, the nature of the reading material that sold in greatest quantities, both in England and in America, makes it plain that the possession of what might be called statistical literacy, doubtfully enriched by the educational experience that produced it, did not encourage the average working-class reader to aspire beyond the magazines and newspapers that were carefully designed for his limited comprehension.

America had at least this one clear-cut educational advantage over Britain: the abler or more fortunate children, mainly in the cities, could continue beyond the elementary grades. In twenty years (1878–98) the number of high schools in the country had risen from fewer than 800 to 5,500, and the number of pupils from fewer than 100,000 to more than half a million. The products of this system might reasonably have been expected to constitute an audience for a somewhat higher level of reading matter than that to which those who had had no more than an elementary education were normally limited. In England, by contrast, no laws as yet provided for state-supported schooling beyond the first few years—a small beginning was to be made with Balfour's Act in 1902—and the existing provision for secondary education was decidedly inadequate. It is true that toward the turn of the century, in belated response to Germany's well-attested superiority in scientific and engineering training that enabled her to surpass Britain in the competition for world markets, a certain amount of technical instruction had been made available in the manufacturing centers. Otherwise conditions had not improved markedly since 1868, when the Taunton Commission declared that two-thirds of English towns entirely lacked schools above the primary level and most of the remaining one-third had schools whose advanced level was noticeable only in name. Analysis of the figures collected at the time that the Bryce Commission inquired into secondary education (1895) has led recent historians to hazard the guess that there were then about 75,000 pupils in the 621 endowed secondary schools reporting; but of these, no more than 30,000 to 40,000 (including the boys in the ancient public schools, which always made some pretense, however anachronistic, of preparing their students for intellectual maturity) were receiving what would be regarded in the twentieth century as a satisfactory secondary education. Altogether, enrollment in secondary schools of all kinds, including non-profit-making schools of varying merit, did not exceed 2.5 per thousand of the population. Education beyond the twelfth or thirteenth year was still widely regarded as a privilege of the middle class, to which only the most exceptional child from the working class was entitled. Inherited notions of class structure and prerogatives thus continued to govern educational thinking, which for the most part was considerably in arrears of the actual social situation.

In Scotland, however, the story was different, as indeed it had been ever since the ideal of schooling for all had been formulated in John Knox's *First Book of Discipline* (1559). During the intervening period, though with a decided lapse in the eighteenth century, an uncoordinated but effective combination of parish and burgh (municipal) effort had made elementary schooling accessible to virtually every Scots child, and secondary education, even university training, to all boys who were qualified, regardless of social class. The universal democratic education toward which England groped throughout the nineteenth century had long since been an established fact north of the Tweed. It was no accident that some of the most influential contributions toward the formation of a mass British reading public had originated in Scotland, with Lord Brougham (the advocate of popular education), George Birkbeck (the originator of the mechanics' institutes), Archibald Constable and the brothers William and Robert Chambers (pioneers of cheap books and periodicals), and Samuel Brown (founder of the "itinerating libraries" in East Lothian, which helped to prepare the way for public libraries). In 1872 the Education (Scotland) Act—which, significantly, omitted the word "elementary" from its description of the education aimed for, and specified "the children of the *whole* people of Scotland" as the intended beneficiaries—took over the chaotic patchwork of Scottish schools from the church, the burghs, sectarian bodies, and private societies and individuals, and brought them together under elected school boards. Although the new demand for uniform quality led to a temporary concentration of national educational energies upon improving the teaching of the "ordinary branches," higher education remained available to the most promising of the young, thanks partly to the opportune channeling of income from obsolete charitable endowments into foundations (scholarships) and bursaries.

To make good the general lack of formal educational opportunity beyond the elementary level, England adopted various schemes. In the period 1825–75, mechanics' institutes had provided courses of evening lectures, libraries, and in some cases classes for the ambitious workingmen, artisans, and clerks of hundreds of towns. In the last quarter of the century, the movement lost its momentum as well as such social homogeneity as it had earlier possessed. In the north of England it continued to serve primarily craftsmen, operatives, and other members of the laboring class and lower-middle class. In 1891 the Yorkshire Union of 280 institutes had some 60,000 members, most of whom belonged for the sake of acquiring a certain amount of technical knowledge. A number of institutes in Yorkshire and elsewhere had, as a matter of fact, already been transformed into technical schools, supported in part by local grants. But at the same time, the Yorkshire Union continued the mechanics' institutes' long-standing practice of circulating books to its members. It maintained a library of 30,000 volumes, which were distributed to 200 remote villages as yet untouched by the public library movement. In the south of England, meanwhile, the clientele of the institutes was predominantly middle class and the emphasis was on general "literary and philosophical" lectures and lighter entertainment. In some instances they, too, continued to maintain their libraries, although in others the mechanics' institute buildings and book stocks had been taken over as the nucleus of a rate-supported public library.

A second important means of providing education beyond the elementary level in England was university extension. Originating in the desire to make university training available to poor students, and given additional impetus by one of the questions left unanswered by the Forster Act—what shall be done with those whose hunger for learning is only sharpened, not satisfied, by compulsory elementary schooling?—the movement got under way in the 1870s. Despite many disappointments and generally slow progress, in the last fifteen years of the century and the first decade of the new, extension courses offered in various towns by Oxford, Cambridge, and London universities attracted some 50,000 men and women each year. These adult seekers after knowledge, however, were chiefly of the middle class. Only between one-quarter and one-fifth of them, and these mainly in the north, were from the ranks of the workers. University extension as originally constituted failed in its aim of bringing a liberal education to the laboring class, partly because the local sponsoring committees were middle class and therefore (as had also been too often the case with sponsors of the mechanics' institutes) suspected of ulterior motives, and partly because of difficulties in financing. Not until 1905 did the universities and the organized working-class movement join in a successful concerted effort to provide part-time continued education to the workers, principally in the form of tutorial classes. It was then that Albert Mansbridge saw a proposal he had made two years earlier flower into the Workers' Educational Association, a federation of the educational arms of numerous cooperative societies and trade unions that was to be the most successful and influential adult-education agency in the new century.

Toward the end of the 1880s, attempts had been made to introduce university extension on the English model into the United States. But the courses organized by a few universities—notably that of Chicago, under its vigorous president, William Rainey Harper—had but a brief success, and only in 1906 was the extension scheme to be revitalized under the leadership of the University of Wisconsin. Meanwhile, its purposes were served in two other, characteristically American ways. The public libraries of some larger cities, obedient to the wider conception of community service through adult education that distinguished the American library movement from the British, sponsored courses of university-level lectures. And, more important, the well-established and popular Chautauqua program was enlarged to include a Literary and Scientific Circle that during the 1890s enrolled some 100,000 Americans, half of whom were between thirty and forty years of age, in courses of home reading. By 1900, some 50,000 such students had "graduated" after four years of directed reading. The British equivalent of this institution was the Home Reading Union, founded in 1889 by James Bryce, the philologist Max Müller, Archdeacon Farrar, the philosopher Frederic Harrison, and others, which sought the same end—education through purposeful fireside reading—by the same means: reading lists, monthly magazines, neighborhood discussion circles, and summer assemblies.

In both Britain and the United States, the tendency in these various instruments of adult education that had the most pronounced effect on the tone of the reading public was the increasing presence of women. Like their transatlantic cousins who had long attended the lyceums (the venerable and influential counterparts of the mechanics' institutes, devoted especially to lectures and libraries), English women had long been active in the cultural and social programs of the mechanics' institutes, especially in those towns where the middle class, rather than the workers, dominated the organization. But now women began to swell the audiences for the afternoon series of university extension lectures and classes, and formed the majority in the home reading circles; and in America they organized the innumerable "culture clubs," dedicated to the more or less earnest study of art and literature, that soon became a familiar and, to some observers, perennially risible part of the social scene. In the United States, where female higher education had met considerably less resistance than in Britain, young women remained at school beyond the elementary grades in ever-growing numbers; in the single year 1900, indeed, 37,000 had gone beyond high school to become students in normal (teacher-training) colleges, and 25,000 more were in regular colleges and universities. On both sides of the ocean, women had generally greater educational opportunities, possessed a larger portion of leisure (thanks to labor-saving appliances and similar blessings), and enjoyed a many-sided "emancipation" that was a widely publicized social phenomenon of the 1890s.

All these factors combined to increase the woman reader's consumption of print. And, as a consumer, she acquired greater power over what was produced for popular consumption than had been wielded even by the middle-class women of previous generations, especially in England, under whose ever-present threat of disfavor such writers as Dickens and Thackeray—to say nothing of all publishers, and the submissive Mr. Mudie of the circulating library—had labored. To adapt Mr. Dooley's dictum to a new use, the hand that rocked the cradle was the hand that ruled the pens of popular authors and commanded the consciences of editors. No analysis of contemporary literary taste and taboo can overlook the numerous and assertive presence of women as wives, mothers, and guardians of morality and decorum.

On balance, the conditions of everyday life in Britain around 1900 favored the cultivation of the reading habit. Because of the gradual increase of real income and the fall of prices, including that of printed matter, the ordinary man, earning say thirty-eight shillings a week, could afford sixpennyworth of reading matter more often than had been possible for his father. Although the crowding that had made private reading so impracticable a recreation in countless Victorian households was not noticeably lessened, another requisite for comfortable application to a book or paper—adequate illumination—had become more available. In the country, to be sure, the dim old standbys, candles and paraffin lamps, persisted; but in town and city, gas lighting (greatly improved by the invention of the Welsbach mantle in 1885), and in the most favored households the incandescent electric lamp, had eliminated what had been, in the earlier part of the century, one of the gravest obstacles to the free indulgence of the reading habit. On the other hand, except for the fortunate few who belonged to the "leisured class," during six days of the week the time for reading was severely limited. In the great majority of occupations one of the classic goals of the labor movement, the eight-hour day and forty-hour week, was nowhere in sight. As late as 1913, the standard working week in Britain was to range from forty-six to fifty-six hours, and in the United States from forty-four to sixty-six.

The small additions to leisure time that changing conditions provided in 1900 had many claimants. Outdoor sports, both participant and spectator, were increasingly popular: the football and the cricket or baseball bat competed with the book for attention. In 1900, furthermore, the bicycle craze that had been one of the great international social phenomena of the 1890s was far from over. In America, where it was estimated that one million bicycles were in use, the rivalry of the pneumatic tire with the printed word was so strenuous that booksellers, it was reported, proposed to fight impending losses by adding cycles to their wares.

Fifty years earlier, in Britain and America, the principle that libraries open to all might be supported from tax funds had won formal acceptance. The passage of Ewart's bill (1850), which enabled local authorities to levy rates for building libraries, was a landmark in the history of mid-Victorian social improvement, the latest in a series of measures that, it was hoped, would ease social tensions and remove the ever-present threat of unruliness (or worse) on the part of the working population. If religion had proved ineffective as the opiate of the people, wholesome reading matter, made freely available in libraries, would succeed; the printed word would also prove a beneficent substitute for the public house. Such hopes, expressed by orators at the dedication of scores of libraries built under Ewart's Act, epitomized the widespread Victorian faith in the power of print. Unfortunately, however, these high expectations had not been fulfilled. The pace of library building, slow in the first decades after the enabling legislation was passed, was still hobbled at the end of the century by various difficulties, such as the statutory provision that no more than a penny in the pound could be levied for library purposes. Once the buildings were erected, further difficulties presented themselves: the selection of books was often grotesquely inappropriate for a lower-middle- and working-class clientele; the atmosphere in some libraries was not conducive to quiet reading; and librarians and the local "friends of the library" were too often censorious and patronizing in the relations with readers and borrowers and in their supervision of clients' tastes.

Nevertheless, by the time of the Queen's golden jubilee in 1887 the public library movement had gathered momentum. The inadequate financial support derived from the rates was supplemented by philanthropists such as J. Passmore Edwards, the millionaire newspaper proprietor, who endowed numerous London libraries, and above all by Andrew Carnegie, whose benefactions, starting in his native Dunfermline in 1881, extended to England in 1897 and were to reach their peak in 1900–5. Assisted by new legislation (1893 for England, 1894 for Scotland) that allowed local authorities to "adopt the acts" by resolution rather than rely on the problematic success of a popular referendum, many communities that had hitherto been without public libraries now acquired them. Between 1880 and 1889, some sixty-five rate-supported libraries were founded; in the next decade 153 more were built. The total number of such libraries in 1900 was approximately 500. Even so, in England there was only one municipal library for every 88,943 of population (in Scotland 93,619), and it was asserted that in every community that did possess a library—a number of populous towns were still without one—95 percent of the people were indifferent to its presence. As a self-styled "Working Woman" candidly put it in *Chambers's Journal* in 1899, the working class, for whom the libraries had been established, had found little use for them. "In spite of modern civilization and modern education, working men, but more especially working women, have . . . 'as much use for learning as a cow has for clogs.' . . . There is absolutely nothing in the home life to encourage a taste for literary pursuits." It is true that a certain number of working-class children used the libraries, but their choice of books merely swelled the total of fiction circulated—which constituted about eighty percent of all books issued, a figure that persistently disturbed librarians and their local sponsors—and in mature life they ceased to borrow books of any kind.

Here again the United States was more fortunate. Public libraries had sprung up in most cities and towns following the establishment of the first major tax-supported library, the Boston Public Library, at mid-century. By 1900 most of the states has passed legislation permitting (and in New Hampshire, requiring) the use of tax funds to establish and maintain such facilities, as well as setting up centralized libraries to serve the whole state. In addition to tax revenues, some thirty-six million dollars in private benefactions (including Carnegie's) had flowed to libraries in the two decades preceding 1900. In that year there were over 1,700 free circulating libraries that possessed book stocks of more than 5,000 volumes, and the total number of volumes owned by American public libraries was about forty-seven million, compared with five million in Britain.

A comparison of the British and American library situations is incomplete and misleading without mention of the English commercial libraries, which had no really important counterpart in America. During the high Victorian era, Mudie's Select Circulating Library had had a central, indeed crucial, role in supplying books to the middle class. When it declined in prosperity at the turn of the century, it was replaced by a host of cheaper rental- and subscription-libraries, the most famous of which, begun in 1900, were those of Boots, the retail chemist chain. Meanwhile the firm of W. H. Smith and Son, which half a century earlier had leased its stands on railway platforms throughout England, was doing a thriving rental business in addition to selling great quantities of newspapers, magazines, and cheap books to the traveler. It was reported about 1900 that, of the 50,000 copies initially printed of a new novel by, say, Marie

Corelli, no fewer than 10,000 were earmarked for the circulating librar-ies. These commercial outlets catered to a major portion of the book-borrowing public, which in America, by contrast, tended to rely on municipal libraries.

The fading of Mudie's library was the direct result of a long-overdue event that occurred in 1894: the demise of the expensive three-decker novel, costing more than thirty shillings, whose survival, sustained by the self-interested collaboration of publishers and circulating libraries, had kept the price of original editions artificially high throughout the century, despite the many successful experiments with cheap reprints that had enlivened British publishing since before Victoria came to the throne. Now, finally, the price of books could (in theory at least) find its natural level. All technical barriers to cheapness had been overcome. Chemistry had made paper much less costly; a series of inventions had made possible the swift setting of type, the mechanized printing, folding, and gathering of sheets, and the prefabrication of casings in large quantities.

To some extent counterbalancing this tendency toward cheapness, however, were two new developments. One was the increased proportion of the total expense of producing a new book that was devoted to adver-tising and to paying authors. By 1900 the old practice of buying a literary property outright from the author had been almost entirely replaced by the royalty system, which meant that in the case of any moderately suc-cessful book, payment to the author continued to be a running charge against profits throughout the book's life instead of being written off, as before, after a relatively short period. Aware, moreover, of the great profits that publishers made with popular books, and stirred (by Sir Wal-ter Besant and his Society of Authors) to demanding what they deemed their fair share of those profits, writers for both book publishers and periodicals were receiving better pay than ever before.

Missing from the Anglo-American publishing scene in 1900, also, was one potent element that throughout the century had kept a certain large category of books in each country artificially cheap, so to speak, and their authors unwarrantedly poor. This was the lack of international copyright, an omission of justice finally remedied in 1891. Because of it, American works had been pirated at will by British publishers, the retail prices being far below those of comparable books that bore British copyrights. American publishers returned the compliment with great enthusiasm and gain. In 1886, for example, Hardy's *The Mayor of Casterbridge* had appeared in seven American editions, only two of which were authorized, ranging in price from one dollar to twenty cents. The books of Robert Louis Stevenson and such individual titles as Mrs. Humphry Ward's *Robert Elsmere* (1888) and H. Rider Haggard's *Cleopatra* (1889), which had at least ten American editions, were appropriated with similar freedom, the result being so many competing editions that often nobody—author, designated publisher, or pirate—made any money. With the introduction of international copyright, the proportion of American to British works on American publishers' lists sharply increased, with an inverted effect, of course, in Britain. Although the impecunious book lover who had bought cheap pirated editions was temporarily the loser, the new agreement had the salutary effect of stabilizing a trade hitherto afflicted with cut-throat competition and of making possible the production and sale of equally cheap books on a legitimate basis.

In 1900 the average British price of a novel in its original edition was 6s.—a welcome decline from the old three-decker price of 31s. 6d. Original nonfiction ranged from 7s. 6d. to 21s. Cloth-bound reprints of original fiction cost 2s. 6d. or 3s. 6d., and a wide variety of books by recent or currently popular novelists (Reade, Collins, Hall Caine, Marion Crawford, Clark Russell, William Black, Stevenson) could be bought in paper covers for only 6d. These sold in vast quantities: a sixpenny *Lorna Doone* (1896), for example, had an advance order of 100,000 copies. But even these bargains were not the cheapest books on the market. Noncopyright reprints of older romances and sensational novels were priced at 3d., and below them were abridgments of standard fiction (such as W. T. Stead's Penny Novelist series), more or less complete texts of tales and novels (Newnes's Penny Library of Famous Books), and collections of poetry (Stead's Penny Poets). By 1900, as I observed in *The English Common Reader,* "books had become so cheap that seemingly the only step remaining was to give them away. But these paperbacks were a credit to the bookmaker only in a strictly technological sense. Aesthetic appeal and durability had been almost wholly sacrificed to economy." The reader who liked his books to be comely was not overlooked, however. In the mid-1890s J. M. Dent had introduced his Temple Shakespeare, one play per shilling volume, in well-designed, convenient, and durable format. This and the immediately following Temple Classics series were the precursors of the immensely successful and influential Everyman's Library, which began in 1906, and of the World's Classics series, initiated by Grant Richards in 1901 but soon transferred to the Oxford University Press. Such series of classic reprints proved that cheap books could also be physically attractive.

The result of all this activity was that books, whether bound in cloth or in perishable paper, were now familiar objects in countless British homes that earlier had known only the Bible, perhaps a few tracts or other examples of gratuitously distributed religious literature, and cheap weekly papers. This was the case also in America, where the flood of cheap books had begun in the 1870s, partly as a consequence of providing paperbacks (especially dime novels) for the soldiers in the Civil War. Where England had, for instance, the remarkably prolific and long-lived Railway Library (Routledge), which by 1898 had reprinted 1,300 novels in 2s., 1s. 6d., and 1s. formats, the United States had its Lakeside, Fireside, Seaside, Franklin Square, and similar "libraries." Some of these cheap series, such as Street and Smith's Log Cabin series, were composed of old but still popular dime novels; others, as in England, were reprints of uncopyrighted current literature.

American prices of new books were roughly equivalent to those in Britain. New novels could be bought for $1.00 or $1.25 in cloth and for fifty cents in paper. Serious nonfiction cost somewhat more. Hardbound reprints were about to appear: shortly after 1900, the firm of A. L. Burt was to reprint many copyright editions by arrangement with the original publishers, soon to be followed and surpassed by Grosset and Dunlap, whose first reprinted title, Paul Leicester Ford's *Janice Meredith* (1903), sold several hundred thousand copies after sales of the original edition had begun to decline.

On both sides of the Atlantic, regular bookshops were outflanked and outsold by newer agencies of distribution. It is true that the bookselling business has at least as much claim to the sobriquet "the fabulous invalid" as the Broadway theatre, but about the turn of the century the perennial complaints of retailers had more substance than usual. The multitude of paperback volumes that flowed from the high-speed presses could be bought at stalls operated at every railway station by the great wholesaling and retailing firms, W. H. Smith and Son in Britain, the American News Company in the United States. In addition, British drapers' shops and American department stores sold books at prices below those asked by booksellers. In the former, the buyer could expect a discount of as much as fifteen percent; in the latter, he could benefit not only by the reduced prices of the department stores' "book bazaars" but also by what are now called tie-in deals: with the purchase of, say a pair of gloves, he was entitled to buy any book in the store for only twenty-five cents. The Net Book Agreement negotiated by British publishers and booksellers in 1899 largely, but not entirely, ended price cutting on books bearing a catalogue price of 6s. or more, but it did not affect cheaper publications. In America, a similar arrangement put a stop to discounts on nonfiction books by most department stores (Macy's, the great New York store, continued to offer discounts for many years) but another decade was to pass before fiction was price-fixed.

Americans could also buy books through subscription schemes peddled by door-to-door salesmen. Their portable "lists" included reference works, sets of poets and novelists, and individual titles by such celebrities as Horace Greeley, P. T. Barnum, Henry Ward Beecher, and President Grant (whose memoirs, published and distributed in this fashion by Mark Twain in a short-lived and disastrous venture in get-rich-quick publishing, sold 312,000 in the first thirty months). In the 1890s the subscription book business had an annual volume of twelve million dollars. Publishers specializing in such books were said to turn a cold eye upon any book offered them that could not be depended upon to sell 100,000 copies.

A third channel of American book distribution, which in 1900 was said to be as important as that of regular bookshops and subscription selling in a land where only two or three percent of the people lived near bookshops, was the mail-order service available from every publisher. Thanks to this, and with the aid of the rural free delivery postal routes inaugurated in 1897, books conquered the great distances that had been one of the chief barriers to the dissemination of culture on the American continent.

The American publishing industry had a long tradition of "respectability" and conservatism. Only toward 1900 had it adopted the policy, cultivated for some years past by the livelier sections of the British trade, of lavish advertising and the use of publicity campaigns specially tailored to sell individual titles for which great hopes were entertained. Once roused from their gentlemanly lethargy, the leading American publishers outdid their British colleagues in promotional activity. In 1900 most houses had an annual advertising budget of $50,000 or more, and one was reported to spend a quarter of a million dollars a year. In 1900 the first full-page newspaper advertisement in trade history started Maurice Thompson's historical novel, *Alice of Old Vincennes,* on its highly prosperous career. If people still did not buy books on the scale publishers dreamed of—though one hears little complaint on that score from the successful firms of the period—it was not for lack of encouragement. Provocative advertising, the hustling salesmanship of department-store book sections, the cajolery of canvassers, the economic attractiveness of premium arrangements such as that which included a free book with every purchase of a quantity of soap (in the mid-1880s the publisher of the Seaside Library had unloaded three million unsold books on soap companies), and the well-publicized presence of mail-order desks within reach of everyone with a postage stamp—all these devices thrust books into the consciousness of every American.

It was only fitting, therefore, that these years should have witnessed the birth of the word "best-seller": an example of language promptly filling an urgent new need. Although the *Dictionary of Americanisms* dates the word only from 1905, it was actually in use as early as 1897, in connection with the list of "the most popular new books" that the New York *Bookman* had been running since its first issue, two years earlier. The periodical's London namesake had been featuring a similar monthly list since it began in 1891. This was, in truth, the great age of the best-seller. Records were set during these years that were to stand for a long time. Between 1900 and 1915 no fewer than nineteen books sold over one million copies each in America: in the next fifteen years, only three books did so (Edith M. Hull's *The Sheik*, H. G. Wells's *Outline of History*, and Will Durant's *Story of Philosophy*). Nearly all of those nineteen, in contrast to one of the subsequent three, were fiction. In 1901, six novels sold 150,000 each in the United States, and nine more exceeded 100,000. A book about a shrewd Yankee horse dealer, Edward Noyes Westcott's *David Harum* (1898), had sold more than 400,000 copies by early 1901, and 750,000 by 1904; riding the wave of its popularity, in a pattern often noticed during the period, a novel with a similar appeal, Irving Bacheller's *Eben Holden*, sold 300,000 copies in 1900 between July and Christmas. A sentimental little book set in the Louisville factory slums, Alice Hegan Rice's *Mrs. Wiggs of the Cabbage Patch* (1901), was on the best-seller lists for two years, in the course of which the printers had to supply 40,000 copies a month. American historical romances were especially in demand. In 1899 the genre was represented by *Janice Meredith*, which had sold 275,000 copies by the end of 1902, and by Winston Churchill's *Richard Carvel*, whose record was 520,000 copies in two years; in 1900 Mary Johnston's *To Have and To Hold* sold 200,000 copies within two months of publication.

Such novels, of course, appealed principally to American tastes. But otherwise, the color of British and American best-seller lists in this epoch was strikingly homogeneous. The historical romance with an American setting was merely one variety of a larger genre that dominated popular literature for at least a decade: the romance of sword-play and high adventure, whether set in historical times or with a contemporary but exotic setting, or having its *mise en scène* in a fictitious realm (such as George

Barr McCutcheon's Graustark). Authors such as Rider Haggard, Anthony Hope, Stanley Weyman, and F. Marion Crawford—three Britons, one American—won success writing this kind of fiction. One particular type of historical novel that was equally popular in both countries was that set in early Christian times, preferably the decadent age of Nero, when religion could be mixed with a faint suggestion of sex—a sure-fire formula for a best-seller then as (occasionally) now. In the wake of Henryk Sienkiewicz's *Quo Vadis?*, which had swept the Anglo-American world in the mid-1890s, came such hits as Hall Caine's *The Eternal City* (1901), which had an American first printing of 200,000 copies, and *The Christian,* which sold 50,000 in the first month of British publication; and Marie Corelli's *The Master Christian* (1900), which had a prepublication printing of 75,000—the largest on record, according to its London publishers.

Tastes in these "fat years of fiction," as they were later to be called, were nothing if not catholic. For a while there was a vogue for *Gemütlichkeit* of the "kailyard school" exemplified by J. M. Barrie's *Auld Licht Idylls* (1888) and *A Window in Thrums* (1889) and by "Ian Maclaren's" *Beside the Bonnie Brier Bush* (1894), which, assisted (as was Barrie's *The Little Minister*) by a defective copyright, sold nearly one million copies in America in a few years. If a reader preferred contemporary theological quandaries wrapped up in fiction, he could select *Robert Elsmere,* whose success in America was even greater than in England; or if he wanted religion tinged with social criticism there was the Rev. Charles M. Sheldon's *In His Steps,* a moral romance that first appeared, without benefit of copyright, in a denominational paper in Topeka, Kansas, was quickly discovered by ten publishers, and ultimately sold, according to conservative estimates, a world total of six million copies, one-third of them in the United States.

Notwithstanding the impression conveyed by these sample sales figures, which certify beyond a doubt that more people were buying books than ever before, it remains true that in both Britain and America the majority of literate men and women, whether by choice or by necessity, never opened a book. Their experience of print, and therefore, in those precinema, preradio, pretelevision days, their only experience of the world beyond the narrow sphere of their daily lives, was confined to magazines and newspapers. In Britain, where experiments in suiting periodicals to the tastes and capacities of the semiliterate masses had been going on ever since the 1830s, dramatic breakthroughs occurred in the last years of the century. Among them, the three titans of late-Victorian journalism, George Newnes (*Tit-Bits,* 1881), Alfred Harmsworth (*Answers to*

Correspondents, 1888), and Cyril Pearson (*Pearson's Weekly*, 1890), developed a formula of anecdotes, jokes, excerpts, riddles—everything simple, nothing profound, something for everyone, and no long attention span required—that won millions of new readers who lacked the education, the intellectual energy, the time, or the money to read anything more substantial. By the end of the 1890s, each of these magazines was selling between 400,000 and 600,000 copies a week, and a prize contest—a much-employed circulation-building device in the journalism of this fiercely competitive epoch—once sent *Pearson's Weekly*'s sales up to a million and a quarter. On a somewhat higher level, meanwhile, the most popular magazines—the *Strand, Windsor,* and *Pearson's,* priced at between 3*d.* and 6*d.*—had circulations of between 200,000 and 400,000. But even these unprecedented figures were soon surpassed by newcomers: in 1898 *Harmsworth's Magazine* started at 500,000 and approached one million, and in the same year Pearson's *Royal Magazine* started at one million and immediately trained its sights on a second. In addition to its nice balance of fiction and topical articles, this class of periodicals exploited the newly perfected technique of photoengraving, which, by replacing the expensive and laborious woodcut with the cheap half-tone, permitted a freer and more flexible use of illustrations. In 1890 there had been five illustrated papers on the English bookstalls; in 1899 there were thirteen.

Similar prosperity visited other segments of this feverishly expanding mass journalism. Women and children, if not the prime targets, were certainly not neglected. *Woman's Life,* a Newnes inspiration, sold 200,000 copies a week in 1896; in the same field, competing with a more or less standard assortment of fiction, needlework patterns, domestic hints, and fragments of easily assimilable general information, were such papers as *Home Chat, Our Home, The Happy Home,* and *Home Notes.* For the factory girl there was *Forget-Me-Not,* and for the errand boy, *Chips;* Harmsworth, whose properties these were, had a special Midas touch with papers for the child and adolescent. Building energetically on the foundations laid long before by Reynolds and Lloyd, the early Victorian penny-dreadful magnates, he established or revived during the 1890s a whole galaxy of sensational fiction papers for boys—*Union Jack,* the *Halfpenny Wonder,* the *Halfpenny Marvel,* and the *Boys' Friend*—some of which flourished as late as the Second World War. Only a few older juvenile papers, notably the Religious Tract Society's *Boy's Own Paper,* survived their keen competition. It was Harmsworth's periodicals, after all, not the more sedate Tract Society's, that year after year featured the detective hero Sexton Blake.

The same ferment and spectacular expansion characterized the American magazine world, which had long profited from the lack of an international copyright law, by an efficient and cheap postal system, and by its ability to command the nation's best writing and editorial talent. The inventive editors of Fleet Street had their counterparts in such figures as S. S. McClure and Edward Bok, a young Dutch immigrant whose innovations, among them a zeal for public-spirited crusades on behalf of causes especially meaningful to the housewife and mother, made his *Ladies' Home Journal* the most popular of all the magazines for the middle-class American home. Priced at ten cents, the *Journal* was typical of the meaty, well-illustrated, general periodicals—*McClure's, Munsey's,* and *Cosmopolitan* were others—that gave better value for the money than had their predecessors selling for twenty-five or thirty cents a copy. The audience discovered and served by these magazines—a substantial part of whose success was due to their use of timely articles and short stories in place of the belletristic essays and travel sketches that had been the staple of their genteel forebears—was immense. In 1885 the only four American magazines with circulations of over 100,000 had sold an aggregate of 600,000 a month; by 1905 there were five times as many, and their total sale was more than 5,500,000 copies. One by one, the chief mass periodicals had arrived at circulations of over half a million: the *Ladies' Home Journal* in 1891, the *Youth's Companion* about 1894, the *Delineator* in 1895, *Munsey's* in 1897. In 1903 the *Ladies' Home Journal* was to pass one million. As in Britain, such records were achieved not only through the expert selection, editing, and arrangement of the magazines' contents, but also by constant advertising and schemes of rewards by which readers who collected groups of new subscriptions were entitled to premiums such as books, sewing machines, jewelry, clothing, and portfolios of views of the Chicago Columbian Exposition.

Meanwhile, certain older institutions continued to flourish. One was the weekly story paper, exemplified in Britain by the *Family Herald,* which had been among the first in the field and was still bought by countless maidservants, and in America by Beadle's *Banner Weekly* and George Munro's *Fireside Companion.* Another was the weekly novelette, complete in one issue, with an indispensable picture of dramatic action on the front page to attract the purchaser's eye. In Britain the Heartsease Library, the Duchess Novelettes, Horner's Penny Stories, and others sold huge quantities of tales with titles such as *The Voice of Blood, The Kiss of Judas, The Bracelet of Death, Betrayed at the Altar, Betrothed to a Brigand,* and *The*

Phantom Boatman. These, presumably, were the kind of papers favored by the barmaid of William Ernest Henley's sonnet, who "tries / From penny novels to amend her taste."

However mightily they prospered at the turn of the century, these were instruments of mass culture that looked backward rather than forward, and the future belonged to the innovators. While Newnes and Bok and their rivals were transforming their respective nations' weekly papers and magazines, the Harmsworths and the Pulitzers were presiding over a concurrent revolution in daily journalism. The technique of presenting the news—or the most vivid items of news—in short, snappy form, with frequent subheadings and other editorial and typographical aids to easy reading was mastered. "Scoops," sensational crusades, signed articles, and timely interviews proved again and again to sell more papers. Politics, the chief concern of the established dailies, had given way to entertainment, sport, and crime news—hitherto largely the special province of the Sunday press—in the halfpenny London papers (the *Star,* the *Echo,* the *Evening News*) of the late 1880s. But the big break with the past came in 1896 with the establishment of the *Daily Mail,* the first halfpenny morning paper. Launched, typically, with an extravagant publicity campaign, Harmsworth's paper, "written by office-boys for office-boys," as Lord Salisbury observed, quickly eclipsed all existing circulation records. Figures of 1901 eloquently tell the story: the *Times* (3*d.*) sold 37,900 copies a day, the *Manchester Guardian* (1*d.*) sold 44,300, and the *Daily Mail* (½*d.*) sold 836,000. The day of the press lords, building journalistic empires with the coppers of millions of readers, had arrived. There could have been no more pregnant symbol of this revolution in journalism—the new domination of mass-circulation papers over the old-established, august journals of opinion—than Harmsworth's (by now Lord Northcliffe's) saving of the ailing *Times* from extinction in 1908 with the profits from the *Daily Mail.*

In the United States, as in Britain, newspaper proprietors and editors fought to increase circulation, not for the sake of the money brought in by actual sales but to attract the more profitable custom of advertisers. Advertising, instead of being merely a welcome incidental source of revenue, became the very lifeblood of modern journalism as viewed from the increasingly potent business office. W. T. Stead's campaigns in Britain for social and political reform (motivated, it is true, as much by altruism as by the hope of increased sales—which did not materialize) were matched in America by those of Joseph Pulitzer, whose transformation of the moribund *New York World* into a paper with a circulation of one million copies by 1898 marked the birth of modern American journalism. The *Daily*

Mail's violent xenophobia, served by carefree doctoring of the news to suit the paper's policy, stirred aggressive British feelings against the Transvaal, and during the Boer War that ensued the paper's circulation rose to almost one million. At almost the same moment, the American William Randolph Hearst, in similarly reckless fashion, propelled his nation into a circulation-boosting war with Spain. The yellow press had acquired the fearsome power of committing a whole people to war.

One American newspaper development, however, did not have its ready analogue in Great Britain. Faced with the competition of the new cheap general magazines, with their brightly written topical articles and pictures, newspapers turned more and more to the production of Sunday supplements, whose *mélange* of "fact, fiction, fun and folly," as the historian Arthur Schlesinger, Sr., once put it, rivaled that of the magazines. In 1890 there had been about 400 Sunday papers, two-thirds of which were Sunday editions of dailies; in 1900 there were 639. In Britain the somewhat increased topicality of the general magazines neither reflected nor spurred any noteworthy expansion of the scope of the Sunday papers—among them *Reynolds' News, Lloyd's Weekly News,* the *News of the World,* and the *Weekly Dispatch,* veterans of more than sixty years' service to the working-man's sabbath—which remained dedicated for the most part to their traditional fare of sensation, scandal, sport, and radical politics.

Quietly persisting in the midst of the hurly-burly of cheap best-sellers and mass-circulation newspapers and magazines was the small but discriminating reading audience of the élite. Far more influential in proportion to its size than it would sometimes concede itself to be, it provided a steady and critical body of readers for the work of those gifted contemporary writers who had neither the skill nor the luck (nor, possibly, the desire) to attract the vast new public. In a world of mass readership, the literary establishment was at pains to uphold critical standards, to condemn not only the cynical greed of the commercial interests that provided the masses with their reading matter but also what seemed to them the irremediably crude tastes of working-class readers.

There is, of course, another side to the picture. Millions of people in both countries now had both the ability and the leisure to read; it was naive to have expected the newly literate to emerge with highly developed critical standards. To some extent, at least, public taste is formed by the quality of the material that is most readily available or most persuasively offered. With the increase in literacy, reading matter became a commodity that could be sold on an industrial scale, and commercial interests responded with the undiscriminating zeal that mass marketing of almost any commodity demands.

The problem faced by a society that has acquired more leisure than it is readily equipped to use in any profitable way is not a new one. Its existence was recognized a century ago, not only by thoughtful social observers but even by American presidents not ordinarily given to cultural analysis or prophecy. Addressing the educational summer school at Chautauqua in 1880, James A. Garfield observed that "We may divide the whole struggle of the human race into two chapters: first, the fight to get leisure; and then the second fight of civilization—what we shall do with our leisure when we get it." The place of the printed word in that leisure remains unsettled, as disturbing to the guardians of quality in our own day as it was in Garfield's.

1972

OCCASIONS

15
Four Victorian Poets and an Exploding Island

Rich though English poetry is in descriptions of events in nature—on the earth and in the skies—we seldom have the opportunity of seeing a single remarkable occurrence through the eyes of several poets. Individual references, of course, are common; thus Chaucer preserves for us a memory of the rare conjunction, in 1385, of the crescent moon, Saturn, and Jupiter in the sign of Cancer, and of the "smoky reyn" that ensued, and Shakespeare, in a well-known passage in *A Midsummer Night's Dream,* describes the disastrously wet and cold weather that oppressed England in 1594–96. But when poets have joined to commemorate a single event, it has ordinarily been one more closely identified with the affairs of men than with the behavior of the winds or the stars. London burns and is rebuilt, and a host of rhymers burst into song; there is a royal marriage or death, and the voice of the Laureate is echoed through the land. Sometimes inspiration works under even greater forced draft, as when a Keats and a Leigh Hunt vie against the clock in writing extempore sonnets on "The Grasshopper and the Cricket," or 112 competitors, sixty-nine of whom invoke the phoenix, seek the honor of delivering the address at the opening in 1812 of the burned-and-reconstructed Drury Lane Theatre.

The results of such competitions belong among the curiosities rather than the treasures of literature. The results of a similar competition in 1883 ("coincidence" would be more accurate, since what happened was wholly unarranged) possess a somewhat greater critical interest, because the poets involved were Tennyson, Bridges, Hopkins, and Swinburne. Thanks to an awesome event whose origins were half a world away, we have the unusual privilege of watching four poets responding independently to a single phenomenon; poets, moreover, who belong to the same broad "romantic" tradition and are all distinguished for their treatment of nature. They all saw the same spectacle in the twilight skies, but, as we shall discover, each poet produced a different version of the sight.

On 26–27 August 1883, the volcanic island of Krakatoa, in the Dutch East Indies, erupted in what has often been called the most stupendous natural explosion in recorded history. Most of the island was destroyed,

View of Krakatoa during the earlier stage of the eruption, May 1883 (*The Eruption of Krakatoa, and Subsequent Phenomena* . . . [Royal Society, 1888])

and over thirty-six thousand people were killed; ships at great distances were engulfed by tidal waves or surrounded by vast seas of pumice; the sound was heard as much as twenty-five hundred miles away. Even more memorable were the dramatic optical effects caused by the dispersion of volcanic debris through the upper atmosphere. Beginning in the Far East and then spreading, week by week, to the skies over North and South

America, Africa, and Europe, these phenomena included prolonged and spectacularly colored twilights, large coronas, green- and blue-colored suns and moons, and unusual hazes. In England they were first visible toward the end of October, reached their peak in November and December, and then gradually disappeared, although occasional recurrences were noted throughout 1884.

British newspapers and scientific periodicals printed hundreds of observations from all over the globe. First came messages from vessels arriving in South Sea ports from the vicinity of the explosion; in due time there were communications from sky-watchers in the gardens of country vicarages. The learned societies were, of course, deeply interested, especially since there was some initial skepticism that the magnificent sunsets were in fact caused by the Krakatoa explosion. In January 1884, the Royal Society appointed a special committee to gather and organize all available information and scientific commentary on the subject. The voluminous report of this committee, published in 1888, tabulates data on the various optical, seismic, magnetic, and meteorological phenomena observed from Japan to Turkey.[1] More than a century later its five hundred pages still communicate to the reader a vivid sense of the excitement and wonder the world-wide effects of the eruption stirred among all who noticed them. In their attempts to describe the brilliant celestial displays, the observers often abandoned scientific terminology in favor of a descriptive style that can only be called lyric—and when the sunsets of late 1883 defied even poetic language the observers resorted at last to pictorial art: they said the sunsets were like those of Turner.

Here and there in the memoirs of the time we find descriptions of the "Krakatoa sunsets" as they were seen by sensitive but nonscientific watchers. The historian G. G. Coulton, for example, recalled in his autobiography:

> the sun went down again and again through that dust in matchless splendour. The afterglow often lingered, even in the eastern sky, for hours. In the brightest west, emerald green was not occasional but almost normal. We seldom see it except as a background to the sunset; strips of sky come out green in contrast to the vivid crimson or vermilion of the clouds which form the main pattern. But in those Krakatoa skies, the green was often in the forefront and more striking than anything else. . . . Those sunset glories . . . once made us drop a game of football and watch for an hour.[2]

At Brantwood on Coniston Water, meanwhile, the most devoted connoisseur of both Turners and sunsets, the aging John Ruskin, gazed from his studio window with Arthur Severn. In a communication to the press Severn wrote that on 24 November he had said to Ruskin:

"Well, I never saw such a sky or clouds, it is exactly like an old master picture, like a rich Titian sky." . . . I said this because what *ought* to have been blue sky was quite a rich green, and some of the clouds rich amber, others red brick colour, and others a yellow green. . . . I was startled, because I knew some of the colours to be unnatural, especially at that time of day (4:30); it was not a green or an amber I had ever seen, and I have watched the sky very carefully for many years. Then, about a week ago [i.e., 3 or 4 December], I saw the same effect again, and on looking round towards the sunset my eye caught the crescent moon; it was of a *pale blue green*. Two evenings before this, I was startled on looking up from my book (and some time after candles had been brought in) to see quite a red glare behind the "Old Man"; it was almost night, I thought it was some large fire, but on going out I saw that it was merely a glare from the sunset; and more to the east near the horizon there were lurid masses of red cloud very far off showing through bars of nearer gray cloud. I thought of running into Ruskin's study and telling him to look, and went as far as his door, but then deemed it better not, as the effect was of so lurid and awful a nature, I thought it might put him off his work![3]

Ruskin's "work" at the moment was "The Storm-Cloud of the Nineteenth Century," an eccentric two-part discourse on smog which he was to deliver in London the following February. Perhaps as a result of Severn's solicitude, Ruskin seems not to have been much impressed by the Krakatoa sunsets. He alluded to them only once, to point up, in one of his new lectures, his sense of his own deepening spiritual isolation and that of late nineteenth-century society. The harmony which once existed between mankind and nature, he wrote, "is now broken, and broken the world round: fragments, indeed, of what existed still exist, and hours of what is past still return; but month by month the darkness gains upon the day, and the ashes of the Antipodes glare through the night."[4]

But most notable among the English sunset-watchers in that winter of 1883–84 were our four poets. Three of the four were not poets only, each being also, in his way, a close student of nature. Hence these viewed the Krakatoa phenomena with a double vision—the scientist's as well as the verbal artist's.

The Laureate, as is well known, had steeped himself from earliest youth in "the fairy tales of science, and the long result of Time." Although Tennyson's most familiar scientific allusions, in *In Memoriam* especially, are to the pre-Darwinian, geological evidences of evolution, elsewhere in his poetry his eyes are frequently lifted to the skies. He was an extraordinarily alert observer of meteorological and astronomical occurrences, and a paper enumerating and briefly explicating Tennyson's astronomical references required no fewer than eighty pages when printed in the *Journal and Transactions of the Leeds Astronomical Society* for 1906.

Tennyson presumably watched the Krakatoa sunsets from his house at Aldworth, Surrey, and stored up what he saw for later poetic use. In a blank-verse narrative, "St. Telemachus," he moved the sunsets back fifteen centuries to provide a lurid background for the life of the saint:

> Had the fierce ashes of some fiery peak
> Been hurl'd so high they ranged about the globe?
> For day by day, thro' many a blood-red eve,
> In that four-hundredth summer after Christ,
> The wrathful sunset glared. . . .

And in line 178 of "Locksley Hall Sixty Years After," written in 1886, the speaker, a crusty old man raging against the sorry state of the modern world, recalls an event of his youth: his last meeting with his sweetheart, Amy, when "the moon was falling greenish thro' a rosy glow." This eerie image was almost certainly inspired by the blue or green tint the crescent moon acquired in the prolonged red twilights of 3, 4, and 5 December 1883. The strange sight was observed throughout England. Severn, as we have seen, noted it in the Lake District. At York the moon had "a most striking green tint"; at Worcester "the crescent of the moon, being just above the fringe of red light, assumed a lively green hue"; in Surrey itself the "crescent moon [was] greenish all the evening."[5]

At Yattendon, Berkshire, a younger man, destined to succeed Tennyson in the Laureateship at one remove, was stirred by the same sunsets. This was Robert Bridges, whose scientific interests were somewhat more professional than Tennyson's, since until his recent retirement he had been a practicing physician. The chief poetic reminiscence of the sunsets in Bridges's poetry occurs in his long verse narrative, *Eros and Psyche,* published in 1885. The time is the age of classical myth:

> Fair was the sight; for now though full an hour
> The sun had sunk she saw a wondrous light
> In shifting colour to the zenith tower,
> And grow more gorgeous ever and more bright.
> Bathed in the warm and comfortable glow,
> The fair delighted queen forgot her woe,
> And watched the unwonted pageant of the night.
>
> Broad and low down, where last the sun had been,
> A wealth of orange gold was thickly shed,
> And touching that a curtain pale of green,
> Like apples are before their rinds grow red:
> Then to the height the variable hue
> Of rose and pink and crimson freaked with blue,
> And olive-bordered clouds o'er lilac led.
>
> High in the opposèd west the wondering moon
> All silvery green in flying green was fleeced;
> And round the blazing South the splendour soon
> Caught all the heaven, and ran to North and East;
> And Aphrodite knew this thing was wrought
> By great Poseidon, and she took the thought
> She would go see with whom he kept his feast.
>
> (pp. 10–11)

In this passage Bridges invented nothing. Every detail of his description—the long persistence of luminosity after sunset, the gradation and variation of the sky colors which reached to the very zenith and the northern and southern horizons, the green moon enwreathed in a green cirriform sky haze—is amply documented in the Royal Society's Krakatoa Report. Bridges, it should be noted, ingeniously implies the connection between the sunsets and some terrestrial convulsion by his reference to Poseidon, the wrathful and mighty sea-cause and earthshaker.

Unknown to Bridges at this time, in Lancashire his friend Gerard Manley Hopkins was studying the crimson sunsets with particular attention. They had come at a fortunate moment, for in the past year Hopkins's interest in sunset phenomena had been so strong as to lead to two of his very rare appearances in print. Two letters of his on "shadow-beams in the east at sunset" had been published in the scientific weekly *Nature,* the first a year earlier, on 16 November 1882, and the second very recently, on 15 November 1883. These contributions, along with one still to come, were the only evidence published in his lifetime of his longstanding devotion to astronomy and meteorology. His private notebooks, however, reveal how carefully, year by year, in every season, he observed clouds, the aurora borealis, the stars, and sunrise and sunset.

The fruits of Hopkins's sky-gazing in late November and December 1883 were contained in a letter dated at Stonyhurst College on 21 December, and printed in *Nature* for 3 January 1884. In this scientific communication Hopkins described the Krakatoa sunsets in language of which few besides poets are capable.[6] There is not space to reproduce the whole letter, but a few excerpts may serve to represent its literary quality. The Krakatoa sunsets differed from ordinary ones, Hopkins wrote,

in the nature of the glow, which is both intense and lustreless, and that both in the sky and on the earth. The glow is intense, this is what strikes every one; it has prolonged the daylight, and optically changed the season; it bathes the whole sky, it is mistaken for the reflection of a great fire; at the sundown itself and southwards from that on December 4, I took a note of it as more like inflamed flesh than the lucid reds of ordinary sunsets. On the same evening the fields facing west glowed as if overlaid with yellow wax.

But it is also lustreless. A bright sunset lines the clouds so that their brims look like gold, brass, bronze, or steel. It fetches out those dazzling flecks and spangles which people call fish-scales. It gives to a mackerel or dappled cloudrack the appearance of quilted crimson silk, or a ploughed field glazed with crimson ice. These effects may have been seen in the late sunsets, but they are not the specific after-glow; that is, without gloss or lustre.

The two things together, that is intensity of light and want of lustre, give to objects on the earth the peculiar illumination which may be seen in studios and other well-like rooms, and which itself affects the practice of painters and may be seen in their works, notably Rembrandt's, disguising or feebly showing the outlines and distinctions of things, but fetching out white surfaces and coloured stuffs with a rich and inward and seemingly self-luminous glow.

And again, speaking of the texture of the streamers' colored surfaces:

After the sunset [of 16 December] the horizon was, by 4.10, lined a long way by a glowing tawny light, not very pure in colour and distinctly textured in hummocks, bodies like a shoal of dolphins, or in what are called gadroons, or as the Japanese conventionally represent waves. The glowing vapour above this was as yet colourless; then this took a beautiful olive or celadon green, not so vivid as the previous day's, and delicately fluted; the green belt was broader than the orange, and pressed down on and contracted it. Above the green in turn appeared a red glow, broader and burlier in make; it was softly brindled, and in the ribs or bars the colour was rosier, in the channels where the blue of the sky shone through it was a mallow colour. Above this was a vague lilac. The red was first noticed 45° above the horizon, and spokes or beams could be seen in it, compared by one beholder to a man's open hand. By 4.45 the red had driven out the green, and, fusing with the remains of the orange, reached the horizon. By that time the east, which had a rose tinge, became of a duller red, compared to sand: according to my observation, the ground of the sky in the east was green or else tawny, and the crimson only in the clouds. A great sheet of heavy dark cloud, with a reefed or puckered make, drew off the west in the course of the pageant: the edge of this and the smaller pellets of cloud that filed across the bright field of the sundown caught a livid green. At 5 the red in the west was fainter, at 5.20 it became notably rosier and livelier; but it was never of a pure rose. A faint dusky blush was left as late as 5.30, or later. While these changes were going on in the sky, the landscape of Ribblesdale glowed with a frowning brown.

This last passage repeated a point made earlier in the same letter, in words which must be quoted here:

Four colours in particular have been noticeable in these afterglows, and in a fixed order of time and place—orange, lowest and nearest the sundown; above this, and broader, green; above this, broader still, a variable red, ending in being crimson; above this a faint lilac. The lilac disappears; the green deepens, spreads, and encroaches on the orange; and the red deepens, spreads, and encroaches on the green, till at last one red, varying downwards from crimson to scarlet or orange fills the west and south. . . . The first orange and the last crimson flush are perhaps pure, or nearly so, but the two most remarkable glows, the green and the red, are not. The green is between an apple-green or pea-green (which are pure greens) and an olive (which is a tertiary colour): it is vivid and beautiful, but not pure. The red is very impure, and not evenly laid on. On the 4th it appeared brown, like a strong light behind tortoiseshell, or Derbyshire alabaster. It has been well compared to the colour of incandescent iron. Sometimes it appears like a mixture of chalk with sand and muddy earths. The pigments for it would be ochre and Indian red.

It is curious: if we compare these passages, especially the earlier portion of the last one quoted, with the second stanza quoted from Bridges's poem, we discover that every color Hopkins uses is present, designated in the same terms, and for the most part arranged in the same order, in Bridges's description (orange, apple-green, rose, red, crimson, blue, olive, lilac). There are other verbal echoes: Hopkins writes "variable red" and Bridges, "variable hue of rose and pink and crimson"; and both describe the spectacle as a "pageant." The *Eros and Psyche* passage, in fact, is hardly more than a versification of certain elements of Hopkins's prose picture. As soon as Hopkins read the poem, he wrote to Bridges (1 January 1885): "The description . . . so closely agrees with an account I wrote in *Nature*, even to details which were local only, that it is very extraordinary: you did not see my letter, did you?"[7] Hopkins's suspicion is decently veiled, but it is unmistakable, and, one feels, not without basis.

"Swinburn[e], perhaps you know," Hopkins continued in the same letter to Bridges, "has also tried his hand—without success." He had, indeed. At Putney on 25 November (he appended the precise date to the poem) Swinburne viewed one of the most spectacular of all the Krakatoa displays, described by an observer at nearby Richmond as "sunset in amorphous indistinguishable cirrostratus or cirrus haze. Green light above sunset, and bright greenish-white growing from about 10 minutes after sunset. Above the greenish-white pale red or pink. Lasted about 45 minutes after sunset."[8] Swinburne promptly worked his impressions into "A New-Year Ode: to Victor Hugo," a tribute to the master on the completion of *La Légende des siècles* and "on the still increasing glories and varying beauties of his work, which if possible grows more splendid and wonderful as the sunset draws nearer. . . . Of course," Swinburne wrote his mother, "you see the allegory that was at once suggested to me on looking at that glorious transfiguration of the sky a little before the sun set, which made everything above and around more splendid than ever it was at morning or at noon."[9]

These are the first three of the six relevant strophes:

XVII

It was the dawn of winter: sword in sheath,
    Change, veiled and mild, came down the gradual air
With cold slow smiles that hid the doom beneath.
    Five days to die in yet were autumn's, ere
The last leaf withered from his flowerless wreath.
    South, east, and north, our skies were all blown bare,
But westward over glimmering holt and heath
    Cloud, wind, and light had made a heaven more fair
        Than ever dream or truth
        Showed earth in time's keen youth
When men with angels communed unaware.
        Above the sun's head, now
        Veiled even to the ardent brow,
Rose two sheer wings of sundering cloud, that were
        As a bird's poised for vehement flight,
Full-fledged with plumes of tawny fire and hoar grey light.

XVIII

As midnight black, as twilight brown, they spread,
    But feathered thick with flame that streaked and lined
Their living darkness, ominous else of dread,
    From south to northmost verge of heaven inclined
Most like some giant angel's, whose bent head
    Bowed earthward, as with message for mankind
Of doom or benediction to be shed
    From passage of his presence. Far behind,

Even while they seemed to close,
    Stoop, and take flight, arose
Above them, higher than heavenliest thought may find
    In light or night supreme
    Of vision or of dream,
Immeasurable of men's eyes or mounting mind,
    Heaven, manifest in manifold
Light of pure pallid amber, cheered with fire of gold.

XIX

And where the fine gold faded all the sky
    Shone green as the outer sea when April glows,
Inlaid with flakes and feathers fledged to fly
    Of clouds suspense in rapture and repose,
With large live petals, broad as love bids lie
    Full open when the sun salutes the rose,
And small rent sprays wherewith the heavens most high
    Were strewn as autumn strews the garden-close
        With ruinous roseleaves whirled
        About their wan chill world,
    Through wind-worn bowers that now no music knows,
        Spoil of the dim dusk year
        Whose utter night is near,
    And near the flower of dawn beyond it blows;
        Till east and west were fire and light,
As though the dawn to come had flushed the coming night.[10]

The insatiate reader may find the remaining strophes in any collected edition of Swinburne. They are no better than the ones quoted.

    The fruits of this unplanned poetical contest are creditable to only one of the participants. It is fairly evident that while Tennyson, Bridges, and Swinburne doubtless saw the sunsets with their physical eyes, the experience was unaccompanied by the imaginative vision that transmutes sensory data into art. The Krakatoa sunsets inspired none of the three to write good poetry. Ironically, the only good poetry that resulted from the celestial display is found in Hopkins's prose.

    Though there is no reason to suppose that Tennyson moodily shut himself up in his den while everyone else at Aldworth surveyed the marvelous western skies, the lines he wrote have no necessary impress of personal experience; they might just as well have been written from a casual glance at the newspapers. Every "poetic" term in the line in "Locksley Hall Sixty Years After"—*greenish, rosy glow*—was current in ordinary journalistic descriptions of the sunsets. And the "St. Telemachus" lines, in essence, are a statement of a scientific fact rather than of an observed sight.

Whether or not Bridges drew upon Hopkins's published description, the *Eros and Psyche* version of the sunsets is mediocre poetry. The extraordinary qualities of the sight are largely neutralized by Bridges's conventional, not to say trite, diction ("fair was the sight," "the fair delighted queen forgot her woe") and by his failure to achieve a clear image. To say that "she saw a wondrous light / In shifting colour to the zenith tower, / And grow more gorgeous ever and more bright" does not really say much about what she saw, and the second quoted stanza does hardly more than enumerate a spectrumlike succession of colors. Nor is the picture of the "wondering," "all silvery green" moon fleeced "in flying green" self-realizing. To see it, the reader must bring to the poem a previous knowledge of the peculiar interplay between the green hues of the Krakatoa moon itself and those of the cloudracks that passed across it. And while the narrative context may have recommended that the queen be bathed in a "warm and comfortable glow," the coziness thus implied is scarcely in harmony with the awesome qualities of the spectacle. Bridges, in short, reduced the unearthly splendors of the Krakatoa sunsets to the artistic level of stage scenery.

Swinburne, in his six strophes, simultaneously sees much more than the sunset and much less than the sunset itself contained. The specific optical effects, such as other observers noted that day, are largely confined to the first half of strophe XIX. The rest of the passage is a hodgepodge of nonrelated images, nondescriptive elements, and wave after wave of vaguely affective language, or Swinburnese. The poet's eye hovers uncertainly between heaven and earth, and what he sees is obscured by what his inveterate poetic habits predispose him to say he sees. Whether or not they are appropriate to this particular experience, all the high-powered Swinburnian words that have served so faithfully on so many different occasions are put to paper once more: *ardent, vehement, utter, doom, ominous, dread, supreme, immeasurable, rapture,* and the rest. There are the inevitable weak personifications, the equally inescapable bursts of alliteration and assonance, and even the familiar Garden of Proserpine accessories, the ruinous roseleaves, the wan chill world, and the wind-worn bowers. But perhaps most characteristic of Swinburne's penchant for holding the mirror of artifice up to nature is his insistence on using his favorite image of *flame* and *fire* to describe sunsets which witnesses agree were marked by diffused rather than concentrated light, by intense and long-lasting radiance rather than by darting tongues of brightness. The best comment, surely, on Swinburne's logorrheic treatment of the sunsets is Hopkins's, in the letter already quoted: "Either in fact he does not see nature at all or else he overlays the landscape with such phantasmata, secondary images, and what not of a delirium-tremendous imagination that the result is a kind of bloody broth: you know what I mean. At any rate there is no picture."

Hopkins, however—and how unfortunate it is that he did not finally transmute his experiences into verse—is an extraordinarily sensitive and minute observer. His prose letter, far from being a set-piece like Bridges's and Swinburne's stanzas, is a delicate blending of scientific description and aesthetic perception. His wealth of metaphors and analogies (inflamed flesh, yellow wax, bright metals, fish-scales, crimson silk, ploughed fields glazed with crimson ice, artist's studios, Rembrandt paintings, shoals of dolphins, waves in Japanese painting, sand, light behind tortoise-shell, Derbyshire alabaster, incandescent iron, chalk mixed with sand and muddy earths, pigments of ochre and Indian red) brings ethereal phe-nomena down to earthly terms. But the figures and analogies are them-selves so freshly evocative, so apt, so far removed from commonplace standards of comparison that they enlarge and intensify, rather than constrict, the reader's experience. In addition, Hopkins enhances the immediacy of the various phenomena, indeed converts the visual into the tangible, by describing them as much in terms of texture and shape (flecks, spangles, quilted, ploughed, hummocks, fluted, burlier, brindled, ribs, bars) as in language of color and light. Far more effectively than the writers in verse, he combines the spatial dimension of the spectacle with the temporal as he describes the subtle arrangement and succession of effects, the impingement, mingling, and shifting of the respective bands of color. In Hopkins's paragraphs, written as scientific rather than poetic discourse, is embodied a true sense of the "inscape" of the scene that millions of Englishmen beheld on those memorable afternoons.

Our knowledge of how Tennyson, Bridges, and Swinburne reacted, privately and immediately, to what they saw is clouded by the dramatic or allegorical contexts in which they eventually set their published versions of the Krakatoa phenomena. Did Tennyson himself—"St. Telemachus" be-ing as yet unconceived—think of the displays primarily as "blood-red" and "wrathful"? Was it Bridges, or only his "fair delighted queen," who found them "warm and comfortable"? And where, in the welter of words Swinburne was moved to utter, can we isolate the essence of his own experience at Putney between 4 and 5 P.M. on 25 November? At least we know quite surely how Hopkins felt. It is the very absence of art that gives his report its unquestionable authenticity. But whatever the particular quality of each man's response, no shadow of physical dread darkened his appreciation of the scene's sheer beauty. To be sure, from those same upper reaches of the atmosphere where the colors were mixed in a colossal palette came a more tangible product, fallout. People collected it on window-panes during rainstorms and snowfalls; but it was harmless volcanic ash, merely a scientific curiosity. Nobody then was imperiled by the dust that had blown halfway around the world.[11]

1960

16

The Volcano and a Coral Reef

The foregoing piece on Krakatoa has a special place in my memories of research undertaken and completed in that it was a subject that made itself; I did not propose it, and for a long time I did not realize just what I had. Whereas the island in the Dutch East Indies ended in violent disintegration and dispersal throughout the upper atmosphere, my little article had a genesis as unnoticed as, say, the beginning of a coral reef in the same quarter of the globe, and it grew just as unobtrusively over a considerable span of time. This is not the way most scholarly articles develop, if we are to believe the textbooks on literary-historical research procedures, and in fact a number of the essays in the present book were produced more or less according to the rules: shape your subject carefully before you begin, outline your plan of attack, and then seek out, as systematically as possible, all the information bearing upon it. But the so-called methodology taught in graduate courses is misnamed: in practice, research is not always as tidy and cut-and-dried as the word implies. When a topic is not already structured and defined, the ideal orderly procedure can seldom be followed. My own first rule of research, in such a case, holds that once a scholar has acquired the indispensable basic working knowledge of the bibliographical tools and source materials in his field, the best thing for him to do is simply to follow his nose. One of the pleasures of research lies in the fact that once a project is under way, whatever the mode of attack, one thing can lead gratifyingly to another—and another—and another, as the following narrative well illustrates.

The Krakatoa essay is surely unique in one respect: it is the only known fruit of research that began with an inert "fact" in an old copy of the *Reader's Digest* and had life breathed into it by a remembered line in one of Tennyson's poems.

The story goes back an unconscionably long way, to a time when Mount Krakatoa was not as famous as it has become in recent years, especially since the eruption of Mount St. Helens, in the state of Washington, in 1980. This unusual event in American territory stirred public interest in the subject of volcanic activity, and the historic example of

Krakatoa acquired new timeliness. It was featured in television documentaries, and the Smithsonian Institution issued a large up-to-date bibliography of the scientific studies it had inspired. The disaster at the Chernobyl nuclear power plant six years later lent urgent interest to one of the memorable effects of the Krakatoa eruption, the wide diffusion of the products of the explosion through the upper atmosphere. But in 1946, when the *Reader's Digest* condensed an article on Krakatoa that had appeared in *Nature Magazine,* probably few of its millions of subscribers had ever heard of the occurrence before.

At least I hadn't; or if I had, the topic had fresh interest for me, because I thought it might bear on the meaning of line 178 in Tennyson's "Locksley Hall Sixty Years After": "the moon was falling greenish thro' a rosy glow." Could this eerie image have been suggested by the optical phenomena described in the article? The connection would, I thought, be worth a paragraph sometime, perhaps in the valuable little periodical begun some years earlier, called *The Explicator.* So I marked a file folder "Krakatoa and Tennyson," tossed into it the pages torn from the *Reader's Digest* and a memo about the Tennyson line, and that, for the time being, was that. I did, however, add to the file the quotation from G. G. Coulton's *Fourscore Years,* which I happened to read because of a passing interest I then had in the lives of modern historians of the Middle Ages.

A decade later, having completed a project I had been working on and being, therefore, momentarily at loose ends, I decided to write up the Tennyson item, perhaps for submission, if *The Explicator* didn't take it, to the venerable British periodical that for more than a century had been devoted to just that kind of odds and ends, *Notes and Queries.* I thought, however, that I'd better learn a bit more about the eruption of Krakatoa and the phenomena it created, especially as they were observed in Tennyson's country, half way around the world. The quest, begun, as I remember, by consulting the university library catalogue, fortunately led me to the geology department library, where I found a large volume published in 1888 by a special committee of the Royal Society appointed to collect all available data relating to the seismic, meteorological, and other effects of the eruption.

Among the hundreds of contemporary articles cited were two by "G. M. Hopkins" dated from Stonyhurst College and published in *Nature,* the premier British scientific journal then, as it remains today. (The American *Nature Magazine* from which the *Reader's Digest* account was taken was unrelated to it.) For a time, I was elated by the assumption that I had come upon a pair of hitherto unknown pieces by the poet. But when

I checked the various volumes of the Hopkins correspondence I found that his *Nature* articles had been reprinted in the volume containing the letters he exchanged with his friend R. W. Dixon. I went through his poems but could find no hint that his observation of the Krakatoa sunsets from Stonyhurst had suggested any images.

I also found a letter from Hopkins to Robert Bridges, referring to his *Nature* contributions and to Bridges's use of Krakatoa phenomena in his poem *Eros and Psyche*. This clue took me to Bridges's poems and to the published critical studies of that poet, who was more highly regarded a couple of generations ago than he is today. In Edward Thompson's study (1944) the relevant stanzas of *Eros and Psyche* were quoted, and a footnote referred to a use of Krakatoa in Tennyson's late poem "St. Telemachus," which had been published in Tennyson's posthumous volume, *The Death of Oenone . . . and Other Poems* (1892). This I hadn't known about, although in the hope of finding other allusions to spectacular sunsets I had read through what I assumed to be all of Tennyson's post-1883 poetry in my copy of the Student's Cambridge edition of his works (1898, and still in print when I acquired it in the 1950s, which was long before Christopher Ricks's superb critical edition appeared). After some effort, I discovered—the publisher's note in the front of the book gave no indication of this—that for copyright reasons this edition did not include the poems of Tennyson's very last years. So I had to go to another edition, the original *Death of Oenone* volume, to find the text of the poem.

Now I had three poets who had written about the Krakatoa sunsets: Tennyson, Hopkins, and Bridges. I checked other possibilities, including Swinburne and Browning, with no results. However, since I had gotten my original lead through the Royal Society report, I thought there might be other clues there which I had overlooked in my excitement about Hopkins. I was right: this time I found a reference to a letter to a London newspaper signed by one Arthur Severn and dated from Coniston, in the Lake District. The name I knew: Arthur Severn was Ruskin's cousin by marriage, and he took care of the failing art critic at Coniston; and Ruskin was a great connoisseur of sunsets. To the massive Cook and Wedderburn edition of Ruskin's works, therefore—and in the magnificently detailed index I found a reference to a brief mention of Krakatoa in one of Ruskin's lectures, "The Storm-Cloud of the Nineteenth Century."

While I was re-examining the Royal Society report, I checked the chronological list it contained of the "dates of first appearance of all the optical phenomena," and found mentioned, under the date 29 November 1883, a letter to the *Pall Mall Gazette* signed by John Addington

Symonds at Davos. My roster of Krakatoa-watching English men of letters gave every indication of growing. After some trouble locating a file of that London daily paper, I obtained a photostat of the letter, which actually appeared in the 29 October issue as a reply to an earlier letter to the *Gazette* on the phenomenon of iridescent clouds. Symonds described in some detail his observations of these clouds during his years in the Alps; the finest display he recalled was, he said, seen from the summit of the Schwarzhorn four years earlier, on 7 December 1879. But no reference was made to the Krakatoa sunsets, which would not appear in Switzerland until late November 1883. The phenomena were unrelated, although a number of Symonds's descriptive sentences anticipated the vivid imagery that made prose poems out of Hopkins's communications to *Nature*. In this instance, I had been betrayed by my source.

At that point, I decided to write up my data into a ten-page article, but partly because I didn't know where to submit it—by this time it had grown too long for *The Explicator* or *Notes and Queries*, it didn't seem right for *Scientific American,* and neither *Victorian Studies* nor *Victorian Poetry* had yet been launched—I put the draft on the shelf. Now came an experience which strengthened my conviction that whenever possible the writer of a scholarly article should delay publishing it until there has been time for quiet reflection and reevaluation; such writing never suffers from moderate aging, and it may well gain from the addition of newly discovered information or newly perceived significance. After the draft had rested for more than a year, I took it down, planning to polish it and send it on its hopeful way to *Victorian Studies,* which had appeared in the interim.

But among my notes was one teasing loose end. In Hopkins's letter to Bridges he had referred to Swinburne's trying his hand at a description of a volcanic sunset. The editor of the Hopkins-Bridges correspondence, C. C. Abbott, queried whether the reference was to a poem Swinburne published in 1880. I knew, of course, that this wouldn't do as far as Krakatoa was concerned, because the dates didn't fit; and I had already gone through the poet's 1884 publication, *A Midsummer Holiday and Other Poems,* without noticing anything of interest. However, the Hopkins remark continued to bother me. From the context, he appeared to be alluding to a recent poem of Swinburne, and one that specifically dealt with a Krakatoa-type sunset. So I went back to Swinburne's collected poems, made a more thorough check of the 1884 volume, and discovered what I had simply overlooked on my first run-through, six strophes of the "New-Year Ode: to Victor Hugo" that used the materials of a spectacular sunset—and the sunset was specifically dated, by Swinburne, "November 25, 1883"! Here, then, found almost as a postscript to my research, was by all odds the longest, though hardly the best, poetic product of the Krakatoa spectacle. Had I not restrained myself from sending off the article when I thought it was in fairly final form, I would have omitted some important material—and exposed myself to the charge, by someone better versed in Swinburne than I was, that I'd not done my homework as impeccably as is required of a scholar. The incident was an impressive demonstration of the abiding scholarly truth that haste is the mother of error.

What had begun as a simple indulgence of curiosity eventually developed, through the use of detective procedures and, I must admit, a series of lucky accidents, into a publishable article, the three poets in the original title having now been increased to four. Since the article appeared, the publication of a previously unknown letter (at Baylor University) raised the possibility that I might expand it somewhat and revise the title once again, extending the number to five. It will be recalled that I had scanned the poetry Browning wrote between 1883 and his death in 1889 and found no Krakatoa allusion. But in *Browning's Trumpeter: The Correspondence of Robert Browning and Frederick J. Furnivall 1872–1889* (Washington, D.C., 1979) William S. Peterson printed a letter from Browning to Furnivall dated at Venice, 9 October 1883, in which he wrote, "October is clearly the best month for visiting Venice—the mornings are fresh, not to say cold,—then follows a clear blue sunny noontide, and the evenings are inaugurated by such sunsets as I believe are only to be seen here—when you float between two conflagrations—that of the day, reflected in the lagune."

Surely these were Krakatoa sunsets? But no: while they may well have been as spectacular as Browning said they were, especially in a Venetian setting, it is highly doubtful that their particular splendors had originated in an exploding mountain half a world away. Upon reviewing the Royal Society report once again, I found that, for one thing, the date was wrong: although the first sightings of the abnormal sunsets in England occurred at Chelsea and Haslemere—near Tennyson's home—between 20 September and 3 October, the spectacle did not reach its full intensity until after mid-November. In southern Europe there were observations in mid-October at Nice ("Extraordinarily beautiful sunsets and long glow") and Lisbon ("Remarkable sunsets with after-glows"), but the maps in the report that trace the distribution of sky effects at several stages from September to the end of the year show that in October Venice was on the very edge of the northern limit. Even during the maximum coverage of the continent in late November, when reports poured in from southern Scandinavia, Germany, Austria, Switzerland, and western Poland, Venice was barely on the periphery of a line running from Warsaw and Vienna southward, then curving southwesterly across the Adriatic and the eastern Mediterranean. It is true that Rome witnessed a "magnificent crimson glare like aurora" on 28 November, but Browning was writing on 9 October, and when he told Furnivall that the conflagrations in the sky were "only to be seen there"—in Venice—he was probably right, in a way he did not intend; for he was in all likelihood unaware that competing sunset displays were beginning to be watched in England. The most that can be salvaged from his praise of Venetian sunsets in early October is the slender possibility that they were slightly intensified—no more—by the approach of the atmospheric dust, and a fresh realization of the truth that historical hypotheses, no matter how attractive and plausible, have to be discarded when crucial dates and places don't fit.

1987

17
Adventures of an Annotator

When Dr. Johnson defined a lexicographer as a harmless drudge, he might well have extended the definition to cover another of his occupations, that of an annotator of literary texts. Both vocations have their share of unadventurous drudgery, though the latter also has its occasional moments of triumph over difficulty; and both, besides being harmless, make a solid, however unappreciated, contribution to our understanding of what the literary texts annotators so conscientiously gloss really mean. While there are undoubtedly larger personal and professional rewards in other forms of scholarly labor, annotating a work or two is good exercise for both the neophyte and the seasoned veteran, if for no other reason than the salutary reminders it provides of the fallibility of one's predecessors and one's own susceptibility to error. I know of no more convincing way for the scholar to learn, or relearn, the profound truth of the well-known axiom that in scholarship the price of truth is eternal vigilance and unremitting skepticism.

Although the tendencies of two major critical movements in the past half century—first the so-called New Criticism of the fifties, then the structuralism and deconstructionism of our own time—have been against the kind of approach to a text that annotation implies, the annotator's importance in the total sphere of literary study has actually increased. Whatever our personal critical allegiances, we must admit that allusions— topical, literary, or whatever—are often an integral part of the texture of a work, a part of the author's strategy as he appeals to a fund of knowledge he presumes a reader to possess; and that for a reasonably complete comprehension of what he is about, of precisely what he meant his first readers to understand by his statement, we must take adequate account not only of the easily explicable surface meaning of his allusions but, even more crucial, the overtones they possess. Although annotation is, in the first instance, a handmaiden of elucidation, in the end it serves the higher cause of interpretation. Allusions, properly illuminated, often turn out to be as full of subtle connotation, even of irony and ambiguity, as are their kinsmen, figures of speech.

Moreover, the patient explanation of allusions becomes more urgent year by year as the scope of information and of literary experience young readers possess steadily shrinks. Teachers of literature have discovered with increasing dismay that with every new generation comes a new level of ignorance. A number of recent studies have revealed to the general public that most products of our American high schools are abysmally ignorant of even the main facts of history. One cannot now be confident that an undergraduate will understand any kind of reference to past events, whether mythological, historical, biblical, or literary—the sort of thing Macaulay's hypothetical schoolboy could spot and explicate at the drop of a ruler. Even allusions to relatively recent topics (recent, that is, in the perspective of one who began teaching literature in the 1940s) perplex the student. As an initial effort to establish the level on which we would be communicating, I once made a practice of asking the students in a doctoral-level seminar I taught who Colonel Blimp was. The response was unanimously glassy-eyed.[1] While it may be asking too much for students to share with me a piece of information I enjoy by virtue of having been a knowledge-retaining adult when they (and nowadays their parents!) were yet unborn, it is regrettable that their fund of such general knowledge as is useful in explaining allusions in literary works contracts further and further, until it is now almost at the vanishing point as far as the great majority of readers, in and out of the classroom, are concerned.

Of course when he or she is reading works of English literature, the American student's legitimate need for annotation increases. Many references that the British student might be able to explain without any trouble are understandably beyond the American's ken, and so editions of English works primarily intended for the American market must be annotated with particular thoroughness. From what I read of the diminishing capacities of British pupils, however, I suspect that their need is approaching our own, and that the extensive annotation characteristic of the best present-day American classroom editions no longer seems, even in England, as gratuitous as it once did when students were in fact reasonably— or at least minimally—well-informed readers.[2]

A number of years ago I proposed to the publishers of the Riverside editions, distinguished in their time (as they still are, although the long series eventually came to a halt) for their scholarly standards of text and annotation, that I prepare for them an edition of Carlyle's *Past and Present,* of which no paperback was currently available and of which, in fact, no satisfactorily annotated edition was available in any form. *Past and Present* is a prodigiously allusive book. Indeed, this was my chief reason for suggesting that it be included in the Riverside series, for Carlyle's idio-syncratic prose, which presents difficulties enough as sheer literary style, needs constant explanatory annotation to a degree hardly matched in nineteenth-century literature. It would seem to follow, then, that the work must have been copiously footnoted by previous editors—that preceding my own exertions, which the publishers of the Riverside editions were pleased to encourage with a contract, there must have been what it is handy to call a substantial "annotating tradition." This was actually the case. To be sure, only one edition of the whole book, that prepared by A. M. D. Hughes for the Clarendon Press in 1918, was annotated with relative fullness and attention to scholarly detail (and this had long been out of print). The few other complete editions, such as Edwin Mimms's in Scribner's Modern Student's Library, contained only a few notes. But since portions of *Past and Present* were included in a number of classroom anthologies of English, or specifically Victorian, literature, or in small volumes of selections such as *The Best of Carlyle,* the notes of their editors added sizably to the total accreted annotation which came down to the new editor.

Now since conscientious annotation is a legitimate branch of literary scholarship, the same rules that apply to scholarship in general apply to it. Annotators, like scholars at large, are perfectly free to build upon their predecessors' work. There is no particular virtue in starting from scratch when a body of potentially useful information is already in print. And in a case such as *Past and Present,* as we shall see, the job still remaining to the editor after he has taken full advantage of his predecessors' industry is so large as to make it foolish indeed for him to refuse to benefit from it out of an adamant insistence on originality. (Whatever lingering scruples he might feel about absorbing someone else's annotation could be quieted by a preliminary acknowledgment of indebtedness.) But the very fact that he has access to the work of previous annotators imposes upon the editor a special scholarly obligation, which is to scrutinize every statement that comes down to him—never, in other words, to accept a previous editor's assertion without subjecting it to the test of critical scholarship. An ex-isting annotation must be examined with the same rigorous concern for accuracy as one gives to one's new contributions to the tradition.

As I proceeded with the task of sifting for possible adoption the annotations I inherited, it was all too easy to apply *New Yorker*-style labels to some of my predecessors. As a group, they might be called "Our Discrepant Annotators." In the very first chapter of *Past and Present,* Car-lyle observes, "Yes, in the Ugolino Hunger-tower stern things happen;

best-loved little Gaddo fallen dead on his Father's knees!" The notes accompanying the passage in various anthologies agreed that the reference was to Dante's *Inferno,* 33; but that was all they agreed on. Witness Annotator A (the italics in each instance are my own): "Count Ugolino who with his *two sons* and *two grandsons* was starved in prison." Annotator B: "He died, with *four sons,* in prison, starved to death." Annotator C: "He was imprisoned with *two sons* and *two nephews.*" Annotator D: ". . . the story of Ugolino and his *two sons.*" Who shall decide when doctors disagree? But that is what fresh annotators are for, and the answer, if we refer solely to Dante's text and not to any possibly obfuscating commentaries, is that Annotator B was correct: it was four sons, no grandsons, and no nephews.

Then there are "Our Dreaming Annotators." In Book 2, chapter 12, Carlyle writes: "And when he had narrated how he went away on purpose till his anger should cool, repeating this word of the philosopher, 'I would have taken vengeance on thee, had not I been angry,' he arose weeping and embraced each and all of us with the kiss of peace." To the quotation—I am glad, for the sake of his soul's resting in peace, that I did not record which annotator it was—was hung, in one edition, the succinct note, "Cicero." But where in Cicero's voluminous writings? I went through English translations without result; as a last resort I tried the desperate expedient of translating Carlyle's quoted words back into a hypothetical version of Cicero's Latin and then consulting the various Cicero dictionaries and concordances under the leading words. These heavy reference works are complicated, very hard to use, especially by a nonclassicist. With much difficulty I traced down the various passages where the individual words of my back-translation occurred, but nowhere could I find any statement resembling that clothed in Carlyle's words. Finally I did what I should have done in the first place, had not an unnecessarily Puritan sense of scholarly pertinacity insisted otherwise: I consulted a colleague in the classics department, who quickly supplied the answer. It was not Cicero at all, but Seneca, *De Ira,* 1.15.3. The anger of which Seneca wrote was as nothing compared with mine when I reckoned up the time I had wasted barking up the wrong tree and inventing clumsy Ciceronian Latin, thanks to some older editor who was satisfied to be guided by fancy rather than stern fact.

Although I have called him a dreamer (a politer term than he deserves), he also holds an adjunct membership among "Our Careless (or Indolent) Annotators," who are a numerous breed. For example, late in *Past and Present* Carlyle cries out against "mad Chartisms, impracticable

Sacred-Months, and Manchester Insurrections." According to one of the best-regarded survey-anthologies of English literature in which excerpts from *Past and Present* appear, "Sacred-Months" is "an allusion to the revolutionary calendar adopted in France in 1793; here, a symbol of the French Revolution itself." While there is no question that Carlyle's mind was steeped in imagery and allusions associated with the French Revolution—his great history of it had appeared a few years earlier—there is little to be gained by tracing the reference to an event that happened fifty years before *Past and Present* was published in 1843, when "Sacred-Months" can be shown to have had an immediately topical force. The term did indeed originate during the French Revolution, but it attained new currency during the Chartist agitation that is one of the book's chief concerns. In 1839 and the years following, the Chartists, a radical activist workingmen's party, proposed, as one means of exerting economic pressure on their employers and thus on Parliament, to hold month-long strikes, which they called "sacred months." It is undoubtedly to these that Carlyle was referring, as is made evident, for one thing, by his use of "impracticable," which would scarcely apply to the "Sacred Months" of the French Revolution.

In the same eight-word phrase Carlyle refers to "Manchester Insurrections," which at least four editors identify as alluding to the Peterloo Massacre in Manchester in 1819. But elsewhere Carlyle attaches the epithet "late" to his references to "Manchester Insurrections," and "late" would hardly be applicable to an event occurring twenty-four years earlier. Furthermore, although Peterloo involved bloodshed, it could not accurately be called an "insurrection," because it had begun as a peaceful assembly and became something more only when the attending troops overreacted, as we say, to what they nervously but mistakenly took to be the imminent threat of mob violence. The fact is that Carlyle was explicitly alluding to millworkers' riots that occurred in Manchester in August 1842, only a few weeks before he began writing *Past and Present*.

In the double error represented by the received annotation of this tiny passage we can read three useful lessons. One is that annotators must not be satisfied with the first possible, even plausible, explanation that offers itself. The facts that Sacred Months did figure in the French revolutionary calendar, and that there was bloodshed in Manchester in 1819, are easily ascertained from reference works, but this is far from proof that Carlyle had these circumstances in mind here. The annotator must be prepared to dig deeper whenever there is any possibility that the superficially obvious answer is not the right one. Secondly, he must take into account the author's demonstrated purpose in writing—the occasion of the book, the overall context. *Past and Present* was meant to be a tract for the times, as topical as the daily newspaper, and for this reason there is a high degree of likelihood that some apparently long-range historical allusions may actually have a close connection with the moment of writing. In choosing between two alternative explanations, therefore, the annotator may safely be guided by the general nature of the book. Thirdly, annotators must also pay close heed to the context of an allusion within the very sentence in which it occurs. In the present instance, one recalls that the phrase went: "Chartisms, impracticable Sacred-Months, and Manchester Insurrections." Although the rule is not absolute, the assumption is that in so closely linked a series Carlyle meant to be understood as referring to all three events as immediately contemporary manifestations of the same phenomenon that was alarming him. The occurrence of "Chartism" at the head of the series surely points to "Sacred-Months" and "Manchester Insurrections" as alluding to events inextricably associated with Chartism, which was a totally new movement in 1838–43.

I found other examples of the same curious short-sightedness on the part of annotators, their failure to recognize the influence of the book's highly topical purpose upon the intention of allusions. Carlyle writes at one place of a "Master Unworker" (that is, an aristocratic landowner) "coercing fifty-pound tenants; coercing, bribing, cajoling; 'doing what he likes with his own.' " One anthology glosses this merely by reference to Matthew 20:15, where the quoted phrase does occur. But (see above, pages 40–41) the point is that Carlyle here is referring to a notorious protest by the crusty, reactionary Duke of Newcastle, who used these words, with their biblical weight of authority, when he was criticized in Parliament for having evicted every one of his tenants who failed to vote for his candidate in the election of 1829. The plea was bitterly disliked at the time, and it was so well remembered that one finds it quoted by Victorian writers many years after *Past and Present* appeared.

It is ironic that the same anthology, which in this case relied on the Bible too exclusively for its annotation, in another case failed to rely enough. Carlyle writes: "for him [the Quack] and his there is no continuance appointed, save only in Gehenna and the Pool." The footnote reads: "The Thames River for several miles below London Bridge," which is more or less accurate. But "Pool" so explained makes no sense here. Actually it alludes to the lake of brimstone in Revelations 19–20, as is made clear by its being linked with Gehenna. This is another plain instance of an editor's failure to take advantage of the light offered by the immediate context.

Another of our careless (or indolent) annotators drops from Carlyle's reference to "Owen's Labor-Bank" the explanation, "Planned by Robert Owen . . . but not achieved." In a second text, the same phrase prompts the note, "An enterprise proposed by the Chartists in 1847." Here we have three errors. (1) The Labor-bank, more properly the Labor-exchange, was a market at which artisans could sell their goods directly to the consumer, without the intervention of a middleman, and price them according to the value of the labor involved in their production. It not only was planned by Owen but actually existed for a time. (2) It was *not* proposed by the Chartists, despite what the second editor asserts. (3) Although it may be unjust to pillory an editor for what may have been an error in his notes or a typographical blunder, still scholarship, if it is worth anything, is obligated to guard against mistaken notes and uncorrected typos; and if we are to accept the statement that the Chartists proposed the Labor-bank in 1847, we are entitled to ask what significance Carlyle's first readers would have found in an allusion to an event that would not take place until four years later. Carlyle wore the mantle of a biblical prophet, but he did not possess a crystal ball.

In the edition of *Past and Present* prepared by Hughes, the only editor for whom I retained almost unalloyed respect once I had concluded my labors, "the late Bribery committee" is said to refer to a committee of the House of Commons appointed in 1835 to investigate some cases of flagrant corruption in the recent election. Had he examined the record of events in 1842 more carefully, he would have found that there was another bribery committee appointed in that year, which is obviously the one that Carlyle had in mind. Again, the force of "late"—which would hardly apply to an example seven years earlier if a more recent one existed—helps point the annotator to the truth.

The toughest, most tantalizing problem in the whole of my enterprise required a search for the answer that consumed, I am sure, considerably more time than is required for the preparation of a well-researched graduate term paper. It went on literally for months. The passage in Carlyle is this—one of the most memorable in the whole book, and having additional interest nowadays in that it describes a primitive model of what has come to be called, in the pontificate of John Paul II, the Popemobile:

The old Pope of Rome, finding it laborious to kneel so long while they cart him through the streets to bless the people on *Corpus-Christi* Day, complains of rheumatism; whereupon his Cardinals consult;—construct him, after some study, a stuffed cloaked figure, of iron and wood, with wool or baked hair; and place it in a kneeling posture. Stuffed figure, or rump of a figure; to this stuffed rump he, sitting at his ease on a lower level, joins, by the aid of cloaks and drapery, his living head and outspread hands: the rump with its cloaks kneels, the Pope looks, and holds his hands spread; and so the two in concert bless the Roman population on *Corpus-Christi* Day, as well as they can.

There was no reason to doubt that Carlyle was describing an actual practice. But neither he nor any of his annotators provided any documentary evidence for it. Naturally, I wanted to know more.

In searching, I made the initial mistake of assuming that the practice was new, or peculiar to the then reigning Pope. This was consistent with the principle I have already mentioned, that in the allusions that dot a book like *Past and Present* one is justified in suspecting a large incidence of immediate topicality. But it is a poor principle that does not have its exceptions, and this is not one of them. I therefore ransacked the university library for whatever information I could find on Gregory XVI, in collected lives of the Popes, the *Catholic Encyclopedia,* articles on the Papacy in contemporary periodicals, even the London *Times* for news articles on recent Corpus Christi Day processions in Rome: but to no avail. The first break in the case came by sheer accident. I was sitting in my study at home, ruminating about something totally unconnected with this mild but as yet unverified example of pontifical deceit, when my eyes happened to light on the shelf where rested my copy of the two-volume diary of Henry Crabb Robinson (1869). Idly I wondered whether, since old Crabb traveled a lot, he might not have witnessed such a procession when in Rome. I took the book from the shelf, and the index directed me, without a moment's hesitation, to such a description, dated 1830, the year before Gregory XVI became Pope. Clearly, therefore, Carlyle was referring not to something that would have been in the papers in 1841–42 but to a regular practice in Rome, not limited to one Pope. With this clue, I renewed my search in the library, this time going to all the available reference books on religious festivals and customs. Some of these went so far as to describe Corpus Christi Day processions, but mainly in connection with medieval mystery plays. They contained nothing on the Pope's public impersonation.

Finally I went to the card catalogue—a procedure that the professional scholar, well acquainted with the specialized tools of his trade, disdains as the ignoble resort of the bibliographically incompetent, but which occasionally rewards even the expert—and looked up books devoted to Roman customs alone. Here I struck pay dirt. In *La Vie quotidienne dans la Rome pontificale au XVIIIe siècle* (Paris, 1962) Maurice Andrieux quotes Fernand Hayward, *Les deux Siècles de la Rome pontificale 1679–1870* (Paris, 1928). I translate: "The Pope, draped with an immense cope of gold cloth, was borne on a kind of platform; he held the sacred Host in a gleaming monstrance. To avoid excessive fatigue to a Pope who often was aged, he was seated on a small stool hidden by the folds of a large robe, so that he appeared to be kneeling before the Holy Sacrament."

The result of this seemingly interminable quest was a one-line footnote in my edition, stating simply that Carlyle was referring to—and in his characteristic way picturesquely embellishing—an established custom in Rome, and citing Crabb Robinson's description. Once the hard-won note was in type, further stuffed Popes, like the duplicate kings in the battle scene at the end of 1 Henry IV, kept turning up. Even before the book appeared, I ran across another description, like Crabb Robinson's dated 1830, in the memoirs of Charles Greville; and two and a half years later I found a third, in William Wetmore Story's *Roba di Roma* (1876).

Such are the pleasures of serendipity. Another case was that represented by the note I appended to Carlyle's reference to "some Morrison's Pill, some Saint-John's corrosive mixture." The Morrison's Pill allusion was, and always had been, crystal clear, because that particular all-purpose nostrum, which claimed to be equally effective against both constipation and diarrhea, was famous; it was advertised, for instance, in the monthly parts in which Dickens's novels first appeared. But what about "Saint-John's corrosive mixture"? No editor had ever explained the phrase, and St. John, as a figure presumably contemporary with Carlyle, was in no biographical dictionary. In going through the periodicals of 1842 for possible enlightenment on other allusions, I happened to find in an issue of the *Quarterly Review* for that year a long and instructive article on the patent medicines and quackery of the day, in which a paragraph or two were devoted to "St. John *Long*," which was almost his full name (a preliminary "John" seems to have been dropped in common usage). There, of course, was the reason why no earlier annotator had identified him and why any studious recourse to reference works was doomed from the outset: whether by error or inscrutable design, Carlyle had referred to him by his middle, rather than his family, name. This gratifying discovery led me to the *Dictionary of National Biography,* where I found more information, and resulted in the following note: "A concoction of St. John Long, quack physician to the carriage trade. Reputed to contain oil of turpentine and mineral acid, it was used to treat consumption, rheumatism, gout, abscesses of the lungs and liver, and insanity. Long was convicted of manslaughter in 1830." Had space permitted, I might have added that he had previously been acquitted of a similar charge, thanks to the testimony of a number of titled and otherwise eminent personages who swore by his curative powers.

I have subsequently made a hobby of pursuing the estimable St. John Long wherever he lurks in the annals of his day. Some further facts are to be found earlier in this volume (pages 39–40). When I was doing research for my book on British art from 1760 to 1900, I ran across the unexpected fact that before he discovered the magical powers of his fiery salve, Long had been an aspiring artist: he was briefly a pupil of the painter John Martin, the master of the cataclysmic sublime, and had succeeded so far as to be allowed to exhibit a picture or two at the prestigious Royal Academy. But my happiest encounter with him was even more accidental. In the interests of another book, I had penetrated into the incipient wilderness of London's Kensal Green cemetery in search of the mausoleum enclosing the remains of the great equestrian showman Andrew Ducrow. Eventually I discovered it, hideously vandalized as are most of the other monuments in those funerary acres, and after standing in melancholy admiration of this once imposing memorial—a miniature Greek temple with Egyptian trimmings and Aesculapian emblems—I took the requisite snapshot and turned away. And there, directly opposite, I was confronted by the equally majestic resting place of St. John Long, who had died in 1834 of the very same disease—consumption—that he had purported to cure in others. No one not acquainted, as I fortunately was, with his gaudy history and the way in which, against all reason, he had inspired the steadfast loyalty of his wealthy patrons could read the ironic subtext that lay beneath the inscribed epitaph, worded as it was with exquisite evasiveness:

IT IS THE FATE OF MOST MEN TO HAVE MANY ENEMIES, AND FEW FRIENDS. THIS MONUMENTAL PILE IS NOT INTENDED TO MARK THE CAREER, BUT TO SHEW HOW MUCH ITS INHABITANT WAS RESPECTED BY THOSE WHO KNEW HIS WORTH AND THE BENEFITS

DERIVED FROM HIS REMEDIAL DISCOVERY. HE IS NOW AT REST AND
FAR BEYOND THE PRAISES OR CENSURES OF THIS WORLD. STRANGER
AS YOU RESPECT THE RECEPTACLE FOR THE DEAD (AS ONE OF THE
MANY WHO WILL REST HERE), READ THE NAME OF *JOHN SAINT
JOHN LONG* WITHOUT COMMENT.

No comment was needed. But if it in fact was required, it had already
been supplied, in italics, by Carlyle's physician brother, writing in *Fraser's
Magazine* (January 1831). After a thorough search of the "records of
quackery," he had concluded that

> *no determined resolute pretender to physic, who had possessed himself
> of a sufficient stock of impudence and knavery, had ever failed to
> succeed in realizing a fortune by public infatuation, and that with a
> rapidity in the exact ratio of his ignorance, and the extravagance of
> his pretensions.*

Much of the satisfaction derived from an extensive course of editing
comes from such pinning down of allusions that have previously been
unexplicated. Carlyle speaks of man as being a "Patent-Digester." What is
the point? Luckily, in his fine edition of *Sartor Resartus* my former colleague, the late Charles Frederick Harrold, bequeathed me a clue; for
in *Sartor* Carlyle refers to "a Papin's-Digester," and Harrold explained:
"Famous 'steam-digester,' a closed vessel in which the boiling point
of water was considerably raised; invented by Denis Papin (1647–ca. 1712),
French physicist, and one of the inventors of the steam-engine." The
"Patent-Digester" in *Past and Present* is obviously a half-punning adaptation of the earlier "Papin's Digester." Later I came upon the same appli-
ance, a kind of early pressure cooker, in chapter 38 of *Pickwick Papers*.
And from this particular exercise in elucidation I enjoyed a spinoff, for
when I came to annotate Browning's *The Ring and the Book* it enabled
me to detect an additional dimension in Browning's use of the strange
word "Papinianian," one of his many coinages. The word is, in fact, a
four-way pun.

There is satisfaction, too, in being able to improve an existing annotation, either by adding fresh information or by making it more specific. Thus when Carlyle cries, "Is it not scandalous to consider that
a Prime Minister could raise within the year, as I have seen it done,
a Hundred and Twenty Millions Sterling to shoot the French?" it is

instructive to go back to the government's financial records for the Napoleonic Wars—the period Carlyle supposedly is alluding to—and discover that, as the resulting note puts it, "Carlyle seems to exaggerate. The largest annual revenue during the Napoleonic Wars was collected in 1814; it amounted to £105,600,000 from all sources. The war expenditure in that year was £71,700,000." It is part of the annotator's responsibility to confront the author's rhetoric with documented facts, and, as a corollary, to help the rhetoric achieve its desired effect when the deficient cultural equipment of a later age makes it probable the point will be missed. Carlyle remarks at one place, dispensing with quotation marks, "Though he slay me, yet will I despise him." Earlier editors properly cited the source, Job 13:15. But they evidently did not feel obligated to explain to modern readers what Carlyle rightly expected his own to detect: namely, that he was deliberately misquoting Job for the sake of the effect that such misquotations, when recognized, often have. Hence I felt it necessary to quote the actual words of the Bible, "Though he slay me, yet will I *trust* in him," to ensure that no one would remain unaware that Carlyle slyly substituted "despise" for "trust" and so inverted the whole meaning of the sentence.

Similarly, I felt called upon to clarify the familiar allusion Carlyle made, not only in *Past and Present* but in several other places, to the supposed exchange at the celebrated trial in 1824 of Thurtell for the murder of Weare. "Q. What sort of person was Mr. Weare? A. Mr. Weare was respectable. Q. What do you mean by respectability? A. He kept a gig." This modest vehicle, the cheapest means of private transportation one could buy, became Carlyle's abiding symbol of fatuous middle-class status-consciousness, and from his pages it sprang to other writers', soon acquiring the currency of a proverbial expression. The truth, of which earlier editors of *Past and Present* seem to have been unaware, is that the reports of the trial contain no such dialogue. Carlyle's source, a writer in the *Quarterly Review* in 1828, who admitted he was quoting from memory, may have been thinking of a sentence in a London newspaper's coverage of the trial: "He always maintained an appearance of respectability and kept a gig." A small point, but there is always something to be said for putting the record straight.

When one is attempting to explicate so catholically allusive a writer as Carlyle, perfect success is not to be hoped for. The unsolved problem that bothered me most as I sent off my manuscript to the publisher was a set of verses at the end of the "Practical-Devotional" chapter:

The Builder of this Universe was wise,
He plann'd all souls, all systems, planets, particles:
The Plan He shap'd His Worlds and Æons by
Was—Heavens!—Was thy small Nine-and-thirty Articles?

The context is plain enough. It refers to the Oxford movement, the decisive manifesto of which, Newman's *Tract 90*, was published about a year and a half before Carlyle began to write *Past and Present*. (There may also be a side-glance at the doctrine of "Natural Theology"—the belief that the order of the physical universe is witness to the existence of a God who did all the planning—which was then in the intellectual news because of the publication of the so-called Bridgewater Treatises, a series of monographs dedicated to proving "the Power, Wisdom, and Goodness of God, as Manifested in the Creation.") But diligent search in all the places I could think of failed to turn up the lines quoted. I had to content myself with dropping a note to the lines, beginning "The authorship of the quatrain seems not to have been established" and going on to capsulize the essential information about *Tract 90* and its place in the history of the Oxford Movement. Only a year ago did I discover that, as when I was tracking down the phantom quotation from Cicero, I had been on a wild goose chase from the outset. A slim volume that sweeps together the fragments of verse Carlyle himself composed includes the quatrain, which was written on a slip of paper affixed to the printer's copy of *Past and Present*.[3] I had allowed for the possibility that Carlyle was in fact the author, but I was justified, I think, in believing that he was quoting someone—a reasonable assumption in view of the complex network of allusions and buried quotations of which the book is composed.

Furnished as the annotator's mind has become with all the diversified subjects he has coped with in his efforts at explication, long after the edition has appeared his antennae remain up, receptive to every bit of relevant information that might, in some instances, have significantly amplified or altered a note as it was printed. In an early page of *Past and Present*, Carlyle mentions "the picturesque Tourist," by which, as my note correctly says, he meant himself. But I might have added that he was quoting a title often used for books belonging to a particular form of travel literature, and in a letter to Ralph Waldo Emerson in June 1841, as I later found out, he had referred to "the whole gang of Picturesque Tourists, Cockney friends of Nature &c &c, who penetrate now by steam, in shoals every autum [sic], into the very centre of the Scotch Highlands."[4]

His reference to "tankards of Heavy-wet" at the conclusion of a passage ridiculing the nation's "Collective Wisdom" (Parliament) is not sufficiently illuminated by the succinct note "Strong ale or stout," which is accurate as far as it goes but does not give the whole story (see above, pages 47–48).

Toward the end of the book, "black Quashee" and "the Haiti Duke of Marmalade" are explained as "General name for a Negro" and "Carlyle's derogatory invention" respectively. What I did not know in time to benefit from it was that "Quashee" or "Quashy" was not only "a negro personal name," as the *Oxford English Dictionary* says, but one that figures in antislavery literature dating as far back as the eighteenth century; that it remained current in Carlyle's time is indicated by Thackeray's mention of "Quashyboo Mission" in *Vanity Fair,* chapter 64. The "Duke of Marmalade" was another generic name but, notwithstanding my own note, it was not Carlyle's invention; Samuel Warren had already used it in his novel *Ten Thousand a Year* (1839–41). How widely current it was at this time is suggested by its presence in a letter James Fenimore Cooper wrote to the editor of the weekly *Brother Jonathan* on 7–11 (?) February 1842: "Christophe [i.e., Jean Christophe, late "Emperor" of northern Haiti] had *his* Dukes of Marmalade, and Lemonade, and, if the European pretension is to be maintained, they were the social superiors of John Jay, and Alexander Hamilton . . ."[5] And so the annotator's work is never fully done, if one allows for the inevitable residue of notes that could stand further refinement.

The use that readers will make of all those small-type lines at the bottom of the page—the gain in understanding to which the elucidations contribute—is reward enough, no doubt, for the time, energy, and patience the annotator has invested. But sometimes the exercise can have larger consequences. Having once got interested in explaining the topical allusions in *Past and Present,* I pursued the subject far beyond the limits of a footnoted edition, convinced that Carlyle's pattern of references to recent and contemporary events and personalities as a basic element of his technique has critical significance. The result, as the reader has doubtless perceived, was the essay printed elsewhere in this volume.

1987

"Our Gallant Colonel"
in *Punch* and Parliament

Public figures who opposed early Victorian progress with the full fervor of their reactionary opinions were not uncommon. They were at least as numerous as the eccentrics with whom the era was replete, and from whom they often were, as in the present case, indistinguishable. Only a few, however, have won a permanent place in the curious annals of Victorian society largely by virtue of their backward-looking views, without the assistance of any memorable accomplishment. Such a man was Colonel Charles DeLaet Waldo Sibthorp of Lincoln, whose facetious fame while alive and subsequent enshrinement in the *Dictionary of National Biography* were—apart from the peculiarities of appearance and manner that made him God's gift to caricaturists and the makers of lampoons—due wholly to his noisy, disrupting, obstructive presence in Parliament for almost three decades.

A fair number of other people held as he held on various issues; some, publicly or privately, fulminated as he did; but only he made so lengthy and comic a display of last-ditch Toryism. Others may have declared in Parliament, as he did, that reform was "a thing which he detested as he detested the devil," and concurred in his view of innovation, which, he said, "was at best a dangerous thing; and he had seen in his own time so many dangerous results from innovations—for instance, the Reform Bill, which had done everything to cause revolution—railroads, and other dangerous novelties—that he felt disposed to oppose everything savoring of innovation."[1] But not many other men with access to the public ear would have enlarged upon his theme, as Sibthorp characteristically did, by confiding to a rapt House of Commons that "he disapproved of the new patent water-closets, and much preferred the old system."

By virtue of its extravagance, truculence, obstinacy, and sheer farcical grandeur, Sibthorp's comprehensive opposition to everything that had even the faintest odor of change was a spectacle that enlivened the English political scene in turbulent, critical years when it particularly needed the saving touch of comedy. The recorded reception of that spectacle in both Parliament and press affords us a lively view of the way extreme conservatism, recklessly expressed, appeared to the dominant spirit of the age,

OCCASIONS

self-consciously "enlightened," liberal, forward-looking, and eager for improvement. Without becoming inappropriately solemn, it is not unfair to suggest that in the quality of Sibthorp's opinions and the notoriety they earned him we glimpse, distorted as in a curved mirror, the outlines of the conflict between outdated past and on-going present that was joined in the early Victorian mind.

Except for a lively article by Christopher Sykes,[2] the Colonel has not received much attention from modern students of his era. Those who note his ubiquitous presence in the early volumes of *Punch* have an understandable tendency to dismiss him as a myth, an all-purpose butt dreamed up around the paper's editorial table. But when one refers to the sober pages of *Hansard,* the myth at once turns into a man: a man not wholly credible, to be sure, but unquestionably present, protesting, and voting no. A systematic pursuit of Sibthorp through the files of both *Punch* and Hansard, though a laborious operation, is not without its rewards.

From 1841, *Punch's* first year of publication, to 1855 "our Gallant Colonel," as the paper's editors called him with a distinct air of proprietorship, was the subject of some 345 references, ranging from two-line quips to extended burlesques; and his unforgettable face stares out at us from over fifty drawings.[3] In the beginning, his name was used ordinarily as a peg on which to hang the pallid puns and melancholy riddles that were *Punch's* first staple. The theory was that if a witticism was not funny enough in itself, attaching the name of Sibthorp would make it so. The frequency with which *Punch* offered packets of assorted facetiae headed "Conundrums by Col. Sibthorp" or "Sibthorp's Corner," or prefaced by "Col. Sibthorp was overheard to say," suggests that it was exploiting a well-established conditioned reflex among its readers. But often the humor was specifically adapted to, or suggested by, the risible figure behind the name. Any remark about whiskers, any pun on *hair/hare/air,* was bound to involve Sibthorp, as was any joke on *goose, ass,* or *wits (lack of).* By the mid-forties the real or reputed opinions of Sibthorp became as much a topic of fun as his personal oddities. Although occasionally the editors became almost sharp in rebuking Lincoln for returning him,[4] there is no question of their affection for him; for a decade and a half the steady flow of Sibthorpian jokes, skits, and cartoons helped sell the paper.

The Colonel came from an influential landowning family long resident at Lincoln.[5] His forebears had represented the town in Parliament since the early eighteenth century, the Colonel's immediate predecessors in the seat having been his father and his elder brother Coningsby. The

••• 268 •••

Sibthorps were, as a matter of fact, adept at keeping seats of more than one sort in the family; the Colonel's grandfather, Dr. Humphrey Sibthorp, passed the Sherardian chair of botany at Oxford, which he had occupied from 1747 to 1784, to his son John. Although subordinated to John in the *DNB,* where the latter, because of his travels and publications as a botanist and his correspondence with Linnaeus, has the dignity of a separate article, Humphrey was not without his achievements. If his zeal for the diffusion of learning was not very marked—in all his years as Sherardian professor he delivered but a single lecture, and that one was a failure—he exerted himself in behalf of his family to the substantial extent of marrying, in succession, two heiresses, each the daughter of a wealthy London merchant.[6]

Charles Sibthorp, the future inheritor of the estate thus augmented, was born on 14 February 1783. He matriculated at Brasenose College, Oxford, in 1801, but left without a degree. His temperamental suitability for academic life is adequately indicated by his remark a half century later, when denouncing Ewart's bill to permit the levying of rates to build free libraries, that "he did not like reading at all, and he hated it when at Oxford." More to his taste was soldiering. He first joined the Royal Scots Greys, exchanging later to the Fourth Royal Irish Dragoons—he married the daughter of a securely seated Irish M.P.—and serving on the Peninsula with Wellington. After the peace of 1815 he gravitated, in the familiar way of English officers, to the militia of his county, in which his father and great-uncle had also held colonelcies.

The tenor of his political life was accurately foreshadowed in 1824, when he fought a duel with one Dr. Charles Shuttleworth over "some uncomplimentary language at a Turnpike Meeting," and two years later, when he stood for Parliament for the first time on a platform based on uncompromising opposition to Catholic emancipation and "any attempts to subvert that glorious fabric our matchless Constitution." The canvassing in 1826 was enlivened by scurrilous lampoons and *jeux d'esprit,* and during the subsequent chairing he was "struck in the face, and much hurt by a stone." But the seat was his, and his it remained until his death in 1855, with but one brief interval, the Reformed Parliament of 1833–34, when he lost it, by eighty-eight votes, to the young radical, Edward Lytton Bulwer. To assuage the Colonel's sorrow over this, his only electoral defeat, the ladies of Lincoln presented him with a silver vase and a handsome diamond ring. He was sent back to Parliament at the next election, but at the same time Bulwer won the other Lincoln seat, which he held until 1841.[7] The constituency's political schizophrenia persisted throughout

Sibthorp's life, repeatedly visiting upon the Colonel, with an irony he no doubt failed to relish, a colleague of liberal views. As the *Times* observed in its obituary notice (17 December 1855), "the predilections of the constituency [were] rather personal towards himself than based on any political grounds." One cannot define with utter certainty the nature of Sibthorp's peculiar powers over the 1,300 electors of Lincoln, whose true sympathies, as evidenced by their vote for the second seat, lay elsewhere than in an ideology considerably to the right of Lord Eldon's; but a clue may perhaps be found in his reaction to the repeated attempts to eliminate corrupt practices in English elections, a topic at which we will glance in due course.

The Colonel had been in Parliament nine years when Charles Dickens looked down on him from the reporters' gallery:

> You see this ferocious-looking personage, with a com-
> plexion almost as sallow as his linen, and whose large black
> mustachios would give him the appearance of a figure in a
> hair-dresser's window, if his countenance possessed one ray of
> the intelligence communicated to those waxen caricatures
> of the human face divine. He is a militia-man, with a brain
> slightly damaged, and (quite unintentionally) the most amus-
> ing person in the House. Can anything be more exquisitely
> absurd than the burlesque grandeur of his air, as he strides up
> to the lobby, his eyes rolling like those of a Turk's head in a
> cheap Dutch clock? He never appears without that bundle of
> dirty papers which he carries under his left arm—they are
> generally supposed to be the miscellaneous estimates for 1804,
> or some equally important documents. You must often have
> seen him in the box-lobbies of the theatres during the vacation.
> He is very punctual in his attendance at the House, and his
> self-satisfied "He-ar He-ar" is not unfrequently the signal for
> a general titter.
>
> This is the man who once actually sent a messenger up to
> the Strangers' Gallery in the old House of Commons, to in-
> quire the name of a gentleman who was using an eye-glass, in
> order that he (the Militia-man) might complain to the Speaker
> that the individual in question was quizzing him! On another
> occasion, he repaired to Bellamy's kitchen—a refreshment-
> room, where persons who are not Members are admitted on
> sufferance, as it were—and perceiving two or three gentlemen

at supper, who he was aware were not Members, and could not in that place very well resent his insolence, he indulged in the exquisite pleasantry and gentlemanly facetiousness of sitting with his booted leg on the table at which they were supping! He is generally harmless, and his absurdities are amusing enough.[8]

Dickens's delight in Sibthorp's grotesque appearance was shared by *Punch*'s caricaturists. No drawing of a representative parliamentary group was complete without him. His face was as much of a humorous cliché as his name. It suggested an unsuccessful brigand: a lean and hungry look, deep-set and fanatically gleaming eyes, and, framing all, the most famous mustache and whiskers of the age. These last were luxuriant in the extreme, but as little touched by scissors, comb, and brush as his mind was affected by the Victorian idea of progress. His exuberant hairiness was both his personal pride and his public fortune. A Sibthorp shaven and shorn would not exactly have been overlooked—there remained his opinions, after all—but he would have had considerably less savor for the pictorial press.

"His dress," the *DNB* remarks in a demure understatement, "attracted attention." A writer in *Fraser's Magazine* in 1847 was less restrained: "It looks," he said, "like the *débris* of what must once have been a *magnifico* . . . [It has] a majestic air of tawdry grandeur. . . . The costume is a perfect kaleidoscope; it belongs to no mundane mode. . . . Now, it gives the wearer the ultra-rakish air of an outsider of the betting-ring; now, a tyrannical idea fuses all clear outlines of coat, vest, and pantaloons into a loose, enveloping drapery, till you behold a sallow and bearded Turk."[9] All this, and fingers laden with "sparkling brilliants" too—and, as irresistible to the caricaturists as the whiskers, an enormous gold quizzing-glass on a stout chain.

Sibthorp's conduct in the House was as spectacular as his appearance, and, to those of his colleagues who wanted to get on with business, infinitely more annoying. Their reaction, when he got up to speak, was a mixture of groans and laughter. His attitude on a given question was predictable enough, as were the words he would couch his ideas in, and the practical tactics he would use. He was, in the judgment of men who had suffered him for years, a bl——y bore.[10] Nevertheless there was always the happy possibility of some new gambit, some fresh display of outrageous candor, some hitherto unrevealed object of his animus, to lighten the Westminster air. And so, after a noisy prelude during which the Colonel stood silent and imperturbable, his disorderly roll of papers tucked under his arm, the House would let him begin. In an uneven voice, sometimes resounding and shrill, at other times inaudible; with right arm beating the air above his head, and his small frame pivoting and attitudinizing, he would proceed to add to the Sibthorp legend.

As Peel once noted on the floor, his speeches were "seasoned with that quality of vituperation which is not unusual, and perhaps is to him natural." Sibthorp's vocabulary of abuse, indeed, was as rank as his whiskers. His mastery of parliamentary billingsgate is indicated by this representative but far from complete list of terms in which he was accustomed to denounce governments, parties, policies, bills, and persons:

> corrupt, truckling, obnoxious, machinations, nefarious, jobbery, infamous, absurd, cowardice, oppressive, humbug, "a disgrace to the country," "inactive, weak, ignorant, useless," unconstitutional, tyrannical, fraudulent, paltry, disreputable, vacillating, abominable, claptrap, "profligate, lazy, inefficient," duplicity, mismanagement, delinquency, arbitrary, inquisitorial, subserviency, expediency, tergiversation, pusillanimous, incompetent, "hollow, treacherous," Jesuitical, "trickery, trumpery, and trash," "mean, dirty, shabby," plunder, "weak, incapable, and irresolute," "imbecility and impudence," "apostasy, hypocrisy, and perfidy."

His speeches were laden with blunt aspersions upon the political morality of his opponents and of the placemen in the ever-expanding bureaucracy. He verged upon slander so often that one must conclude that by silent agreement he was treated with an indulgence withheld from less picturesque members. Probably the people he attacked with such monotonous iteration resigned themselves to it; after all, they must have reflected, it was only old Sibthorp talking, in the only language he knew. To make an issue of his choice of words would merely have wasted more time.

Which is not to say, of course, that, once begun, he was listened to with unfailing gravity and patience. Many were the speeches that were interrupted by "[Laughter]," to which Sibthorp customarily responded with the ominous assurance that "Hon. Gentlemen might laugh, but the day would soon come when their countenances would bear a very different appearance. . . . He cared as little for their smiles as he did for their frowns." Perhaps even more frequent than laughter, and proof that

Sibthorp's auditors were by no means always amused, were "[Loud cries of 'Adjourn! adjourn!' or 'Divide! divide!']" and other "considerable indications of impatience" which the reporter did not further describe. But Sibthorp was never rattled. "Let the gallèd jade wince," he was fond of observing, "his withers were unwrung." When the noise died down, he plunged forward with dauntless equanimity.

His positive accomplishments were few. In August 1831, to be sure, he narrowly missed earning a place in the history books. During the debate on the Reform Bill, he moved an amendment to enfranchise the fifty-pound tenant farmer. But (as was his unlucky habit) he miscalculated his timing, and was declared out of order; it therefore fell instead to the Marquess of Chandos to embody the proposal in a successful amendment which substantially altered the nature of Reform. By this quirk of parliamentary fate, the amendment became known as Chandos's rather than Sibthorp's. The indignant Sibthorp protested that his motion had been first according to the clock, if not the rules; and, again typically, he found his Latin questioned. "Hos ego versiculos scripsi, tulit alter honores—" he observed. A member suggested that Virgil's word was *feci*, not *scripsi*. "Well, *scripsi* or *feci*," replied Sibthorp, unabashed, "I don't know which, though I wrote it down. But *scripsi* or *feci*, I did both, and I take credit for both."

In 1840 Sibthorp successfully urged the reduction of the annuity of Prince Albert (a foreigner) from £50,000 to £30,000—a deed to which the newly married Queen is said to have responded by vowing never to visit Lincoln so long as Sibthorp represented it. His chosen function, however, was that of the perpetual naysayer, the dedicated and resourceful obstructionist. When a bill he disliked was introduced, he would announce that "he would oppose it in every stage, and clause by clause": a threat he never failed to make good down to the smallest detail. When he himself introduced a motion, it was almost never a constructive proposal, but rather an amendment that would in effect simply nullify the intent of the original bill; or, just as often, a maneuver which, if successful, would bury the bill for good. On uncounted occasions he moved the "six months' amendment," which in parliamentary practice is equivalent to rejection. Time after time his fellow members pleaded with him not to press the motion; but with few exceptions, he insisted on a division, which he almost invariably lost. Another form of obstructionism (sometimes justified, it is true, by the government's steam-rollering tactics) was to move for adjournment on the ground that the hour was too late to permit adequate discussion of a measure.

Probably no other member was responsible for so many unnecessary divisions, his insistence on which was always motivated, as he took pains (and time) to point out, by his simple sense of Duty, from which he would not be swayed by appeals from impatient members on either side of the House. At a conservative estimate, he found himself in the minority nineteen out of every twenty times the House divided. It is probably fair to say that no member of Parliament in his time was more ineffectual— and certainly no member equaled him in the flamboyant way in which he accomplished nothing. Nothing, that is, except delay and irritation.

If he was hard on his fellow members, he was no easier on official-dom. He loved to demand extensive statistical reports from government offices. In 1838, for example, he called for a return of "the present valu-ation. . . . of all the property . . . which originally belonged" to all the church institutions that had ever been alienated, as well as of "the names of the individuals to whom, and the periods at which, such were granted, and by whom they are now severally enjoyed." The horrified attorney-general protested that a form would have to be sent to every landowner in England and Wales, and at least a million titles searched for the past four centuries. "He supposed that the motion of the hon. and gallant Officer was intended merely as a piece of pleasantry, and to amuse the House." Sibthorp retorted, as always when his earnestness was questioned, that he was perfectly serious, and "he treated the observations of the hon. and learned Gentleman with the most sovereign contempt."

The next year Sibthorp, suspicious of the extravagant expenditures that reportedly had attended the Durham mission to Canada, moved for a full accounting, down to the last fur cloak and champagne cork. Lord John Russell observed that as the motion stood, "it was not very consistent either with common sense or with the English language." Sibthorp "re-pelled the insinuation with sovereign contempt, in as strong language as the House would allow him to use, in answer to the unbecoming lan-guage of the noble Lord. He could tell the noble Lord, that he would not venture to make use of such observations out of that House." For this, he drew a warning from the Speaker. But he insisted that "he would have his return or no return at all. . . . He did not care whether his motion pleased the noble Lord or not, or whether he thought that it was consistent with common sense and good grammar, as he was sure that he could never learn anything from the noble Lord; and he was determined that he would never follow in his footsteps." At length, however, he was persuaded to accept Russell's rewording of his motion, which was then passed.

Given the latitude of expression Sibthorp claimed, and the roadblock tactics he delighted to use, it is remarkable that he got into trouble so seldom. Actually, he was quicker to take offense than were his adversaries. In 1836, when he was pressing as usual for adjournment, Sir John Cam Hobhouse declared, "If public business was to be impeded, let it be understood by whom it was so impeded [laughter, amidst which, the laugh of Col. Sibthorp was distinguishable]. There is a well-known Latin proverb, which rendered into English, signifies, that 'nothing is so foolish as a foolish laugh.' " Sibthorp, finding the words personally objectionable, left the House in a huff, only to be brought back by direction of the Speaker. Then he made the lordly speech he kept ready for such contingencies, ending: "Sir, I have but one course to pursue; it is the maintenance of, I hope, unimpeachable honour, and, I trust, unimpeachable courage. I have no hesitation in saying, Sir, that I did receive those words, and that I shall continue to receive them, in a manner offensive to me. As a man of honour, I have but this course to pursue; and this being the case, it is my inflexible determination to pursue no other." But eventually he let his ruffled feathers be smoothed. It was hard to predict when he might take exception to the remarks of others and when he might not. When a member characterized as "below contempt" Sibthorp's allegation that "a more idle and deceitful set of men [than the present ministers] were never allowed to fill such important offices," Sibthorp went to sulk in the corridor. Yet some years later, when another member declared that "nothing had fallen from the hon. and gallant Gentleman the Member for Lincoln [in a speech just concluded] that was worthy of notice," Sibthorp contented himself with a genial "Hear! hear!"

However grievous their provocation, surprisingly few members articulated their feelings toward Sibthorp in the House itself. If they did, it was usually in the relatively innocuous vein exemplified by the remark that "the hon. and gallant Member was in the habit of sitting growling and grumbling like Etna, and then a crater would burst, and out would come—nothing but smoke and rubbish." Probably the neatest job of needling Sibthorp was accomplished by John Roebuck, who, following up a Sibthorpian tirade, let drop the word "buffoonery." But he hastened to beg that Sibthorp "will not at all take any thing to himself," even if buffoonery—a word indelibly associated with the Colonel in a parliamentary context—was mentioned. Sibthorp was justifiably suspicious of Roebuck's intent, and, demanding to be assured that no personal reference was indeed meant, launched automatically into his speech about his public and private character. The Speaker broke in: "The words which fell from

"Portrait of Colonel Sibthorp on hearing that he had signed the Chartist petition." (*Punch*, 22 April 1848)

the hon. and learned Member for Sheffield in no way applied to the hon. and gallant Officer." And Sibthorp had to be satisfied.

In his first years at Westminster, before he became somewhat thicker skinned, he was just as sensitive to the press's treatment of him. In 1831 he moved that the printer and publisher of the *Times* be brought before the bar of the House for gross breach of privilege. The alleged offense was the uncalled-for lavishness with which the paper had sprinkled "[Laughter], [Continued laughter], [Cries of 'Question, question']" and other "expressions of derision" throughout its report of a recent Sibthorp speech. Despite attempts by such men as Hume and O'Connell to convince him that the matter was not "important or solemn," he persisted in his motion, which was beaten, 73–7. The episode probably served only to intensify the papers' interest in this strange being, and year after year, even before *Punch* joined the sport, their columns played him up, especially by way of reporting hilarious rumors—the more improbable the better.[11] It was in this spirit that a person or persons unknown inscribed his name at several places on the Chartist petition of 1848: a monstrous libel on his views which he denounced in the House.[12]

At the same time that they spoke of him as a licensed jester, the doyen of early-Victorian parliamentary freaks, his contemporaries gave Sibthorp

"Sibthorp has no confidence in either party" (*Punch*, 23 March 1850)

full credit for the terrible sincerity with which he clung to his principles. He described himself, with entire accuracy, as "unchangeable in opinion and unchangeable in conduct"; and therein resided both his glory and his tragedy.[13] For Sibthorp devoted himself to the lifelong task of sweeping back the sea of change with a broom. His attachment to the old order forbade that he should ever accommodate his views to the shifting political tides.

He began as a fairly orthodox Old Tory, though he always scorned a party label and on countless occasions vaunted total independence as his proudest political virtue. When parliamentary reform was first discussed he described himself as a "moderate reformer" and even introduced a petition in favor of the bill from his constituents. But he took fright as soon as the bill's true implications appeared, and quickly became one of its most ferocious opponents. He was, of course, no friend of the Whig régime in the early thirties; but when the sail-trimming (i.e., moderate) Tories were returned briefly late in 1834 he found them no better, and from then until the end of his life he was truly a man without a party. Though his sympathies obviously were more Tory than Whig, in his eyes one party behaved just as badly as the other. "He had no confidence in either of the contending parties," he declared in 1850; "they were all rogues and jobbers together." But if forced to a choice, "he could place more confidence in a Whig than he did in a Tory Government, as there was less deceit and hypocrisy in the former than in the latter."

He could never be accused of naiveté where political motives were concerned, but in the latter part of his career his suspicions became so indiscriminate as to border on the pathological. No matter what the issue under discussion, he smelled log-rolling, jobbery, deception, conspiracy everywhere. "Scratch me and I'll scratch you" was a phrase he imputed, time after time, to the occupants of the Treasury bench, who were his particular detestation. The ultimate *reductio* of Sibthorp's distrust of every-body was expressed in a speech he made in 1849. "He confessed that, as that Government was at present constituted, he could not even support a measure emanating from it, which should bear the stamp of justice, lest there should be some sinister purpose lurking beneath, which would con-vert the boon into a curse." In such a state of mind, which often led him to punctuate his speeches with dark mutterings about "man-traps and spring-guns," he would have voted No even in the unlikely event of a member's bringing in an omnibus Sibthorpian dream-bill.

Convinced that both parties and all factions thereof were composed of greedy, ignorant, calculating self-servers, Sibthorp was no more gen-erous in his estimate of individuals. "Fair words," he once reminded the Hon. Spencer Walpole, "buttered no parsnips. He had never done it, and he never would do it. He had never flattered man, woman, or child." To this principle he was utterly faithful. Beginning in the late thirties, Lord John Russell was his special *bête noire:* "he did not know one single act of the noble Lord which had met with the approbation of the country." Admittedly, for a brief time in 1841–42 he had hopes for the Tory min-istry, feeling that "Sir Robert Peel was the only man who could really save the country." But when in 1846 Peel made his sensational reversal on the Corn Law issue Sibthorp confided to the House that "he had entertained suspicions of the right hon. Baronet ever since 1829." Whenever they had in fact begun, they were flourishing by 1845. "There was no measure which he did not believe the right hon. Baronet, as a Minister, capable of introducing for the spoliation and ruin of the Protestant Church," he had said during the debate on the Jewish Disabilities Bill, and a few months later he gave it as his considered judgment that "if there was one man more likely than another to destroy the country, it was the right hon. Baronet."

After taking pains to disclaim religious prejudice, he would proceed to brand as treasonous whatever proposals were made for concessions to non-Protestants. No debate on the perennially vexatious Maynooth

College grant was complete without several statements from the Colonel, whose position on this matter was so familiar and uncompromising as to evoke "[Laughter]" whenever he arose. Catholic priests, in his opinion, were "little better than devils incarnate." The Ecclesiastical Titles Assumption Bill of 1851, while governed by the proper spirit, was far too mild. "Cardinal Wiseman was certainly a dangerous person, and, when he made his appearance here with his new authority from the Pope, ought to have been at once sent out of the country." But the force of this statement, as applied to Wiseman, was somewhat dulled by a necessary afterthought: "The noble Lord [John Russell] was not, however, much better."

Ultra-Protestantism was the greatest cause of his life, and I am inclined to select as the rhetorical apogee of his career the peroration of a speech he made on the subject during the Maynooth College debate of 1845. He was driven to it by the impudence of a member from Cork, who quoted the journalist James Grant as having represented nine years earlier, in his *Random Recollections of the House of Commons,* that Sibthorp "will do and suffer a great deal for his party and principles, but rather than submit to be shaved, he would see Tories, Constitution, and all scattered to the winds." Sibthorp's reply was as repetitious and rambling as usual, but noticeably more impassioned; and he ended thus: "This, Sir, is no time to indulge in ribaldry—which the hon. and learned Gentleman has done. This is not the time, Sir, for any such thing, when the people of England are looking to the House of Commons to defend their rights, to defend their liberties, and to defend their faith. This, Sir, is not a time to turn into ridicule their petitions and their feelings; and I tell the right hon. Gentleman [Peel] I will never support him. I'll never support any man who acts contrary to the duty that he owes to his Sovereign, to the people, and, last of all, and greatest of all, to his God. I never will support any man who does this; and though the hon. and learned Gentleman told me that I would sooner sacrifice my principles than I would be shaved,—I tell that hon. and learned Gentleman that I had rather not only be shaved, but have my head shaved off, than forget I am a Protestant; born a Protestant, bred a Protestant, educated a Protestant—and God grant that I may die with similar feelings, and in that faith!"[14]

While Peel's religious liberalism was one reason for Sibthorp's detestation, another, at least as potent, was his ultimate stand on free trade. Sibthorp was an extensive landowner in five counties, and until the disaster of 1846 all was tranquil on his smiling acres. In 1844 he assured the House that the Lincolnshire laborers, enjoying full employment, were "perfectly content with every thing but the movements of the Anti-Corn

Law League." But with the repeal of the Corn Laws, all was changed, and thereafter Sibthorp frequently lamented the depressed state of agriculture and the near-starvation of the farm workers in Lincolnshire and elsewhere.

Sibthorp was always a stern advocate of economy in government. In the early thirties and again in 1851 he protested spending large amounts of money to remodel royal residences; and, with an unexpected flash of aesthetic perception, in 1850 he opposed further expenditures on the new houses of Parliament. "What was the edifice after all?" he asked. "A piece of mere frippery and flummery, not fit to accommodate the Members of that House, and much more suitable in style for a harem than a place of meeting for a grave and important legislative body." This insistence on economy was a natural corollary to Sibthorp's opposition to all but the irreducible minimum of taxation; except, as he remarked in 1840, where a new tax would have the highly desirable effect of making the incumbent ministry more unpopular.

If Catholic priests were, as he said, devils incarnate, "the very name of a Commissioner stunk in his nostrils." Sibthorp opposed the successive Poor Law Amendment bills, partly because of the miseries wrought by the Poor Law Bastilles (a stand which brought him into incongruous momentary alignment with humanitarians like Dickens), but much more because of his hatred of centralized government. Bureaucracy, as exemplified by the Poor Law Commissioners, was prominent among the symbols of the emergent modern England that Sibthorp hated more with the passing of each year: an England governed, not by Parliament, but by overpaid sinecurists and their officious deputies. Hence he never missed a chance to sabotage a bill that proposed to create a new commission or add to the powers or emoluments of an existing one. He was alarmed by every possibility that the sanctity of the Englishman's castle might be violated by prying agents of government. When a project was afoot to have parish schoolmasters gather certain agricultural statistics Sibthorp rumbled: "Let me catch a schoolmaster on my land—that is all. The only question would then be whether he would venture to come a second time or not." He stood against every Health of Towns bill on the same ground, though an element of local pride was involved: while London was to be exempted from the operation of the act, Lincoln—a fine, clean city—was not. Whatever extensions of government control over living and working conditions were achieved in the early Victorian era owed nothing at all to the Colonel's cooperation.

Nor could he countenance the outrageous notion that there should be legal curbs on the conduct of parliamentary elections. From the time the

Sibthorp as Don Quixote, tilting against the railway (*Punch*, 14 February 1844)

"A dangerous character. Policeman Sibthorp. 'Come, it's high time you were taken to the House, you've done quite mischief enough.'" (*Punch*, 19 June 1847)

outlawing of bribery and other means of influencing voters was first proposed to the very end of his career, he dominated debate on the issue, not the least of the reasons being his awareness of the widespread opinion that he was one of the open-pursed sinners most in need of checking. To outlaw Eatanswill, he maintained, would be un-Christian, because it would make a criminal of any candidate who followed his humane impulses by giving succor to a poor woman or a cup of tea to a tradesman-acquaintance. "He wished to see more expense and more merriment at elections. . . . Some people were afraid to spend a sixpence at elections— they had not the heart to do it; but for his part he liked to see his constituents enjoy themselves; and he would never strive to curtail their innocent pleasures. It was an old and established maxim, *In vino veritas.* Give a man some genial liquor to drink, and he will open his heart to you." He was proud of his philanthropic as well as his festive expenditures: "he was in the habit of giving coals to the poor amongst his constituency, and never passed the sick chamber of a man who had voted for him without leaving some relief." He failed to describe what he did for a sick man who had *not* voted for him; however, his disinterestedness may be inferred from his giving charity to the (voteless) widows of men who had helped elect him. He would persist, Sibthorp told the House, in his custom of spending money for the comfort and entertainment of his fellow men, no matter what busybodies were sent out from London to make "a secret and a scandalous inquiry into the private concerns not only of the constituency, but of Members of Parliament, their characters and conduct." But anxious as he was for the protection of a man's privacy, the secret ballot was something else: "of all the dirty things in this world, of all the un-English, disgraceful things, the ballot was the worst."

Another Sibthorpian abomination—probably the one that delighted England more than any other—was railways. Priding himself upon being the oldest four-in-hand coach driver in Commons, and one who had never had an accident, he ceaselessly denounced this new phenomenon in English life, which sliced up the green countryside, stimulated grandiose and ruinous speculation, and, furthermore, was dangerous. "He hoped . . . the day was coming when a director and an experienced surgeon would be compelled to travel in every railway carriage, in order that both might be present at once in case of accident." In 1841 he cherished the hope "that all the railway companies would be bankrupt, and that the old and happy mode of travelling on turnpike roads in chaises, carriages, and stages, would be restored." He made a virtuous point of never riding on the rails except to move at election time to one after another of the several shires where he held "county votes." Lincoln remembers him today with mixed feelings as the man who saw to it that the city was spared being put on the main line from London.

As a full colonel in the South Lincolnshire Militia[15] he could be relied upon during debates on military matters to offer his farthing's worth of expert advice. His particular malicious delight during his last years, the era of the Crimean War, was to envision his opponents, who, he said, knew nothing whatsoever of military affairs, forming an awkward squad under his command: he would teach them a thing or two. In the same vein, from time to time, he ridiculed those numerous Admiralty officials who had never been to sea. Of one of them Sibthorp liked to observe that he would get sick in a punt under Westminster Bridge.

He committed himself, of course, on his fair share of less momentous topics. Although he opposed a bill to eliminate the "resurrectionist" trade by legalizing the dissection of unclaimed cadavers, he recommended designating for that purpose the bodies of horse-thieves, "those most rascally of all criminals." He denounced the operators of London barrel organs for disturbing the peace, frightening horses, and obstructing traffic. Having spent £25 for cab fares in six weeks in 1831, he felt qualified to announce that "if anything was likely to produce cholera morbus in London, it was the filthy condition of its hackney-coaches. A more disorderly and uncivil set of men, more miserable vehicles in the shape of coaches, or more wretched horses, could not exist than at present afforded the only means of conveyance in this great metropolis." But when omnibuses were introduced Sibthorp found them equally unsatisfactory, what with their overcrowding and their drivers' "disgusting, threatening, and alarming" language. In what vivid terms, one wonders, did the verbally resourceful and socially disrespectful London bus driver address so irresistible a target as Sibthorp?

The Colonel's last five years were colored by a new obsession: a virulent xenophobia, which had been generally latent until 1850 but which then excited him to new heights of frantic utterance, summarized in 1854 by the declaration that "it would take ninety-nine foreigners to make one thorough good Englishman." He fought England's joining the continental electric telegraph convention on the ground that "by this scheme the Government was only encouraging the intrigues of the foreigner, and rendering this country subservient to him." About the same time he urged that "the lamentable influx of foreigners into this country" be taxed. [Laughter.] "He knew he had been often laughed at in that House and out of it," he went on, "—and he did not know but that he might be mobbed, but he would always declare, that it was deplorable to see the sums of money that were carried out of England by foreign opera dancers and singers. Foreigners were encouraged too much in this country. They interfered with native talent. He was sorry to say that the higher classes encouraged all foreigners, whether of character or not—male and female."

This hatred of foreigners sprang partly from the Colonel's devotion to Protestantism, but it was also an obvious concomitant of his bitterness as a defeated protectionist. The connection is apparent in the speeches he made during his last great campaign—a masterpiece of tenacity, invective, recalcitrance, and exaggeration which guaranteed his career would near its end in a blaze of hilarious glory. It was directed against "one of the greatest humbugs, one of the greatest frauds, one of the greatest absurdities ever known," than which "a more wildgoose chase, a more undefined scheme, a more delusive or dangerous undertaking never had been attempted by any man," "a concern full of trickery, fraud, and immorality—a concern by which morality, virtue—[Much laughter]—he was not surprised to hear virtue and morality sneered at in that assembly—by which virtue, morality, religion, social good feeling, prudence—by which all these things would be destroyed." To wit, the Great Exhibition of 1851.

The trouble began with the preparatory cutting down of some of the trees in Hyde Park: an act of desecration blameable upon relative newcomers to Sibthorp's list of bureaucratic tyrants, the Commissioners of Woods and Forests. "The Commissioners came like a thief in the night, and cut down those beautiful trees. . . . If the Commissioners had left the beautiful elms alone, and cut down some decayed trunks which were used for purposes objectionable to the olfactory nerves, the public would not have censured them." But censured they now were, and Sibthorp followed up his attack by urging an injunction against putting up any buildings in the park for exhibition purposes. This move got nowhere, and in the months that followed, Sibthorp's passion for viewing with alarm was exercised as never before. In July 1850 he saw menace in the fact that on the preceding day no fewer than 1,500 foreigners had landed in the country, "many of whom, no doubt, had been surveying the ground where this Exhibition was to take place, and looking after matters with a view to their own interests." When the Crystal Palace was built, the trickle would swell to a flood of sinister visitors, "talking all kinds of gibberish. Of course, the English people would not understand them, and they would get into all kinds of disturbances. Suppose a case: A foreigner called a cabman, and told him to drive him to a certain place; the cabman could not understand him, and before he knew what he was about he would have something like a stiletto in him."

Sibthorp therefore recommended that London immediately build a new jail, larger than any then existing, to accommodate the hordes of criminals who would descend on the metropolis. Although the foreign element naturally would be most conspicuous among the malefactors, the exhibition would also act as a magnet for native talent. "All the bad characters at present scattered over the country would be attracted to Hyde Park as a favourable field for their operations, and to keep them in check an immense body of police must be constantly on duty night and day. That being the case, he would advise persons residing near the park to keep a sharp look-out after their silver forks and spoons and servant maids."

Nor was it only the unlucky neighbors who were to be victimized. A year before the opening, workingmen all over the country were saving to bring their families to the fair. "The poor labourers were to come up to London, helter-skelter, where they would suddenly find themselves amidst the temptations of a great metropolis—were they? What would become of the chastity and the modesty of those who might become the unsuspecting victims of those temptations? . . . Their property, their wives and families would be at the mercy of pickpockets and whoremongers from every part of the earth. Oh, it would be a beautiful sight!"

Even more dreadful was the threat, indeed the certainty (for Sibthorp scorned fine distinctions), of espionage. "Her Majesty's Government, and, he grieved to say, many of our gentry were 'hail, fellow! well met,' with every foreign ragamuffin . . . nothing would suit the Government but that those amicable strangers should be allowed to pry into our dockyards, and inspect the Tower and our arsenals. The whole nakedness of the country," he warned, would be laid open to them. The only fit punishment for so treasonous a government was to ship the whole lot to Botany Bay.

The nation, however, was obstinately deaf to the bewhiskered prophet from Lincoln. The Crystal Palace opened on 1 May 1851, but without Sibthorp's blessing. The blessing it did receive, he vehemently protested in the Commons the same evening. He had not attended the ceremonies, he said, because of "His duty to his God. ['Oh!'] Yes, he repeated, neither his duty to his God, nor his duty to his country, would suffer him to visit that showy bauble. He considered it a paramount duty as a good Christian and a good subject to absent himself from the Crystal Palace. He deeply regretted to hear that the head of the Protestant Church

"Sibthorp in the Crystal Palace" (*Punch*, 15 February 1851)

of this realm should have been there invoking a blessing—invoking the assistance of Him who suffered for the sins of mankind. ['Oh!'] Yes, he expressed his opinion as he felt—he declared without reserve the faith that was in him." And, just as he had prided himself a decade earlier on never going near Downing Street, "for he hated the sight of the place," he declared that a thousand guineas would not induce him to look in at the Palace; "the very sight . . . almost sickened him."[16] He wished then, as he had done several times before, for the structure's total annihilation. "Would to God," he had cried when it was still under construction, "that a heavy hailstorm or a visitation of lightning would put a stop to the further progress of that work!" The proposal to make the building a permanent structure fed his fury. He had a victory of sorts when the Palace in Hyde Park was torn down. This turned to defeat when it was re-erected at Sydenham. But the final, though belated, victory was his, and we can imagine his shade rejoicing when the by then decrepit Palace burned down in 1936.

The Sibthorpian rage, adequately covered by *Punch* and the rest of the press, added a pleasantly tart flavor to the nation's festival spirit. At its root was the simple circumstance that Sibthorp, a dedicated representative of the now dethroned farmer protectionists, had to look on while the triumphant free traders built a shining monument to British industry. If the Crystal Palace had been meant to advertise native agriculture, Sibthorp might well have sung a different tune. But from the very beginning of his attack, it was obvious that he hated the Palace because he hated free trade.

"Sibthorp out for a holiday" (*Punch,* 7 June 1851)

And though to most Englishmen the Great Exhibition seemed a huge success, to Sibthorp its effects were unmitigatedly evil. To be sure, he had no chance to call Parliament's attention to the crime wave that engulfed London, because no such wave occurred. Otherwise, however, he found it possible to announce that his blackest prophecies had been fulfilled. As of mid-summer 1851, the Crystal Palace had caused "the desecration of the Sabbath—the demoralisation of the people—a disunion of parties—and increasing poverty to a most serious extent; for he had heard, and with pain, that the poor of this country had been seduced to come up to this Exhibition." The economic consequences were the most deplorable.

"Performance of our friend Sibby, in the lobby of the House of Commons, after the decision to pull down the Crystal Palace" (*Punch,* 8 May 1852)

"One-half of the tradesmen in the metropolis and the provincial towns would tell them [i.e., members of Parliament] that their trade was lost—that they had no customers—all had gone to the Crystal Palace, not merely for amusement, but, what was worse, to make future orders for the goods of foreigners, who came here to undersell the honest, industrious, and heavily-taxed people of England." On one occasion he held up, as an example of what he loved to call "cheap and nasty" products of foreign manufacture, a decanter. [Laughter.] "Yes, a decanter—an engraved decanter, and the price of this imposition was sixpence. Now, he asked, how was a man in this country, who was accustomed to eat roast beef and drink strong ale, after the manner of a Christian, to compete with those nasty foreigners who lived on brown bread and sour krout, and who manufactured decanters at sixpence a piece?" The indignity was compounded because the government, under the lax design and patent laws, encouraged the unprincipled foreigner to appropriate English inventions, which he would then manufacture and ship to England to "undersell the ingenious and laborious mechanics of our own land."

Thus did the Colonel's voice echo across the early Victorian age, not always loud, not always clear, but invariably cantankerous.[17] Ridiculous though he often was, and rendered more so by the loving attentions of the humorous press, his grim devotion to his principles was not only admirable but, to a certain extent, intelligent. In his injudicious way the Colonel was sometimes a cogent critic of the tendencies of his age. He saw through the pretensions and delusions—the frippery and flummery, as he would have put it—that too often were hailed by interested parties as evidence of the March of Civilization and the Triumph of British Institutions. However ludicrous an enlightened England found his detestation of railways, for example, the facts gave him impressive support: railways did cause the greatest speculative frenzy since the South Sea Bubble; they did disfigure the face of England; they did doom the coach lines and coaching inns; and they were the scene of one dreadful wreck after another. Behind his attacks on bureaucracy—compare Dickens in *Little Dorrit*—and on governmental waste and inefficiency—compare any candid account of the War Office at the time of Crimea—lay plenty of substance.

Moreover, to sum up the grotesque glory that was Sibthorp by saying that he had the courage of his crotchets would be to neglect the fact that some of the convictions which the extravagance of his manner turned into seeming aberrations were seriously and, in some cases, widely entertained by his thoughtful contemporaries. His hatred of the railways was echoed by the aging Wordsworth and by Ruskin; his fright at the encroachment of democracy was echoed by innumerable members of his class and was given eloquent voice by, among others, Carlyle; his conviction that England had never been better governed than she was before 1832 was shared not only by Wellington but, more significantly, by that quintessential Victorian, Gladstone; his detestation of Papists and Frenchmen was hardly shriller than that of *Punch* itself in the fifties. In these and other respects, he was no more a picturesque, lonely anachronism than the mouthpiece of attitudes which, while not necessarily fashionable in the bustling, sanguine climate of his day, nevertheless had plenty of adherents. His role, therefore, was not merely one of broad comic relief in the agitated parliamentary decades of Melbourne and Peel, Palmerston and Disraeli. His conversion of respectable ideas into farce offered his delighted audience (had anyone cared to interpret it thus) a long-running illustration of an important human truth: that in extreme commitment, unleavened by moderation, open-mindedness, discrimination, reasonableness—or what Matthew Arnold, a decade after Sibthorp's death, would call "criticism"—lurks the uninvited germ of absurdity.

1965

POSTSCRIPT: THE COLONEL REVISITED

When I published this appreciation of the redoubtable Colonel Sibthorp, based as it was on a systematic pursuit of the person and the image through the two historical sources in which he is most prominent—the many volumes of *Hansard's Parliamentary Debates* and the first fourteen years of *Punch*—I had little reason to believe I had not done him substantial justice. At that time, as my endnotes suggest, I had drawn upon a number of other sources to round out the portrait of my favorite early Victorian "character." But I still did not realize either the full extent of the peculiar celebrity he enjoyed (I think the word is justified) while he lived, or the variety of contexts in which it is preserved.

The recent revival of interest in the Crystal Palace as a landmark in the history of Victorian popular culture and the development of modern architectural design has inevitably restored the Colonel to public notice in that connection. Patrick Beaver's *The Crystal Palace 1851–1936* (London, 1970) went so far as to adopt him and his ferocious opposition to the enterprise as a sort of comic leitmotif. One question, though, remains unanswered: Did he or did he not sneak into the exhibition despite his resounding vow that he would never stoop so low? A month after the show opened, a *Punch* cartoon (7 June) showed him being dragged, kicking and screaming, to the season ticket window by an avuncular Mr. Punch. This was, of course, *Punch*'s predictable response to Sibthorp's declaration of principle, now that the object of his latest obsessive phobia was a fait accompli. But unlike *Punch,* the *Illustrated London News* was not a humorous paper, and in its 28 June issue, reporting that the voices of adverse criticism had finally been stilled, it said, "Even the gallant and eccentric Colonel, who uttered his fervent wish that the hail and storms of heaven might batter and overthrow the Building, has relaxed his hostility, and condescended to visit the beautiful Abomination." The paper did not give the source of this bit of headline news, and it is possible that the festive spirit of the moment had induced it to lower its journalistic standards sufficiently to pass on a mere unsubstantiated rumor. But if Sibthorp did enter the gleaming edifice in Hyde Park, the news did not reach Edward FitzGerald in rural Suffolk, who seems to have remembered only the initial fulmination. "I have not yet been to London—and shall probably not go down, as you say, a fly on old Sibthorpe's beard," he wrote his friend Stephen Spring Rice on 11 August. "Is that what you said? Something in that way of metaphor, relative to our, neither of us, visiting the exhibition."[18] And, whether or not the Colonel succumbed to the mass enthusiasm, it is certain that FitzGerald did not go to the Crystal Palace that year, although later, when the building was re-erected in Sydenham, he visited it regularly during his trips to London.

The Colonel seldom appears in modern political histories of his age, and when he does, it is usually as the hapless M.P. who narrowly missed getting credit for the "Chandos clause." But the local circumstances under which Lincoln returned him, time after time, are described in the chapter "Politics 1832–68" in Sir Francis Hill's *Victorian Lincoln* (Cambridge, 1974), which clarifies the relationship between Sibthorp and the other famous onetime representative of the constituency, Sir Edward Bulwer (-Lytton). Bulwer referred to his adversary in a footnote in the first edition of his *England and the English* (1833): ". . . Every body knows what you are when you are merely a gentleman, they begin to doubt it when you become a man of letters. In standing for Lincoln, a small second-rate country squire was my opponent. One of his friends was extolling his pedigree, as if to depreciate mine. 'Do you not know that Mr. B's family is twice as old as Col. S——'s, if *that* be any merit in a Legislator?' was asked of this gentleman. 'Impossible,' replied he, 'Why, Mr. B—— is an *Author!*' "

The second volume of Thomas Pinney's edition of Macaulay's correspondence (Cambridge, Mass., 1974) sheds a little light on Sibthorp's activity as a political martinet during the feverish days immediately after the passage of the first Reform Bill. In a letter dated 8 August 1832 Macaulay wrote to Lord Mahon, the M.P. for Wooton Bassett:

> Nothing would give me more pleasure than to accept your invitation. But we [are] strictly on duty. No furloughs, even for a dinner engagement or a sight of Taglioni's legs, can be obtained. It is very hard to keep forty members in the House. Sibthorpe and Leader [M.P. for Kilkenny] are on the watch to count us out; and from six till two we never venture further than the smoking room without apprehension. In spite of all our exertions, the end of the Session seems further and further off each day. If you would do me the favour of inviting Sibthorpe to Chevening Park, you might be the means of saving my life, and that of thirty or forty more of us who are forced to swallow the last dregs of the oratory of this Parliament;—and nauseous dregs they are. (2:171)

But the plea was too late, as far as the immediate needs of the weary corporal's guard of steadfast M.P.s were concerned. Writing the very next day to his sisters, Macaulay described the all-night session he had just gone through, the debate on the bill to prohibit Orangemen's processions in Ireland having required no fewer than seventeen divisions. The chief obstructionist on this occasion was the fanatical Protestant politician from Dublin, Sir Frederick Shaw. "Of the two who supported him at the beginning of his freak," said Macaulay, "one soon sneaked away. The other, that hairy, filthy, blackguard, Sibthorpe, staid to the last,—not expressing remorse, like Shaw, but glorying in the unaccommodating temper which he shewed and on the delay which he produced. At last the bill went through" (2:174).

It appears from this that in his earliest years at Westminster the Colonel, as zealous then as he always would be to spot the lack of a quorum, was a strict disciplinarian, as befitted his military status. Indeed, the anecdote quoted in note 11 implied something of the sort: he marshaled his troops (in this case, the evangelical crusaders for Negro emancipation (the "Saints") with whose cause Sibthorp was in sympathy) by preempting for them seats in the spectators' gallery during the debate on the question. What I overlooked in that anecdote was the further implication of the ribaldry. On the principle that where there is smoke there is likely to be fire, I should have realized that associating the Colonel with a bawdy house was an in-joke that deserved to be followed up, as a hint of an aspect of his private life that neither *Hansard* nor *Punch,* for obvious reasons, made public. He was, says Sir Francis Hill, a well-adjusted and happily married man while still a soldier; but when he succeeded to the family seat in Parliament following the death of his elder brother, "the change in his circumstances changed the man, and he became heartless and purse-proud, leading a life of intemperance, riot and wickedness. . . . 'A perfect mountebank in manner and appearance,' wrote Cracroft [a local diarist upon whom Hill relies heavily in his chapter on Lincoln politics], 'yet I must do him the justice to say that he was a most fearless man.' " When Sibthorp died in 1855, Cracroft remarked, "the only good point in his past life to look back to with any comforting thought of him is his reconciliation with his wife, and his family surrounding him in his last days—else all's blank, and much worse."

The ominous implications of "all's blank, and much worse" cannot be filled in. But we do know that the wife with whom Sibthorp was belatedly reconciled was not his first. The *Times* for 8 December 1829 reported the conclusion of a lawsuit brought against the Colonel by his then wife, charging him with adultery and petitioning for a formal separation and the payment of alimony to the amount of £2,000. This was granted by the Dean and Chapter Court at Westminster, but the Colonel refused to pay and an appeal in his behalf to the High Court of Delegates was lodged by the best counsel money could buy, the great Henry Brougham, who was shortly to become Lord Chancellor and elevated to the peerage. When Brougham addressed the court, however, it was only to announce that "the party with whom their proceedings originated"—Mrs. Sibthorp—had died, and the issue therefore was moot. Their lordships then directed that the appeal be disposed of in the usual form.

From these fragments of evidence it appears that from an unspecified time before the first Mrs. Sibthorp charged her husband with adultery to very near the end of his life a quarter century later, he was a disreputable rake. This side of his character must have been common knowledge, the basis of much gossip which underlay the innuendo of Greville's bawdy-house story and which surely must have spiced, for knowledgeable readers, those hundreds of superficially innocent allusions in *Punch.* If it was worth the trouble, one might scrape together additional bits of contemporary scandal. An American visitor to England, for instance— one David W. Bartlett, whose *What I Saw in London* was published in Auburn, New York, in 1852—recorded, along with the familiar items of Sibthorp's appearance and conduct in the House of Commons, that he was "a great racer, gambler, and wine-drinker. . . . He is one of the aristocracy—a kind of pet of theirs, and yet is an exceedingly coarse and vulgar man in many things. . . . The proper place for such a conceited idiot is not in Parliament, but in a Lunatic Asylum. . . . Colonel Sibthorp is also a notorious libertine, and we are told by excellent authority that upon the death of a favorite mistress an English bishop condoled with him upon his loss."

In one of several political squibs Dickens contributed to the *Examiner* newspaper in August 1841, he recycled the Sibthorp material he had first used in his profile of the Colonel in *Sketches by Boz*. In the course of recommending "Subjects for Painters (After Peter Pindar)" Dickens wrote:

—To all who practise art, or make believe,
I offer subjects they may take or leave.

Great Sibthorp and his butler, in debate
—(*Arcades ambo*) on affairs of state,
Not altogether "gone," but rather funny;
Cursing the Whigs for leaving in the lurch
Our d——d good, pleasant, gentlemanly Church,
Would make a picture—cheap as any money.

Or Sibthorp as the Tory Sec.-at-War,
Encouraging his mates with loud "Yhor! Yhor!"
From Treas'ry benches' most conspicuous end;
Or Sib.'s mustachios curling with a smile,
As an expectant Premier without guile
Calls him his honourable and gallant friend.

Or Sibthorp travelling in foreign parts,
Through that rich portion of our Eastern charts
Where lies the land of popular tradition;
And fairly worshipp'd by the true devout
In all his comings-in and goings-out,
Because of the old Turkish superstition.[19]

(The chief, if not the only, value of these lines is their proof that Dickens was never cut out to be a poet, even a humorous one.)

With the unpredictability that one repeatedly discovers among Victorian public figures, this flamboyant, coarse, licentious politician was also an art lover. It is startling to discover in the diary of Joseph Farington, painter and Royal Academy potentate, under the date of 27 April 1804, the statement that J. M. W. Turner's guest at the private view of that year's Academy exhibition was "Coll. Sibsthorpe."[20] The new complete edition of Farington's diary is regrettably unannotated, but this could scarcely have been our man, who was then only twenty-one, a recent Oxford dropout, and was as yet a captain, not a colonel. But the coincidence is remarkable, not to say unsettling: a *duplicate* Colonel Sibthorp (however spelled) before the real one appeared at the exhibitions? There is, in any event, uncontrovertible evidence that the ill-kempt, whiskery M.P. who was his colleagues' despair and humorists' delight, regularly paid his shilling to see the latest pictures, as did the commander under whom he had served in the Peninsular War, the Duke of Wellington. Benjamin Robert Haydon wrote in his diary on 17 March 1840 that at the Suffolk Street Gallery (headquarters of the Society of British Artists) he "met Colonel Sibthorp. I asked in the course of conversation what was the principal cause of being successful as a Speaker in the House of Commons. 'Never let your points be deferred till the dinner hour,' said he; 'always finish a little before.' "[21] When Haydon met Sibthorp again, at the exhibition of the Water Colour Society on 2 May 1843, the conversation was more appropriate to the occasion. "I said, 'Well, Sir, this is full of talent and Color. What have you bought?' He took me [to see] a Bird nest with two Eggs! I said, 'There is a beautiful thing of the Colysaeum by Palmer, with a dark blue Hill, & oracle or some other.' Away he went to look at it! —& I cut him, for he was awfully conspicuous, with half shaved face, embroidered waistcoat, gold chain, fly-backed coat—yet I like the Colonel for his frank contest in the House."[22]

The collection, housed at his residence in Eaton Square, to which Sibthorp presumably added the watercolor of a bird nest with two eggs continued to grow. In 1855, only months before his death, he bought some of the best pieces at the great Bernal sale of medieval treasures, including a thirteenth-century enameled brass chase portraying the murder of St. Thomas à Becket. The *Illustrated London News* (12 April 1856) covered the sale of the collection at Christie's. No paintings were included, but there was a wide variety of other objets d'art: bronzes, inlaid cabinets (one from the Bernal sale), clocks of various sizes (including a clock-watch "said to have belonged to the Emperor Napoleon I"), elaborately carved ivory tankards, groups of marble and alabaster figures, Raphael and Palissy ware, Limoges enamels, wood carvings . . . "A more heterogeneous gathering," the *Art Journal* for May 1856 tartly commented, "has seldom passed under the hammer, and, considering the quantity, the quality was far below average. The sale, however, attracted considerable attention, and realised good prices"—£1,506 11s. 0d. to be exact.

Quite plainly, Charles DeLaet Waldo Sibthorp was a more complicated man than his most familiar role as an antic performer who was constantly in the public eye would suggest. "He was," says Sir Francis Hill, "a strange mixture; a man of public principle and private vice; of great courage, good temper, and consistency, and a hard worker; of limited intelligence; shrewd, with flashes of wit, but a buffoon." Which should one choose: this judicious summation, or the typically dissident judgment of the crotchety historian of the economics of artistic taste, Gerald Reitlinger: "Popular history books, based on the goodness and inevitability of mechanical progress, have made a silly man out of Colonel Sibthorp, who preferred the Middle Ages to 1851, yet Don Quixote among his windmills is still the most sympathetic character in the book"?[23]

1988

19

An Uncommon Curiosity:
In Search of the Shows of London

Back in 1966, I tossed a memorandum into the suggestion box I keep, what Henry James might have called his donnée file. "Wouldn't it be fun—and instructive," I asked my future self, "to do a short book on the various kinds of exhibitions that were a prominent feature of the London scene during the nineteenth century? The various panoramas (and other '-amas'), George Catlin's exhibitions of his Indian paintings, Haydon's catastrophic display of his large canvases, perhaps shows on the Barnum order, for example, the presentation of General Tom Thumb. And Tussaud. There was great variety. And the nature of the shows, changing no doubt from generation to generation, would reveal much about the popular interests of each period, and probably something of the attempt to combine entertainment with instruction. The exhibitions would be an out-of-the-way, but significant, index to cultural conditions.

"Moreover," I continued, "there are probably many stories connected with them. Some were smash hits and immediately had imitators; others were flops. Were there entrepreneurs who made a living setting up such exhibitions? Where were they held? How many people attended? How long did they last? What were their publicity methods? Were there different kinds of exhibitions for different classes?"

Six years later, having finally cleared my desk, I began to seek the answers to such questions. When the resulting book was published in 1978, I looked at that memo again. "Short book" indeed! *The Shows of London,* as it came from the press, ran to 553 double-columned pages and included 180 illustrations. Reviewers, otherwise well disposed, vied with one another to suggest various practical purposes to which the oversize volume could be put, such as serving as a bed board for people with backache.

But I was right about the fun and instruction. I experienced plenty of both as I explored what turned out to be an enormous field of English social history that nobody had ever bothered even to map. To be sure, a solitary voice had been raised in 1899, in that wonderful old rag-bag of obscure, trivial, and wildly miscellaneous information *Notes and Queries.*

A sensational London show: exhibition of Napoleon's carriage, taken at Waterloo, in the Egyptian Hall (drawing by Thomas Rowlandson)

"The subject of exhibitions in London," observed a correspondent, "is of great interest, and so far as I know, is one of the few subjects of which no reasonably comprehensive history has been published." But seemingly nobody else had recognized the subject's very existence, let alone its potential importance. For the next several years, I immersed myself in the records of the London entertainment business, the scope of the research inexorably widening until the beginning of the narrative was pushed back to Tudor times and the full roster of topics came to include almost everything that three centuries of curiosity-hungry Londoners paid to gape at. These ranged from the mountebank booths at Bartholomew Fair and the "ragged regiment" of royal effigies at Westminster Abbey to exhibitions of freaks, automatons, waxworks, architectural models, famous paintings reproduced in needlework, and—particularly—the several kinds of pictorial shows, called mechanical theatres, panoramas, dioramas, and cosmoramas, which were in their various ways the ancestors of the modern cinema.

During all this research, there were few dramatic moments such as one associates with the celebrated saga of the Boswell papers, the unmasking of Thomas J. Wise's bibliographical forgeries, or the discovery of the true circumstances of the murder of Christopher Marlowe in a Deptford tavern. Coming upon a seventeenth-century printed copy of a play by

Elkanah Settle bound up in an old volume labeled "London Pamphlets" was an isolated event. But there are other pleasures, as well as frustrations, in research. In the case of *The Shows of London* these came mainly from the fact that I was following in no one's footsteps. There were no bibliographies bearing on the history of London exhibitions, no preliminary sketches of the territory. All I had to work with was a body of information that might be imaged as a huge (sometimes it seemed limitless) ball of tangled yarn from which thousands of loose ends dangled. Instead of following a more or less systematic procedure, all I could do was tug at those strands, one by one, and see where they led.

Some broke off almost at once; they led nowhere. Others proved to be intricately entwined in other tangles that had to be sorted out. One small clue might lead to ten more clues. I learned afresh the wisdom of Roger Williams's sage remark (1643): "A Little Key may open a Box, where lies a bunch of Keyes." The process of gathering raw material was so tortuous that it would be impossible to reconstruct the successive steps that led to any single fact. Sometimes, happily, one small lead took me to a bonanza I had no reason to anticipate. In a routine check of William Matthews's bibliography of British diaries I found a reference to a two-volume work by three Persian princes, describing their visit to London in 1836. The reference merely stated that they had attended an exhibition of "erudite fleas." But when located the book proved to contain many passages recording their detailed, if more picturesque than trustworthy, impressions of several of the leading London shows of the day.

The more I worked, during the several periods I spent in London libraries, the more open-ended my project appeared. Although a substantial amount of repetition is inevitable in any wide-scaled program of research, there was always the possibility of new and illuminating data awaiting the next turn of the page or the arrival of a new batch of dusty books at my desk. Often, when the law of diminishing returns seemed about to operate in a given library, fresh prospects opened up that brought me back the next day, and the day after that.

There was drudgery aplenty, though long experience equips the scholar to make the necessary mechanical labor his work involves as efficient as it can be. His eye, trained like an electronic scanner to respond whenever it meets one of the hundreds of significant words that constitute the vocabulary of his current investigation, runs swiftly down column after column of indexes or page after page of unindexed books, while his disengaged mind occupies itself with other things. When the eye meets a

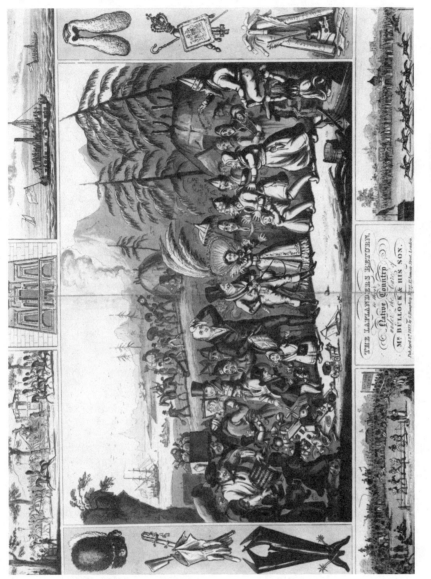

Exhibition of Laplanders and their artifacts, at Bullock's Egyptian Hall (1822)

The last week of Exeter Change, London's indoor menagerie (1818)

pertinent word, it automatically stops and alerts him. He then reaches for his ballpoint pen and pad of note slips.

But in the midst of drudgery, boredom never set in. Not with so colorful and lively a subject as mine, offering, as it did, constant revealing insights into the daily lives and the diversified imaginative experiences of ordinary Londoners from the reign of Elizabeth I to the death of Victoria's prince consort. Sometimes the brightness of a London summer day beckoned: when the sun shines in England, the American anglophile hates to linger indoors. But total absorption in the English past is a pleasure too, even when the sheer bulk of information mounting up makes the return of British Library call slips reporting that a desired book is "Missing" or "Destroyed by Bombing" an occasion for secret, guilty rejoicing.

Although every research library, no matter where located, has a flavor, a presence of its own, in England those differences are more pronounced—just as English society has always nourished the personal differences that, in extreme cases of nonconformity, breed the cherished

Perspective view of the interior of the great gallery of the Polytechnic Institution,
London, a pioneer science and technology museum (ca. 1838)

English eccentric. The London Library, where I broke ground for my
research because it has over two hundred shelf-feet of books on London
history and topography, was established in 1841 when Thomas Carlyle
and some of his fellow writers decided they could no longer put up with
the annoyances and distractions in the British Museum reading room.
Carlyle testified before a parliamentary investigating committee that respectable families used the room as a convenient day-care center for their
weak-minded uncles or sons, among them an alleged lunatic who blew his
nose punctually every half hour. Furthermore, Carlyle complained, the
reading room harbored the biggest fleas known to science. The private
subscription library which these refugees founded, facing leafy St. James'
Square just south of Piccadilly, has counted among its members hundreds
of well-known authors and scholars, including in modern times such

luminaries as T. S. Eliot and E. M. Forster. The visiting American student, who for a modest fee may have access to London's best stock of serious books outside the British Library, finds himself reading alongside men and women whose names are familiar to every reader of the *Times Literary Supplement*.

The largest collection of books, prints, maps, manuscripts, and printed miscellany dealing with the City of London proper, as well as with much of the surrounding metropolitan area, is at the Guildhall Library, not far from the traffic-clogged Bank corner. When I worked there (it has since moved to ultramodern quarters nearby), the spacious reading room under high gothic arches was quiet and uncrowded, although, to be sure, the presence of a young man who spent hours at his table making paper airplanes stirred unsettling memories of Carlyle's lunatic. Aided by a cataloguing system particularly designed to organize the library's specialized resources, I was served day after day with a wealth of rare pamphlets, volumes of out-of-the-way periodicals that could have been found only with difficulty, if at all, in America, and teeming scrapbooks of prints and playbills.

The Gabrielle Enthoven Collection is to the historian of English drama and other theatrical entertainments what the Guildhall is to the specialist in London history. For many years it had been housed, as it was when I worked there, in an obscure corner of the Victoria and Albert Museum. (It has recently found a new home in the British Theatre Museum, Covent Garden.) The Enthoven is London's most extensive collection of English theatrical memorabilia not in private hands—flimsy playbills by the tens of thousands in their riotous mélanges of typefaces and exclamation points, prints, photographs, posters (some, for circuses, as big as bed sheets, and accordingly hard to store and handle), programs, promptbooks, designs for scenery, even maquettes of stage sets, dating from as long ago as the eighteenth century.

The biggest all-embracing collection of books in London is, of course, the British Library—a new name that is hard to get used to, because for over two centuries, until 1973, the institution was known as the library of the British Museum. It is to the old name, not the new, that a sentimental aura belongs, an aura composed of memories of Karl Marx, Dickens, George Eliot, George Gissing, and the countless other writers and scholars who have worked under the great cream, gold, and blue dome. Every scholar feels a certain affection for it, if not precisely reverence: it is the place where many of the books on English literature and history that contributed to his education were gestated. At the same time, though, the visiting researcher is bound to become impatient as the hours

Staircase of the old British Museum, Montague House (ca. 1845?)

pass and the ill-paid attendants in their soiled jackets, moving among the desks that radiate spokelike from the platform that serves as the circulation nerve center, seem always to be delivering books to other desks than his. Apart from reading the morning newspaper, repairing to the Museum pub across the street during licensing hours, browsing in the formidable array of reference books that line the room's walls, or speculating on who one's fellow researchers are, where they come from and what they are reading, there is little to pass the time.

The waste is all the more regrettable when the probability is that some of the books, when they do arrive, will be glanced through and cast aside, as of no value, within a few minutes. But there is a way of circumventing the deliberate pace of British Library service. Adjoining the reading room is the North Library, where certain classes of books, rare or bulky, are delivered. By setting up two pieds-à-terre, one in the reading room and one in the North Library, it is possible to keep two streams of book requests and deliveries going at the same time. Since the British Library nowadays is not as crowded as it was a few years ago, when readers had to be there at opening time if they were to find a seat, there is nothing really unethical about this arrangement apart from the fact that keeping a double establishment in London somehow implies kinship with the respectable Victorian gentleman who kept one house for his family in Bloomsbury and another for his mistress in St. John's Wood.

I must mention one other rich collection which is, as yet, little known or used: the John Johnson Collection of Printed Ephemera at the Bodleian Library in Oxford. From 1925 to 1946 John Johnson, "printer to the University," was the man in charge of producing the books of the Oxford University Press. He was deeply interested in the history of his occupation, especially in typography and printing as they figured in everyday life. In pursuit of this vocational avocation, he collected all kinds of printed material generated by the needs of commerce and social life and intended to be thrown away after use—handbills, advertising and public-notice posters, restaurant menus, grocery wrappers, beer bottle labels, railroad timetables, cigarette cards, business forms, souvenirs of holiday resorts, postcards, mail-order catalogues, fashion plates, even mere price tags and tram tickets. Now they are mounted on stout cards in some three thousand tall filing boxes arranged in such classifications as "Soaps," "Patent Medicines," "Motor Cars," "Dress," "Politics," "Slavery," and "Military Affairs." There are upward of 176 boxes on "Theatre" alone. My own interest drew me to the dozens of boxes labeled "Wax Works," "London Play Places," and "Panoramas." Next to museums of everyday life, with which England abounds, one of the best ways to sense the pulse of a bygone era is to delve into the printed matter that accompanied people's daily activities. And so John Johnson's collection, made to illustrate a particular aspect of technological history, actually is a rich source for the study of social history at large.

The contents of the boxes I used typified one major category of raw material indispensable to the history of entertainment. Elsewhere I found those same kinds of "primary documents" not only gathered in loose form in boxes but pasted into scrapbooks which proved to be both the joy and the bane of my daily research. The joy, because the scrapbooks preserved, in addition to playbills and prints, page after page of tiny advertisements and news items clipped from eighteenth- and nineteenth-century newspapers, thus sparing me the inordinate labor of going through whatever files of those newspapers happened to survive. The bane, for two reasons. One was the sheer bulk of those folio volumes, so big and unwieldy that they could not be propped up and therefore had to be examined while I stood bending over them. (At the Victoria and Albert

Museum I once called for a scrapbook of London scenes that proved to be so heavy it could not be lifted but had to be dragged from the delivery cart to my table.) But more irritating was the fact that the compilers of those scrapbooks, antiquarians and hobbyists long since dead, often failed to note the date and source of each clipping as they pasted it in. My gratitude for their labors consequently was tempered by exasperation and worse, not only because of the lack of dates but because those scrapbooks were mute evidence of the wholesale destruction of what were deemed at the time totally expendable sources (nothing but old newspapers!) but which were actually irreplaceable. I could not help remembering that during the Second World War, some thirty thousand bound volumes of newspapers from the eighteenth and nineteenth centuries were lost when the British Museum's newspaper repository in the northern suburb of Colindale was wrecked by bombing and several ensuing days of rain turned its exposed contents into tons of soggy pulp. There, the destruction was the price of a savage war. The scrapbook makers' intentions, by contrast, were wholly honorable and innocent, but through either negligence or short-sighted policy they turned out to be vandals. So I could not help execrating them at the same time that I benefited from their visionary confidence that someone eventually would come along to make use of what they had so laboriously assembled.

My debt was especially great to the reverend antiquary Daniel Lysons (1762–1834), who left to the British Museum six great folio scrapbooks entitled *Collectanea: or A Collection of Advertisements from the Newspapers* beginning in 1661. Lysons was sufficiently prominent to merit an article in the *Dictionary of National Biography.* But others of my unwitting bene-factors remain nameless, for example one "G. S.," a resident of Peckham in 1840, who farsightedly put together for me a scrapbook called *Exhi-bitions of Mechanical and Other Works of Ingenuity,* from the preface to which I got the epigraph for my book.

Another set of backbreaking scrapbooks at the British Library is the nine volumes that apparently constitute the house archives of the Surrey Zoological Gardens, an outdoor summer amusement place that flourished for the first thirty years of Victoria's reign not far from the better-remembered Vauxhall Gardens. In addition to the menagerie, it had a lake, flower gardens, a conservatory, and nightly displays of fireworks against the background of Brobdingnagian wood-and-canvas "picture models" representing such locales as London in the fire of 1666 and Rome at festival time. I confess that my heart sank when those nine folios were dumped on my table in the North Library. If he is lucky, there are times in a scholar's life when he has feasted so long that a short interval of famine is welcome. In the event, I extracted from this *embarras de richesses* what I needed and left the rest, with its invaluable records of the gardens' business affairs, including deaths in the menagerie and the fees Barnum charged for General Tom Thumb's nightly appearances, to some future historian of that popular Victorian enterprise.

I wish I could thank by name the man, perhaps a librarian late in Victoria's reign, who thoughtfully compiled another series of scrapbooks that chronicle, in clipping, print, playbill, and miscellaneous paste-ups, the sights and doings in the very center of Victorian London's amusement world, the parish of St. Martin in the Fields and particularly the perennially raffish neighborhood of Leicester Square. They are seemingly unknown to theatrical historians because they are not in the British Library or the Enthoven Collection but in the local history collection of the Westminster City Library in Buckingham Palace Road, opposite the west side of Victoria Station. One does not usually associate a metropolitan public library like this with academic research. Its chief purpose is to serve Londoners who need to use its reference books or draw current books for at-home reading. But researchers learn to adapt themselves to the nature and conditions of each library where there is a chance of finding pertinent material.

Sometimes, to squeeze the maximum benefit from libraries, regardless of their individual character, tricks of the trade are needed which are not described in books on the art of literary or historical research. It is not always easy, for example, to gain access to some English libraries. The British Library, it is true, normally offers no difficulties. It requires only a perfunctory declaration that the work one proposes to do cannot be done elsewhere in London, followed by a Polaroid mug shot and the issuance of a reader's ticket. But other libraries are more reluctant to admit the American who comes in from the street without previous introduction. On such occasions, the art of chatting up the presiding functionary comes in handy. If a discreet employment of trans-Atlantic affability does not suffice, Providence may come to the rescue, as it once did for me when I was able to identify myself as the author of a book I opportunely spied on the librarian's select ready-reference shelf. In a pinch, another variety of one-upmanship may save the day. At one library, I could not gain access to certain material because for some unstated reason it was restricted to holders of an endorsed reader's card. I hadn't even a reader's card, let alone an endorsed one, whatever that was. But I quickly remembered that the head librarian was a scholar who had published articles in my own field of Victorian literature. "Oh, but

I'm sure Mr. X would want me to see those books," I said, and before long I saw them.

In some situations, calculated craftiness is plainly inappropriate and would not work anyway. At the British Museum, the Department of Manuscripts and the Department of Prints and Drawings own so much precious material that security must be maintained at a high level. The latter may not have closed-circuit surveillance, but it is a little disquieting to be aware of its equivalent, an official constantly overseeing the room from a chair at the rail of the surrounding gallery. At the other extreme, I know of an institution in central London (it had better be nameless) where, when I asked leave to look through its archives, no note was taken even of my name. I was led at once to a corner closet in the library, shown the large cardboard and metal boxes where the records were kept, and left alone. I could have departed with some irreplaceable manuscripts in my briefcase and nobody would have been the wiser.

Most English librarians, like their opposite numbers in the United States, are not only hospitable but, in general, knowledgeable. After all, it is their business to command a wide expanse of bibliographical, if not substantive, information to meet the diverse and often unpredictable requirements of their clientele. Sometimes, as is only to be expected, the visiting specialist knows a good deal more about his specialty than do the librarians. But at least a few men and women on the staffs of London libraries are scholars in their own right, and they willingly place their expertise at the disposal of the visitor. I think with particular gratitude of the information and leads I got from the director of the Enthoven Collection and the keeper of prints and maps at the Guildhall Library.

In the absence of such helpful hosts, the scholar must do his own prospecting and digging. His bibliographical knowledge and the catalogues of the individual libraries may take him only so far; and, as was the case with sources of *The Shows of London,* some kinds of obscure and ephemeral material, abundant though they may be, are either poorly catalogued or not catalogued at all. And so, sooner or later, systematic procedure must be abandoned in favor of freewheeling exploration. Above all, the scholar must somehow break down the barriers that separate him from the storehouse itself. In the British Library, access to the stacks is virtually impossible. Elsewhere, however, it is possible for a scholar who is patient and tactful to win freedom of the inner shelves. Between the London Library's reading room and the basement stacks are three flights of narrow iron stairs, negotiated with difficulty if one has an armload of books. But the frequent trips I made up and down every day were a small price to pay for the convenience of working methodically along the shelves and opening every book that might conceivably have something for me.

At the Westminster City Library, the whole local history collection is shelved in the very room where both the staff and the scholar, once he has found an empty space at one of the tables, work. In such circumstances, nothing prevents him from ranging the shelves—and the under-the-counter cases. It was under the counter, a lode unmentioned by any staff person, that I came upon those bountiful Leicester Square scrapbooks. Such serendipity is ample compensation for the noisy, cramped quarters where the scholar must perforce work. And one's daily presence in the midst of busy staff going about their tasks can help break down whatever initial reserve they might have. Once assured of the visitor's serious purpose (and, as occasion permits, his intimate knowledge of a little sector of the field in which their collection specializes), they take a friendly interest in his work and thus are more likely to toss him useful information than if he were separated from them.

When I finished gathering material for *The Shows of London,* I felt, with some confidence, that though there may well have been concealed references I still didn't know existed, they were few indeed, and someone else was welcome to discover them in my wake. As things turned out, I have been finding little chips of additional information ever since. But during those days and weeks in London libraries, I learned quite enough about London exhibitions to satisfy me and, I suspect, my readers as well.

1981

20

Victorians on the Move;
Or, 'Tis Forty Years Since

In the dim, dear, distant days when academic paperwork got done perfectly well without the aid of computer printouts, course enrollments were tallied on a row of blackboards in the college gym, where registration, cafeteria-style, was held every term. It was at one such college, on one such occasion in September 1941, that somebody discovered that, for reasons not immediately clear, an announced course in Victorian poetry had attracted enough students to warrant its being given, and nobody had been assigned to teach it.

The task fell to the newest and lowest occupant of the departmental totem pole, a young instructor who was grateful, as any freshly fledged Ph.D. would be, for the chance to teach an advanced literature course. His qualifications to undertake a survey of Victorian poetry, however, hovered between the minimal and the nonexistent. Such information as he had acquired in graduate school was mostly about eighteenth-century English literature and Romanticism. As an undergraduate at the same college, he had once taken a course in Victorian prose, but the intervening three or four years had sufficed to erase the memory of most of what he had read then, and, apart from the usual extracurricular indulgence in Dickens and possibly a few glimpses of other writers, that was the extent of his acquaintance with Victorian literature.

Of necessity, therefore, he had to learn as he taught. As it happened, the fact that his knowledge of Victorian matters was, at the outset, a *tabula rasa* proved to be not so much a disadvantage as a stroke of luck, because it represented the general state of affairs as of 1941. If he was not actually present at the creation, he was certainly on hand in the very earliest stage of the scholarly study of Victorian literature and life. For if the appearance of an annual bibliography of publications can be said to mark the moment a scholarly discipline is officially recognized, this one was just eight years old, the first issue of the Victorian Bibliography, covering the publications of 1932, having been published in the May 1933 issue of *Modern Philology*. One who joined the nascent discipline in the early 1940s was privileged to watch it grow with what seems in retrospect to have been dramatic speed, and to learn along with everybody else as Victorian studies passed, as it were, from the dark ages into the light of its own Renaissance. The development amounted to a textbook case, a paradigm, a microcosm of the way specialized scholarly disciplines burgeoned in English and American culture after the Second World War.

Few specialists who joined the profession in, say, the 1960s can fully appreciate how recently, and from how low a starting point, this particular branch of English literary study rose. Medieval studies had long been established as a lofty and fertile field of humane learning. Decades earlier, scholars had found the English Renaissance colorful, intellectually and aesthetically exciting; the English eighteenth century had been discovered to be full of Palladian dignity as well as Hogarthian animation; the Romantic age had its own well-established claims to attention, despite the demotion its poets had suffered at the hands of Paul Elmer More and the New Humanists and, more recently, the critical school of T. S. Eliot. And, thanks largely to the surge of nationalism in the fermenting 1930s— the rediscovery of America's unique past as well as a renewal of faith in its promise—the study of American literature had begun to generate its own excitement.

But *the Victorians*—! The very word was ineffaceably and banefully associated with Lytton Strachey and, even worse, his tinhorn imitators. In 1941, the twenty-three-year-old shadow of *Eminent Victorians* cast a retrospective pall, as well, over the whole long era that bore the name. Most of the popular writing that had been done on the Victorians since the First World War was wearisomely jokey, simply because the Stracheyan image of the age required it to be. Practically nobody under the age of fifty took the Victorians seriously. Yet Victorianism survived: people over fifty in the 1940s were Victorians by birth and often in spirit too, which rendered them fair targets for the iconoclasm of the new age. The Victorian era was still too close to the present to have any chance of being viewed with reasonable objectivity. Moreover, in the academic study of literature the unwritten criterion of a writer's suitability for serious consideration was that he be comfortably dead, preferably for a century or so. No one then envisaged that by the 1950s academic dissertations were to be devoted to authors who were not only alive but had hardly had time to acquire a reputation. To be sure, the Germans had never had any such ground rules: they had unapologetically prepared "philological" dissertations on Victorian authors while those authors were still alive, and were continuing to do so. But who, not least in the aftermath of the First World War and in the first years of the Second, cared what pedantic German scholars did? In the United States as well as in Britain, it was hard to justify studying Carlyle or Tennyson when so many older English authors still demanded attention.

The Victorians' fine arts likewise were so little valued that in 1935 John Martin's last apocalyptic canvases, a trilogy so sensationally popular in the 1850s that they had been toured in Britain and America as a profit-making exhibition, had brought at auction a total of seven pounds. The nadir, however, was reached about the same time when a London dealer offered to *give* a customer one of John William Waterhouse's paintings, which was taking up space in his showroom. The customer, who was broadminded and had nothing to lose, would have removed it, except that he found he could not get it inside a taxi. The routine destruction of Victorian buildings in the interests of "modernization" called forth no protests. On the contrary, people cheered as the wrecker's ball demolished the ornate Ruskinian facades. In music, only the continuing popularity of the Savoy operas reflected appreciation of the Victorians' achievement; their oratorios were as little esteemed by the discerning as the moral maxims of Martin Tupper.

Given such an atmosphere, it is no wonder that when a few academics began to take a serious interest in Victorian literature, they suffered a collective inferiority complex (a term that was outliving its vogue even then). The low opinion entertained of Victorianism in general lent, so it seems as one looks back, an air of embarrassment to their cottage indus-try. There was some encouragement to be found in the fact that they had nowhere to go but up. The trouble was that the basic materials for schol-arship in their field still were lacking. Medievalists had their Wells *Manual* for bibliographical help, their long row of *EETS* texts, and Karl Young and E. K. Chambers to provide a firm foundation for the study of the early drama. The eight volumes of Manly and Rickert's *The Text of the Canterbury Tales* were fresh from the press in 1940. Shakespeare schol-arship could draw on the riches of the New Variorum, obsolescent as some of the volumes were, and on the first fruits of McKerrow, Greg, and Pollard's "New Bibliography." Miltonists had in hand Masson's seven-volume *Life*, a legacy of the Victorian age itself, and in 1940 the last volume of the Columbia *Milton* had been published. In eighteenth-century studies the letters of Addison, Steele, Sterne, Gray, Goldsmith, and Burns had been edited according to modern principles; R. K. Root and George Sherburn had laid the basis for the intensified study of Pope; and the eighteen-volume set of *The Private Papers of James Boswell from Malahide Castle* energized Johnsonian scholarship, though the Yale editions of Boswell and Johnson were still in the future and only a handful of people knew how large and rich a body of documents remained unpublished. Specialists in the Romantic period had the De Selincourt edition of Wordsworth's letters, Buxton Forman's of Keats's, and Grierson's of Scott's; they had Newman White's newly published life of Shelley, Howe's *Complete Works of Hazlitt*—and *The Road to Xanadu*.

No such array of bibliographies, editions, and biographies was available to the pioneering Victorian scholar. The only bibliography of earlier commentary which attempted comprehensiveness (it actually fell far short of that), Ehrsam, Deily, and Smith's *Bibliographies of Twelve Victorian Authors*, had appeared in 1936. A mere glance through it today would reveal how thin and superficial was the existing body of printed scholarship and criticism down to that time. The collected annual bibliographies for 1932–44 and C. F. Harrold's methodical survey of "Recent Trends in Victorian Studies, 1932–1939" in a 1940 issue of *Studies in Philology* are chiefly remarkable today for their demonstration of how few of the newly published books and articles they cite remain unsuperseded, and of how by far the greater part of our present knowledge has been acquired since then. The quantum leap that occurred in scientific knowledge after the Second World War had its counterpart in literary studies generally, but in Victorian studies especially.

Among collected editions of Victorian authors, the vast Cook and Wedderburn *Ruskin* stood out in lonely grandeur. Although, as Helen Gill Viljoen was to show, it was not without flaws, its comprehensiveness, minuteness of apparatus, and incredibly detailed index made it a model, for the time, of what a "definitive" edition should be like. There were no other models. Quite the contrary: the received texts of Victorian authors, if not always object lessons in How Not To Do It, were products of a prescientific age when texts were not sacrosanct and corruptions multiplied from edition to edition. The Bonchurch edition of Swinburne was unfortunately typical of most textual sources that Victorian scholars had to be content with unless they had access to the original printings.

There were then no biographies of Victorian writers to equal Wilbur Cross's lives of Fielding and Sterne. One read about Tennyson in his son's two-volume "memoir," a notorious masterpiece of suppression, evasion, and filial devotion, or in Harold Nicolson's shorter book, which was considerably livelier but identifiably a product of its time (1923). For Carlyle, there were David Alec Wilson's six heavily prejudiced volumes, more a compilation than a coherent, interpretive narrative. For Browning, there was the totally undistinguished Griffin and Minchin; for Rossetti, Mégroz and, of all people, Evelyn Waugh; for Morris, J. W. Mackail; for

Charlotte Brontë, Mrs. Gaskell, still "standard" after over eighty years; for Dickens, Forster, considerably more informative than most biographies of great Victorians but by no means even-handed or well proportioned. In addition, there were the readable but slick and trendy biographies by such popularizers as "Hugh Kingsmill" and Hesketh Pearson; and the best that could be found on several lesser figures were the slim volumes in the English Men of Letters series, none of which provided a firm basis for intensive scholarly work.

Apart from Hugh Walker's severely dated *Literature of the Victorian Era* (1910), the only general history was Oliver Elton's belletristic two-volume *Survey of English Literature 1830–1880* (1920). Holbrook Jackson's *The Nineties* (1913) did a better job with the *fin de siècle* than anybody had succeeded in doing with the preceding fifty years. Whatever their deficiencies, these works nevertheless were more useful, except as a source of lively anecdotes to spice lectures, than such vulgarizations as "Frances Winwar's" best-selling biographical extravaganza starring the Pre-Raphaelites, *Poor Splendid Wings.*

The fund of criticism that could help a novice in 1941 get his bearings is best described by reciting a few names. The essayists—one shrinks from invoking the word "critics" in this context—who had written on the Victorians since the beginning of the century included Stopford Brooke, A. C. Benson, Arthur Symons, and F. L. Lucas. Between-the-wars commentators, who typically were belated Edwardians like Edmund Gosse or Georgians like J. C. Squire, either were candidly hostile to the Victorians or, in a dutiful but plainly unenthusiastic attempt to make the best case for them, succeeded only in showing that the best case they could make was not very convincing. Most of the wisdom on Dickens was concentrated in the volumes, still respected today of course, by Gissing and Chesterton.

For social background, one had Esmé Wingfield-Stratford's Strachey-esque three-volume kaleidoscope of many colors, characteristically titled *Those Earnest Victorians, The Victorian Sunset,* and *The Victorian Aftermath.* There were, as yet, few serious studies of ideas as embodied in Victorian literature, nothing comparable to A. O. Lovejoy's *The Great Chain of Being*; among those few was Joseph Warren Beach's *The Concept of Nature in Nineteenth-Century English Poetry.*

Like their colleagues in American literature, then, Victorian specialists had to build the systematic foundations of their knowledge—the materials of biography, text, social and intellectual milieu—at the same time that they were erecting the superstructure of informed interpretation and criticism.

By 1941 there were enough straws in the wind to permit one to believe that something was up. Now, at last, the once-over-lightly causeries, long on grace and short on substance, were starting to give ground to the products of hard-headed research. Perhaps it could be said that the skeptical investigatory spirit which is indispensable to scholarship was first notably introduced into Victorian studies by Carter and Pollard's exposé of Thomas J. Wise's forgeries in 1934, which encouraged every thoughtful student of books, not least Victorian books, to distrust appearances and received "truths" wherever found, and whomever they might concern. (Fannie Ratchford's efforts to implicate the elder Buxton Forman and, less successfully, Gosse in the Wise fraud were still in the germinal stage in 1941.) In 1935 the first edition of DeVane's *Browning Handbook* efficiently organized the existing body of information on the individual poems, with the overdue and salutary effect of relegating Mrs. Sutherland Orr's *Handbook* (1885) and E. P. Berdoe's *Cyclopaedia* (1892) to the back shelves. In 1937, Harrold's edition of *Sartor Resartus* set a standard for annotated editions of individual texts that was seldom to be matched.

The next year appeared Harrold and Templeman's massive anthology of prose (1,743 double-columned pages, printed on the secular equivalent of Oxford Bible paper), a prime instance of a textbook, in some respects in advance of its time, which stimulated rather than merely reflected scholarship in its field. Its magisterial sixty-seven-page introduction provided teachers and students alike with a well-informed, panoramic survey of the Victorian social and intellectual background. In 1939, Lionel Trilling's *Matthew Arnold*, a revision of his Columbia dissertation, offered a model for prospective explicators of an author's leading ideas. Nobody could have foreseen it at the time, but two almost successive items in the Victorian Bibliography for 1940, Orwell's essay on Dickens in *Inside the Whale* and Edmund Wilson's "Dickens: The Two Scrooges" in the *New Republic*, marked the beginning of what was arguably the most momentous development of all in post-war Victorian scholarship and criticism, the discovery of Dickens as a towering and complex artist. In the same year was published the *Cambridge Bibliography of English Literature*, whose third volume, notwithstanding its many errors and omissions, supplied Victorian scholarship with what was to be its single most frequently consulted tool.[1]

Contemplating the sheer magnitude of the Victorians' printed output (one estimate was to place the number of novels published in Britain during the nineteenth century at roughly 40,000), no ground-breaking researcher had cause to fear that his resources would be exhausted. In addition to the countless books and files of periodicals from the era, untold quantities of manuscript material in both institutional and private hands awaited discovery and examination. Some known caches, to be sure, were inaccessible. Rossetti's letters to Jane Morris, possibly containing secrets of their love affair, were kept under lock and key at the British Museum, not to be opened until 1964. The collection of Tennyson literary manuscripts in the library of Trinity College, Cambridge, including drafts of *In Memoriam*, was under the "perpetual interdict" ordered in Hallam Tennyson's will; to the exquisite frustration of scholars, the papers could be looked at but not quoted from. "Never" promised to be a long time.

Now, in the 1940s, literary study began to be institutionalized, and nowhere was the tendency more evident than in the Victorian field. Far from being, as it had been in large part, the domain of literary journalists and enthusiastic but unsystematic and uncritical amateurs, it became the province of professionals. Organized with what British onlookers regarded as a fearsome efficiency of which only Americans, fortunately, were capable, subsidized with imposing (but never quite sufficient) amounts of money for research and publication, equipped with all the machinery the post-war world of learning devised to speed the process—societies, periodicals, bibliographies, and research guides—literary scholarship flourished as never before.

It was fitting that of all the fields of literary study, Victorian scholarship became one of the most thoroughly organized. Firm believers as they were in the efficacy of the printed word in spreading information and ideas, the Victorians themselves had had equal faith in the power of mass effort to achieve ends that were beyond individual capability. Like F. J. Furnivall, in this respect the Victorian prototype of the modern scholar, they delighted in setting up a new society whenever one seemed desirable. Modern students of Victorian literature piously followed their example. In the elaborate structure of the Modern Language Association they had, and of course still have, their own section, which sponsored not only paper-reading programs and overpriced luncheons at the annual meetings but, more valuably, the preparation of convenient reviews of published research in Victorian poetry, fiction, prose, and periodicals. From the parent organization, regional Victorian studies associations hived off, to multiply the benefits of communal discussion by holding annual meetings of their own. Beyond these, numerous special-interest groups, chiefly devoted to the study of individual authors, sprang up, with varying life expectancies.

Alongside the organizations appeared journals for the publication of research. Dominating the Victorian field since 1957 has been the august *Victorian Studies*. Originally conceiving it as a journal whose contents would exemplify and stimulate the cross-fertilization of disciplines, its editors found that articles that genuinely reached across two or more fields were hard to come by, so that they had to settle for a good quarterly mix of articles addressed to separate portions of its constituency, social, economic, political, and cultural historians as well as students of literature.

Concurrently with *Victorian Studies* have flourished (in most cases) several specialized periodicals, the venerable prototypes of which were the *Transactions of the Brontë Society*, founded in 1898, and *The Dickensian*, dating from 1905. Until after the Second World War, the latter was the organ of an amiable cult in harmony with the mental set and activities of the Pickwick Club. Then, in response to the temper of the times and the advent of a new, tough-minded generation of Bozolators, it was gradually converted into a scholarly periodical of some importance. The first postwar journal to be devoted to a Victorian novelist was *The Trollopian*, which soon found that the wartime enthusiasm for Trollope's novels did not leave enough momentum to propel a quarterly periodical exclusively concerned with him, and therefore transformed itself into the highly respected, broad-gauge *Nineteenth-Century Fiction*. Another American journal, *Victorian Poetry*, has been somewhat more uneven in quality, but it has always printed the best essays submitted to it.

In the foothills sprang up numerous publications of more specialized interest. Like their sponsoring organizations they had varied life expectancies, some not surviving their editor's loss of dedication and/or financial and moral support, and the successful ones tending to turn themselves from modest news letters into fairly pretentious "reviews." Thus there were, and in some cases still are, informal information-exchanges or quarterly journals devoted to Browning, Gissing, Kipling, Mill, Disraeli, Morris, Shaw, Samuel Butler, Hopkins, Arnold, the Pre-Raphaelites, Lewis Carroll, Walter Pater, even John Forster. Some of the interests represented in this array were specialized indeed. One wonders how many subscribers the *William Carleton Newsletter* attracted during its brief lifetime in the mid-1970s.

Even the abnormally energetic Furnivall did not think of founding "research centers" for the coordinated study of Chaucer, Wycliff, Shakespeare, Shelley, or Browning. But these proved to be a natural outgrowth of the postwar societies for the study of individual authors as well as of the establishment in American universities of "factories" devoted to preparing definitive critical editions of Hawthorne, Melville, Thoreau, and William Gilmore Simms, projects of such scope and complexity as to require a staff of textual and research specialists and the support of rich related library collections. Some such enterprises, like the Tennyson Research Centre at Lincoln and the Disraeli Project at Queens University, Canada, contented themselves with "researching" the life and works of single writers; others, like the Victorian Studies Centre at Leicester University and the nameless *de facto* one at Indiana University, took all (Victorian) learning as their province.

As a natural accompaniment and consequence of this organized activity, the major British and American research libraries themselves became informal headquarters for Victorian scholarship. Masses of letters and literary manuscripts, some of which they had owned for generations, were brought to light, studied, and published for the first time, and into the British Museum Library, the Berg Collection, the Morgan Library, the Huntington Library, and the special collections rooms at such American universities as Harvard, Yale, Princeton, and Texas flowed a golden stream of newly acquired manuscripts.

And so Victorian scholars possessed not only the will but the way to catch up with their colleagues in other fields. Gradually they remedied their lack of dependable working tools. One of their most urgent needs was for reliable critical texts. This was met more slowly than could be wished, but the results, when they came, were worth the wait: the Clarendon Press *Dickens*, for example, though regrettably unannotated, and the Michigan edition of Arnold's prose. The ambitious critical edition of Browning unfortunately was beclouded by an acrimonious dispute over the choice of copy text, and another much-needed edition, that of Newman, was abandoned by its publishers after the untimely death of its editor.

The study of some authors was handicapped by the sheer unavailability of some of their works, which had long been out of print and were to be found in few libraries. Efforts to restore them to print, in unedited form, were not uniformly successful. The Oxford University Press launched a complete edition of Trollope's novels only to drop it, for lack of sufficient sales, after several volumes had been published. The various facsimile reprint series which flourished in the period when the libraries of newly established institutions of higher learning were being built from scratch did not make much of a dent in the list of Victorian titles of which no modern editions were available.

The appearance of scholarly editions of authors' letters had proved to be of great assistance to workers in other periods. Now it was the Victorians' turn. The Pilgrim edition of Dickens's letters, with its formidable apparatus of explanatory notes; the Edinburgh-Duke edition of the Carlyles' correspondence; the letters of Thackeray, Macaulay, George Eliot, Newman, Meredith, Pater, Swinburne, FitzGerald, Carroll . . . a brave company. Not that they were all without blemish. The Doughty-Wahl edition of Rossetti's letters, besides lacking an index, was so incomplete and unreliable that a completely new edition had to be undertaken, and even such an initially useful edition as Booth's of Trollope was superseded by N. John Hall's much larger one.

By the 1950s an awareness grew of the commanding importance of contemporary periodicals in the study of Victorian literature and life. Several volumes had been published on the history of major individual magazines and reviews, but these paid scant attention to their contents as a mirror of the culture of the time. The *Wellesley Index to Victorian Periodicals*, as it proceeded from its first volume in 1966, effectively displayed the contents of some fifty influential journals, and, thanks to its editors' dazzling feats of tenacious investigation, succeeded in identifying nearly ninety percent of the authors of unsigned articles. The Research Society for Victorian Periodicals applied itself to bringing further order out of that particular realm of chaos, but except for the severely criticized "Phase I" of the *Waterloo Directory of Victorian Periodicals*, its record of sponsorship so far has been longer on major projects envisaged than major projects accomplished.

The growing number of scholars who prospected for ore in library files of bound periodicals found themselves assisting, however unwillingly, at a process already under way, the inexorable physical disintegration of those irreplaceable volumes. In many libraries, the sad condition of much-used periodicals like *Punch*, the *Athenaeum*, and the *Illustrated London News* testified alike to their value as source material for a wide variety of literary and cultural studies and to the impermanence of wood pulp (a proud Victorian invention). Ironically, with the substitution of microfilm copies, supposedly an emblem of technological progress, scholars found themselves no better off than medieval bureaucrats had been when they were obliged to unwind long, sewed-together and rolled-up parchments to get at a single document.

A substantial number of library-stack explorers, though their ID cards identified them as members of English department faculties, reached into areas outside literature and contributed toward the achievement of what may well be regarded as the supreme goal of Victorian scholarship, the weaving of a seamless web of historical knowledge that embraces all aspects of the age's life and expression. No previous century in any country, said Kitson Clark, had left behind so staggering a mass of documentary and graphic evidence, and, even as literary scholars were widening their knowledge of what Victorian poets, novelists, and essayists had written, historians were examining the whole social-cultural-intellectual condition of Victorian life. There were, in fact, two simultaneous and related "knowledge explosions," with the result that Victorian writers, as conceived by a new generation of scholars, took shape against a steadily more detailed and authentic historical background. Such seminal books as Walter Houghton's *The Victorian Frame of Mind* dissipated the parochialism which in effect had separated literature from the history of Victorian social, philosophical, moral, and religious attitudes. The rediscovery of Henry Mayhew's *London Labour and the London Poor*, first by way of Peter Quennell's three volumes of selections and then through the Dover facsimile reprint of the entire work, performed a like service at the opposite end of the social and cultural scale.

As a consequence of all this activity, among those in the know, at least, the former summary dismissal of Victorianism as a lengthy aberration of the cultural process was recanted, and in its place developed an almost excessive regard for the age's literary and artistic products. The indifference with which wartime Londoners had watched the destruction of Victorian warehouses and office blocks while they lamented the disappearance of Wren churches gave way to a new version of Morris's "Anti-Scrape" crusade, the purpose this time being the rescue not of Gothic churches imperiled by self-styled "restorers" but of Victorian structures threatened by "developers." This did not, in the end, prevent the destruction of the Euston Arch or the Coal Exchange, but the preservationists gave the speculators a harder fight for their money.

In the realm of the fine arts, however, the most spectacular development was the rehabilitation of Victorian painting. One of the three Martin canvases which had fetched a total of seven pounds in 1935, *The Great Day of His Wrath*, was hung in a prominent location in the Tate Gallery, its worth being estimated at an amount befitting its huge size. As auction prices soared, public galleries in London and the provinces put on exhibition after exhibition of the work of such artists, celebrated in their own time and now revalued, as Etty, Dyce, Maclise, Mulready, and Frith; there were at least a dozen shows given over to the Pre-Raphaelites alone. The Tate and the Victoria and Albert Museum both installed the cream of their

Victorian collections in newly appointed rooms. In literary studies, this release of long-suppressed interest in Victorian art generated a thorough re-examination of the Pre-Raphaelites' dual role in poetry and painting, the intellectual and emotional connotations of nature in poetry and landscape art, Ruskin's art criticism generally, and typology and iconology in poetry and painting. Especially suggestive was the demonstration, by several scholars, that the illustrations in Dickens's novels were considered by both novelist and artist to be integral extensions and amplifications of the fictional text.

The Victorian book was also studied as an artifact and commodity, the product of such extra-literary forces as publishing economics, technological innovations, and popular reading taste. Michael Sadleir's *XIX Century Fiction*, a bibliographical record of a collector's passion for the popular literature of the epoch, laid out the colorful background of three-deckers, shilling shockers, and railway novels against which the more permanent heritage of Victorian literature might profitably be studied. Although sadly reduced during the war, when such unexplored archives as those of Cassells and Longmans perished in the Blitz, the surviving stock of Victorian publishers' records, some still in the firms' hands, some in libraries, became available to students of the publishing practices that determined how much an author was paid to write and what the public was offered to read.

As is true of other periods of literary history, the precise degree to which contextual research illuminated the literary document is open to debate. There are those (certainly including the formerly young instructor) who would argue that forty years of intensive biographical and historical scholarship have profoundly affected the way Victorian texts should be read if they are taken to be more than autonomous linguistic events occurring independently of author and milieu. The various formalist schools of criticism were to have a delayed and rather uneven impact on the reading of Victorian literature. In 1940, as Theodore Morrison suggested in a gently satirical piece in *Harper's Magazine* called "Dover Beach Revisited," there were four academically respectable ways a poem could be read: as a poetic expression of the age's sensibility, as a "criticism of life," as a mirror of the poet's psychic condition, and as an indication of whether he was a Marxist or not. Noticeably absent from these alternatives was the perspective of the New Criticism, which at that moment was beginning its ascent to the peak of influence it would reach in the 1950s. If Morrison meant to imply that "Dover Beach" was not considered to be amenable to New Critical analysis, he was right—for the moment, at least. The ironies, paradoxes, tensions, and ambiguities that were being discovered in Donne and Pope seemed in short supply in Tennyson, Browning, and Arnold, with the result that the methods of the New Criticism were applied in Victorian studies much less often then they were in, say, the study of seventeenth- and eighteenth-century poetry. The only poet who benefited substantially in those early years from the modernist mode of criticism was Hopkins, whose reputation steadily rose as his poems were examined, thanks largely to his great influence on later poets, with an inspired minuteness not then lavished on any other Victorian poet's canon.

Eventually, of course, few approaches to literature that were devised in those yeasty years went unrepresented in the criticism of Victorian authors. With Lewis Carroll, these approaches ranged from psychoanalysis and the anatomy of nonsense to game theory, symbolic logic, and the theory of comedy. Nobody evidently tried to present Carroll as a Marxist, though that feat would seem to have required no more ingenuity than the attempts that were made to identify Dickens as a proto-existentialist. It was, in fact, Dickens's seeming ability to accommodate almost every current variety of fiction criticism that was responsible for his becoming the most written-about of all Victorian authors. In the earlier years, when he was given a break between sessions on the couch he was signed up as a Marxist, even though the closest he ever came in life to that beatific allegiance was his theoretically possible encounter with Karl Marx as a fellow reader at the British Museum. In the course of time, all fashionable critical instruments were tried out on him, with predictable results: illumination in the case of those that were genuinely applicable, fiasco in the case of those that were not.

So far as quantity was concerned, the high water mark of Dickens scholarship and criticism was reached in the years 1970–72, when some eighteen double-columned pages of the Victorian Bibliography were needed to record the output. The reason for this great additional burst of interest was the centenary of his death in 1870. The first such celebration to stimulate the flow of scholarly and critical articles in Victorian studies was the hundredth anniversary of Hardy's birth. Hardy studies were already thriving then, thanks to the indefatigable sponsorship of Carl J. Weber, but the extra momentum picked up in 1940 was sustained without interruption in the years that followed. Four later centenaries, including Dickens's, were responsible for similar outpourings: in 1944, that of Hopkins' birth, when nearly one hundred articles appeared, some of them in special Hopkins issues of the *Kenyon Review*; in 1945, that of Newman's conversion to Rome; and in 1959, that of the first publication of *On the Origin of Species*, which touched off four years of commentary on Darwin before the tide ebbed. The year 1959 is also memorable for the example it afforded of the way current events sometimes play into the teacher's hands, for it witnessed the famous rematch between Science and Culture in the persons of C. P. Snow and F. R. Leavis respectively. Even before the Age of Obligatory Relevance, a purgatorial term of years which no teacher of pre-1950 literature looks back upon with nostalgia, it was always expedient to prove, if one could, the Victorians' inveterate timeliness.

Events like the centenary observances naturally gave a healthy boost to the critical stock market, where, despite the fluctuations in individual prices that were inevitable when so mixed a list of stocks was involved and the critical atmosphere was so volatile, the Dow-Jones index of shares in Victorian reputations moved steadily upward. George Eliot was the combined IBM and Xerox stock of the postwar era. In the seven years 1942–48 the annual bibliography listed a total of only twenty-six items about her, ten of which were mere scraps in *Notes and Queries*; in 1949 not a single new item on Eliot was published, in 1950 only three, and in 1951, one. Eliot's critical standing at that moment was not unfairly represented by Samuel Chew's unenthusiastic account in the Baugh *Literary History of England* (1948):

> No other Victorian novelist of major rank is so little read today. The effort to lift fiction to a higher plane than that upon which her predecessors and contemporaries were satisfied to work, though it brought her temporary prestige, has ultimately been responsible for this decline. . . . [I]n George Eliot's hands the novel was not primarily for entertainment but for the serious discussion of moral issues. If these issues are no longer felt to be vital, as the Victorians felt them, and if the solutions proposed now seem unsatisfactory, the *raison d'être* of the stories which are but vehicles for these ideas is enfeebled, if, indeed, it does not vanish altogether.

There is not a little irony in the fact that this evaluation was published in the same year that Leavis's *The Great Tradition* appeared, with its pioneering praise of what W. J. Harvey called Eliot's "serious, subtle and adult view of the moral life."

A few blue chip stocks, mainly those of poets—Tennyson, Browning, Arnold, Hardy, Hopkins—were equitably priced at the outset of the period and rose steadily in value; they were notably exempt from the vicissitudes of the market. Stock in Thackeray, grossly undervalued in the 1940s, would have returned good profits to a farsighted speculator. Little scholarship was devoted to him before the mid-forties (the 1944 bibliography cited but a single item, again in *Notes and Queries*), and despite the publication of Gordon Ray's edition of Thackeray's letters and Stevenson's and Ray's biographies, it was not until the sixties that he achieved his present place in the hierarchy of novelists. Trollope would have been an equally profitable investment, though one would have had to wait longer, until the past decade in fact, to realize the maximum return. Two lesser-known stocks that were underpriced forty years ago have performed well—Gissing and Mrs. Gaskell. A third, that of Arthur Hugh Clough, enjoyed much activity in the sixties but seems in retrospect to have been somewhat overvalued. From time to time there were signs that an over-the-counter stock might qualify for a higher rating—Landor and "Mark Rutherford" come to mind—but the flurry of interest in them proved short-lived.

On the other hand, two stocks that have always been on the big board have had indifferent records. George Meredith never appealed to more than a few investors, and despite a small boom in the seventies, trading in him has generally been light. In 1959 a writer in the *Manchester Guardian* remarked, "It looks as though Macaulay were in for a revival. His life and his work are part of that nineteenth-century tradition of liberal thought to which we are increasingly turning." But nothing much happened, despite the appearance of his collected letters and the first volume of John Clive's biography. Instead, the revival of interest in Victorian liberal thought chiefly benefited John Stuart Mill, the rise in whose stock was signalized by the early volumes of a collected edition.

Two stocks have had an erratic record and their prospects are, at this moment, uncertain. During the early part of the period there was a continual output of Stevensoniana, much of it of no great critical importance. By the mid-fifties the production of both criticism and research was dwindling, and by the early seventies surprisingly little was being written about him. A similarly curious phenomenon was the variable fortunes of Kipling. In 1942 *Scrutiny* greeted T. S. Eliot's *A Choice of Kipling's Verse* by observing that "certainly Mr. Eliot should never have lowered himself to advocating a revival of interest in such a writer." But the imprimatur by Eliot counted for more than the Leavisites' fastidious dismay, and Kipling enjoyed a modest revival, though most of the commentary on him, to be sure, was concentrated in the *Kipling Journal*.

The recent brisk activity in Rossetti and Morris scholarship is attributable in part to nonliterary circumstances. One poet has benefited from the resurgence of interest in Victorian painting, the other from the concurrent rediscovery of the arts and crafts movement. Morris, in addition, bears political credentials which have served him well in a time when Victorian radical socialism became a lively subject of study.

The rise and fall of critical reputations could be discerned only in long perspective. But Victorian scholarship produced plenty of spot news, the printed chitchat and scandal of the marketplace—misguided or overambitious enterprises, controversies, squibs that failed to go off, revelations. The first and (as it proved) only volume of a massive projected life of Ruskin barely managed to get his parents off on their honeymoon. Helen Rossetti Angeli denounced Violet Hunt for her culpable misrepresentation of the story of Elizabeth Siddal Rossetti's suicide. A scholar tried unsuccessfully to convince the community that Christina Rossetti had been secretly in love with William Bell Scott. Sir Charles Tennyson drew aside the curtain that had concealed for so long the terrible truth about home conditions at Somersby as well as rattling some other skeletons in the family's well furnished closet, a process recently carried further by Robert B. Martin's relentlessly but tactfully candid biography of the poet. It became common knowledge that the official biography of Hardy, nominally by his second wife, was in fact the work of the novelist himself. There was a protracted squabble over the issue of whether Hardy had or had not had an affair with Tryphena Sparks, and whether the child she bore, if she bore one, was Hardy's.

It was to be expected that this, the side of their lives that the Victorians most resolutely kept from public view, was responsible for the greatest furor when hidden aspects did come to light in a less reticent age. The sensation was all the greater in the case of the Victorians because it involved the destruction of conceptions—"images" was the new term—sedulously cultivated by the people in question and perpetuated by their descendants. During these same years, the revelation, in his *London Journal*, of Boswell's invincible raunchiness came as no surprise to those acquainted with the sexual libertinism of his time, however hard it may have been for them to accept the dim hint, from other evidence, that Dr. Johnson once craved the touch of the whip. F. W. Bateson's controversial argument that there was an incestuous element in the relations of William and Dorothy Wordsworth was received with relative calm by a scholarly public long since accustomed to the presence of Annette Vallon in Words-worthian biography, to say nothing of their even longer-standing accep-tance of Shelley's and Byron's sexual irregularities. But once again: *the Victorians*—?

Some hint that Dickens, the genial Boz, the welcome guest at every fireside where *Pickwick Papers* was read aloud, had had a mistress had surfaced as early as 1934. But it was not until the 1950s that the fuller documentation of the Ellen Ternan affair, by Ada Nisbet and others, stirred the most vehement rearguard resistance by Dickensians for Con-jugal Fidelity. The most furious controversy, however, occurred when Admiral Sir William James, grandson of Effie (Ruskin) Millais, published documents relating to the intimate facts of Ruskin's unconsummated mar-riage which reflected favorably on his grandmother, and J. H. Whitehouse countered with another document (Ruskin's own statement) which pre-sented the other side of the story. Most interested spectators denounced this well-publicized display of the family laundry as grossly unedifying and irrelevant, but they overlooked the greatest irrelevancy of all, the fact that Effie's fierce octogenarian defender had many years earlier, even prior to being dressed in his first sailor suit, modeled for Millais's picture of Bubbles, world-famous from its appearance in Pears' soap advertise-ments. By the time the Ruskin sensation had run its course in the scholarly headlines, people were prepared to accept with equanimity Phyllis Grosskurth's frank treatment of John Addington Symonds's homosexu-ality and even the disclosure that the Reverend Charles Kingsley had enjoyed making highly explicit erotic drawings for the delectation of self and, presumably, spouse.

Now the forbidden caches of papers were opened, one by one. Cecil Lang was able to print in his edition of Swinburne's letters the account of the poet's sexual proclivities which Edmund Gosse had prepared but, not daring to publish it in his life of the poet (1917), had deposited in the British Museum against the day when such revelations would not shake the foundations of society. Markedly less interesting when they were opened were the long-embargoed letters from Rossetti to Jane Morris; they proved to contain little that was not already known. And, though here no personal gossip was involved, the Tennyson manuscripts at Cam-bridge were thrown open for unrestricted scholarly use, just too late for Christopher Ricks to use them in his critical edition of Tennyson's poems.

It must not be inferred from the foregoing pages that the history of Victorian studies lacks instances of inefficiency and waste. Unlike other busy industries, academic ones have no safeguards against the squandering of energy and no reliable means of quality control. Repetition of effort and overemphasis of the trivial are prices that seemingly must be paid for the freedom of activity that every scholar and critic enjoys. Complaint can justly be made of what David DeLaura has called "the endless circling around the same questions" that has distinguished the criticism of Victorian literature in recent years. So much remains to be learned that the talents of the profession need not—should not—be deflected to redoing what has already been done, restating with an air of discovery what has already been adequately canvassed. For despite the depletion of forty years, the reservoir of provocative subjects for initial or justifiably renewed investigation and discussion remains well supplied. Some are minor questions, on the order of "Who, if anyone, was George Eliot's model for Casaubon?" Larger issues cannot, by their very nature, always be settled for good, requiring, as most do, fresh attention from each passing generation. What *was* the genetic relationship between the Romantic and Victorian periods: was there a severe disjunction, or were the continuities of thought and sensibility more significant than the divergences?

One pressing need is for a synthesis of the best that scholars and critics have discovered and proposed, in the form of a reasonably large-scale history of Victorian literature. (There seems to be no sign that the long-promised volume of the Oxford History of English Literature covering the period is imminent.) None of the short treatments, such as that in the Penguin Guide to English Literature, is very satisfactory. Despite the consensus that a great deal of what is most important to learn about the Victorians is embodied in their periodical literature, no scholarly or even semischolarly history of Victorian periodicals as a class exists. Nor is there a well-informed overall account of Victorian publishing. Formal large-scale primary bibliographies of most of the major authors, on the model of Richard Purdy's bibliography of Hardy, should be priority projects. A large mass of important prose demands annotation in an age when most of the topical as well as the literary references baffle the imperfectly educated: who, for example, will undertake to footnote the five volumes of Carlyle's "Critical and Miscellaneous Essays" in the Centenary edition?

There should be full-length studies of the "higher journalists" who figure in John Gross's *The Rise and Fall of the Man of Letters* and, more extensively, in the author lists of the *Wellesley Index*, for these were the influential people who had the ear of the public throughout the Victorian era. The shelves devoted to scholarly editions of authors' letters still have some gaps. Some fiction writers of the second rank or below would reward attention if our understanding of the total literary and cultural environment of Victorian literature is to be expanded. Robert Wolff's large book on Mary Elizabeth Braddon exemplifies what might be done for a number of popular writers about whom ample information might be accumulated with sufficient determination and a bit of luck: Surtees is a prime example. . . . The list, needless to say, could continue. The more we possess, the more we quite reasonably think we need.

It has been an engrossing spectacle to watch, this academic industry which, after a late start, has taken its place among the most fruitful of its kind, enabling us, as it has, to know with ever-increasing intimacy the Victorians as they lived and their literature as they wrote it. Thousands of men and women have joined to dispel the ignorance and pervasive misapprehension in which notions of the Victorian age were still wrapped in 1941. Knowledge, understanding, and tempered sympathy have replaced condescension or—worse—facetious disdain. And yet, as this cursory reckoning nears the bottom line, the chilling thought occurs: Has all this bustle been only machinery, in the Arnoldian sense of the word? What end, apart from the enlightenment of an infinitesimally tiny fraction of society—practicing students of Victorianism, talking to each other—has it accomplished? Have Victorian studies passed one test by which the fruits of historical research are judged, their effect on the public understanding of a past society? Are the major Victorian writers now read more widely, and more intelligently, than they were forty years ago? Is the popular conception of Victorianism—all the clustered images and associations the word now conjures up—significantly different from what it was then? The spirit of Furnivall's Browning Society, after all, still broods over a shrine in Texas, and in today's argumentative vocabulary the epithet "Victorian" retains some of its former derogation.

Furthermore, for whatever it may be worth, one longtime Victorian-watcher must reluctantly testify, from the depths of his consciousness, that a few of the crude stereotypes he already entertained that bright September day in 1941 have stubbornly resisted the corrective action of forty years. But this is witness only of the obstinate durability of impressions acquired in receptive youth, and it is inadmissible evidence when the larger issue is confronted—as neither space nor inclination permits here. Unless academics do, in fact, work in the ivy-covered, hermetically sealed tower attributed to them in the laity's hoary myth, the processes of scholarship and criticism must, in subtle, mysterious, unmeasurable osmotic fashion, influence the attitudes society holds toward the subject of their study. And the advancement of learning, in any case, is not "machinery";

its value is not contingent on some clear demonstration of its social utility. So let the chilling thought be withdrawn and the account finally balanced to this effect: The success of the great Victorian studies enterprise, stretching from the innocent days of the New Criticism to the brave new world of postdeconstructionism, is beyond question. To end a backward glance like this in a warm Macaulayan glow would seem alien to the modern spirit, a shameful reversion to the Victorians' own complacency. But Progress, in this connection, is neither illusion nor cant. It is a matter of abundant record.

1982

Notes

Chapter One

1. One of the few annotators to question whether "the poem illustrates Browning's characteristic philosophy of aspiration" is Walter E. Houghton, in the Spencer-Houghton-Barrows anthology, *British Literature* (Boston, 1952), 2:714. My own skepticism considerably antedates the publication of this provocative note.

2. "Tennyson, Browning, and a Romantic Fallacy," *University of Toronto Quarterly* 12(1944): 175–95.

3. Browning shared the strong and widespread Victorian preference for doing rather than thinking, for experience over learning. Compare such characteristic statements of the attitude as these, from Samuel Smiles's *Self-Help* (London, 1859): "a man perfects himself by work much more than by reading, . . . it is life rather than literature, action rather than study, and character rather than biography, that tends perpetually to renovate mankind" (p. 6); "the experience gathered from books, though often valuable, is but of the nature of *learning*; whereas the experience gained from actual life is of the nature of *wisdom*; and a small store of the latter is worth vastly more than any stock of the former. . . . And it must be admitted that the chief object of culture is, not merely to fill the mind with other men's thoughts—and to be the passive recipients of their impressions of things—but to enlarge our individual intelligence . . ." (p. 258). "It is not how much a man may know, that is of so much importance, as the end and purpose for which he knows it. . . . We must ourselves *be* and *do*, and not rest satisfied merely with reading and meditating over what other men have written and done. Our best light must be made life, and our best thought action" (p. 259).

   That the grounds for the attitude toward the grammarian which I here ascribe to Browning were in harmony with prevailing Victorian values is further implied in Thackeray's comments (*Pendennis*, chap. 29) on the relative worth of the lives led by his own versions of the students' "low man" and "high man"—the two templars, Warrington, who takes the world as it comes, and the grimly studious Paley: "The one could afford time to think, and the other never could. The one could have sympathies and do kindnesses; and the other must needs always be selfish. He could not cultivate a friendship or do a charity, or admire a work of genius, or kindle at the sight of beauty or the sound of a sweet song—he had no time, and no eyes for anything but his law-books. All was dark outside his reading-lamp. Love, and Nature, and Art (which is the expression of our praise and sense of the beautiful world of God), were shut out from him. And as he turned off his lonely lamp at night, he never thought but that he had spent the day profitably, and went to sleep alike thankless and remorseless."

4. To the students' further plea that he at least "take a little rest," he might have replied as did Antoine Arnauld, the seventeenth-century theologian, quoted by nineteenth-century English authors as diverse as Isaac Disraeli (*Curiosities of Literature*), Carlyle (*Sartor Resartus*), and Smiles (*Self-Help*): "Rest? Rest? Shall I not have all eternity to rest in?"

5. First, apparently, by Joseph F. Payne in the introduction to his edition of Linacre's *Galen* (1881); see Sir John E. Sandys, *A History of Classical Scholarship* (Cambridge, 1903–8), 2:228. Payne, according to a correspondent in *Notes and Queries* 194(1949):284, also put forward the idea in his Harveian Lecture of 1896 on *Harvey and Galen*. Mario Praz (*TLS*, 6 December 1957, 739), referring to the lines beginning "So, with the throttling hands of death at strife, / Ground he at grammar," quoted Heinrich Strömer's letter to Johannes Cochleus on Erasmus's death: "Totus erat, omnium vir doctissimus, in restituendo Graeco origine; cui sic erat, iam iam morbi vi quam maxime urgente, addictus, ut ab illo non citius discesserit quam mors ipsa e manibus scribentis calamum extorserit." A striking, though wholly accidental, demonstration of the "peculiarly Erasmian" nature of Browning's religious ideas may be found in Wallace K. Ferguson's

article, "Renaissance Tendencies in the Religious Thought of Erasmus," *Journal of the History of Ideas* 15(1954):499–508. Browning is nowhere mentioned; but the ease with which his name may be substituted for Erasmus's throughout the article suggests that the intellectual sympathies that bound him to the great humanist were numerous and strong.

6. The translation is by Hoyt Hudson (Princeton, 1941), 72.
7. *The Praise of Folly*, 50–51.
8. Ibid., xxxv–xxxvi.

Chapter Two

1. L. C. Collins, *Life and Memoirs of John Churton Collins* (London, 1912), 79. Collins described this interview, or possibly the earlier one referred to in this passage, in an article, "Poetry and Symbolism," *Contemporary Review* 93(1908):65–66. Collins suggested a symbolic interpretation of "Master Hugues" which has nothing in common with the one offered here, but Browning stoutly denied any such intention.
2. "Poetry and Symbolism," 67.
3. It is tempting to relate the spider-webs here and in later lines, with their clear reference to men's futile search for religious truth through ratiocination, to Tennyson's lines:

I found Him not in world or sun,
  Or eagle's wing, or insect's eye,
  Nor through the questions men may try,
The petty cobwebs we have spun.   (*In Memoriam*, 124)

The stanza, with its additional thrust at Paleyan natural theology, must have been peculiarly gratifying to the Browning who later wrote "Caliban upon Setebos."
4. *Dust-clouds* in the first edition.
5. Writing to the Rev. Henry G. Spaulding, 30 June 1887, Browning commented: "The 'mode Palestrina' has no reference to organ-playing; it was the name given by old Italian writers on Composition to a certain simple and severe style like that of the Master; just as, according to Byron, 'the word Miltonic means sublime' " (Herbert E. Greene, "Browning's Knowledge of Music," *PMLA* 62 [1947]:1098–99).
6. "If Caesar can hide the sun from us with a blanket, or put the moon in his pocket, we will pay him tribute for light" (*Cymbeline*, III.i.43–45). Note that "hide the sun . . . with a blanket" may have suggested "Blot ye the gold, while your spider-web strengthens, / Blacked to the stoutest of tickens" (lines 99–100). For some reason *Cymbeline* was in the back of Browning's mind as he wrote this poem; like the roof of the baroque church, "the roof of [Imogen's] chamber," according to Iachimo (II.iv.87–88), "With golden cherubins is fretted." The *rotten-planked* of the penultimate line, incidentally, became *rotten-runged* in later editions.
7. Philipp Spitta, *Johann Sebastian Bach* (English trans., New York, 1951), 1:360.
8. Bach himself was caught between the two warring camps. His inherited allegiance was to Lutheran orthodoxy, yet during his brief tenure at Mühlhausen (1707–8) he found himself not only in the very citadel of pietism but organist in a church whose pastor was a fervent pietist. His later career as the supreme master of the fugue leaves little doubt where his mature musical sympathies lay; at the same time, he also proved that in the straitest, the most intellectual and rule-ridden of musical forms there was still room for the poignant utterance of the human soul. (For a detailed study, see Leo Schrade, "Bach: the Conflict between the Sacred and the Secular," *Journal of the History of Ideas* 7 [1946]: 151–94.) Browning did Bach no more than simple justice in denying any resemblance between him and Master Hugues.
9. "Allegory in Baroque Music," *Journal of the Warburg and Courtauld Institutes* 3(1939): 20–21.

Chapter Three

1. The text used is that of *Men and Women* (London, 1855).
2. *The Poetical Works of Matthew Arnold*, ed. C. B. Tinker and H. F. Lowry (London, 1950), 247.

Chapter Five

1. Page 41. All references are to the Riverside edition of *Past and Present* (Boston, 1965), which reprints the text of the first edition.
2. Stulz's fame persisted for many years. He is referred to in Ruskin's *Modern Painters* (1843); Disraeli's *Coningsby* (1844); Thackeray's *Book of Snobs* (*Punch*, 1846–47), *Pendennis* (1848–50), and *The Newcomes* (1853–55); Bulwer-Lytton's *The Caxtons* (1848–49); and Reade's *Hard Cash* (1863). Even the putative Sir Roger Tichborne claimed that Stulz had "always" been his tailor; see W. P. Frith, *My Autobiography and Reminiscences* (London, 1887), 2:44.
3. Again like Long and Stulz, the Duke of Newcastle continued to hold a place in the rhetorical vocabulary of Victorian writers, many years after ceasing to be immediately topical. Dinah Maria Mulock recalled his query, in the anachronistic setting of 1800, in *John Halifax, Gentleman* (1856), and Trollope mentioned it in *The Way We Live Now* (1874–75).
4. See Owen Chadwick, *The Victorian Church* (New York, 1966), 1:214–15.
5. It is not impossible that Carlyle also intended a hidden reference to quacklike adulteration in his "Duke of Logwood" (p. 92). "The alleged use of logwood in colouring spurious or adulterated port wine was at one time a frequent subject of jocular allusion" (*Oxford English Dictionary*).
6. Other events of the parliamentary session to which Carlyle alludes are the passage, at last, of the Talfourd-Mahon Copyright Bill on 24 June (pp. 107, 131, 201), and the "Goulburn Baring Budget" (p. 208).
7. The immediacy of any argumentative work like *Past and Present* is enhanced by the introduction of neologisms, including the author's coinages. According to the *OED*, Carlyle's use of "red tape" attributively (pp. 14, 30, 198, 229) had only very recent precedents, in 1838 (Bulwer-Lytton's *Alice*) and 1840 (Carlyle's own *Heroes and Hero Worship*). "Puseyism" (pp. 119, 133, 163, 292) was equally a novelty: John Sterling had first used it in his *Essays and Tales* (1838) and Mrs. Carus Wilson in 1840. Carlyle's " 'millocracy' so-called" (pp. 143, 174), which he is credited with inventing, was an adaptation of Mrs. Trollope's "millocrat" in *Michael Armstrong* (1839–40).
8. On Laurie, see Philip Collins, *Dickens and Crime* (Bloomington, Ind., 1968), 184–88. Collins notes that, notwithstanding the widespread belief that Laurie had used the precise phrase ascribed to him, there is no solid evidence of his having done so.
9. On the Ecclesiastical Commission and Church Extension, see Chadwick, *The Victorian Church*, 1:136, 340.
10. See Trevor Blount, "The Documentary Symbolism of Chancery in *Bleak House*," *Dickensian* 62(1966):49–51.
11. Norman Gash, *Sir Robert Peel* (London, 1972), 38. The crisis of 1842, mentioned in the first paragraph of this essay, was of a different kind, though no less alarming.
12. Charles Hindley, *The Life and Times of James Catnach* (London, 1878), 215–16. See also *Annual Register 1830*, Chronicle, 77–78, 84–86.
13. Need it be pointed out that Carlyle's rhetoric here (not uniquely) did some violence to history and etymology? *Sans-culottism* in its original usage referred to the masses' egalitarian preference for trousers over knee breeches, not to their total lack of nether garments. But for the sake of a vivid image and the contrast with literal shirtlessness, Carlyle fixed upon the expanded meaning of the word.

14. How deeply the French Revolution continued to influence the public mind in the early Victorian era is still an open question, deserving of more study than it has yet had. Cf. the somewhat revisionist view of George Watson, *The English Ideology* (London, 1973), 44–46: By the time of *Past and Present* the Revolution "is a fading popular memory which excites ardour, as a political analogy, of an increasingly factitious kind. . . . Most English views of the Revolution itself, though not of the Terror that followed it, are relaxed to the point of acceptance. . . . The bogey of revolution was never accepted as an argument by educated Victorian opinion."

15. As the creator of Diogenes Teufelsdröckh, Carlyle's attention would naturally have been arrested by a speech during the Commons' five-night-long debate on the alleged iniquity of truck shops. On 7 March the fractious member for Knaresborough, Busfield Ferrand, renewed an accusation that the millowners supplied inferior goods to the employees who were obliged to patronize the company shops: "Did they know nothing of the flour paste [used in making calico]; nothing of the shoddy trade; nothing of the old rags and the devil's dust?" Later in the same speech he quoted a letter from an Oxfordshire textile manufacturer, eager to do his northern rivals in, who spoke of "the Yorkshire people always underselling them through the use of 'shoddy' or 'devil's dust' " (*Hansard*, 3rd ser., 61 [1842], cols. 141, 149). Hence the passage in *Past and Present* (p. 143): "The Honourable Member complains unmusically that there is 'devil's dust' in Yorkshire cloth. Yorkshire cloth—why, the very Paper I now write on is made, it seems, partly of plaster-lime well-smoothed, and obstructs my writing!" Devil's dust was "the flock to which old cloth is reduced by a machine called a devil" (*OED*).

Chapter Six

1. Page references are to the New Oxford Illustrated Dickens edition (1952).
2. Matthew Arnold commented trenchantly on school reading books, as well as on other aspects of contemporary education touched upon in *Our Mutual Friend*, in his inspector's reports for 1860–69. See *Reports on Elementary Schools, 1852–1882*, ed. Sir Francis Sandford (London, 1889), 82–152.
3. Philip Collins, *Dickens and Education* (London, 1963), 159. Pages 159–71 of this book contain the fullest discussion of the subject. See also Asher Tropp, *The School Teachers: The Growth of the Teaching Profession in England and Wales from 1800 to the Present Day* (New York, [1957]), chap. 3, "The 'Social Condition' of the New Schoolmasters."
4. Collins, p. 160. Mary Sturt, *The Education of the People* (London, 1967), 198, quotes a professional paper of the time, *The School and the Teacher*: "It is no strange thing that men who in education, tastes and habits have all the qualifications of 'gentlemen' should regard themselves as worthy of something very much higher than the treatment of a servant and the wages of a mechanic. What in short the teacher desires is that his 'calling' shall rank as a 'profession'; that the name of 'schoolmaster' shall ring as grandly on the ear as that of 'clergyman' or 'solicitor'; that he shall feel no more that awful chill and 'stony British stare' which follows the explanation that 'that interesting young man is only the schoolmaster,' " Such a passage enables us to understand the precise intonation and intention of Eugene's repeated contemptuous use of "Schoolmaster" ("a most respectable title") as he addresses Headstone in the scene in the Temple (pp. 288–93).
5. Although the immediate cause of Lowe's resignation was the charge that he had doctored the inspectors' annual reports to suppress criticism of the Committee of Council's doctrines, it is clear that his sponsorship of "payment by results" had much to do with it. Chaps. 6 and 7 of Tropp's book, cited in note 3, supply a detailed narrative of the whole Revised Code controversy.
6. Lizzie's education exemplifies a notable trend in the years just before the novel was written. The literacy rate among girls of her generation (i.e., those who were able to sign

the marriage register) rose from 54.8 percent in 1851 to 65.3 percent in 1861. This increase of 10.5 percentage points was the largest recorded for either sex in any single Victorian decade.

7. George Gissing, *Charles Dickens* (New York, 1924), 257.

8. Dickens may be casting a side glance at the popularity of Mrs. Beeton's *Book of Household Management*, which in its first year of publication, 1861, had sold 60,000 copies.

9. Unless the event was duplicated nearer the time of the novel, the bill Dickens mentions alludes to an incident of 1840, when two sisters were prevented from jumping off Southwark Bridge, "both firmly tied together round the waists with two strong scarfs knotted, and which went round their bodies two or three times" (*Annual Register* 1840, Chronicle, 122–23).

10. In ironic contrast, the walls of the murderous Bradley Headstone's schoolroom were decorated with "peaceful texts from Scripture" (p. 555).

11. The paper industry was much in the news in the years just before Dickens wrote *Our Mutual Friend*. In 1861, as was noted above, the excise duty on paper was repealed. The growing insufficiency of standard raw materials, mainly rags, to meet the increased demand for paper stimulated a search for other materials which resulted in the adoption of esparto grass and, later, of wood pulp. For one example of the popular interest in the topic, see "Paper," *Cornhill Magazine* 4(1861):609–23.

12. One interpretation of the place of paper in *Bleak House* is Trevor Blount's: "the paper symbolism of Chancery documents, begging letters, and philanthropic correspondence . . . [is] meant to show the substitution (as Dickens saw it) of paper resolutions, vapid theorizings, and wordy protestations for actual help when and how it was needed" ("Poor Jo, Education, and the Problem of Juvenile Delinquency in Dickens' *Bleak House*," *Modern Philology* 62 [1965], 331). For another, more comprehensive statement, see Alan R. Burke, "The Strategy and Theme of Urban Observation in *Bleak House*," *Studies in English Literature* 9(1969):666–67, 672–73.

13. But at least two commentators have linked paper with Shares—that is, as physical symbols of the worship of stock-exchange values which is a dominant motif of the novel. Arnold Kettle quotes from the second paragraph of chap. 10, "As is well known to the wise in their generation, traffic in Shares is the one thing to have to do with in this world" (p. 114), and observes: "The dust-heaps are the dominant visual image of the accumulation of wealth and power; but it is a feature of that power that it operates mysteriously, through bits of paper: wills, promissory notes, the offer of reward which Rogue Riderhood clutches, above all, through shares" ("*Our Mutual Friend*," *Dickens and the Twentieth Century*, ed. John Gross and Gabriel Pearson [London, 1962], 219). J. Hillis Miller, in his Afterword to the Signet edition of the novel, quotes both the former passage and the one with which the present paper ends as the basis for his remark, " 'Shares,' which, in their inexhaustible power to duplicate themselves and make everything of nothing, Dickens describes as the virtual god of a moneyed society." In Dickens's text, however, shares are not explicitly spoken of as pieces of paper.

14. See his letter of 7 June 1850, quoted on p. 252 of the Papermac edition of Collins's *Dickens and Education*.

15. This brief passage contains one further topicality. The "electric" wires are, of course, those of the telegraph (pp. 252, 253), which had come into general use for the transmission of private messages only a few years earlier. By 1865 the several independent companies had offices throughout commercial London. When Society, assembled at the Veneerings', reviews and passes authoritative judgment on the late melodramatic events up the Thames, the Wandering Chairman gives it as his opinion that the proper reward for Lizzie's heroism would be to "have got her a berth in an Electric Telegraph office, where young women answer very well" (p. 818). This bran-new occupation was one of the very first which enabled women to enter the Victorian business world.

Chapter Seven

1. Since this article was originally drafted, additional aspects of the relation between chapter 1 and the rest of the novel have been pointed out by Robert Newsom (*Dickens on the Romantic Side of Familiar Things* [New York, 1977], 19–28). The text used here is that of the Norton Critical Edition, ed. George Ford and Sylvère Monod (New York, 1977). Citations are first to chapter, then to page in this edition. [After this essay appeared, Ford threw additional light, as it were, on one of its chief topics in "Light and Darkness: Gas, Oil and Tallow in Dickens's *Bleak House*," *From Smollett to James: Studies in the Novel and Other Essays Presented to Edgar Johnson*, ed. S. I. Mintz et al. (Charlottesville, Va., 1981), 183–201.]

2. Cf. *OED*: "*Pugilism*. (From the tenacity and absolute control with which the Court of Chancery holds anything, and the certainty of cost and loss to property 'in chancery'.) A slang term for the position of the head when held under the opponent's left arm to be pommelled severely, the victim meanwhile being unable to retaliate effectively; hence sometimes figuratively used of an awkward fix or predicament." The first cited occurrence of the term is in Captain Marryat's *Newton Forster* (1832).

3. Francis Dowling, *Fistiana, or the Oracle of the Ring* (London, 1841), quoted in Alan Lloyd, *The Great Prize Fight* (New York, 1977), 32.

4. *Past and Present*, ed. Richard D. Altick (Boston, 1965), 133–34.

5. Dickens's familiarity with the jargon of the ring is evident in several passages of his novels, particularly in connection with the "Game Chicken" in *Dombey and Son*: "The Chicken himself attributed this punishment to his having had the misfortune to get into Chancery early in the proceedings, when he was severely fibbed by the larkey one, and heavily grassed" (chap. 44). In *Bleak House* itself, pugilistic terms recur, mainly in connection with the bearlike Chadband. Mr. Snagsby observes, "And when a time is named for having tea, it's better to come up to it" (i.e., "come up to scratch," explained by the Norton editors as "a reference to a line drawn across the center of the ring in the early days of prize-fighting"). " 'To come up to it!' Mrs. Snagsby repeats with severity. 'Up to it! As if Mr. Chadband was a fighter!' " (19.235). The same term is later attributed to Bucket (49.595). Chadband's oily smile threatens Snagsby with "an argumentative back-fall presently if he be not already down" (25.320), and in his powerful homily on "Terewth" prophesies, somewhat redundantly, that "you shall fall, you shall be bruised, you shall be battered, you shall be flawed, you shall be smashed" (25.321). Chadband accepts that for Jo's sake "I should have to wrestle, and to combat and to struggle, and to conquer" (25.322). In the next scene, the much-battered Phil Squod offers himself as a sparring partner in Trooper George's shooting gallery-gymnasium. "They can't spoil *my* beauty. I'm all right. Come on! If they want a man to box at, let 'em box at me. Let 'em knock me well about the head. *I* don't mind! If they want a light-weight, to be throwed for practice, Cornwall, Devonshire, or Lancashire, let 'em throw *me*. They won't hurt me" (26.328).

6. Although Rockingham Castle, the original of Chesney Wold, was in Northamptonshire, Dickens moved the Dedlocks' acres to Lincolnshire to take advantage of that county's celebrated wetness. Drainage of the fens had begun as early as the Norman conquest, but efforts were being intensified at the time *Bleak House* was written. In 1851 Parliament empowered the Lincolnshire Estuary Company to recover from the sea "extensive tracts of lands, abutting on the Lincolnshire coast of the Great Estuary, called The Wash," by making new channels and outfalls for the rivers Witham and Welland (*White's 1856 Lincolnshire: A Reprint of the 1856 Issue of History, Gazetteer, and Directory of Lincolnshire*, by William White [New York, 1969], 36, 279–80).

7. See Susan Shatto, "Byron, Dickens, Tennyson, and the Monstrous Efts," *Yearbook of English Studies* 6(1976):144–55.

8. On the scientific background of the novel's analogies, see Ann Y. Wilkinson, "*Bleak House*: From Faraday to Judgment Day," *ELH* 34(1967):225–47, and William F. Axton, "Religious and Scientific Imagery in *Bleak House*," *Nineteenth-Century Fiction* 22(1968): 349–59.

9. It is tempting to trace this unnatural confusion of time and light to *Macbeth*, echoes of which reverberate throughout *Bleak House* more insistently, perhaps, than anywhere else in Dickens. The scene (II.iii) following the "unnatural" murder of Duncan contains reports of "dire combustion [cf. Krook!] and confused events" (II.iii.54), and Ross later says to the Old Man:

> By th' clock 'tis day,
> And yet dark night strangles the travelling lamp.
> Is't night's predominance, or the day's shame,
> That darkness does the face of earth entomb
> When living light should kiss it? (II.iv.6–10)

10. But although we are told, on one occasion, that "bedroom fires blaze brightly all over the house [Chesney Wold]" (28.349), they do not necessarily protect the inhabitants against the damp chill. In fact, the fires are as ineffectual in providing heat as the lamps and candles usually are in providing light. See 28.347 and 58.693–94.

11. Tulkinghorn's rustiness is repeatedly mentioned (e.g., he is "rusty to look at" [2.13], "rusty, out of date" [10.119]). Rust—the result of dampness, especially exposure to the elements, and often of age as well—is found throughout the novel. Krook owns to a "liking for rust and must and cobwebs" (5.50), and included in his inexhaustible stock of junk are hundreds of rusty keys (5.49); in Nemo's room upstairs is a "rusty skeleton of a grate" (10.124). The votive shrine near which Lady Dedlock prays in "gloomy" Notre Dame Cathedral is a "rusty little gridiron-full of gusty little tapers" (12.139), later recalled by the "rusty grate" on which Trooper George grills his rasher of bacon (26.325). The London legal neighborhood in the summer vacation is covered with "a great veil of rust" (19.233). In the street where the Dedlock mansion stands, disused ironwork is "rusty foliage, sacred to the memory of departed oil" (48.575). The railway construction sites Mrs. Bagnet and Mrs. Rouncewell pass on their way to London contain "torrents of rusty carts and barrows" (55.654), and Trooper George finds the yard of the Rouncewell iron works littered with "mountains of . . . broken-up, and rusty machinery" (63.742).

12. As if to reinforce the image of Chadband's shining dome, Dickens portrays several other men as bald: Mr. Jellyby (4.41), Snagsby (10.117), Gridley (15.187), and Bagnet (34.429).

13. The near-homophone "laggard" describes the mist that hangs over Cook's Court on the night of "the appointed time" (32.393).

14. Dickens made thrifty use of the windfall that names in English history afforded him. By naming young Rouncewell "Watt" he invoked not only the symbolic harbinger of the new industrial society but, by fortuitous identity of sound, Wat Tyler, the symbol of popular rebellion—thus offering Sir Leicester more than one occasion to choke over the word. In the present context, Dickens availed himself of the fact that Volumnia's fashionably pronounced "Lord" echoed the name of the legendary Ned Ludd, a more recent symbol of violent working-class discontent. At a remove of little more than a page, her "Lud" touches off, by an association of ideas, "all Sir Leicester's old misgivings relative to Wat Tyler, and the people in the iron districts who do nothing but turn out by torchlight" as had the Luddite machine-breakers in the second decade of the century (28.352).

15. It would be stretching things unacceptably far to detect significance in the fact that among the leftovers from the Smallweeds' tea which Judy scrapes together for Charley Neckett are "worn-down heels of loaves" (21.262).

16. The matches and lavender were the customary stock of London street sellers. Is Dickens implying that Miss Flite herself has been reduced to this form of beggary, or, by his silence, intimating that though she is equipped to beg, she does not do so?

17. See Michael Steig, *Dickens and Phiz* (Bloomington, Ind., 1977), 132–36.

Chapter Eight

1. Had a copy of that then extremely scarce work been available when the data were being assembled, Frederic Boase's *Modern English Biography* (Truro, 1892–1921) would doubtless have reduced somewhat the number of authors who died after 1850 and on whom the requisite data were not obtained.

2. In the first chapter of his *New Trends in Education in the Eighteenth Century* (London, 1951), Nicholas Hans analyzes the social origins and education of 3,500 "men of national repute," born between 1685 and 1785, who have places in the *Dictionary of National Biography*. Unfortunately he does not treat authors in a distinct category, and, so far as I know, there is—apart from Williams's brief passage in *The Long Revolution* (pp. 234–36)—no study of eighteenth-century authors comparable to the one I am here presenting of later generations. There is a somewhat similar survey of American authors: Edwin Leavitt Clarke's *American Men of Letters: Their Nature and Nurture (Studies in History, Economics, and Public Law* 72, no. 1 [Columbia University, 1916]).

3. See, for example, P[atrick] Colquhoun, *A Treatise on the Wealth, Power, and Resources of the British Empire* (London, 1814), 106–7; G. D. H. Cole and Raymond Postgate, *The Common People, 1746–1938* (London, 1938), 70, and the 1947 edition of the same book, p. 63; O. F. Christie, *The Transition from Aristocracy 1832–1867* (London, 1927), 66–71; and Leone Levi, *Wages and Earnings of the Working Classes* (London, 1885), 25.

4. The apparent supremacy of Eton as a nourisher of literary talent is to some extent a statistical illusion. In the past two centuries the school has always had at least twice as many students as any of its rivals.

5. Hans's figures (*New Trends in Education,* p. 32) on seventeenth- and eighteenth-century scientists do, but only by a narrow margin. One hundred and twenty-five scientists went to Cambridge, 116 to Oxford.

6. *Fifty Years Ago,* new edition (London, 1892), 176–77. Besant's figures, to put it mildly, lack substantiation. The official census returns for England and Wales throw only a fitful and dubious light on the number of persons who regarded themselves as professional writers. In the 1841 census, the first to include detailed occupational breakdowns, 167 persons were entered as authors and 459 as newspaper editors, proprietors, and reporters. In 1851, 2,671 "authors" were counted (but the fact that 123 of them were under twenty years of age is a measure of the seriousness with which we should regard all these figures!). In 1861, 1,673 men and women were included under the heading "author, editor, writer." In 1871 the classification was monstrously enlarged by the inclusion of "students" among "authors" and other "literary persons," with the result that the total was 139,143. For the next six decades the classifications were fairly consistent, although in the last two (1921, 1931) the limitation to England and Wales was removed and figures for all of Great Britain used instead:

	MALE	FEMALE	TOTAL
1881: Authors, editors, journalists, reporters, shorthand writers	5,644	467[8%]	6,111
1891: Authors, editors, journalists, reporters	7,485	787[9%]	8,272
1901: Authors, editors, journalists, reporters	9,811	1,249[11%]	11,060
1911: Authors, editors, journalists, reporters	12,030	1,756[13%]	13,786
1921: Authors, editors, journalists, publicists	12,240	2,166[15%]	14,406
1931: Authors, editors, journalists, publicists	17,190	3,409[17%]	20,599

Chapter Nine

1. George H. Ford's *Dickens and His Readers* (Princeton, 1955) is indispensable for any examination of Dickens's reception. But as the book's subtitle (*Aspects of Novel-Criticism since 1836*) makes clear, its concentration is on how critics rather than common readers responded to Dickens.

2. The fullest account of the sale of *Dombey and Son* is in Robert L. Patten, *Dickens and His Publishers* (Oxford, 1978), chap. 10

3. Cited by Ford, *Dickens and His Readers*, p. 76n.

4. Charles and Frances Brookfield, *Mrs. Brookfield and Her Circle* (New York, 1905), 1:248. Wilkie Collins wrote, much later: "That *Chuzzlewit* (in some respects the finest novel he ever wrote) delighted his readers, and so led to a large sale of his next book, *Dombey*, I don't doubt. But the latter half of *Dombey* no intelligent person can have read without astonishment at the badness of it." (Quoted in *Dickens: The Critical Heritage* [London, 1971], 212. This volume will be cited hereafter as *Critical Heritage*.) But Wilkie Collins was wrong about *Martin Chuzzlewit*, which had a hard time with the public and whose sales never exceeded 23,000; and the sustained sale of *Dombey and Son* would suggest that plenty of intelligent persons endured to the end, their "astonishment at the badness of it" notwithstanding.

5. *Critical Heritage*, 64, 173, 206. For convenience' sake, excerpts from contemporary reviews are quoted whenever possible from this volume. Other quotations are taken from the original sources.

6. Edgar Johnson, *Charles Dickens: His Tragedy and Triumph* (New York, 1952), 2:613.

7. Henry Mayhew, *Voices of the Poor*, ed. Anne Humpherys (London, 1971), 60, 131.

8. See *Critical Heritage*, 157–58.

9. So, at least, says Amy Cruse in *The Victorians and Their Books* (London, 1935). Dr. Michael Slater, an expert on the publication and reception of *Nicholas Nickleby*, is unable to confirm the assertion.

10. For a sensible summary of Dickens's limited fame among the working class, see Ford, *Dickens and His Readers*, 77–81.

11. *Sharpe's London Magazine* 6(1848):200. Italics supplied.

12. *Critical Heritage*, 70.

13. See Kathleen Tillotson, *Novels of the Eighteen-Forties* (London, 1954), 18–20.

14. *Critical Heritage*, 176.

15. Cruse collects evidence of readers' reception of *Dombey and Son* on pp. 157–58.

16. Quoted in *Dickensian* 65(1969):112.

17. *Critical Heritage*, 191.

18. See Malcolm Morley, "Enter *Dombey and Son*," *Dickensian* 48(1952):128–29. The comment quoted is from the *Theatrical Times*, 14 August 1847, by way of S. J. A. Fitzgerald, *Dickens and the Drama* (London, 1910), 223.

19. Plagiarisms and imitations of the various early novels are useful indicators of the features the popular audience enjoyed most, but these, too, are lacking in the case of *Dombey and Son*. "Baron" Renton Nicholson's *Dombey and Daughter: a Moral Fiction*, published in penny numbers in 1847, was a slum story which, though it contained many "Dickensian" elements that had made the fortune of earlier spinoffs from the novels, borrowed little but the title, and the fame, of *Dombey and Son*. See Louis James, *Fiction for the Working Man* (London, 1963), 68–69.

20. Paul D. Herring, "The Number Plans for *Dombey and Son*: Some Further Observations," *Modern Philology* 68(1970):162.

21. *The Letters of Charles Dickens*, ed. Madeline House and Graham Storey (Pilgrim Edition, Oxford, 1965–), 4:593, 629.

22. *Critical Heritage*, 232.

23. The most extensive treatment of Dickens's theatricality is Robert Garis, *The Dickens Theatre* (Oxford, 1965). On his intimate relationship with his readers, see also William F. Axton, *Circle of Fire: Dickens' Vision and Style and the Popular Victorian Theater* (Lexington, Ky., 1966), especially pp. 10–15; and J. D. Jump, "Dickens and His Readers," *Bulletin of the John Rylands Library* 54(1972):384–97.

24. *Critical Heritage*, 43, 70.

25. *Critical Heritage*, 77.

26. *Fraser's Magazine*, April 1840 (*Critical Heritage*, 90).

27. *Critical Heritage*, 233–34.

28. Garis, *The Dickens Theater*, 29–30.

29. *Quarterly Review* 64(1839):89–90.

30. In the course of a swingeing attack on the theatricality of *Dombey and Son*, Part 1 ("Cursed be the hour—should say a sincere admirer of Mr. Dickens' genius—that he ever set foot within a theatre, or became intimate with theatrical people"), Samuel Warren demanded, "Is it not certain that Mr. Dickens . . . had his eye on Tilbury or Bedford" (two popular character actors) enacting the role of Mr. Chick? (*Blackwood's Magazine* 60 [1846]:636–37).

31. See *Critical Heritage*, 216–17.

32. *Critical Heritage*, 140.

33. Marvin Rosenberg uses *Dombey and Son* as a prime example in arguing that "anyone who has not heard Dickens read aloud has probably never savored the novels to the full. Even the most discerning critics, reading silently, may fail to hear in the soundless symbols on the printed page some of Dickens's richest and sweetest nuances." Particularly Captain Cuttle: "like many of Dickens's characters, he must be heard to be believed" ("The Dramatist in Dickens," *Journal of English and Germanic Philology* 59 [1960]:11–12).

34. For example: "keeping her poor place so clean that an individual might have ate his dinner, yes, and his tea too, if he was so disposed, off any one of the floors or stairs," and "He hasn't the courage to meet her hi-i-i-igh . . . but steals away, like a felion. Why, if that baby of mine . . . was to offer to go and steal away, I'd do my duty as a mother by him, till he was covered with wales!" (39:532–34 in the Clarendon edition of *Dombey and Son*, ed. Alan Horsman [Oxford, 1974]). Subsequent references, inserted in the text, will be to chapter and page in this edition.)

35. Robert L. Patten, "The Fight at the Top of the Tree: *Vanity Fair* versus *Dombey and Son*," *Studies in English Literature* 10(1970):762.

36. See J. W. T. Ley, "Sentimental Songs in Dickens," *Dickensian* 28(1932):320–21.

37. William Axton has argued at length ("*Dombey and Son*: From Stereotype to Archetype," *ELH* 31 [1964]:301–17) that two popular dramas, Albert Smith's burlesque *Dick Whittington and His Cat* (1845) and Douglas Jerrold's *Black-Ey'd Susan* (1829, and frequently revived), supplied Dickens with the "mythical" materials by which the characters, plots, and imagery of *Dombey and Son* acquired universal significance. It is doubtful, however, that contemporary readers would have been aware of these deeper meanings. If they saw the plays in question, they would have remembered them on the literal level of the plot alone, and whatever response drew the plot and the mythic elements together as they read the novel would have occurred on a subliminal, not conscious, plane. The furthest *Dombey and Son*'s first readers would have gone in respect to the Whittington legend would have been simply to identify Walter Gay, as Dickens intended, as a modern avatar of that hero, irrespective of the elaborations and alterations to which Smith subjected the story in his burlesque. And Dickens's application of the epithet "Black-ey'd" to Susan Nipper would have recalled only the old song by John Gay, "Sweet William's Farewell to Black-Ey'd Susan" or the title, not the plot, of Jerrold's immensely popular nautical drama.

38. "T. Kent Brumleigh" [T. W. Hill], "Notes on *Dombey and Son*," *Dickensian* 39(1942–43):32.
39. See *Letters of Charles Dickens*, 4:598.
40. See Michael Steig, "*Dombey and Son* and the Railway Panic of 1845," *Dickensian* 67 (1971):145–48.
41. There is more on "grinders" in my article, "Victorian Readers and the Sense of the Present," *Midway* 10(1970):104, 114–15.
42. *Life and Works of Lord Macaulay*, Edinburgh edition (London, 1910), 10:211.
43. *Critical Heritage*, 217.
44. The contagion originated in the novel itself. Earle R. Davis has calculated that before the serialization ended, Florence had suffered no fewer than "eighty-eight separate weeping spells" (*The Flint and the Flame* [Columbia, Mo., 1963], 78). This record of persistence may be matched only by the number of times Carker flashes his teeth and is decidedly greater than the number of occasions, frequent though they are, on which Edith's bosom heaves or is otherwise brought to the reader's attention.
45. Quoted by way of Forster in *Critical Heritage*, 232.
46. Madeline House and Graham Storey usefully let some air out of the legend of the universal sorrow that attended the death of Little Nell (*Letters of Charles Dickens*, 2:ix–xii). The same caution should be observed in respect to Paul Dombey.
47. *Quarterly Review* 64(1839):93.
48. *Critical Heritage*, 179.
49. Brookfield, *Mrs. Brookfield and Her Circle*, 1:255. In the printed text the letter is dated November 1847, but the wording suggests an earlier date, nearer the time when part 5 appeared (February 1847).
50. See Mary Edminson, "Charles Dickens and *The Man in the Moon*," *Dickensian* 56(1960): 50–59.
51. *Critical Heritage*, 69.
52. *Critical Heritage*, 188.
53. One wonders what Dickens's readers would have made of Toodle's contrived use of railroad metaphors as he imparts advice to his assembled children: "If you find yourselves in cuttings or in tunnels, don't you play no secret games. Keep your whistles going, and let's know where you are. . . . I starts light with Rob only; I comes to a branch; I takes on what I finds there; and a whole train of ideas gets coupled on to him, afore I knows where I am, or where they comes from. What a Junction a man's thoughts is . . . to-be-sure!" (38:512–13). Here, literary invention in the cause of topicality struck a false note.
54. *Letters of Charles Dickens*, 4:113.
55. *Critical Heritage*, 230.
56. *Critical Heritage*, 44.
57. Horsman's edition, 59 n.2.
58. *English Review* 10(1848):267.
59. A junior Toodle also turns successively purple and red under stress (38:514,517). No critic has yet explored the relationship between the apoplectic tendency in these children and Major Bagstock's equally alarming and changeable complexion. It is noteworthy that only lower-class children like Alexander MacStinger are physically maltreated in *Dombey and Son*. Perhaps Dickens is implying that children of superior station, like Mrs. Pipchin's and Dr. Blimber's pupils, have to put up with much greater and permanently harmful torment—in their tender spirits.
60. *Critical Heritage*, 63.
61. Most of these objections were raised in *Sharpe's London Magazine* 6(1848):201–2. Similar questions occur in other reviews.
62. These and other questions are raised in Colin Brooks, "Mysteries of the Dombey

Family," *Dickensian* 46(1950):31–32.
63. See *Critical Heritage*, 612–14.
64. *Critical Heritage*, 190.
65. Michael Steig, "The Critic and the Illustrated Novel: Mr. Turveydrop from Gillroy [*sic*] to *Bleak House*," *Huntington Library Quarterly* 36(1972):57.
66. See Michael Steig, "Iconography of Sexual Conflict in *Dombey and Son*," *Dickens Studies Annual* 1(1970):161–67.
67. Steig, "The Critic and the Illustrated Novel," 57–58, 67.

Chapter Ten

1. This essay was first read before the English Institute in 1952 as a pilot study for *The English Common Reader*, which was published five years later. It includes considerable factual material that was not incorporated into the book.
2. Wilkie Collins, "The Unknown Public," *Household Words* 18(1858):217–24. The essay was reprinted in Collins's *My Miscellanies* (London, 1863), 1:169–91. In the same year, the subject was treated in an article in *Blackwood's Magazine* 84(1858):200–16; and, in the next year, in the *British Quarterly Review* 29(1859):313–45.
3. Official returns in *Census of Great Britain, 1851: Population Tables* 2 (Part 1) (1854), p. cliv.
4. Registrar-General's returns for England and Wales only; Graham Balfour, *The Educational Systems of Great Britain and Ireland* (London, 1898), 305. An article by Robert K. Webb, "Working Class Readers in Early Victorian England," *English Historical Review* 65(1950):333–51, critically surveys the evidence on the literacy rate among the masses in the thirties and forties.
5. Clarence Gohdes, *American Literature in Nineteenth-Century England* (New York, 1944), 29–31.
6. Charles Tennyson, *Alfred Tennyson* (New York, 1949), 248. Sir Charles's actual phrase, "in a few months," must not be interpreted too strictly. There were five editions of the poem between June 1850 and November 1851; the first and fifth were of 5,000 copies each, and probably the others were of about the same size or slightly larger (Edgar F. Shannon, Jr., *Tennyson and the Reviewers* [Cambridge, Mass., 1952], 146, 156). But even if, as is likely, the figure of 60,000 represents sales over a period of several years rather than months, it is still a remarkable short-term total for a book of poetry. One must remember that the records achieved by other Victorian best-sellers in this class of literature were built up over a generation or more. Robert Pollok's *The Course of Time*, for example, sold 78,000 between 1827 and 1869 (*Publishers' Circular*, 16 January 1869, p. 3); John Keble's *The Christian Year* sold 379,000 during the whole life of the copyright, 1827–73 (John Collins Francis, *John Francis, Publisher of "The Athenaeum"* [London, 1888], 2:193n); and the most famous of them all, Martin Tupper's *Proverbial Philosophy*, passed the 200,000 mark in 1866, twenty-eight years after the first series appeared (Derek Hudson, *Martin Tupper: His Rise and Fall* [London, 1949], 40).
7. Edgar Johnson, *Charles Dickens: His Tragedy and Triumph* (New York, 1952), 2:752, 756, 759. *Bleak House*, according to Dickens, had a circulation "half as large again as *Copperfield*," which sold about 25,000 a number (2:670).
8. Henry Curwen, *A History of Booksellers* (London, 1873), 106.
9. F. A. Mumby, *The House of Routledge, 1834–1934* (London, 1934), 86. This figure may appear high, but Mumby says elsewhere (p. 77) that J. G. Wood's *Common Objects of the Country* (1858) sold out an edition of 100,000 in a week.
10. *Edinburgh Review* 96(1852):451.

11. Curwen, *History of Booksellers*, 428. Curwen also says that Mudie took 2,500 of *Enoch Arden* and 3,000 of Disraeli's *Lothair*. The latter, however, proved an unfortunate speculation.

12. "The Circulation of Modern Literature," *Living Age* 76(1863):314; a rich source, incidentally, for contemporary sales figures.

13. Ibid.

14. This figure was given by Charles Knight in the preface to the first bound volume of the magazine (1832). He repeats it in his *Passages of a Working Life* (London, 1864–65), 2:184. However, in 1855, replying to an inquiry addressed to him on behalf of the Chancellor of the Exchequer, Knight wrote: "In the first year (1832) it sold about 100,000; in the second, 160,000. The largest sale was in the third and fourth years" (Alice A. Clowes, *Charles Knight: A Sketch* [London, 1892], 225–26). Since the paper was unstamped, government returns are of no help in establishing the precise facts. It is at least certain that the circulation of 200,000 was not long sustained, and by 1845 it had fallen to 40,000 (ibid.).

15. The 1849 figure is from William Lovett's testimony printed in [House of Commons] *Select Committee on Public Libraries* (1849), Q. 2787. In 1851, a witness before another committee gave the *Family Herald*'s circulation as 147,000, while another witness put it at "over 200,000" ([House of Commons] *Report from the Select Committee on Newspaper Stamps* [1851], Qq. 973, 2498). The figure of 1855, given in the text, is from Charles Knight (Clowes, *Charles Knight*, 226). To confuse matters still further, it may be noted that in the same year, 1855, a speaker in Parliament placed the *Family Herald*'s circulation at 240,000 (*Hansard's Parliamentary Debates*, 3rd ser., 137 [1855], col. 783. This is merely one example, out of many that could be cited, of the contradictory evidence facing one who wishes to obtain a fairly accurate picture of the audience for mass-circulation periodicals in the nineteenth century. Since the papers were unstamped for the most part, the government returns are useless, and in any event, the stamp duty was removed in 1855. There was no Victorian equivalent of the Audit Bureau of Circulation, and so a periodical publisher's sales figures could be a matter strictly between himself and God. His public boasts are of little value, for as the *Bookseller* remarked (1 April 1869, p. 298), "many of our contemporaries . . . publish particulars respecting their circulation which must somewhat astonish their printers." Lacking the actual account-books of the various publishers, the researcher must be content with such figures as were hazarded at the time, on good authority or bad, and try not to become too exercised over the frequent disagreement among witnesses.

16. Knight's figures again, as of 1855 (Clowes, *Charles Knight*, 226). But in the same year, the Chancellor of the Exchequer told the Commons that the *London Journal* sold 510,000 (*Hansard*, 3rd ser., 137 [1855], col. 783).

17. An estimate as of 1849 (*Select Committee on Public Libraries* [1849], Q. 2788).

18. *Hansard* as cited in note 16, cols. 781–82; H. R. Fox Bourne, *English Newspapers* (London, 1887), 2:124, 226–27.

19. Collins, "The Unknown Public," 218.

20. *Select Committee on Public Libraries* (1849), Q. 1308.

21. Michael Sadleir, *XIX Century Fiction* (London, 1951).

22. On this whole subject, see, in addition to Sadleir's bibliography, John Carter and Michael Sadleir, *Victorian Fiction* (London, 1947), 2–14.

23. The free traders' side was presented by Chapman in an article, "The Commerce of Literature," *Westminster Review*, n.s. 1 (1852):511–54; reprinted as *Cheap Books and How to Get Them* (1852). See also the *Athenaeum*, 22 May 1852, 575–77.

24. The publishing trade's indignation over the "underselling" practice may be studied *in extenso* in the columns of the *Publishers' Circular* for the whole period.

25. Leone Levi, *Wages and Earnings of the Working Classes* (London, 1885), 48.
26. Ibid., 52.
27. G. D. H. Cole and Raymond Postgate, *The Common People, 1746–1938* (London, 1938), 296.
28. There is a vast contemporary literature on the subject, a sampling of which will prove that the vivid account given in chap. 11 of J. L. and Barbara Hammond, *The Age of the Chartists* (London, 1930) is not exaggerated.
29. *Report of Her Majesty's Commissioners Appointed to Inquire into . . . Certain Colleges and Schools. . . .* 4 vols. (1864). See, for example, the testimony on Rugby (4:294–95) and Eton (3:123, 4:249).
30. *Hansard*, 3rd ser., 109(1850), col. 839.
31. See John Minto, *A History of the Public Library Movement in Great Britain and Ireland* (London, 1932), and Sidney Ditzion, "The Anglo-American Library Scene," *Library Quarterly* 16(1946):281–301.
32. The best study of the W. H. Smith railway library enterprise is Robert A. Colby, "That He Who Runs May Read," *Wilson Library Bulletin* 27(1952):300–6. A brief bibliography is appended to this account.
33. *Select Committee on Public Libraries* (1849), Q. 2751.
34. Maurice J. Quinlan, *Victorian Prelude: A History of English Manners, 1700–1830* (New York, 1941), gives in chaps. 8 and 10 an excellent summary of the effect of Evangelicalism upon the reading public down to 1830—an effect that persisted long after that date. Francis E. Mineka, *The Dissidence of Dissent* (Chapel Hill, N.C., 1944), chap. 2, collects evidence of the Evangelicals' distrust of imaginative reading-matter.
35. Charles Knight, in his *Popular History of England* (London, n.d.), 8:846, decided, after an analysis of the *Classified Index to the London Catalogue of Books, 1816–1851*, that of 45,510 books listed in that catalogue, 10,300 were "works of divinity"— as against 3,500 works of fiction, 3,400 of drama and poetry, and 2,500 of science.
36. Not even Dickens, despite the statement so often encountered that he appealed to every class, high and low. It is true that there was great demand for cheap imitations and parodies of his earlier works, and unauthorized adaptations from the novels were popular in the cheap theatres; but that is not the same thing as acquaintance with the genuine article. Dickens's was essentially a middle-class audience.
37. Collins, "The Unknown Public," 218.
38. *Hansard*, 3rd ser., 121(1852), col. 596.
39. *The Times*, 8 February 1854; reprinted in *Living Age* 43(1854), 122. The whole article (pp. 118–22) is a blunt attack on the "unsoundness of the position held by the great publishing houses."
40. In 1852 the "cheap" edition of Dickens, at 3s. 6d. to 5s. a volume, was only getting under way; a title was not included in this series until six to ten years after original publication. Thackeray's *Henry Esmond* was available only at the standard three-decker price of 31s. 6d., *Pendennis* was 26s., and *Vanity Fair* 21s. Only after a similar lapse of time would these titles be reissued at six or seven shillings. Among the principal works of Carlyle, *Heroes and Hero Worship* was 9s. in 1852, *Chartism* (a short work) 5s., *Latter-Day Pamphlets* 9s., *Past and Present* 10s. 6d., and *Sartor Resartus* 10s. 6d. Macaulay's *Essays* was 21s.
41. *Select Committee on Newspaper Stamps* (1851), Qq. 2481–93.
42. Ibid., Q. 2508 ff.; cf. Qq. 598–601, 1214–17, 1325.
43. Johnson, *Dickens*, 2:946. It is instructive to compare this figure with that of the *Athenaeum*, which had "the largest circulation of any literary periodical," appealing to a more intellectual audience and selling at double the price. Although Leslie A. Marchand has estimated the *Athenaeum's* sale in 1853 at between 18,000 and 24,000 (*The*

Athenaeum: A Mirror of Victorian Culture [Chapel Hill, N.C., 1941], 81), in 1855 Commons was told, on the authority of the periodical's proprietor, that its total press run, stamped and unstamped, was but 7,200 a week (*Hansard*, 3rd ser., 137 [1855], col. 781).

44. [Leonard Huxley], *The House of Smith Elder* (London, privately printed, 1923), 98–100; *Publishers' Circular*, 1 May 1862, 199.

45. [This paragraph was based on the small amount of source material on the Cassell firm that was then available. Subsequently, Simon Nowell-Smith's *The House of Cassell 1848–1958* (London, 1958) filled this particular gap—one of many—in our knowledge of the history of Victorian publishing houses.]

Chapter Eleven

1. [This essay was contributed to a volume marking the centenary of the Victorian *annus mirabilis*, 1859. Dealing as it does with the literary scene at the end of the 1850s, it is in effect a companion piece to the essay preceding it in this book, where I study the situation earlier in the same decade from the viewpoint of a market-conscious publisher. Here I adopt a somewhat different perspective, examining a cross-section of the printed output of a single year in an effort to describe the full range of reading matter available to all levels of the growing audience.]

2. "Popular Literature—the Periodical Press," *Blackwood's Magazine* 85(1859):98–99. This article (pp. 96–112) and its continuations (85:180–95, 515–32, and 86:681–89) are perceptive treatments of various aspects of popular literature in 1859. Three other contemporary discussions are [Wilkie Collins], "The Unknown Public," *Household Words* 18(1858): 217–22; [Margaret Oliphant], "The Byways of Literature: Reading for the Million," *Blackwood's Magazine* 84(1858): 200–16; and "Cheap Literature," *British Quarterly Review* 29(1859): 313–45.

3. *The George Eliot Letters*, ed. Gordon S. Haight (New Haven, 1954–56), 3:234n.

4. Charles Tennyson, *Alfred Tennyson* (New York, 1949), 319. (Charles Morgan, however, in his *House of Macmillan* [New York, 1944], 52, says that 10,000 copies were sold in the first *month*.) Another indication of the public's receptivity to poetry is the fact that by June 1859, a cheap one-volume edition of Barham's *Ingoldsby Legends*, issued a year earlier, had sold 21,000 copies (*Publishers' Circular*, 15 June 1859, 282).

5. Francis Darwin, *The Life and Letters of Charles Darwin* (New York, n.d.), 2:1, 31, 61.

6. After the first edition of 1,250 copies, there was a second of 3,000, published 7 January 1860, and a third of 2,000 copies in April 1861 (Darwin, *Life and Letters*, 2:51, 149).

7. Advertisement in the *Athenaeum*, 12 November 1859, 623.

8. This material is taken from Mudie's advertisements in the *Athenaeum*, various dates, 1859.

9. *George Eliot Letters*, 3:33.

10. Of the 200,000 volumes Mudie bought between January 1858 and October 1859, 87,780 were fiction, 56,472 history and biography, and 25,552 travel and adventure (*Athenaeum*, 22 October 1859, 538).

11. *George Eliot Letters*, 3:40.

12. With good reason, because it was in this year that Mudie, after ordering 300 copies of *Richard Feverel*, yielded to the outrage of certain patrons and banned the book from his shelves (Lionel Stevenson, *The Ordeal of George Meredith* [New York, 1953], 72).

13. *Letters of Charles Dickens*, ed. Walter Dexter (Nonesuch edition, Bloomsbury, 1937–38), 3:92.

14. Advertisement in the *Athenaeum*, 12 March 1859, 366.

15. See [*The Times*] *Tercentenary Handlist of English and Welsh Newspapers, Magazines and Reviews* (London, 1920), 91–92.

16. Edgar Johnson, *Charles Dickens: His Tragedy and Triumph* (New York, 1952), 2:946.
17. *Letters and Private Papers of William Makepeace Thackeray*, ed. Gordon N. Ray (Cambridge, Mass., 1944–46), 4:158–59.
18. *Letters and Private Papers of Thackeray*, 4:160.
19. George M. Smith, "Our Birth and Parentage," *Cornhill Magazine*, n.s. 10(1901):9.
20. *George Eliot Letters*, 3:207.
21. Collins, "The Unknown Public" (see note 2 above).
22. *Publishers' Circular*, 31 December 1866, 98.
23. Oliphant, "The Byways of Literature" (see note 2), 207–8.
24. Margaret Dalziel, *Popular Fiction 100 Years Ago* (London, 1957), 36.
25. Charles L. Graves, *Life and Letters of Alexander Macmillan* (London, 1910), 130.
26. Samuel Smiles, *Autobiography* (New York, 1905), 223.
27. Advertisement in the *Athenaeum*, 5 March 1859, 336.
28. Samuel Smiles, *Self-Help* (London, 1859), 249, 265–66.
29. Ibid., 268.
30. *Athenaeum*, 31 December 1859, 888.
31. *Athenaeum*, 29 January 1859, 153; *George Eliot Letters*, 3:15n.
32. Advertisement in *Publishers' Circular*, 1 December 1858, 593.
33. For the decline of *Cornhill*'s fortunes after its brilliant beginning, see Leonard Huxley, *The House of Smith Elder* (privately printed, 1923), 119–20.
34. *Publishers' Circular*, 31 December 1866, 988.

Chapter Twelve

1. *Publishers' Circular*, 19 June 1897, 725.
2. "World's Classics," *Times Literary Supplement*, 25 May 1946, 247.
3. G. F. Palgrave, *Francis Turner Palgrave* (London, 1899), 73.
4. "Literature and Power," *Kenyon Review* 2(1940):435.
5. *Edinburgh Review* 31(1819):470.
6. Frederick Maurice, ed., *Life of Frederick Denison Maurice* (New York, 1884), 1:313–17.
7. *Essays About Men, Women, and Books* (London, 1894), 143.
8. See Margaret Cole, *Books and the People* (London, 1938), 20.
9. *Essays About Men, Women, and Books*, 144.
10. Henry Curwen, *History of Booksellers* (London, [1873]), 138, 150–51; *Bookseller*, 6 January 1874, 4; *Publishers' Circular*, 1 October 1866, 587.
11. *Bookseller*, 1 July 1868, 451; *Publishers' Circular*, 15 June and 1 July 1868, 329, 353.
12. A year later, another classic reprint series made headlines for a different reason. The appendix of the Marlowe volume in the Mermaid series, edited by young Havelock Ellis, referred to certain blasphemous opinions attributed to the dramatist. The resultant uproar "in various quarters" caused Henry Vizetelly, the publisher, to prepare a new edition in which the objectionable passages were suppressed, as well as cancels for insertion in unsold copies of the original edition. A little later, after Vizetelly's imprisonment for selling translations of Zola, and his subsequent death, the series was acquired by Fisher Unwin, who dismissed Ellis from the editorship, removed his name from the volumes, and incurred his life-long contempt. See Ellis's *My Life* (London, 1939), 208–10, and *Publishers' Circular*, 1 April 1887, 357.
13. See *The House of Dent, 1888–1938* (London, 1938), passim; Ernest Rhys, *Everyman Remembers* (New York, 1931), 230–42; Rhys, *Wales England Wed* (London, 1940), 163–69; and Frank Swinnerton, *Swinnerton: An Autobiography* (London, 1936), 65–85.
14. *Publishers' Circular*, 15 March 1864, 152.
15. *Bookseller*, 31 October 1866, 992.

16. Michael Sadleir, ". . . Bibliographical Study of Books of the XIXth Century," *The Bibliographical Society 1892–1942: Studies in Retrospect* (London, 1945), 154.
17. Occasionally a series bore a name obviously designed to capitalize on the success of another. The existence in 1874 of a Cottager's Library (W. Nicholson and Sons, Wakefield) and of a Cottar's Library (William Walker and Sons, Otley, Yorkshire) is a tribute to the fame of Milner and Sowerby's Cottage Library, which for over twenty years had enjoyed a large sale in the provinces. When the successful Camelot series, owned by the Walter Scott Publishing Company of London and Felling-on-Tyne, was renamed the Scott Library early in 1892, it may or may not have been sheer accident that a *Stott* Library was undertaken within a few months.
18. *Publishers' Circular*, 1 September 1868, 509, and 1 July 1870, 389.
19. Series in 32mo. included the Cottage Library, Bell and Daldy's Pocket Volumes, the Miniature Cabinet Library, the Miniature Library of the Poets, the Pocket English Classics, and Tegg's Cabinet Series. A magnifying glass may not always have been needed to read them, as it frankly was in the case of William Pickering's 24mo. Diamond Classics (1820), but it often would have helped.
20. *Correspondence of Leigh Hunt*, ed. Thornton Hunt (London, 1862), 2:217–21.
21. *Some Reminiscences* (London, 1906), 2:406.
22. *Life of Henry Morley* (London, 1898), 335. Cf. the obituary of Morley in the *Athenaeum*, 19 May 1894, 645–46.
23. *Punch* 106(1894):251.
24. *Life of Henry Morley*, 357.
25. *Publishers' Circular*, 15 November 1870, 756, and 17 December 1870, 1024.
26. *Publishers' Circular*, 1 May 1872, 284.
27. *Publishers' Circular*, 1 September 1884, 823. The Victorian merchandising mind is shown at work in an ingenious device offered in connection with Kent's Miniature Library edition of Shakespeare, issued in a set of thirty-six volumes. For 3s. 6d. extra, one could buy a French morocco pocket book, complete with patent clasp, pencil, and compartment into which he could fit either a conventional engagement book or a miniature volume of Shakespeare (ibid., 15 July 1882, 617).
28. *Publishers' Circular*, 1 July 1884, 613.
29. *Publishers' Circular*, 21 April 1894, 428.
30. *Publishers' Circular*, 3 March 1894, 232.
31. *Publishers' Circular*, 11 August 1894, 131.
32. *The House of Dent*, 63, 273.
33. Frederic Whyte, *Life of W. T. Stead* (London, 1925), 2:229; *Newsagents' Chronicle*, 7 November 1896, 30.
34. The sales of many titles in Milner and Sowerby's Cottage Library, 1837–95, are reported from the firm's own records in Herbert E. Wroot, "A Pioneer in Cheap Literature," *Bookman* (London) 11:169–75.
35. Joseph Shaylor, "Reprints and Their Readers," *Cornhill Magazine*, n.s. 18(1905):541.
36. *Private Papers of Henry Ryecroft* (Modern Library edition), 59.
37. "Taken as Read," *Academy* 64(1903):319–20.
38. Charles Dickens, *Collected Papers* (Nonesuch edition, Bloomsbury, 1937–38), 2:403.
39. This sentiment was most lavishly expressed, perhaps, in the testimony before two Parliamentary committees of inquiry, those on public libraries (1849) and the abolition of the newspaper stamp (1851). George Dawson, a mechanics' institute lecturer, told the former committee (Qq. 1368–75) that poetry "is a great deal read" by the working class, "and of course the result is, very much poetry is written by working people. Anybody connected with a newspaper knows what an enormous flood of poetry the working classes send in the course of a year." "The higher class of poetry," he continued, was "very much read by the working people. . . . Shakespeare is known by heart, almost,"

and Milton also was "much read." But it would be idle to assume that these assertions were true of any but a tiny minority of the working class.

40. Edward G. Salmon, "What the Working Classes Read," *Nineteenth Century* 20 (1886):116.

41. William Laird Clowes, "The Cheapening of Useful Books," *Fortnightly Review*, n.s. 70(1901):93. The whole article (pp. 88–98), like Shaylor's, cited in note 35, sketches the main tendencies in reprint publishing during the nineteenth century and surveys the situation at the beginning of the twentieth.

42. Curwen, *History of Booksellers*, 247. For the history of the *Cyclopaedia*, see a centenary article, " 'Pantheon of English Writers,' " *Times Literary Supplement*, 12 and 19 December 1942, 612, 624.

43. *Publishers' Circular*, 1 February 1887, 126. A full bibliographical record of the series is found in *A Bibliographical Catalogue of Macmillan and Co.'s Publications from 1843 to 1889* (London, 1891); see index, 610–11.

44. *Publishers' Circular*, 1 July 1886, 725.

45. Phyllis Bartlett, "Hardy's Shelley," *Keats-Shelley Journal* 4(1955):15.

46. Ellis, *My Life*, 208.

47. Burt, *An Autobiography* (London, 1924), 143–44.

48. Hammerton, *Books and Myself* (London, [1944]), 72.

Chapter Thirteen

1. The compiler of the section on nineteenth-century periodicals in the *Cambridge Bibliography of English Literature* did the *Tobacco Plant* justice by including it on the same page (3:830) which contains entries for the *Fortnightly*, the *Contemporary*, *Tinsley's*, *St. Paul's*, and the *Nineteenth Century*. But the paper paid for the honor by having its life reduced, in the *CBEL* record, from eleven years to a mere four.

2. None of the original records of the enterprise appear to survive. The secretary of the Cope firm wrote to the late A. E. Culpin, of Wirral, Cheshire, on 23 October 1948: "When we closed down our own printing presses, John Fraser, Junior, commenced business on his own account as a printer and would no doubt have been in possession of some of the original matter relating to these publications. At his death, his business was taken over by Messrs. Hill & Reeder of this city [Liverpool]. . . . Unfortunately, their premises were very badly damaged by enemy action during the war and all their records destroyed."

3. Carlyle gives a vivid picture of him—"a poor Scotchman named Maccall, who is in very bad case just now"—in a letter to his mother, 13 February 1853; *New Letters of Thomas Carlyle*, ed. Alexander Carlyle (London, 1904), 2:144–45.

4. Imogene B. Walker, *James Thomson (B.V.): A Critical Study* (Ithaca, N.Y., 1950), 124–26. Excerpts from Thomson's diaries and letters referring to his work for the *Tobacco Plant* are also found in the biographies by Henry S. Salt and Bertram Dobell.

5. Some forty brief extracts from these contributions were published as "Selections from Original Contributions by James Thomson to *Cope's Tobacco Plant*" (*Cope's Smoke Room Booklets*, no. 3, 1889). A number of the essays were reprinted in their entirety in volumes of Thomson's prose. For a general discussion of his contributions to the *Tobacco Plant*, see Walker, *James Thomson*, 139–41, 144. Except for the omission of the reviews of the English Men of Letters volumes, Walker's list of Thomson's contributions (pp. 191–92) seems complete.

6. Readers accustomed to the terse style of modern cigarette-company publicity and, except for the legally required Surgeon General's Warning, its evasion of the health issue, may wish to ponder the polished circumspection of an advertisement of "Cope's Cigaretos" in the number for August 1875: "These Cigaretos are made from a peculiar kind

of Oriental Tobacco, which we ourselves import. The smoking of this Tobacco is said to give relief in cases of Asthma. It will be most interesting to us to know if the Tobacco does possess the peculiar property attributed to it; and, with the view to proper investigation, we are willing to supply, post free and without charge, to Medical Gentlemen, Packets of these Cigaretos for experiment. We do not require or expect in return any letter or certificate for advertising purposes, but we shall be glad to receive a private and confidential note of result from any who take an interest in the question."

7. He could even write about opera—so long as the opera had some relation with tobacco, as did *Carmen*, which he discussed in February 1879.

8. Number 13 of the *Smoke Room Booklets* (1893), "John Ruskin on Himself and Things in General," consisted of a six-page introduction by Walter Lewin followed by fifty pages of quotations from Ruskin's writings, chiefly *Fors Clavigera*. "This publication was the subject of proceedings in the Chancery Division before Mr. Justice Stirling on November 24, 1893, Messrs. Cope submitting to an order for a perpetual injunction" (*Works of John Ruskin*, ed. E. T. Cook and A. D. O. Wedderburn [London, 1902–12], 38:115).

9. Clarence Gohdes, in the bibliography of his *American Literature in Nineteenth-Century England* (New York, 1944), lists the principal reviews, but none of the excerpts from the writings of the authors themselves that I discuss here.

10. The editor noted: " 'Jim Bludso' is by a hitherto unknown author in this country, and, sooner than our readers should be deprived of the pleasure of perusing it, we have struck out an advertisement. To print 'Jim Bludso' has caused our exchequer a loss of about £50." But one suspects that it was only a paper loss, as the canceled advertisement was probably for Cope's own products.

11. *Walt Whitman: the Man and the Poet* (London, 1910), xxxiv. Dobell made the error, in which he was followed by Harold Blodgett (*Walt Whitman in England* [Ithaca, N.Y., 1934], 153), of assigning the essay to the years 1881–82. Actually it ran in the *Tobacco Plant* in May, June, August, September, and December 1880.

12. Clara Barrus (*Whitman and Burroughs, Comrades* [Boston, 1931], 179) quotes a letter from Whitman to Burroughs, 11 June 1879: "I send you the 'Tobacco Plant' with a piece of mine [which] will interest you. (You'll see I have used one of your letters of last winter.)—How nicely those English get up their print things."

13. Thomson to Bertram Dobell, 19 October 1879; quoted by Henry S. Salt, *The Life of James Thomson* (London, 1889), 138.

14. Quoted by Salt, *Life of Thomson*, 152.

15. On the notorious "Coming K——" series, see Michael Sadleir, *XIX Century Fiction: A Bibliographical Record . . .* (London, 1951), 2:27–30.

16. On these, see Salt, *Life of Thomson*, 135–36, 249 and Walker, *James Thomson*, 140.

17. [I have allowed this ending to stand as it was printed in 1951, because the passage of years has not invalidated the point. That a tobacco firm would subsidize a popular literary review is even less conceivable now. But cigarette manufacturers do keep a place in their promotional budgets for funds to support other forms of cultural events, notably art exhibitions.]

Chapter Fifteen

1. *The Eruption of Krakatoa, and Subsequent Phenomena: Report of the Krakatoa Committee of the Royal Society*, ed. G. J. Symons (1888), hereafter referred to as *Krakatoa Report*.

2. G. G. Coulton, *Fourscore Years: An Autobiography* (New York, 1944), 148.

3. *Nature* 29(1883–84):177–78. First ellipsis and italics in the original. This volume of *Nature* is rich in eyewitnesses' accounts of the Krakatoa phenomena at their height.

4. *Works of John Ruskin*, ed. E. T. Cook and A. D. O. Wedderburn, [London, 1902–12], 34:78. Ruskin added in a footnote: "Written under the impression that the lurid and

prolonged sunsets of last autumn had been proved to be connected with the flight of volcanic ashes. This has been since, I hear, disproved again. Whatever their cause, those sunsets were, in the sense in which I myself use the word, altogether 'unnatural' and terrific; but they have no connection with the far more fearful, because protracted and increasing, power of the Plague-wind." See also p. 63 of the same volume. The "plague-wind" is Ruskin's term for what he considered a devil-made phenomenon new to the nineteenth century: a malign wind that propelled across the English skies dun and poisonous clouds laden with gases and carbon from the factory chimneys.

5. *Nature* 29(1883–84):131, 151.

6. Hopkins's *Nature* articles are reprinted in Appendix 2 of *The Correspondence of Gerard Manley Hopkins and Richard Watson Dixon*, ed. Claude Colleer Abbott (London, 1935), 161–66. As a minuscule addition to Hopkins bibliography, it might be noted that the last of these communications was summarized in the *Krakatoa Report*, p. 172: the first occasion upon which Hopkins was, in a sense, "reprinted."

7. *Letters of Gerard Manley Hopkins to Robert Bridges*, ed. Claude Colleer Abbott (London, 1935), 202.

8. *Krakatoa Report*, 161. For numerous additional descriptions of the sunsets of this and immediately following days, see pp. 299–308. The *Report* reproduces six chromolithographs, made from crayon sketches, of the progress of the sunset the next afternoon (26 November) as seen from Chelsea.

9. Letter of 25 January 1884, in Mrs. Disney Leith, *The Boyhood of Algernon Charles Swinburne* (London, 1917), 68–69.

10. *A Midsummer Holiday and Other Poems* (London, 1884), 55–60.

11. [This topical allusion lost its applicability when the testing of nuclear devices in the atmosphere was banned in 1963. It regained all its original force in 1986, when the accident at the Chernobyl atomic reactor poured lethal "dust" into the upper air.]

Chapter Seventeen

1. For the glassy-eyed among my present readers, I may cite the recent supplement to the *OED*: "Colonel Blimp, a character invented by David Low (1891–1963), cartoonist and caricaturist, pictured as a rotund, pompous ex-officer voicing a rooted hatred of new ideas."

2. As I was revising these pages, I came upon two massive volumes recently published by the American firm of Clarkson Potter, which has made something of a specialty of issuing "annotated" editions of standard works such as *Alice in Wonderland* for the general public. These volumes, edited by Edward Guiliano and Philip Collins, contain the texts of six of Dickens's novels, plus *A Christmas Carol*, flanked in the margins by a perfect cascade of explanatory notes. At the same time, a British publisher is issuing a series of volumes each of which is devoted to annotating a single Dickens novel; the reader under this arrangement supplies his own copy of the text. The striking thing about both of these necessary enterprises is that they explicate thousands of allusions in familar works that would have required far less glossing in earlier days.

3. *The Collected Poems of Thomas and Jane Welsh Carlyle*, ed. Rodger L. Tarr and Fleming McClelland (Greenwood, Florida, 1986), 66.

4. *The Collected Letters of Thomas and Jane Welsh Carlyle*, ed. Charles Richard Sanders et al. (Durham, N.C., 1970–), 13:162.

5. *The Letters and Journals of James Fenimore Cooper*, ed. James Franklin Beard (Cambridge, Mass., 1960–68), 4:239.

Chapter Eighteen

1. All quoted remarks by the Colonel and his fellow-members are taken from *Hansard's Parliamentary Debates*.

2. *History Today* 1(May 1951):14–20.

3. Writing of Sir Peter Laurie, the Middlesex magistrate who won fame and ridicule for his various pronouncements from the bench, most notoriously his avowed determination to "put down suicide" (see above, p. 45), Philip Collins remarks, "Sir Peter probably surpasses even Colonel Sibthorpe, MP, as the favorite butt of *Punch* throughout the 1840s. . . . There are thirty[-one] jokes in the first half-yearly volume, and I have counted over one hundred attacks on him during *Punch's* first decade; doubtless I failed to notice many others" (*Dickens and Crime* [London, 1962], 186–87). I must, however, insist on Sibthorp's clear primacy in this regard. *His* record in the first half-yearly volume was sixty-eight jokes, and in the first decade, 266.

4. See especially *Punch* 23(1852):39.

5. Information on the Sibthorp family and the Colonel's preparlimentary life is from Arthur A. Maddison, *An Account of the Sibthorp Family* (Lincoln, 1896).

6. Humphrey's second wife is said to have been descended from the Elizabethan man of letters, Sir John Harington. Another fortuitous—and equally remote—connection Colonel Sibthorp had with English literature was obtained through his sister Mary Esther, who in 1801 married John Hawkins, uncle of Edward John Trelawny (Lady Anne Hill, *Trelawny's Strange Relations* [Stanford Dingley, 1956], 7).

7. "That they should return Sibthorp and reject Bulwer," wrote Dickens to John Forster on 5 July 1841, "is by Heaven, a national disgrace. . . . I don't wonder the devil flew over Lincoln. The people were far too addle-headed, even for him" (*Letters of Charles Dickens*, ed. Madeline House and Graham Storey [Oxford, 1965–], 2:323).

8. "A Parliamentary Sketch," in *Sketches by Boz*; originally two articles in the *Evening Chronicle*, 7 March and 11 April 1835. See William J. Carlton, "Portraits in 'A Parliamentary Sketch'," *Dickensian* 50(1954):100–9.

9. "Colonel Sibthorp," *Fraser's Magazine* 36(1847):462–65. Another eyewitness description of Sibthorp, from which I have derived a few details, is in [James Grant,] *Random Recollections of the House of Commons, from the Year 1830 to the Close of 1835* (London, 1836), 137–43. [Still another appreciation appeared in the series of "Popular Portraits" featured in the newly established *Illustrated London News*, 9 July 1842, 141.]

10. Typical of the comments one finds in the memoirs of his fellow parliamentarians is this, by Lord Broughton (John Cam Hobhouse): "This evening [9 July 1840] a disagreeable discussion ensued at the House of Commons, when Mr. Barrington moved an Instruction extending out-of-door relief on our Poor-Law Continuance Bill. Colonel Sibthorp treated us to some of his usual impertinence. Amongst other amenities he said he wished Ministers had to live in the workhouse, or go to the treadmill" (*Recollections of a Long Life* [London, 1910–11], 5:277–78).

11. One story that seems not to have found its way into print at the time was set down by Greville in 1829: "M'Intosh, in the course of the recent debates, went one day to the H. of C. at eleven in the morning to take a place. They were all taken on the benches below the gangway, and on asking the doorkeeper how they happened to be all taken so early, he said, 'Oh, sir, there is no chance of getting a place, for Colonel Sibthorpe sleeps at the bawdy house close by, and comes here every morning by eight o'clock and takes places for all the Saints'" (*Greville Memoirs*, ed. Lytton Strachey and Roger Fulford [London, 1938], 1:287; in earlier editions *tavern* was substituted for *bawdy house*).

12. *Punch* (14[1848]:175), with even greater unlikelihood, pictured Sibthorp marching in the

Chartist procession, under a banner reading, "Sibthorpe and Down with our Old Institutions."

13. The granitic quality of his opinions was in extraordinary contrast to those of his brother, the Rev. Richard Waldo Sibthorp, an indecisive priest who ricocheted between the Anglican and Roman churches. The story of this clerical Sibthorp, which won the family additional notoriety in Victorian times and must have caused the Colonel exquisite suffering, is told by Christopher Sykes in *Two Studies in Virtue* (New York, 1953). A more dependable clergyman-brother, the Rev. Humphrey Sibthorp, is said to have been "of the greatest service to him" in all his election contests.

14. This outburst earned Sibthorp a full-column notice and a picture, showing him presenting his severed head to Britannia on a platter, in *Punch* 8(1845):188–89. The letterpress was devoted to an ode on the occasion, composed allegedly by Wordsworth and actually by Thackeray. Two other *Punch* tributes to the Colonel are known to be Thackeray's: "An After-Dinner Conversation" (14[1848], 182–83), in which he is entertaining "Mr. Benjamin Dizzy" and a gentleman from Philadelphia, and the "Pontifical News" item (19[1850], 182), announcing that Sibthorp is to become a Capuchin friar.

15. When he told Commons of his being gazetted to a full colonelcy, *Punch* (27[1854]:261) commented, "We were aware that the Colonel was tolerably full of something or other." The preceding year (24[1853]:230) it had printed "Sibthorpe's Address to his Army," a parody of Henry V's speech before Harfleur.

16. One sometimes meets the assertion that Sibthorp did, in fact, pay a visit to the Crystal Palace (see, for instance, Asa Briggs, *Victorian People* [Chicago, 1955], 35]. If there is contemporary evidence of that occasion, apart from the inevitable libelous rumors that were circulated, I have overlooked it.

17. It fell silent only at his death on 14 December 1855. He left four sons, one of whom, Major Gervase Tottenham Waldo Sibthorp, succeeded him in the House of Commons.

18. *The Letters of Edward FitzGerald*, ed. Albert McKinley Terhune and Annabelle Burdick Terhune (Princeton, N.J., 1975–80), 2:34.

19. *Miscellaneous Papers*, ed. B. W. Matz (Gadshill edition, London, 1897–[1908] 36:471).

20. *The Diary of Joseph Farington*, ed. Kenneth Garlick et al. (New Haven, 1978–84), 6:2309.

21. *The Diary of Benjamin Robert Haydon*, ed. Willard Bissell Pope (Cambridge, Mass., 1960–63), 4:615.

22. Ibid. 5:270.

23. Gerald Reitlinger, *The Economics of Taste: The Rise and Fall of the Objets d'Art Market since 1750* (New York, 1965), 107.

Chapter Twenty

1. It is worth noting, in confirmation of the tenor of the present essay, that when the *CBEL* came to be revised, the third volume was the first to be published (1969), because it was the one that had most urgently required updating. As the editor remarked, "In the 1930s Victorian literature, and especially the Victorian novel, had with rare exceptions barely entered into the accepted range of scholarly activity. . . . The study of the eighteenth century, and of the Middle Ages and Renaissance, has swollen in extent over the last generation; but it has not transformed the subject as recent studies of romantic and Victorian literature have done."

Index